Norms of Language

Theoretical and Practical Aspects

Renate Bartsch

LONGMAN

LONDON AND NEW YORK

Longman Group UK Limited,
Longman House, Burnt Mill, Harlow,
Essex CM20 2JE, England
and Associated Companies throughout the world.

*Published in the United States of America
by Longman Inc., New York*

© Longman Group UK Limited 1987

First published 1987

British Library Cataloguing in Publication Data

Bartsch, Renate
Norms of language: theoretical and
practical aspects. – (Longman linguistics library)
1. Standard language
I. Title II. Sprachnormen. *English*
418 P368

ISBN 0-582-01475-1 CSD
ISBN 0-582-00419-5 PPR

**Library of Congress Cataloging in Publication
Data**

Bartsch, Renate, 1939–
Norms of language.

(Longman linguistics library)
Translation of Sprachnormen, Theorie und Praxis.
Bibliography: p.
Includes index.
1. Standard language. 2. Linguistic change.
3. Language planning. I. Title. II. Series.
P368.B3713 1987 410 86-27515
ISBN 0-582-01475-1
ISBN 0-582-00419-5 (pbk.)

Produced by Longman Singapore Publishers (Pte) Ltd.
Printed in Singapore

Contents

Preface

This book is a translation of *Sprachnormen: Theorie und Praxis*, which was published in 1985 by Niemeyer Verlag, Tübingen. At some points the German version has been shortened or rewritten, or previously written articles which appeared in English have been taken as the basis for some chapters of the present book. The chapters of the book can be read separately. To facilitate this the definitions of those notions of the theory of norms that are central in a chapter have been repeated in its beginning.

The history of this book is long: I began working on the relationship between norms and truth while writing my dissertation (1969), where I had defined and treated three notions of semantic correctness. This thread I took up again in three articles (Bartsch 1979a, b, c), which deal with the central role of correctness notions in semantics and pragmatics, especially their role in the interpretation of linguistic utterances. The first chapter of this book, 'Correctness and norms of language', is based on this material.

Chapters 2 and 3 about norms in general and juridical and linguistic norms in particular were written in 1977 in their main outlines, inspired by Ullmann-Margalit's book *The Emergence of Norms* (1977). The questions that I tried to answer are: What are the essential properties of norms, and how do norms of language differ from norms in the area of law? How are existence and validity of norms constituted, and does this happen in a different way in the two areas of norms? In answering these questions I refer to Hart (1961) and Raz (1975). With respect to how norms emerge and how they function, I refer mainly to Lewis (1969), Ullmann-Margalit (1977), Luhmann (1972), and Gloy (1975). In comparing linguistic and juridical norms I tried to reconstruct the justificational and the institutional foundations of the existence and validity of linguistic norms. These foundations are related to empirical and practical matters in the later chapters on language planning and norm conflicts.

The relationship between linguistic norms and the rules of grammatical systems (linguistic rules) has been a point of special attention throughout this book. It is a major topic in Chapter 4 ('Norms and rules in linguistics'), and in Chapter 5 ('Linguistic change in the light of the theory of norms'). The basic insight in these chapters is that in taking into account the heterogeneity of linguistic systematizations on the one hand and of linguistic norms on the other, the complex relationship between linguistic systems and linguistic norms can be understood. The main concepts for construing this relationship are based on Schnelle (1976). The two kinds of heterogeneity are also important for understanding linguistic change. As far as this field is concerned I refer mainly to insights we find in the work of Vennemann and in the work of Labov, and draw conclusions from my criticism of notions of linguistic complexity (1973).

Working on Chapter 6 ('Linguistic norms in language planning and development'), I have greatly profited from discussions with Björn Jernudd in 1980 and 1984, when I had the opportunity to stay at the Institute of Culture and Communication of the East-West Center in Honolulu. Dr Jernudd also supplied me with lots of relevant literature, especially about multilingualism and language planning in India. Besides Dr Jernudd, I have to thank Dr K. S. Rajyashree and Monsur Musa who also commented on my manuscript during my stay at the East-West Center in 1984.

As a non-native speaker of English I have written this book in a version of one of the many varieties of the super-variety International English, namely the German variety of English. I hope this will not discourage native English readers.

I thank North-Holland Publishing Company (Amsterdam) for the permission to re-publish extensive parts of my articles (1979a, 1984b) from *Journal of Pragmatics* and (1982a) from *Lingua*, and CWK Gleerup (Lund) for the permission to republish my article (1985b) from *Studia Linguistica* in Chapter 6 of this book.

Last, but not least, I thank my students for providing a stimulating environment for writing this book, by listening to a series of lectures I gave about its topics, posing questions, and initiating discussions. Many things became clearer to me while thinking about appropriate answers.

Muiden, September 1986   Renate Bartsch

Introduction

In recent years, linguists, and especially socio-linguists, have paid much attention to the fact that languages are made by people along with the cultural, political, and historical development in general. On the other hand, linguists are aware of the fact that much of the structural properties of languages is due to processes of systematization that go on in the heads of language learners and users, restrained by universal properties of human cognition. These systematizations and structurings are basically unbalanced and unstable, and thus are subject to permanent change. Linguistic communities curtail change that is going wild by accepting or not accepting certain changes. They also initiate language change by adjusting language to the requirements of communication and development of knowledge. Linguistic systematization is blind with respect to these requirements, and it is by selecting changes caused by systematization processes and by introducing new linguistic items and forms of speech that language gets modelled according to the needs of changing societies.

A language like English has changed during its history under both these aspects, and at present we are facing the coexistence of a set of varieties of English due to the wide spread of speech communities of this language and its broad international use. There are the branches of native speakers of English, such as British, Irish, American, Australian, New Zealand and South African English, and a small group of native speakers of Indian English. But there are also varieties of English as a second language, such as Indian English and Philippine English as common languages in the respective countries, and German English, Dutch English, etc., which are versions of English as an

international common language. The norms of the several varieties of English differ to some degree, and efforts have to be
made repeatedly to keep these varieties close enough to each
other in order to secure the usability of English as a common
international language. On the other hand, the differences are
there because of reasons that make them acceptable, at least as
long as mutual understandability is guaranteed. The 'non-native'
versions of English are generally confined to certain registers;
namely to those of science, technology, politics, and traffic. As
far as they are used to express topics of culture, their semantics
may be coined more by the cultural backgrounds of their
speakers than by the cultures of the 'native' varieties of English,
for example by Indian culture in the case of Indian English.
There are, for example, translations of novels from Indian
languages into English by speakers of Indian English, which are
translations into Indian English, and not into British English. To
native speakers of British English such translations may seem odd
due to, for example, the difference between the sets of old
metaphors in Indian and in British English. There are old
metaphors in Indian languages that are transferred into Indian
English, where they are understood likewise as old metaphors,
i.e. not as real metaphors but as normal words, like in English
foot of a mountain, or *bit of a key*, which are no longer understood as metaphors. Such a word is, for example, *nest* in Indian
English, which means 'home' (where one has all one's social
ties). British readers will understand it as a new metaphor, and
by this the text will sound somewhat odd and emotionally exaggerated, although it does not have this quality in its original form
or in its Indian-English interpretation.

Something similar holds for intonation, pronunciation, and
even syntactic structures.

Some people oppose a common international language
'English' because they see it connected with a new world-wide
cultural, economic, and political imperialism (*cf* Skutanabb-
Kangas and Phillipson 1986 in three papers). If we, nevertheless,
find a common international English desirable, we certainly
should give way to its varieties in their local use, like Indian
English as a common language in India, and we really have to
do so with respect to cultural manifestations in these varieties in
order for them to be understood in their own language area. But
we need to be concerned with the international language in a
normative manner such that lexicon, syntax, pronunciation, and
orthography remain close enough between the varieties in order
to secure the usability of the language in the main registers of

international contact. There has thus to be a balance between a necessary tolerance with regard to varieties and normativity with regard to common international settings of language use.

A similar problem of finding a balance between variety and normativity exists for all speech communities that have a standard language and a set of regional and social varieties. Gloy (1975) and others, and recently Mey (1985), have heavily criticized the norms and correctness notions of standard languages as a means of suppression, which according to them serve to reproduce the power structure of capitalist societies. The present book, though in agreement with basic views of these critics, investigates this view, criticizes it, and takes a different stand based on norm-theoretic considerations.

This actual practical background motivates the development of a theory of norms of language that can provide some conceptual order within the complex social reality of language, and can provide well-founded arguments in the discussions about the justification and the validity of standards, as opposed to the richness of creativity in forms and usage of linguistic and communicational means.

In recent years socio-linguists have been interested in developing a theoretical frame for their many empirical findings. A theory of linguistic norms is meant to provide part of the background for such a theory of socio-linguistics.

The book starts with an overview of the various kinds of correctness notions with regard to the forms and the use of linguistic means (*ie* expressions). Firstly, the role of notions of correctness in linguistics is discussed, and then the different types of correctness of language are distinguished: the correctness of phonetic and orthographic units, of lexical units, of syntactic form of written and spoken language, and of texts. As far as the use of expressions is concerned, the principles of semantic and pragmatic correctness are formulated, based on Bartsch (1979a) from the *Journal of Pragmatics*. The main claim of Chapter 1 is that correctness notions are necessary in order to secure recognizability and interpretability of linguistic expressions. Further, the relationship between notions of correctness and norms is spelled out: norms are the social reality of correctness notions. What this social reality amounts to is worked out in principle in Chapters 2 and 3.

These chapters lean heavily on theories of juridical norms, as they are developed by Hart, Raz, Ullmann-Margalit, and Luhmann. I distinguish between theories that deal mainly with existence and validity, and those that deal with existence and functions of norms. The findings with respect to juridical norms are compared with the social reality of notions of linguistic correctness, and the degree and the boundaries of comparability between these different kinds of norms are investigated. Special attention is directed towards the conditions under which linguistic norms can be issued such that they can be valid, and the possibilities of justifying the existence and validity of linguistic norms and their changes. In this context, the claim is rejected that the norms of standard languages, *ie* insistence on correctness from this point of view, serve to suppress lower classes and to keep intact the capitalist power structure. The main result of Chapters 2 and 3 is the definition of the ways of existence of (linguistic) norms as a practice, as valid norms, as accepted norms, as adopted norms, and as justified norms. These notions are used as analytic tools in later chapters of the book.

The fourth chapter is devoted to working out the distinction between linguistic norms and linguistic rules. This is a category distinction that has not always been seen by linguists. This chapter is based on Bartsch (1982a), which appeared in *Lingua*. I show how necessary the clarification of this distinction is by discussing the use of the notions 'norm' and 'rule' in linguistics, provide definitions of the notions, and present classifications of types of rules and norms. The difference between linguistic rules and linguistic norms gives rise to a basic distinction between the objects and aims of socio-linguistic research on the one hand, and those of so-called 'theoretical' linguistics, or, better, theoretical grammar, on the other. Learnability and systematization of linguistic norms are the topics of psycholinguistics, which is therefore related to both major parts of theoretical linguistics, the theory of linguistic norms and the theory of grammatical rules. It is norms that are to be learned, but they are learned not only under restrictions by social conditions but also under restrictions by human ways of systematizing all kinds of data. Thus psychology of language has to attend to the social aspect as well as to the grammatical. Norms of language have to be learned by the child (and the adult), and that this is possible with regard to such a huge set of norms is due to systematizations of the' linguistic data that are formed unconciously in our heads. Products of these systematizations can be accepted by language users as long as they do not contradict that which is already socially accepted. These products thus instantiate correctness notions and give rise to norm practice, or even to valid norms. These systematizations are the psychic realities of sets of potential or actual norms, next to all kinds of lists of linguistic norm contents that are gathered in our heads.

In this book I have treated norms as the social reality of correctness notions. I did not address psychological questions about norms; there lies a field which has hardly been worked on up to now: which psychic and attitudinal factors play a role for acceptance and adoption of norms; which different points of view of systematization play a role in learning norms; how is the psychic existence and representation of norms organized from different points of view: grammatical, epistemic, practical. This field is especially fundamental because, ontologically speaking, contents of norms somehow exist as correctness notions in the heads of people and thus depend on subjective factors. The contents of norms achieve intersubjectivity in what I call 'the social reality of norms'. This is a network of observable regularities in human behaviour, namely of regularities on the level of exemplifying the content of norms in our natural and social surroundings, and of regularities on higher (meta-) levels of behaviour as we find them in acts of criticizing and correcting lower-level behaviour, as well as in acts of formulating and codifying norm contents. This objectivity and intersubjectivity of norms make it possible for the individual to build up (subjective) norm concepts in such a way that he and others can think of them as objectively and intersubjectively valid. Although norm concepts are in our heads, so to speak, they are intersubjective thanks to their social reality.

Chapters 5 and 6 deal with change of language. Firstly, norm-theoretic aspects of linguistic change are formulated and several types of change are distinguished. The interplay between the normative and the grammatical conditions of linguistic change is focused upon, especially with respect to so-called 'natural' or spontaneous change of language. Secondly, the change of semantic norms is treated as a change of minor norms under the presupposition of the principle of rationality as the highest norm and the precondition of context dependence of the meanings of lexical items. This part on semantic change is a short version of Bartsch (1984b), which appeared in the *Journal of Pragmatics*.

Chapter 6 is devoted to kinds of linguistic change that are evidently controlled or initiated by (conscious) human actions. The first part is about the role of linguistic norms in planning of the status of a language: the choice of official and national languages is discussed from the point of view of what such a choice means with regard to the norms of the languages chosen and those not chosen; the same point of view guides the discussion of language standardization with respect to the standard varieties and the non-standard ones of a language. Special topics are the process of standardization and the role of the standard, the question whether the standard is, metaphorically speaking, a 'point' or a 'range', the status of the norms of the standard and the status of the norms of the non-standard varieties, and the question whether a classical language can be the norm that provides the standard of a language. (This part on standardization is, except for small changes, identical with Bartsch (1985b), which appeared in *Studia Linguistica*.) The second part of Chapter 5 is about planning of the corpus of a language. There, the influences of elaboration and cultivation on linguistic norms are investigated. The main influence is one of stabilizing the norms of a language and broadening the domains of its use with respect to the population the language is used by, and the functions the language is used for.

The topics of the last chapter are the definition and classification of linguistic norm conflicts between groups in a population, and within situations of communication. Some of these conflicts play a role in the chapter about linguistic change, where, among other causes, linguistic norm conflicts are considered as a motor of change. This is a special case of the role conflicts generally play as a cause of change. But in Chapter 7 conflicts in the area of linguistic and cultural norms are not discussed from the point of view of social change. The chapter is motivated by the aim of providing an analytic tool for becoming aware of the different kinds of conflict, and of what they mean for the people involved. This last chapter gives a classification of norm conflicts that can be used in a norm-theoretic analysis of multilingual and multicultural societies.

Chapter 1

Correctness and norms of language

1.1 Correctness in linguistics

'Linguistic correctness' has always been a basic notion in traditional grammar, which has been concerned with what the correct expressions in a language are (conditions of well-formedness of expressions) and what the correct use of these expressions is (conditions of use of expressions). Lexicons and grammar books have provided lists of correct basic expressions (words and idioms) and patterns and examples of correct complex expressions, plus examples and descriptions of their use. These two basic aspects are traditionally called 'form' and 'function' of language. In the last sixty years or so, methods of linguistic description came into focus, and later the focus shifted towards the construction of theories which could provide explanations for various linguistic phenomena, *eg*, that language is learned (in certain ways), that language changes (in certain ways), and that linguistic expressions can be interpreted and can serve as a means of orientation about the world and as a constitutive part of actions. In all these later endeavours, from the development of linguistic description to theory formation from certain points of view, the notion of linguistic correctness has played a central role in all kinds of correctness judgements, those of linguists themselves and those elicited by linguists from native speakers. Their intuition about correctness in different respects was the starting-point for the reconstruction of linguistic structures and even processes that were supposed to underlie these intuitions as a kind of mechanism.

Itkonen (1974, 1976) has pointed out that correct expressions and the correct use of these form the data for theoretical linguistics, and that this involves collecting not only utterances, but also judgements about the correctness of these utterances, because only correct utterances should be the basis for constructing grammar. He has looked at these judgements as intuitions about norm-governed behaviour and at the activities of the grammarian as conceptual analysis of the normative notions that regulate this behaviour. In his view, grammar is the same kind of non-empirical science as is mathematics or logic. According to Itkonen, linguistic rules, as we find them in theoretical linguistics, are different from rules of language, of which speakers can become aware when they try to explicate their intuitions. The first are hypotheses of the most effective and elegant way in which the second, the rules of language, can be described.

Although I think Itkonen is right in making a distinction between rules of language and rules in theoretical linguistics, that distinction is rather complicated; moreover, it is not the same for different types of linguistic theory. Nor can I agree with his claim that theoretical linguistics is a non-empirical science, mainly because what the most adequate way of describing linguistic expressions is depends on what assumptions are made initially, and these assumptions can be empirical claims about the organization of human cognitive faculties or even claims about the physiological and biological organization of the brain. Descriptions are then adequate not only in so far as they deliver the correct linguistic expressions, but also in so far as they are formulated on the basis of these assumptions and thus depend on empirical claims. The problem is that these claims cannot be proven in linguistics, and certainly not by pointing out that the description based on them gives the correct linguistic results, because such an argument is simply circular.

Other basic assumptions that involve certain empirical claims and lead to certain ways of constructing a grammar are facts of actual language behaviour, different from judgements about correctness and often in conflict with these judgements, or facts of language change, which should be explained by linguistic theory (for these aspects see Labov 1972a). These facts require that behaviour be interpreted by taking into account both social norms and possible systematizations of the patterns of actual linguistic behaviour in the human cognitive faculties. The notion of norm, on the one hand, and the notion of systematization, on the other, make it possible to analyse change, linguistic heterogeneity, and repeated deviance from correctness in terms of conflicts among norms, among systematizations, and between norms and systematizations, and in terms of strategies for solutions of these conflicts.

Further, adequate description depends on whether one wants to make empirical assumptions of this kind at all, because even without such assumptions, adequacy of description, besides providing for the correct expressions of a language, depends on considerations of generality of the rules, simplicity of the application of the rules (for example, preference for intrinsic rule order above extrinsic rule order), the size of the set of basic notions, and the possibility of broad application of whole complexes of rule applications in subroutines. A further basis for determination of adequacy might be possible integration of linguistic theory, especially grammar, into the general theory of action. This point of view leads to grammars that can be part of a theory of interpretation, as we find in the philosophy of language, where formal grammar is based on notions of truth and, more recently, also on information, such that grammatical rules are compositional and recursive, parallel to the build-up of truth conditions of a sentence from the meanings of its parts.

From the above considerations, it follows that there is not just one relationship between intuitions of correctness, formulated in correctness judgements, and rules formulated by theoretical linguists, but there are as many relations as there are different goals and assumptions under which grammars are constructed.

Besides the theoretical points of view mentioned, there is, of course, the point of view of language teaching, which does not permit simply taking one of the theoretically oriented grammars as the basis for teaching languages. Traditional functional grammar, aided by some structuralist methodology such as substitution, still dominates language teaching in schools, and not just because of a theoretical deficit among language teachers. It is widely recognized that language teaching requires its own theory, depending on the special goals of teaching language and the conditions under which it has to take place. In Chapter 4 it will be argued that it is not the theoretical linguistic rules that have to be learned, but the norms of the language; and for that it is necessary to present the correctness notions. The present chapter therefore has some relevance for language teaching.

Although, apparently, all scholars and teachers of language start from the basic assumption that a grammar or, more broadly, a linguistic theory should take into account correct expressions and the correct use of these expressions and somehow describe them in a comprehensive manner, the ways and kinds of description differ considerably, depending on different basic assumptions and goals. Especially, the degree of empiricality differs, as does the degree of normativity. In so far as a linguistic theory claims to describe and produce correct expressions, it is always normative at least to the extent that it reinforces existing judgements of correctness.

But note that description of norms of a language is itself empirical, and it is descriptive rather than prescriptive, because it describes which norms hold in a speech community. One can describe these norms without at the same time advocating them. A special theory of language norms is a descriptive endeavour; it represents the empirical fact that in community X the norms A hold, and in community Y, the norms B. A special theory of linguistic norms reports an empirical fact, which is a social fact. In being empirical in this way, it is very different from mathematics or from logic. A general theory of norms is partly empirical and partly philosophical, but it is not a normative theory in the sense that it advocates certain norms: it investigates types of norms, their function, their justification with respect of assumed values, and their systematic properties.

In what follows, I want to elaborate on the foundations of certain notions of correctness associated with linguistic means of communication (*ie* linguistic forms), and their use, and call attention to the kinds of norms that provide for the establishment and consolidation of these notions of correctness. Roughly, we can say that the norms are the social reality of the correctness notions: the correctness notions exist in a community by being the contents of norms. In this way, correctness concepts, which as concepts in a certain sense are psychic entities, have a social reality and objectivity above or outside the individuals that grasp them by constructing a psychic representation of them. Their correctness is socially established in varying degrees of formality, from providing models of correctness to providing codifications of the norms. It is a task of the theory of norms to make clear how the social reality of norms and, with that, the objectivity of correctness concepts (and our common concepts generally) comes about, is constituted, and is achieved in a society.

1.2 Types of correctness in language

1.2.1 Correctness of the basic means of expression

As far as correctness of the sounds of a language is concerned, there are two questions: which ones are sounds of the language, and what is the range or latitude of pronunciation that delimits a sound such that it is recognizable as that sound, is easily recognizable, or is nearly perfect, such that it can serve as a model for imitation of the sound? Actually, perfectness of a sound as a certain sound is not an inherent quality, but rather a social phenomenon: speakers who are accepted as providing the models by their pronunciation determine what the sound has to be like. A sound is perfect, or nearly perfect, if it is like the sounds of the kind produced by the people who give the models.

Phonology, traditionally, answers the question of which sounds are in a language. The question is answered in two parts: first, what are the basic sounds, and second, what are the combinations? The sounds are classified into those which form functional oppositions (they distinguish meanings), and those which do not and thus are identified with each other in a sound system in which equivalence is defined as 'making no difference with respect to meaning'. Other definitions of equivalence are 'making no difference with respect to social connotations', or 'making no difference with respect to regional connotations'. According to these notions of equivalence, sounds can be classified as being typical for a social class or a certain region. There are language-specific rules about combinations: for example, /ps/ is not possible in word-initial position in English; and in German, stops in final positions are voiceless. That this rule is called 'final devoicing of stops in German' suggests that a process is involved, in which a voiced stop is devoiced. Such a rule, interpreted as a process, is not a norm, because a norm only says that every stop in final position is without voice; a speaker does not have to imagine a voiced stop in this position and then devoice it when pronouncing it. Linguistic norms that define the correctness of linguistic means of communication never say how these linguistic forms have to be made. For the function expressions have in society as a means of communication, it does not matter how they are produced; only the final result of pronunciation matters. The norms regulate or norm only the product, *ie* the appearance of these means, not the production.

People exhibit strong normative attitudes and behaviour with respect to phonological correctness. Sounds of their language are selected by their perception apparatus from all sounds received. What is perceived, out of what is received, is that which makes a difference from the relevant points of view – conveying information, be it semantic information or social information. People welcome and reward sounds of their language produced by babbling infants, thus reinforcing the production of these sounds; they disregard and discourage the production of other sounds.

Auditory correctness of an actual sound means that it lies within accepted boundaries for the realization of a sound concept; these boundaries are relative to the context in which the actual sound occurs. The accepted range of quality of a sound X is thus a complex of sound-realization types $(X_1, X_2, \ldots, X_n)$ for the n typical contexts in which it occurs in the language under consideration. An example of such a complex would be the set of types of contexts in which voiced dental stops can occur, where each type of context affects the quality of the stop in a different way. But sound concepts, or percepts, can also be organized with respect to additional, morphological–semantic points of view. We can construct a complex including the context types and the qualities of voiced dental stops in these context types, which additionally include the context types in which the voiced stop is realized not in a voiced but in a voiceless manner; then one X_i of the complex would be <[dental stop, − voice] in context type ___ #>. In German, the concepts of voiced stops would thus contain the fact that they are voiceless at the end of a syllable. From a morphophonemic point of view, these are adequate concepts of voiced stops in German. The corresponding concepts in English will be different, since they do not include final devoicing. Each X_i itself is a range of realizations of the sound with small qualitative differences. These realizations are recognized as typical for the linguistic community that speaks the language in question as its mother tongue.

Another group of notions of auditory correctness defines acceptable boundaries for loudness and for pitch or tone. The norms that govern these aspects are often different for different social strata: talking in a loud voice when this is not required because of intervening noise may, for example, be a sign of lower class. For natural reasons women speak with higher pitch than men; in England, however, where pitch of middle-class speakers is higher generally than in continental Europe, social convention requires middle-class women to speak in an even higher voice in order to maintain normal pitch distance between male and female. Prime Minister Thatcher had to unlearn talking in very high woman's pitch: as in public speaking generally, this dominant marker of femaleness was likely to destroy the effectiveness of the Prime Minister's political message, distracting from the content of what she had to say, because whatever she said would be very strongly marked by high pitch as 'women's talk' – even more so in foreign countries than in England.

The norms that keep intact the notions of auditory correctness are never presented to people by description, but by models. There are models for correct pronunciation and tone who have had speech education at teacher academies or theatre schools. Most speakers on television and radio in Germany have received speech education at theatre schools and television academies. The norm of High German pronunciation (*Bühnen-Aussprache*), fixed eighty-six years ago by Siebs (1898/1961, 1969), has been used by teachers of speech up to the present.

Another medium for the realization of language, besides speech, is writing. This second medium can be related directly to the semantic content and to the syntactic functions of the language, or it can be related to the primary medium, sound, and via this detour related to semantic content and syntactic functions. With the direct relationship, we obtain a script consisting of characters or pictures. With the other, we obtain a letter-based script which in more or less detail is a mapping of sounds; in the extreme case of the phonetic alphabet, it is a one-to-one mapping. English, in the beginning of its literalization, had certainly been of the latter kind; but in the course of its history, sound deviated more and more from spelling, so that spelling seems close to becoming a medium independent of sound, which is typical of the first kind of writing, the writing by means of characters. In any event, the script had to be fixed by explicit conventions. These conventions are subject to deliberate change now and then in the history of a language, and they are subject to negotiations and regulations in case there are competing systems of writing and spelling. In the Netherlands, there have been several committees in the last century which revised the spelling, lately mainly from the point of view of congruency with the phonetic distinctions and equivalences. This point of view has been taken to even greater extremes in the system of spelling for Afrikaans (*cf* Berits 1983).

Different points of view lead to contradictory results in devising spelling: historical considerations about roots and the derivation of words, morphological considerations such as the representation of identical meaning in an identical fashion in different contexts of appearance, and phonological, as well as phonetic considerations. The results are often a compromise between points of view and are thus inconsistent from any one point of view. The whole discussion about Dutch spelling reforms is an excellent example of the conflicts involved (*cf* Booij 1979 *et al*; Schaap 1980). The results reached by the officially appointed committee on spelling are codified and become obligatory. There are two different codes of spelling in the Netherlands at this time: one more conservative with regard to morphological history, and one that follows to a greater degree the phonological and even phonetic development of the language. From its main point of view, each code shows inconsistencies due to compromise with the competing point of view. Though both codes are in use, people are required to stick exclusively to one or the other within a text. But to many, including educated writers, this is difficult. On a single page, we often find several spellings of the same word or one code applied to one word, the other code to another. It is the task of secretaries, editors, and proof-readers to create a unified spelling for a text. Here, certainly, two separate codes lead to a great deal of insecurity in writing and additional work in editing.

1.2.2 Correctness of lexical items

In every language there are restrictions on word morphology. Possible stems or root words are mainly affected by phonological restrictions. Possible morphological derivations and compound words are mainly affected by morphological restrictions, which are partly phonologically based because they must conform to the possible sounds and combinations of sounds in a language. Not everything that is morphologically possible in a language is realized. For example, there is no verb *deliminate* in English, though there is *eliminate*, and there is no verb *hospital*, though there is the noun *hospital*. Instead English has the verbs *delimit* and *hospitalize*. The actual words are a conventionally determined open list, *ie* a list to which new words can be added under certain circumstances. The set of actual words consists of a subset of the morphologically possible words plus a subset of loans that are not yet adapted to native morphological restrictions; after adaptation the latter are counted as members of the first subset. Since words are coded separately (organized, that is, in lists rather than in rules), the correctness notion is very simple: what is in the list, *ie* the lexicon, is correct. The lexicon is stored in the 'collective memory' of the speech community. Often it is codified in lexica in the form of books or computer discs. For the individual speaker, on the other hand, basically what is familiar to him, as a word of his language, is correct. He will base his correctness judgements on his own memory in the first place, but accept additionally what is stored in public lexica.

Not all speakers of a language have the same vocabulary: there is a common stock of everyday words, and people in specialized fields of knowledge know words which most people outside that field may not know. The whole vocabulary of a language is organized in subgroups of items for which certain subgroups of people know and handle the correctness notions with respect to the form of a word and with respect to its use ('division of linguistic labour' – a term coined by Putnam 1975).

The simple correctness standard of being on the list or not cannot be applied to new words or to loans newly introduced into the language. Since these words are not on the list, they are incorrect at first sight, or at least do not belong to the set of correct words. Here, the notion of acceptability plays a role: is the word formed according to the patterns of word formation of the language out of existing roots, stems, affixes such that the parts are semantically compatible if combined according to at least one of the semantic combinations that correspond to the type of construct? If it is a new word that is not constructed out of existing morphemes, then the method of introducing it plays an important part: is the context of use sufficient to supply enough information about what its content can be? Or, for a loan word: is it a word of a language with some prestige, or of a language known at least to the leaders of the group which would have to accept it first? Is it a word from a native dialect which is spoken by people who play a role outside their native region, in areas where the standard language or neighbouring dialects are used? Is the loan word adjustable to the phonological and morphological restrictions of the language such that its origin is still recognizable and its original meaning can to some extent be ascertained from knowledge about the original language and culture in which it was or still is used? And, important in all these cases, is there a need for a new word, or is there already a word that performs the tasks of the new word well enough and without stigmatization? Acceptability depends on all these points. The last criterion, for example, excludes *deliminate* and a verb *hospital*.

If a new item is acceptable to a significant subgroup, then it will be adopted first by that group and later in the speech of the community as a whole, to the extent that it is useful there. The moment a word is adopted by a group, *ie*, has been put into use, it acquires correctness standards: there are now criteria for its further use and for recognition of its proper form and appearance.

1.2.3 Correctness of syntactic form

There is not much syntax needed as long as language use is restricted to reporting about the immediate speech situation; the hearer can see for himself what is going on, and language is used more to direct attention to certain parts of the situation than to give a precise description. This is true not only with respect to indicatives, but also with respect to questions and to imperatives or requests that can be satisfied directly in the situation of utterance. Here, what is said and what happens occur more or less simultaneously or follow each other immediately. This has been the situation in teaching language to apes and to small children. It is a situation where not much talk is necessary for successful communication, and word order and inflection are not really important to prevent serious problems of ambiguity. Thus, a notion of syntactic correctness is not necessary, since interpretation can fare well without it. Also in early pidgin stages (see Bickerton 1977), there is no notion of syntactic correctness employed, nor does one exist as yet for the pidgin; everything that works is acceptable. Generally, notions of correctness are not developed for their own sake, but are developed and employed only when they are really necessary. This is also the reason that spoken language is much more free in its syntax, even ignoring syntactic form altogether in utterances for which the interpretation is largely supplied by other than linguistic information – by the situation itself or by previous knowledge of the content of what is said. There are many situations where people do not speak in sentences, but say only one or several words, in an order that is certainly not syntactic, and where contextual, gestural, and intonational clues suffice for interpretation. These situations hold especially when emotions are being expressed: the content is known to the hearer already, and the speaker knows this. If interpretation of speech is secured anyhow, syntax does not matter. A very regular instance of this is in answering questions. Since the question itself supplies the presupposed information in a syntactically explicit manner, it can be answered by just one word or by pairs of words, such as *John Mary, and Bill Suzy* in answer to *Whom do John and Bill love?* An answer in which the missing syntactic form is supplied by the previous question is just a special case of the general condition for minimal or no syntactic form: that the information necessary for interpretation can be presupposed.

Spoken language is syntactically less restricted in general, besides having certain syntactic patterns that are not used in written language. In speech people normally accept this freedom from a strict notion of syntactic correctness, except in situations where it would hinder understanding, and in teaching situations. In the latter, even when communication works well with unregulated constructions, parents and teachers usually correct children and language learners so that they can learn the syntax needed in situations lacking sufficient clues for interpretation, as in communication about unknown events, things, relationships, and for written language generally. Motivation for learning syntax depends on several factors: the prestige of the people providing models of correct speech, the wish to please them and to avoid neglect and other penalties, and the drive to get to know parts of the world that are next door and further away. Communication about things and events that are not present or are unknown, with the purpose of gathering knowledge about them, generally requires a set of consistent syntactic signals, such that in the syntactic forms the facts are represented clearly.

Syntax has to get the facts straight, so to speak. In order to learn how this is done, one first has to learn syntax *vis-à-vis* the facts. Thus far, the somewhat naive picture of how sentences represent information about facts is true: there has to be a mapping between facts and texts, but it can be defined in different ways for different languages. In any case, it has to be defined one way or the other. This means that in **just** those situations where syntax is not really necessary for successful communication (that is, where speech does not transmit information that is really new, but only directs attention to it), syntax has to be learned for the sake of communication about other, strange, and far-away situations and their interrelations. Situations of learning syntax are to that extent certainly 'unnatural': they themselves do not provide motivation for learning syntax because in them, syntax is not really needed.

This might be part of the trouble with the efforts to teach syntax to apes. They do pretty well at learning words and combining them up to three items, even forming new compound words, but syntactic restrictions pose a problem for them because these are not needed in the situation in which apes apparently live and communicate; signs are used for directing attention towards something within the situation of communication itself or a direct continuation of it. Children, on the other hand, at least appear to have broader interests and abilities that make it necessary for them to communicate about situations and things out of reach and out of sight and about possible relationships among these. For the representation of such relationships, there have to be cognitive means available, and it is possible that the syntax of a language is to a great extent just a mapping of these, such that it preserves basic cognitive relationships, such as, for example, the relationships between an action and the different actors and circumstances involved. Different syntaxes are, so to speak, different mappings of these relationships, which preserve cognitive structures to a degree sufficient for orientation about the world by means of language.

On the other hand, the syntax of a language provides a socially

controllable intermediate structure between basic cognitive operations, or at least possibilities for specifying such operations, and
publicly accessible and controllable states of affairs. Thus syntax,
which is learned *vis-à-vis* the facts, provides a socially induced
structuring which the facts permit, on the one hand, and which
basic cognitive types of operation permit, on the other. We can
say that syntax, with respect to situations and events and their
interrelations, selects structures in a socially coordinated way.
Situations and their relationships represented under this selective
view are what we call facts. Thus facts are language-dependent
selections of structurings and systematizations which the world
permits, by being as it is. In this way, a certain homomorphism
between syntax and facts is secured, and what the facts are,
though not whether something is a fact, is socially determined in
so far as the human possibilities of cognitive operations leave a
range of freedom. Facts are situated within the possibilities left
open by the basic cognitive restrictions on handling data provided
by perception and lexical information, in a recursive manner. It
is recursiveness of syntax and, likewise, of cognitive operations
that makes it possible to build up complex information from parts
that are basic relative to syntactically complex representations of
information.

Written language *per se* is largely independent of the situations
of writing and reading. It has to make explicit, by description,
information which in daily speech can be available in the situation. Besides the use of more lexical items, this requires a large
amount of socially controllable syntactic construction. There are
also situations in which spoken language requires strong syntactic
restrictions. Formal speech is an example, as in lectures about
involved matters. Strict syntactic form is also necessary in stories
and songs that report history, not only for facilitating recollec-
tion, but for keeping the facts straight about events that
happened long ago and are not recoverable independently. The
same precision is required in formulating predictions or plans
about the future: if once distorted by ambiguity in the historical
text, history cannot be recovered; if predictions and plans are
distorted by ambiguity, one does not know what to expect and
what to do. The exactness required in these matters is not possible without proper syntactic form. Those responsible for
conveying the history of non-literate peoples, who had to learn
the old stories by heart in exact form and wording, performed
for their language a task similar to that performed by written
language in literate societies. Syntactic form is stabilized in
'frozen texts' generally, whether oral or written ones; that these

frozen texts are reference points or models for the notions of syntactic correctness has led, in the history of languages, to different degrees of standardization and also to tensions between conservative models and new models that are a compromise between the old models and new developments due to change in spoken language, change in conditions of life, and modernization.

The question, now, is whether there are separate notions of syntactic correctness for written and for spoken language or only one, that of written language, to which formal speech, less formal speech, and informal speech are adjusted to greater or lesser degrees. Schoolteachers, up to now, have assumed the latter, as is shown by their correction behaviour: in school, spoken language has always been criticized and corrected against the standard of written language. Especially in primary schools, teachers require pupils to answer in syntactically fully explicit sentences, although a one-word answer, a pair-answer, or a chain of these would be perfectly correct, both semantically and pragmatically. Perhaps this is done for the purpose of teaching syntax, but the trouble with such exercises is that they occur in contexts where syntactic explicitness is not only unnecessary but pragmatically incorrect: it expresses information that need not be expressed because it is fully available from the context in an unambiguous way. The availability of information from the context is systematically taken into account in the production of texts and is conceptualized in the notions of correctness of texts. We have examples of texts (question–answer dialogues) in which the sentences are perfectly correct but which become less acceptable, not to say incorrect, as texts, by over-extending a notion of syntactic correctness so that every statement, whatever the context, has to be expressed as a fully fledged sentence. It is a case of hypercorrection with respect to the use of syntactic form.

In everyday speech, correction activity, oriented towards the written or formal standard, depends on how much one is aware of speaking a language different from written language. In Switzerland, spoken language, Swiss German, is accepted as an independent language, side by side with written language, Standard German. This acceptance shows in the use of Swiss German in semi-formal situations in business and school. Written language there has no influence on everyday speech, though it has some normative force with respect to formal oral language use. Likewise in Austria, spoken language is not subject to the norms of written German, but is independent, though less so than Swiss German, the orientation towards written Standard German being stronger in Austria. The political independence of these two countries certainly contributes to the awareness of having their own spoken languages that are not Standard German. In these cases we can certainly speak of different sets of syntactic norms (as well as other linguistic norms) for written and spoken language. In Bavaria, a German state with a strong notion of identity that is also recognized by other Germans, the Bavarian variety of German is conceived of as having local prestige, though it is considered a dialect of German. Spoken language in Bavaria, depending on region, is influenced by Bavarian but also by Franconian and Swabian dialects in the respective regions; many of the overall South German features are accepted or even promoted in schools, even in written language, certainly as far as lexical items are concerned, and this practice is backed up by Bavarian politics. The notions of correctness for writing are mainly those of Standard German, but some regional notions of correctness are incorporated, at least as alternatives, though not replacing standard forms obligatorily. Formal spoken language, of course, contains more regional features than written language.

In other German states, where there is less feeling of tribal or regional identity, correction of spoken language to conform to Standard German is accepted in all school situations and by people of middle and higher social strata; there, except in informal conversations in villages, between local people with local occupations, the standard of written German is also the measure that is incorporated in the notions of correctness for spoken language. This acceptance of correctness notions of written language does not mean that everyday spoken language conforms to them: tolerance for deviance from these standards of correctness is great or small, depending on social position and type of situation. Although dialects are, of course, constituted by their own notions of correctness, as any language necessarily is, the norms that stabilize these notions have a lower normative force because they are superseded by the norms of the standard language in nearly all situations of public life. This is what makes languages (in the linguistic sense of the word) dialects, which are not accepted as separate languages. There are too many situations in which forms that are correct according to the norms of a given dialect are evaluated according to the correctness notions of the standard language and thus considered incorrect. Dialects are not languages in the sociological sense, because their correctness notions are superseded by those of the transregional standard in all official or transregional contexts, and especially in schools. In these contexts, the norms of the standard language clearly are the valid ones, and this means that there the notions of correctness of the standard language are the only ones: every utterance that does not conform to them is incorrect. This notion of correct and incorrect speech has very decisive consequences outside school: in Germany, a person who does not use the case markings correctly is considered unfit for any white-collar job. Different word order is more acceptable; order of norm phrases that fill in the places, or valencies, of the verb is relatively free in German anyway, especially in spoken language, where these different orders, together with information coded in intonation and the use of certain particles, have different text-pragmatic values. In spoken language special referring constructions are used that are not part of the syntax of written language: *Mein Vater, der ging weg* ('My father, he went away'), or even *Er ging weg, mein Vater* ('He went away, my father'), instead of *Mein Vater ging weg* ('My father went away'); and sometimes we hear something like *Mein Vater, der ging weg ging er*, used systematically by some people in story-telling. These construction types occur systematically in spoken language, but are not part of written language, at least not in German. A more famous example is the use of the definite determiner in front of proper names (*der Hans, die Frieda*). More than twenty-five years ago, Riesel (1959:45) asked whether this form, which has been used by authors, *eg* Anna Seghers, should be considered a new norm of written language. Though this is now a feature of standard spoken language in conversations generally, in all social strata, it is not accepted in written language, except perhaps in personal informal letters, and not in formal speech. With regard to these examples, everyday spoken language seems to have its own notions of syntactic correctness.

Another case involves patterns of word order that deviate from the position of finite and non-finite verbs in sentences of written German. Certain patterns of this kind are also considered incorrect in spoken language. *Hast Du genommen mein Buch?* and *Du hast genommen mein Buch* are incorrect versions of *Hast Du mein Buch genommen?* and *Du hast mein Buch genommen* ('Have you taken my book?' and 'You have taken my book'). The first two will be accepted as occasional infelicitous sentence constructions of a speaker who does not do this systematically, but the systematic use of these expressions by Germans is strongly stigmatized and corrected; they are accepted from non-Germans, however, without correction. They are a marker of being a foreigner and had been associated with the variety of German spoken by East European Jews, just as the following forms are now associated with being a guest-worker: *Du Buch nehmen* ('You take book') instead of *Willst Du dieses Buch nehmen?* or *Du nimmst dieses Buch* or *Nimmst Du dieses Buch?* or *Nimm dieses Buch!* The difference between the first type of deviance and the second is that the former is correct in inflectional morphology and unambiguous, whereas the latter, lacking the correct inflectional morphology, is at least four times ambiguous. Although the first is interpretable according to the rules of the language, and the second is interpretable in situations that give sufficient additional information, these constructions are generally unacceptable except when spoken by someone of whom one does not expect anything better.

We thus have a hierarchy of notions that pertain to acceptability and correctness of syntactic form:

1. Syntactically correct according to the standard of written language;
2. Syntactically incorrect according to the written standard, but acceptable in everyday spoken language;
3. Syntactically incorrect and not acceptable in everyday spoken language of native speakers;
4. Otherwise incorrect and unacceptable but can, if at least understandable and interpretable, be acceptable when used by people of whom one does not expect correct speech.

What is not understandable and not interpretable is absolutely unacceptable. If one has higher expectations with regard to the ability of a person to handle the correctness notions of a language, one will find that person's production of incorrect speech more unacceptable; with higher expectations, that is, acceptability of incorrect speech is lower. Note that sometimes perfectly correct speech with respect to the correctness notions treated so far can be unacceptable, as, for example, in situations in which more casual speech is appropriate, or less explicitness is required. Here other correctness notions than the grammatical ones come into play to determine acceptability.

Thus far I have discussed notions of correctness that pertain to linguistic form of communicational means; I did not include notions of correctness of texts because a text, in my opinion, is not a linguistic form. There are standard forms of different kinds of text that make them recognizable as a text of this kind or that: a letter, a story, a poem, a report, etc., but there is no notion of a text-form *per se*. This is because there must be a property of coherence which makes a text a text, distinct from a mere collection of sentences; and this property cannot be captured on the formal level of the text itself. It can only be captured on the basis of interpretation, by considering reference to established referents, presupposition and other assumed knowledge of speaker and hearer, goals, and motivations of behaviour. Therefore, the notion of 'text-grammar', which has been widely criticized (for example by Dascal and Margalit 1974) since it was introduced in the early days of text linguistics by van Dijk (1972), is not comparable to a sentence grammar and is, in the linguistic sense, no grammar at all. Formulating correctness conditions for texts is not a matter of finding correctness conditions for linguistic forms. Correctness of texts, in some of its aspects, belongs under the heading of correctness of use of linguistic forms, together with semantic and pragmatic correctness; in other aspects, it belongs under the heading of correctness of actions and series of actions. Two different kinds of correctness are involved in both, pragmatic correctness, including aspects of stylistics, and correctness of texts:

1. Correctness of the use of linguistic means or forms;
2. Correctness of communication as a part of rational interaction.

In fact, when judging from the first of these points of view, we always presuppose correctness from the second. This is necessary because when we judge the adequacy of the use of linguistic forms for performing certain communicative actions or series of these (as in texts and dialogues), we have to be able to find out the intended action before we can judge whether the linguistic expression used in that action is adequate for performing that action. On the other hand, to determine the performed action, we generally have to rely on the correct use of the linguistic forms; indeed, this is presupposed in interpretation. In cases in which one finds semantic or pragmatic contradictions if an utterance is interpreted according to the correct use of its parts and syntactic structure, and no indirect interpretation can be derived by pragmatic principles, one can assume that the linguistic forms are used in a way that is different from established use and thus are used incorrectly. One also presupposes in such cases that the intended actions are, in fact, consistent, but wrongly performed with respect to the use of the linguistic means of communication.

The general notion of correctness of texts is mainly based on the notion of text coherence, about which work in text linguistics has been done for more than fifteen years, cf for example van Dijk (1977). Notions of semantic and pragmatic correctness have been treated in Bartsch (1979a, b, 1985a). A more formal treatment of aspects of pragmatic correctness, especially with respect to questions and answers, has been given by Groenendijk and Stokhof (1984).

1.2.4 Correctness of texts

Interpretation of utterances, and especially of texts, is based on the accountability of the use of linguistic means of communication, and on the accountability of the relationships between knowledge, goals, and actions, based on practical reasoning. These two aspects of accountability require notions of what can be expected with regard to the use of certain linguistic means in certain situations, and with respect to actions in these situations. Expectations, and expectations of these expectations of speaker and hearer, are made possible and are justified by the existence of notions of correctness with regard to these two aspects. As far as texts are concerned, the notion of text coherence is the broadest correctness notion. In this chapter, I want to treat only one component of this correctness notion, namely 'thematic correctness' of the continuation of a text at any point. This kind of local correctness plays an important role for the interpretation of lexical items. (For a formal treatment *cf* Bartsch 1984c.)

When we hear the utterance *John does well*, we can only interpret this, *ie* know which state of affairs is represented, if we know in which respect we have to interpret *do well* in this sentence: well with respect to his health, with respect to his career, with respect to his economic position, with respect to his family, etc. These different respects I call 'thematic dimensions', in which words like *good/well, strong, satisfactory*, etc. have to be interpreted. Words which are dimensionally undetermined to some degree can be used with respect to a set of thematic dimensions by which they acquire additional semantic content which is not included in their meaning, but is provided by the context. The context specifies the thematic dimension in question. Questions are possible at any point of a text which will be answered by the continuation of the text (*cf* also Drop and De Vries 1980; Hellwig 1982). These questions define the thematic dimensions within which the interpretation of the continuation of the text takes place. I call these questions 'thematic questions'. (How much the interpretation of indicative sentences depends on expressed or assumed questions is shown and formally worked out in Groenendijk and Stokhof 1984.)

As has been pointed out in the literature on text linguistics (*cf* van Dijk 1977, 1980), the build-up of texts and their coherence are globally determined by the general theme, the 'macro-structure' of the text, and the kind of text, the 'superstructure' or *Textsorte*. Text coherence in larger as well as in smaller parts of a text is determined by identity of referents, relationships between referents (including entities, stretches of time, places, situations) and causal, motivational, and argumentational relationships. The so-called 'scripts' and 'frames' provide a structure of expectations about the progression of a text and at the same time mark the unexpected details of information that are filled into their slots when the text proceeds.

The generation of thematic questions and, with these, the opening up of thematic dimensions, are located within this model of text structure. Especially the request for information about unpredictable, unexpected details within the boundaries of the overall frame and with respect to introduced referents gives rise to thematic questions. A thematic question is based on the preceding text and provides part of the coherence properties, which connect the following text with the preceding text.

Next to restrictions provided by text coherence with respect to frames and text referents, the kind of text determines limits for what can reasonably be asked at any point of the text so that the answer stays well within the delineations of the text type.

Because thematic questions require filling in the unexpected details within a frame, they can pertain to further properties of, or relationships between, introduced referents; these are preferably properties and relationships that explain events or actions in causal or motivational ways, referring to events or actions and attitudes of people.

We can distinguish at least three kinds of thematic questions:
(A) Technically and factually oriented questions;
(B) Person-oriented questions concerning motives and attitudes;
(C) Communicatively oriented questions concerning motivation of certain speech acts and moves in dialogues.

If thematic questions are explicit within texts, as they are, for example, in dialogues, they explicitly provide the thematic dimension by either referring to it with a noun phrase, like *John's health* in *How is John's health?*, or by predicate-limiting adverbial phrases like *with respect to his health, healthwise, as far as his health is concerned*, etc.

If the thematic question is not explicitly stated we can assume that the speaker supposes the hearer to have certain thematic questions, and that he continues his text under these suppositions.

These suppositions can be illustrated by the following examples, in which the interpretation of the Dutch adjective *flink* depends on the assumed thematic dimension (*cf* also 5.2):

> Text 1. *Jantje was met zijn moeder naar de tandarts. Het viel nogal tegen; maar hij is een flinke jongen.* 'Johnny went with his mother to the dentist. It was bad; but he is a brave boy.'

The second sentence is an answer to the B-type question *Has it been bad for him?* The last sentence is an answer to a further B-type question, namely *How did he take it?* On the basis of this question, the adjective *flink* is interpreted within the thematic dimension 'endurance with respect to adverse situations': *flink* here means 'brave'.

> Text 2. *Jantje was met zijn moeder naar de tandarts. Hij had een flinke ansteking onder een van zijn kiezen. Hij kon daarom vandag niet naar school.* '. . . He had a heavy inflammation under one of his back teeth. Because of this he could not go to school today.'

Here, the second sentence is an answer to an A-type question, namely *What was wrong with his teeth?* The last sentence is an answer to a C-type question, namely *Why do you tell this?* The answer is that the speaker wants to give an explanation for Johnny's missing school today. In this way we can reconstruct these short texts as dialogues, where one person askes the thematic question and the other answers.

Example 3 is a real dialogue. We shall see that it becomes a coherent text when the explicit questions are skipped:

> Text 3. R: *Hallo. Wat heb je hier, Erik?*
> E: *Een bakfiets.*
> R: *Is die van jou?*
> E: *Nee, hij is van mijn baas.*
> R: *Stuurt hij moeilijk?*
> E: *Nee, hoor.*
> R: *Ik vraag, omdat die voren twee wielen heeft.*
> E: *Nee, niet moeilijk, maar het is toch even wennen.*

'Hello. What have you got there, Erik? – A cart-cycle. – Is it yours? – No, it belongs to my boss. – Is steering it difficult? – No, not really. – (Now R assumes that E thinks 'Why does she ask this?') I ask because it has two front wheels. – No, not difficult; but you have to get used to it.'

This dialogue can be condensed to become a text produced by Erik, assuming the initiating question 'What have you got there, Erik?' The text then runs:

> Text 4. *Look, I have a cart-cycle; it belongs to my boss. It is not difficult to steer, once you have got used to it.*

Text production presupposes an initiating question posed by the hearer, or anticipated by the speaker, the speaker anticipates the hearer's questions. The answers to these questions constitute the produced text.

In text interpretation, the hearer guesses which questions the speaker supposes him, the hearer, to have. This means that the hearer interprets the text as answers to these questions.

Anticipation of thematic questions requires that there are limits within which these questions can be located. Questions have to be correct in this sense, or at least reasonable with regard to these limits. Aspects under which correctness of questions is determined, are:

1. The situation of communication; it depends on which type of text is appropriate, and along with this, what kind of questions (person oriented, fact oriented, communication oriented) are appropriate.
2. The overall theme of the text; for texts that are mainly directed towards providing information it can be represented by a question. Answering this question is the main goal of the text, next to possibly other goals, such as presentation of self, protection of the image of the other, establishing and strengthening personal relations, teaching, etc.

The two aspects are important for the global organization of the text: thematic questions have to be rational with respect to these aspects, *ie* they have to be directed and adequate with respect to the main goal and the other accepted goals. In case of conflicts between strategies for reaching different goals, some leeway is given to pursuing the minor goals, but it is limited by the requirements of the overall goal (*cf* 7.2).

Next to these global conditions there are local ones on which the satisfaction of the global goals depends: generally, we can say that some action contributes to a goal if it brings us closer to reaching that goal. Goal adequacy depends not only on the goal, but also on initial conditions. If the goal is to provide certain information then the initial conditions are the information that is already available to the hearer. With respect to other goals, such as influencing the attitudes and actions of the hearer, initial conditions include not only relevant information, but motivations, attitudes, and actions performed and planned by the hearer. Considering all this, a text is a set of utterance acts that is rationally organized with respect to main and minor goals, and initial conditions.

If the main goal is to provide information about a certain state of affairs, then a piece of text contributes to the guiding thematic question if it gives at least a partial pragmatically correct answer, *ie* an answer which, in combination with other information available to the hearer, excludes some possible answers. (Compare Groenendijk and Stokhof 1984 for these and other related notions of answerhood.) The basis of judgements about text coherence is the main goal and further related goals towards which the text is expected to be directed.

For the speaker to anticipate correctly the hearer's questions, he needs to have the following information (initial conditions) at each point of the process of text production:

(a) Information about orientation and motivation of the hearer: is he or she, at that point, interested in persons, in facts, or in the reasons for certain moves in communication? The kinds of information are delineated by the kind of text, as some texts do not allow person-oriented questions, others do not allow fact-oriented ones. Both orientation and motivation of the hearer change in the course of a text.

(b) Information about the hearer's knowledge with respect to the topic and theme of the text. Some of it can be assumed as general knowledge about the world and especially about 'scripts' of different kinds of situations; some information is particular to the hearer in question and the situation of speech, as well as the preceding text.

We thus have to consider global and local orientation, motivation, and information. A thematic question has to be directed towards gathering of new information, *ie* it has to ask for new information, and it has to be correct with respect to the overall orientation of the text and the local orientation mentioned under (a) and (b).

The continuation of a text has to give at least a pragmatically correct partial answer to a pragmatically correct thematic question, *ie* it has to give an answer that is pragmatically correct with respect to the hearer's accepted goals, motivation, and local information. Roughly, a continuation of a text is pragmatically correct if it gives a pragmatically correct answer to a pragmatically correct thematic question.

The admittance of thematic questions, and with that the possibility of thematic dimensions relative to which interpretation of lexical items and whole sentences has to take place, is restricted by the notions of correctness just mentioned. The hearer assumes the speaker to behave correctly with respect to the points of view discussed above, and the speaker assumes the same about the hearer and about the hearer's assumptions with respect to the speaker and his assumptions. The establishment of thematic dimensions takes place within these boundaries, defined by the above notions of correctness of texts, which are just specifications of the general principle of rationality; and the interpretation of a text, at each point, is delineated by these dimensions accordingly.

So far this can be stated very generally, and it can be applied and demonstrated in individual examples with precise results. But these notions of correctness of texts can be formalized only in a formal semantics and pragmatics of texts. The difficulty, or even impossibility, of making them explicit as formal properties of texts themselves lies in the fact that large portions of the processes that are guided by these notions of correctness have no uniquely determined linguistic expression, or are not expressed linguistically at all. Notions of correctness of texts are at least partially about content and not about form of texts. This can easily be seen with respect to question–answer pairs: from a formal point of view, *Fred with Mary, Peter with Karin, and Thea with Charles* is an answer appropriate to the question *Who comes with whom?*, but it is as well an answer to *which people come together?*, which is of quite a different form. It is types of contents of questions to which certain answers fit; and these contents can be expressed by linguistically different forms.

The whole endeavour of explicating the notions of text correctness is not so much one of linguistics, *ie* of looking for formal linguistic properties of texts, but of the general theory of action, applied to communication by linguistic means.

1.2.5 Semantic correctness

Semantics is that part of the theory of meaning that explicates what expressions contribute to the fulfilment conditions of sentences, and especially to the truth conditions of indicative sentences.

In the philosophical theory of meaning, the concept of 'meaning' in one of its essential aspects is explicated on the basis of the concepts 'truth' and 'evidence'. The first leads to a theory of meaning for a language that is a theory of truth for that language (*eg* Davidson 1969), the second leads to a theory of meaning that is a theory of evidence for the language (*eg* Quine 1964). 'Truth' is the starting-point of so-called logical semantics; 'evidence' is the starting-point of so-called empiricist semantics. Davidson, in his programmatic article 'Truth and meaning' (1969) coined the since then well-known slogan 'The meaning of a sentence is its truth conditions'. This statement, referring to indicative sentences and restricted by the formulation 'the meaning of a sentence in one of its relevant aspects', rests on the fact that to understand a sentence, that is to know what it means, consists especially in knowing under which circumstances the sentence would be true.

Starting with the notion that the meanings of indicative sentences are their truth conditions, one wants to determine the meanings of the constituents of an indicative sentence as the contributions they make to the truth conditions of the whole sentence; and, in principle at least, they make the same contributions in any sentence in which they occur. Those parsings of a sentence into constituents are, then, semantically adequate as the basis on which one can formulate a recursive theory of truth for a language L. A theory of truth for a language L is a theory that describes the application of the predicate *true* to indicative sentences of this language, *ie* a theory that says under which conditions an indicative sentence of L is qualified to be called 'true'. A theory is recursive if it does this in a recursive way and therefore can say, by means of a finite set of rules, how we can give, or withhold from, potentially infinitely many sentences the qualification 'true'. A recursive theory of truth of a sentence calculates the truth value with respect to any universe or realm of discourse from the interpretations of its parts that are relevant for its truth value with respect to this realm. This is precisely what a formal grammar of a natural language (also called 'logical grammar' of that language) is designed for. A formal or logical grammar of a language L gives a semantics of that language which abstracts from the analysis of separate lexical items, except those that are taken to be part of logical syntax itself. Such a grammar treats words with respect to their syntactical category only, and with respect to some subcategorial markings. It gives what one can call a *sentence semantics*. To understand a sentence, *word semantics*, in addition to sentence semantics is, of course, essential. Word and sentence semantics together provide us with the sense of a sentence; to be able to value the sentence as true or false, we have to make reference to the speech situation, at least if the sentence refers in a deictical manner to place, time, and to individuals. This aspect of natural language is explicated in so-called *indexical semantics*. The truth valuation of a sentence is formulated as dependent on 'indices' of the speech situation, to which deictic expressions refer, such as *here, now, yesterday, I, you*, or *he*. A complete semantics for languages with deictic expressions has to be an indexical semantics that includes sentence semantics and word semantics.

1.2.5(1) Meaningfulness and semantic correctness
The notions of meaningfulness and correctness have to be defined

with respect to the goals for which language is used as a means. Therefore, these notions, in the first place, have to be defined for language use, that is, for sentences in use, and specifically for utterances. As far as semantics is concerned, we consider the use of expressions for representing states of affairs. *A sentence utterance* is *semantically meaningful* with respect to a realm of discourse if one can judge whether the assertion expressed by the sentence is fulfilled by the referents of its referring expressions in that realm; with respect to the utterance of an indicative sentence this means that its truth value with respect to that realm can be judged. This can also be the case if the predicates in the referring descriptions in the sentence are not really true of the referents but at least can serve to identify the referents, or do not hinder identification of the referents if this is done deictically. A sentence utterance is *conventionally semantically meaningful* if its being fulfilled or not fulfilled can be judged in a conventional manner, *ie* on the basis of an interpretation according to the conventional meanings of its parts.

The *utterance* of an indicative sentence is *semantically correct*, if it is used in a referentially and predicationally correct way, *ie* if we can judge that its referring expressions refer in the conventional way and if its predicative expression is appropriate as a characterization of the referents in question. Semantic correctness of an assertive utterance thus is recognizable appropriateness of its literal (conventional) content with respect to the world that is partially represented by it. *Semantic correctness of expressions* will be judged with respect to speech situations and situations of verification or fulfilment of the utterance of the expression.

Judging about semantic correctness of the use of expressions is therefore open to exactly the same problems as the decision about whether or not something can count as the verification of an indicative sentence with respect to a theory or a network of beliefs as a background (in the sense of Quine 1963, 1964). This implies that semantic correctness of utterances, *ie* expressions in their use, becomes a meaningful notion only against the background of common convictions of the speech community about the world and about conduct, *ie* about beliefs and norms. As will be pointed out with respect to problems of contextual intentional correctness, heterogeneity of the speech community with respect to convictions can lead to very different judgements about the correctness of use of expressions with religious, scientific, and political backgrounds.

Furthermore, the ability to judge about the semantically

correct use of certain expressions can differ for different people,
depending on their degree of general and special education with
regard to fields that are the background for religious, theoretical,
or moral concepts. The judgements of people in these areas are
differently highly-valued, and are therefore of different relevance
as standards for others. These problems of establishing semantic
norms, and along with them, the problems of the validity of the
correctness conditions of expressions in their descriptive use, are
more or less known to the members of a speech community, and
they are solved to some degree by accepting a 'division of
linguistic labour' (Putnam 1975). This means that not every
member of the speech community has to be able to use every
expression correctly, but that he should abstain from the use of
certain expressions in situations where full knowledge of their
correctness conditions is required, and leave this use, in case of
doubt, to specialists in this area. Semantic competence, *ie* being
able to handle the concept 'semantically correct', is, with regard
to different parts of the vocabulary of a natural language,
unevenly distributed among the members of a speech community.
This is, of course, necessary since memory capacity and lifetime
of humans are restricted to such a degree that division of
linguistic labour has to relieve the individuals; and, at the same
time, this makes it possible for a speech community as a whole
to use and create, in cooperation, a very rich language that is
highly developed in all essential areas, and that can serve technical and social progress.

Semantic heterogeneity not only implies partial semantic
incompetence, but it also implies deviations between the
semantic competence of members of a speech community with
respect to one and the same field where they consider themselves
to be specialists, and even fights between proponents of
competing schools with regard to the competence, or even authority, to determine what the proper use of certain expressions is.
Yet there are boundaries set to semantic inhomogeneity by the
different agencies of socialization that play a role in homogen-
izing the speech community to at least some bearable degree
(for example: parents, school, universities, language and
dictionary institutes, churches, official political statements by
leading figures in politics and economy, or by their agents in the
mass media).

The concept of semantic correctness so far has been based on
the notion of 'counting as evident or true for a population P with
a language L', rather than on the notion of 'true in L'. If we were
to base our correctness concept on this latter notion, we would

define a concept of correctness according to which expressions would be correct, even if we were unable to judge whether they were correct, and sentences would be structurally correct even if there were no possibility of verifying them. Such a concept we call 'truth'-semantic correctness, in opposition to 'use'-semantic correctness, which we have dealt with so far. This concept would make the famous sentence *There is a golden mountain that never will be detected* structurally semantically correct, since it may be true; but it is in principle not verifiable, since it negates its own verifiability. The same sentence might be use-correct in a fairy-tale where other convictions hold than in our culture at present; for example, that there is the all-knowing author who knows that the sentence is true, although none of the people of fairyland will ever be able to recognize that the sentence is true. But if these people strongly believe this sentence to be true, it counts for them as evident, and then it would be correct, not only truth-semantically, but also use-semantically. The relationship between truth-semantic correctness and use-semantic correctness is the same as between 'true' and 'counting as true or evident'. The first is a regulating idea for the second, which is a historically, socially, and culturally bound notion. There is, in our society, a certain kind of cognitive behaviour which explicitly strives for truth, namely scientific behaviour. And what counts as true and evident for a scientist in his field has the prestige to determine what rightly may count as true or evident, at least for the time being. Thus there is an idea of semantic correctness that seems to give us the right to be intolerant against the 'use'-correctness that holds for certain subpopulations of the speech community which, in our opinion, are not guided as much by scientific principles as we think we are. But, as long as something counts as true for a population, it is true for them. To realize the difference between 'true' and 'counting as true' a historical and comparative perspective is required, and this is not the perspective of everyday language use.

Despite the difficulties mentioned that arise when the notion of semantic correctness is filled content-wise and applied, this notion is a central notion, because it formulates the foundation of one essential use of language, namely, language as a means of representation, or, in other words, the descriptive use of language. Precisely by paying attention to the notion of semantic correctness, the problems mentioned become visible: it is not applied homogeneously across the speech community and thus gives rise to misunderstanding in communication; as far as it is homogeneously applied it just makes understanding possible.

Without semantic correctness as a regulating idea, there would be no use of expressions that is sufficiently uniform among the speech community to make communication possible. The use of expressions has to be uniform in two respects, namely with regard to the objects in the world (according to the correspondence aspect of truth), and with regard to the members of the speech community such that only that way of use can be judged to be correct which agrees with the others' use of the expression in question. The concept of semantic correctness embraces these aspects of uniformity, and it is, at the same time, a notion the application of which depends on social, cultural, and historical factors.

1.2.5(2) The frame for regular use of expressions

We use expressions in a non-arbitrary way. To do that we need criteria on the basis of which we distinguish between cases in which we use a certain expression from those in which we do not. This means that we must be able to ask and answer the question whether this or that use of a certain expression is correct. This question we cannot ask if we use a sign only once, but only when we can ask 'Do **we** use the expression which we use in this case **in the same way** as we have done **up to now**?'

In this question, reference is made to:
1. Other members of the speech community;
2. Different points of time or situations;
3. Commonalities between situations.

These aspects define the restrictions known as 'intersubjectivity', 'generality' with respect to situations, and 'regularity'. We thus take into account series of utterances containing expression A, connected with a series of situations in which, or with respect to which, these utterances are used with approval by the members of the speech community. (This approval is, as far as assertions are concerned, Quine's 1964 and 1973 notion of 'assent'.) These situations are satisfaction situations of the utterances. There are points of view determined by current interests of speakers and hearers that determine what the boundaries are, and which traits are salient in these situations:

(1) $R(u_1, s_1)$, $R(u_2, s_2)$, $R(u_3, s_3)$, . . ., where the u's are utterances of A, the s's are the corresponding satisfaction situations, and R is the relationship of approval between utterance and situation.

In the series of utterances u_1, u_2, u_3, . . . a trace is found which is the recurrent appearance of expression A, and in the corresponding situations a trace is found which is assumed to correspond to A, namely Reg(A), the regularities of the use of A. Use 'in the same way', or regular use in, or with respect to, different situations of satisfaction (conditions 2 and 3) would even be necessary for a private language, which a single person could entertain for himself: according to (2) and (3) the use of an expression A is based on the judgement that one has used A in accordance with the use of it in, or with respect to, other situations. This judgement, if it is to be reliable with respect to real properties of the situations, requires that one has a reliable memory. According to condition (1), correct use of A is based furthermore on a judgement of the language user that the other language users of the same linguistic community will also use A in this case, and in accordance with their use up to now. This likewise depends on their having a reliable memory. The speech community as a whole, so to speak, has to have a reliable public memory: it has to be excluded that all or many users of the language remember something different about former use of the expression, even if they use the expression in the same situations. To agree on the use of the expression in each single case is not sufficient: the correlation between the expression and its situations of satisfaction has to show a constancy, and in this way has to be correct, and not be a different one, though socially agreed upon in every single case of use of the expression. A population with such an agreement without a constancy in the situational regularities could handle a notion of correctness, but this would be unreliable with respect to regularities in satisfaction situations and thus could not give rise to a notion of truth or satisfaction: their judgements about sameness of use would be wrong in a way such that language could not be used as a means of orientation in the world. Intersubjective agreement about the correlation between expression and satisfaction situation is reliable from an objective point of view only if we can assume that memories are individually and collectively functioning well; then recollected regularities with respect to an expression A have an objective counterpart, namely Reg(A). This means that social agreement is not a sufficient basis for the notion of truth. The agreement itself has to be based reliably on regularities in situations and on a sufficient memory. The three conditions together form the frame in which regular use of an expression A, or the use of A in the same way, is determined. It gives rise not only to an intersubjective notion of correctness, but at the same time also to an objective notion of truth, which, of course, is intersubjective.

The criteria for the use of a predicative expression (in short: predicators, *ie* nouns, verbs, adjectives, adverbs, prepositions, postpositions, and non-logical conjunctions) form a 'concept in the narrow sense'. This notion is neutral with respect to the question of whether the criteria are more of a prototypical nature, or have the form of a set of propositions in which the relevant features are spelled out, and are weighed with respect to how central they are for the concept in question. This much-discussed difference does not matter as long as it is clearly indicated under what aspects comparison with the prototype has to deliver identities that, in a graded fashion, constitute the required similarity. The 'concept in the broader sense', also called 'connotation', or sometimes split up into 'concept in the narrower sense' and 'connotation', also contains stereotypical or connotational information that need not be true in a satisfaction situation, but is supposed to be true in the so-called normal cases.

The criteria for the use of a one- or more-place predicator have to be such that, firstly, there exists intersubjective agreement with others about the use of A. But it is not sufficient that there merely is agreement, rather the basis on which this agreement is founded has to be of a certain kind, namely, that secondly the situations themselves, if they are satisfaction situations, have to exhibit commonalities under the points of view that determine salience. The agreement between satisfaction situations must, next to use of the same expression A, also lie in features of the things, actions, and relationships within these situations which appear regularly together with the use of non-negated A in satisfaction situations. These are the regularities bound to A. The referent about which A is predicated shows the regularities that are the criteria for the correct use of A. Thus, referring to something by means of a description containing A is based on a judgement about qualities and relationships. The use of a predicator is determined by two kinds of agreement: by intersubjective agreement, and by objective agreement in the regularities within the situations of satisfaction.

1.2.5(3) Satisfaction situations and language learning

Concepts are criteria or patterns in the minds of language users guiding the use of expressions. They have an intersubjective and objective character because they are formed under social control and remain socially controlled by a public normative force enacted in the speech community on its members by approval or disapproval in situations of use of the expressions that express these concepts. This intersubjective and objective aspect of a concept is thought of as somehow a projection that is outside the individuals, a public concept, which regulates all the individual subjective concepts in the heads of the speakers in such a way that these fit within the projection. The public concept has its reality in the trait of regularity that corresponds with the occurrences of its expression in satisfaction situations; the judgement about whether the expression has been applied correctly or not is guided by aspects of relevance under which certain regularities are a matter of attention. For this judgement it does not make much difference whether the comparison between the cases of application of the expression A is performed via mental representations of prototypical cases, or with a pattern that is a description consisting of a set of propositions in which the main features of the subjects to which the expression applies are predicated.

Since the respects or points of view under which identity is considered may vary with speech situations, the applications of expressions can be judged to be correct under these various respects, and, likewise, the notion of truth will then be 'true under this or that respect'. In this way the traditional notion of 'concept' is replaced by a complex of (traditional) concepts which are each expressed by A under different context types $c-i$ which define the relevant respects or points of view for the judgement of correctness or truth. (This notion of context-dependent meaning has been formalized in principle by Montague (1974) and Kaplan (1979) for deictic expressions, and by Sag (1981) and Bartsch (1984a, c) for the formal treatment of polysemy as a function from context indices to intensions.) The decision about applicability of an expression depends on whether the traits of agreement of its semantic pattern (or of a complex of patterns that are variations of the pattern) with the situation in question are salient enough also for the potential hearer to agree to the application of the expression, in accordance with the regularities that for him constitute the pattern which is the concept or complex of concepts he has formed in a socially controlled way.

On the basis of the decisive role of criteria or patterns for the use of expressions in satisfaction situations, we can think of propositions that are necessarily true as sentences that explicate the criteria of application of the expressions used in them. In this vein Donnellan (1962:658) characterized necessity as 'ideal rigidity in our judgements about what we would say in hypothetical cases', and similarly Carnap (1956) in his explanation of his pragmatic notion of intension. The modal notion of *de dicto* necessity is finally based on a normativity that is formulated in D. Lewis's (1969) 'convention of truthfulness' – which really should not be called 'a convention' because it does not have a rational alternative. It is a principle, and a norm of prudence, namely that we conform to linguistic and especially semantic norms; this means that we take into account the notions of correctness in order to make communication possible. We know what the satisfaction of sentences containing certain expressions in certain categorial roles **must** be because of the criteria for the use of these expressions in satisfaction situations. These criteria are fixed enough to function as the basis for decisions about whether an expression may be used in, or with respect to, such a situation. At the same time the normative force enacted in the public use of an expression according to its criteria has to be relaxable if a higher norm requires this (*cf* 5.2).

The role of criteria in decisions about truth and satisfaction, and the acquisition and determination of the criteria, have to be explained in such a manner that their determination is derived from their function as an instrument of decision. On the other hand, this function of decision has to be made possible by what the criteria for the use of expressions are. To explicate this interdependency of function and determination of criteria requires that situations of learning them are situations of satisfaction. These satisfaction situations that, in principle, are also learning- and teaching-situations, I call 'ESL-situations', *ie* 'evidence/satisfaction/learning-situations'.

In ESL-situations the notions 'correct' with respect to the use of a predicator *A* and 'true' with respect to the sentence *This/Here is A* collapse: the sentence *This is a chair* is true if and only if we can apply the predicator *chair* correctly to what is referred to by the deictic expression *this*. In order to call something *A* or refer to it by *an/the A* the criteria of use of *A* have to be satisfied. The meta-linguistic assertion *This is something we can call 'A'* is at the same time a judgement about the quality or the relational properties of the object referred to. To determine the truth of the sentence *This is A* means to determine that *A* is used correctly with respect to that which is meant by *this*. A correct use of *A* in an ESL-situation means truth of the corresponding assertion.

A boundary case in which the decision about truth/satisfaction or correctness is not possible is the situation of first use of an expression *A*. Here, truth or correctness is out of question: it is simply posited. It does not yet have any informational content, except the meta-linguistic information that expression *A* is true/correct here. Only with further use of *A* in other situations can an objective content correspond to the use of *A*, namely that these situations have a relevant common trait together with the situation of first use. If something salient has been singled out uniquely in the situation of first use of *A*, the expression can be assumed to have this as its objective content. The boundary case of first use is regularly experienced by children learning a language. They do not yet have criteria and thus for them a thing simply is what it is said to be: when they ask 'What is this?' they just ask what it is called. An answer consisting of a complex description by means of words they already know would be out of place. They do not want an analytical description of what they see in front of them, but a name.

Since for children, and language learners generally, an expression applies to what is salient for them in the situation attended to, they further apply the expression to everything that is connected with the proper denotation in a salient fashion, be it by similarity or by factual relations within the situation of use itself. From the point of view of someone who is competent in the language, the first application looks like an overgeneraliz-ation or like a metaphor, and the second like a metonymy. Metonymical transfer of a word takes place via traces of spatio-temporal coincidence, action–result, means–ends, material–product, container–content relationships, and other factual connections that are salient within the ESL-situations of use of the word. Because the language learner has not yet learned the correctness conditions for the word, these metaphors and metonymies are not the same for him as they are for the competent language user, who realizes the metaphors and meto-nymies to be deviations from the semantic correctness notions of the word. For the language learner the application of an expression to everything salient in a situation is the starting-point; and therefore his first attempts to use the word, starting from a learning situation, and proceeding to other situations, seem metonymical to competent language users. Likewise further use on the basis of similarities seems metaphorical. Both ways involve a lot of over-extension of the use of the expression compared to established public usage. Disapproval and correc-tion serve to eliminate cases of over-extension of the use of the expression. Correction acts of the type *This is not an A, but a B* provide the oppositions necessary for delimiting the use of the expression further on: some salient features are put into oppo-sition with others, parallel with the opposition of expressions *A* and *B*.

Oppositions are integrated if we consider ESL-situations for sentences containing several predicators in a system of contrasts: we have a set of utterances, *U*, and a set of corresponding satisfaction situations, S, which both exhibit a corresponding structure of similarity and opposition. An example for such a contrast system is:

$$U = \{u_1, u_2, u_3, u_4\}, \text{ and } S = \{s_1, s_2, s_3, s_4\} \text{ with:}$$

u_1: *John is reading a book* s_1: ABC
u_2: *John is reading a letter* s_2: ABD
u_3: *John is writing a letter* s_3: AED
u_4: *Peter is writing a letter* s_4: FED

From this we can construct similarity circles (Carnap's 1928 *Ähnlichkeitskreise*), which are equivalence classes under similarity. Each equivalence class among expressions defines a quasi-constituent, (*ie* a part), and the corresponding equivalence class among the ESL-situations defines a quasi-concept of situations. What evolves as quasi-concepts is dependent on the available set of oppositions, and it is also restricted by the points of view which define salience of traits in the situations.

Using the available opposition, we can break down the expressions and the situations into their quasi-constituents or parts, which are relative to the oppositions provided by the contrast system. Starting from such systems of contrast, new sentences can be formed by the principle of variation of content by substitution of parts and corresponding quasi-concepts in a chain of oppositions. This method has been called 'projection' by Ziff (1960); for the restrictions on these projections see Bartsch (1969).

For expressions that are not satisfied within the speech situation or within a satisfaction situation we have to construct pairs, triples, or chains of situations, or even series of such pairs, triples, and chains of situations. The expression *John will come tomorrow*, for example, requires construction of pairs consisting of the speech situation and situations that have the relationship to it, namely 'within the next day', one of which has to be a satisfaction situation of *John is coming*, if the sentence should be true. I call such a construction a 'satisfaction constellation'. The satisfaction constellation of a sentence that is not satisfied within the speech situation itself consists of the speech situation and one or more satisfaction situations for the descriptive (referential and predicative) content of the sentence, whereby a relationship holds between the speech situation and the satisfaction situations which is specified by the context or by an expression in the sentence. There are temporal, spatial, causal, and motivational relationships between satisfaction situations or whole constellations expressed in sentences, as in *John will come if Mary will*

come or in *John will come because Mary is here.* In the latter
sentence, for example, we have a satisfaction constellation that
consists of a causal or motivational relationship between a satisfaction constellation and a satisfaction situation. If a satisfaction
constellation consists of the speech situation and a satisfaction
situation and both collapse, the constellation reduces to the
speech situation, as for the sentence *Mary is here.* There are
many expressions in languages that have to be learned in full-
blown satisfaction constellations, for example, quantifiers, time-
and space-adverbs and connectors, causal adverbs and connectors, etc. But this requires first that language use in satisfaction
situations is learned, because the construction of satisfaction
constellations requires the incorporation of satisfaction situations.

A dissatisfaction situation of *A* is a situation in which
This/Here is A is not satisfied. There *A* is used incorrectly, and
not A is used correctly. This means that in a situation in which
This/Here is A is false, *This/Here is not A* is true. A dissatisfaction
situation of *A* is a satisfaction situation of *not A*. In case of
existential quantification a constellation is a dissatisfaction
constellation if it does not contain a satisfaction situation. A
sentence with existential quantification (restricted by a predicator
and restricted to a universe of discourse, as for example *a boy*,
restricted to a sports team) is false if within the domain of the
restrictions given there is no constellation that contains a satisfaction situation. The sentence *John will come tomorrow* is true
if and only if there exists a satisfaction constellation, *ie* if and
only if not all constellations defined by the relationship
'tomorrow' are dissatisfaction constellations. A sentence with
universal quantification is true if and only if all constellations are
satisfaction constellations. Truth conditions can be defined in
terms of satisfaction constellations and constellations of these
constellations. Judging from the literature about teaching
language to apes, apes only manage truth conditions, and thereby
correctness notions, at an elementary level, namely at the level
of satisfaction situations. The higher levels of satisfaction constellations, which involve complex constructions that consist of
speech situations, satisfaction situations, and constellations, seem
to be out of reach for them.

1.2.5.(4) Notions of semantic correctness
We first define semantic correctness with respect to situations
and then with respect to constellations. On the basis of this, a
notion of structural semantic correctness is defined which is
independent of situations of language use. The definitions are

formulated for indicative sentences, *ie* for assertions; this makes the interdependence between semantic norms and the notion of truth especially evident. For other types of sentences the definitions have to be formulated accordingly in terms of their satisfaction conditions. Since these conditions are formulated by indicative sentences the semantic correctness conditions for predicative expresssions and referential expressions are the same as in assertions.

(*a*) *Correctness with respect to situations*: A speaker/hearer uses a predicative expression *A correctly in s or with respect to s* if and only if the sentence in which it occurs is true in *s*, or satisfied in *s*. The predicator *A* is used positively correctly in *s* if and only if *This/Here is A* is true in *s*, and negatively correctly if and only if *This/Here is not A* is true in *s*.

In this kind of situation the truth conditions of an assertion are at the same time the conditions of correct use, *ie* use conditions. All parts of the assertion are used correctly if and only if the whole assertion is used correctly. *A* can also be the descriptive content of the whole sentence; for exmple, *The castle is burning* is used correctly if and only if *Look, the castle is burning* or *Here is the burning castle* are true.

(*b*) *Correctness with respect to constellations:* A speaker/hearer uses expression *A correctly with respect to a constellation* if this constellation makes the sentence containing *A* true, or satisfies it.

According to these definitions, in a false sentence there is at least one expression not used correctly. Therefore, people cannot lie *vis-à-vis* dissatisfaction situations. In such a case their assertion would not be a lie, but deviant language behaviour. Even a liar has to correct and adapt his assertions when confronted with a decisive dissatisfaction situation.

Generally, we employ a weaker notion of semantic correctness in which no immediate reference is made to situations and constellations of satisfaction or dissatisfaction, rather a more indirect reference. The employment of this notion of weak semantic correctness by a speaker or hearer is what we mean by 'semantic competence'.

(*c*) *Weak semantic correctness*: An expression *A* is used *weakly semantically correctly* in an utterance if the speaker/hearer who uses *A* accepts the distribution of satisfaction and dissatisfaction constellations with respect to this utterance. That means when confronted with a constellation, he will identify the constellation correctly as a satisfaction or dissatisfaction constellation, *ie* when confronted with a constellation he will use the expression correctly.

This notion of weak semantic correctness is thus a dispositional notion, which according to Carnap's treatment of dispositional terms can only be partly reduced to non-dispositional terms by the following formulation:

A speaker S uses an expression A weakly semantically correctly in a speech situation: if S uses A in a satisfaction or dissatisfaction constellation or situation then it holds that S uses A weakly correctly if and only if S uses A correctly.

The test situations for whether someone is a semantically competent speaker/hearer, *ie* generally uses expressions weakly semantically correctly, are the satisfaction and dissatisfaction constellations. A speaker/hearer can be asked to describe these constellations verbally, and thus can be examined on his semantic competence with respect to an expression A. To use an expression incorrectly means to come up with an incorrect distribution of satisfaction and dissatisfaction constellations. The notion of semantic correctness is as much a public notion as the constellations and situations of satisfaction and dissatisfaction are public.

A notion that applies to expressions themselves and not to the use of expressions, or to utterances, is the notion of structural semantic correctness. It is based on the notion of semantic correctness of utterances.

(*d*) Structural semantic correctness: An expression is *structurally semantically correct* if there is a possible constellation or situation in which it is used semantically correctly. It is structurally semantically incorrect if no such constellation is possible.

A contradiction or an analytically false sentence can never be used positively correctly, and therefore it is structurally semantically incorrect. A tautology or an analytically true sentence can never be used semantically incorrectly, except if negated, and therefore it is a structurally semantically correct sentence. An expression is structurally semantically correct if and only if it is possibly semantically correct. Linguistics, as far as it pays attention to semantics, is only occupied with the notion of structural semantic correctness. Philosophy of language also takes into account its basis, namely the notion of semantic correctness.

1.2.5(5) The second level of concept formation
The second level of concept formation is built on the first, namely on the level of formation of basic notions of semantic correctness:

the series $\{a{-}i_1, a{-}i_2, a{-}i_3), \ldots\}$ of utterances of different expressions $A{-}i$ together with their corresponding series of satisfaction situations $\{s(a{-}i)_1, s(a{-}i)_2, s\ (a{-}i)_3, \ldots\}$ are compared by comparing the traces of these series which are formed by regularities Rij that we find in the use of an expression $A{-}i$ in different context types $c{-}j$. Each comparison that can lead to logical ordering relationships of quasi-concepts of the first level of concept formation, such as taxonomies, has to be done under constant $c{-}j$, because this keeps constant the notion of truth, which is 'true under respect $c{-}j$'. This means that chunks of the series, namely situations of use of expressions under the same points of view, are considered in comparison. The logical comparison takes place under the questions of whether each satisfaction situation for $A{-}i$ is also one for $A{-}j$ (inclusion), whether the set of satisfaction situations for $A{-}i$ and $A{-}j$ exclude each other, *ie* are complementary (contradiction), or whether one is a proper subset of the complement of the other (contrariness). These considerations give rise to hyper- and hypo-relationships and to the relationships of contradictoriness or contrariness of quasi-concepts, restricted with respect to certain types of contexts of use $c{-}i$.

Quasi-concepts with such a systematization of hierarchical and vertical ordering are the traditional concepts of the second level. This method of concept formation has a long tradition in the classification of natural kinds, from Aristotle and Theophrast on to modern taxonomies (*cf* Slaughter 1982). It is a special way of searching for order among things, which presupposes the view that natural kinds are built up from components that make them similar and different, and that these are the result of specialization that builds up from a common ground of origin. Concepts constructed as members of semantic networks of this kind are a special kind of theoretical concepts which are the result of this special way of looking for order in the world.

Generally, order among quasi-concepts that makes them part of semantic nets and theories, and thus makes them concepts in a strict sense, is the result of theory formation. The first steps of this second level of concept formation are delineations of the material acquired on the first level by making explicit the relevant respects of the use or context types of certain expressions, and after that, logical, causal, or other structural relationships are empirically studied or even stipulated on the basis of the study of some clear cases. This analytical work can be called 'labour of concept formation'. and it is done in medium and higher education and in science. Its results can be formulated in theories, sets of analytic sentences or meaning postulates, taxonomic tables, and the like. In doing this, criteria of use of expressions get fixed with respect to certain contexts of use and within certain systematizations.

When we compare the series or chunks of series of utterances and corresponding satisfaction situations, we abstract traces, *ie* related regularities, in such a way that we decide for good how the series or chunks of the series can be continued from a certain point of view $c-i$. These decisions are necessary since the logical relationships within the systematizations should hold for the actual as well as the possible satisfaction situations. When we establish systematizations, which delimit concepts from each other, we deal not only with actual satisfaction situations or constellations, but with the abstracted regularities instead of these; in this manner we also take into account all possible situations of use. Between these abstracted contents we notice and codify relationships which provide restrictions on the use of expressions that hold in certain contexts of use $c-i$. This means that the second level of concept formation provides for a stricter normalization of the use of expressions, which makes it possible to provide reliable derivations and arguments for statements formulated by using these normalized concepts within these contexts or fields of language use (*cf* also 7.2.1). Labour on concept formation means to develop a reliable theory of truth about a realm of reality under certain respects of discovery. This theory says when and where the notion 'true' is applicable in the same way, *ie* under the same respects, and where, within such a single field defined by these respects, the boundaries lie for the use of the expressions employed in this field. Such a theory, of course, is a semantics for a language used in a special field.

There are expressions which only function within a certain systematization or theory, and there are others that function in broader areas too. The latter ones can be formalized to some degree by formal education, but also largely remain on the first level of concept formation. Both levels function together: the first is not simply replaced by the second; language use happens on both levels, and these interfere with each other and influence each other.

The strategies of metaphorical and metonymical transfer of an expression to situations which are new kinds of satisfaction situations for this expression are typical of the formally less restricted first level. But they are also used when the notion of semantic correctness is fairly rigidly restricted and they are then cases of semantically incorrect language use; but at the same time they are semantically meaningful if, on the basis of the cases of correct use and points of relevance within the new situation, it can be calculated to which aspects of the new situation the metaphorically or metonymically used expression applies (cf Bartsch 1984b). A sentence containing such an expression cannot, without reservation, be called 'true'; but with further usage on the basis of the new regularities the concept of truth can apply, restricted to a new way of application of the expression in new types of situations or contexts $c-j$. When these provisions are made explicit the strategies of metaphor and metonymy can also be used on the second level of concept formation, including different scientific fields. The only precaution that has to be taken is that the notion of truth is not obstructed. Such an obstruction can always be prevented by marking the new contexts of use of the expression in question clearly, thus making the notion of truth context-dependent. One later on examines which properties (regularities) the expression has transferred to the new context of use, and which it has newly acquired there. This examination, which consists in asking and answering a series of questions inspired by the old use and the new surroundings of use, is part of a heuristic process to acquire new knowledge about something under the new respect $c-j$ under which the expression has not been used before.

A great number of the semantic correctness notions of the second level seem not to be part of the linguistic competence of the average speaker/hearer. Nevertheless they can be looked at as correctness notions that the speech community as a whole can employ by the way of a division of linguistic labour, which to a large extent is identical with the division of scientific and technical labour in a community.

1.2.6 Pragmatic correctness

Up to now we have only treated one aspect of the meaning of expressions, the semantic aspect. But to understand an utterance, we also have to be able to judge whether it is meant as a judgement, statement, guess, question, wish, request, promise, warning, etc. This aspect of understanding is the pragmatic aspect.

1.2.6(1) The pragmatic aspect of understanding

When we understand a written or spoken utterance as a *judgement* or *opinion* we understand it under two aspects:

1. We understand the semantic content of it (*ie* the truth conditions);

2. We understand that the language user connects a truth claim with this content (*ie* the truth claim).

In addition to these two aspects, a *statement* is understood under a third aspect, the interactional aspect. When an expression *A* is used to make a statement, *A* is meant as a judgement that is spoken to somebody with the goal of giving him certain information, *ie* making him believe that *A* is true, or at least making him believe that one believes *A* oneself, in connection with the claim that the hearer should believe that, too. Only this claim explains the hearer's possible reactions: to accept without comment, to accept with approval, not to accept by casting doubt on what has been stated or by negating it; and it explains why, by stating something, the speaker takes over the commitment to show himself willing to support his statement if he is called upon for justification. A statement is always an interaction, other than an opinion or judgement, which somebody might entertain for himself.

To understand an utterance implies recognizing what kind of action is meant by the utterance. To recognize the meaning of an utterance implies at least these two factors:

1. To recognize the semantic content of the utterance;
2. To recognize the illocutionary potential, or action potential.

Illocutionary indicators serve for the recognition of the action potential. They indicate which action or which sorts of action can be performed in the utterance act. These indicators can be explicit lexical items which describe the act, such as performative verbs like *request, promise, ask*, or indicators such as word order and intonations, or partial indicators like the context, tense, mood, person, type of verb, *eg* an action verb.

Factors (1) and (2) determine interpretation in the narrower sense. Full interpretation of an utterance *A* consists at least of the following three factors:

1. Recognizing the semantic content of the whole utterance (including explicit and partial illocutionary indicators and the complementary propositional content);
2. Recognizing whether in uttering *A* in a situation *s* the speech act *H* is performed;
3. Recognizing the role this action *H* plays in the interaction taking place in *s*.

Steps (2) and (3) of the interpretation occur mostly in interdependence, *ie* according to (2) often several actions are possible interpretations of an utterance which do not always exclude each other. For example, the sentence *There is a bull in the field* can, according to (2), be interpreted as a statement, and then, on the basis of the valuation it acquires according to (3), be understood as an answer to a question, as a warning, as an encouragement for a fight with a bull, as a hint at the natural beauty of country life, or something else, depending on the whole situational and interactional context.

Since only actions that count create institutional or social facts (social relations, especially rights and duties), we have to know under what conditions the utterance *A* counts as an action *H*. (These conditions have been explicated in Searle 1969.) In a theory of interaction, at least the following four kinds of conditions on the use of speech for the performance of acts have to be distinguished:

1. *Conditions of recognition*: normal conditions for production and apprehension of speech; step (1) of interpretation of the utterance according to the conventional meanings of the expressions;

2. *Conditions of correctness*: preparatory conditions, sincerity conditions, intention of the speaker that his utterance counts as expression of his illocutionary intention (essential condition);

3. *Conditions of validity* (*ie conditions for 'counting as'*): the conditions of recognition (1) are fulfilled and the conditions of correctness (2) are not openly violated;

4. *Conditions of acceptability*: conditions for rational and cooperative reaction of the hearer, *ie* conditions for accepting, for rejecting, or putting off a definitive reaction.

The pragmatic correctness conditions under (3), formulated according to Searle (1969), follow from the principle that acting must be rational, namely goal directed and goal adequate, where the goal is the illocutionary goal of the speech act in question. This goal is coded by the semantics of the corresponding performative verb.

Evident pragmatic incorrectness has as a consequence nonvalidity; and as long as the opposite is not evident from the situation of utterance it is assumed that the correctness conditions are fulfilled. This means that the satisfaction of the correctness conditions is a presupposition for the truth or falsity of the proposition that says that this or that speech act is performed by the speaker. Therefore, performative utterances like *I promise to come* are self-verifying (*ie* true by just being uttered) only in situations in which correctness conditions are not openly violated. In negating a description of a speech act, for example in *I have not promised to come*, it is in the first instance negated that the conditions of recognition are fulfilled. If the negation is based on the fact that the correctness conditions have openly not been fulfilled, then a qualification of the negation is necessary pertaining to that fact. A hidden violation of correctness conditions by a speaker, *eg* hidden insincerity, does not impair the validity of the speech act. It still counts as that speech act, and this is why the speaker is held responsible for its consequences. The same is true if, later on, the speaker admits or makes evident, that he had violated the correctness conditions: this does not make him less responsible for what he has said.

1.2.6(2) Notions of pragmatic correctness
The four kinds of conditions for the performance of acts are topics of the theory of action and interaction, generally. The restriction and application to linguistic pragmatics occur when the role of linguistic means in interaction is taken into account. Therefore, the key notions of linguistic pragmatics are 'pragmatically appropriate utterance' and 'pragmatically meaningful utterance', and with them the relative concepts 'pragmatically appropriate expression with respect to situational factors $x, y, z, \ldots$' and 'pragmatically meaningful expression with respect to goals $u, v, w, \ldots$'. Pragmatic correctness embraces these two notions.

Speaker-subjective correctness is correctness from the speaker's point of view. It implies speaker-subjective validity, but not the reverse: if a speaker believes that the conditions of recognition and correctness are fulfilled, then he also believes that his utterance counts as this or that speech act. But he can be aware of the fact that some utterance of his counts as this or that speech act and at the same time know that it was not correct. If the speaker knows that some correctness condition is not fulfilled, and this is not evident for the hearer, and if the speaker does not give hints to the hearer to indicate that, then his utterance is subjectively incorrect as this or that speech act, but it nevertheless counts as correct. Thus, it counts as objectively correct and therefore as valid, that is, it counts as this or that speech act.

Hearer-subjective correctness has to be distinguished from speaker-subjective and from objective correctness. If hearer-subjective correctness does not coincide with objective correctness, which could be verified by an observer who knows the language, the habits, the convictions, and the social norms of the speech community, then we judge that the hearer is deluded in his apprehension (perception and interpretation) of the speech situation, and that therefore his expectations, based on his apprehension, are not justified, and thus not claimable.

It is by no means easy to judge whether an expression A is objectively correct in an utterance u for the performance of a speech act H. The problems here are due to the heterogeneity of a speech community with respect to convictions, knowledge, and norms. Allwood (1976) has made it clear that the distinction between speaker's intention, hearer's apprehension, and, in some cases, observer's apprehension of an utterance can be important. An utterance is correct from the speaker's point of view on the basis of his, the speaker's, convictions; the hearer apprehends the utterance on the basis of his, the hearer's, convictions; and the observer does the same on his, the observer's, convictions.

It may happen that what the hearer apprehends and reconstructs as the speaker's intention does not coincide with the speaker's intention; and the same can happen with the observer's apprehension. These possibilities of communication failure are restricted by considerate behaviour of the speaker with regard to the hearer and the other way around; this means that one tries to take into consideration the convictions of the other. Such behaviour promotes the general goal of communication, namely understanding each other's messages, and therefore is required by the principle of rationality as adequate behaviour for achieving a commonly accepted goal. If a speaker behaves in this way, then he, in the optimal case, formulates his intention on the basis of the convictions of the hearer. Assuming this optimal case, the hearer is wise not to interpret the utterance simply on the basis of his own convictions, or simply on the basis of his assumptions about which convictions the speaker has, but on the basis of his assumptions about which assumptions the speaker makes about which convictions he, the hearer, has. Depending on how considerate the hearer assumes the speaker to be, he will rely more on the last sort of assumptions than on other possible assumptions relevant for the interpretation. If the hearer is really egocentric and inconsiderate with regard to the speaker, or if the speaker is a total stranger to him, he will interpret the speaker's utterances on the basis of his own convictions. If the speaker knows the hearer as very speaker-considerate, with respect to him personally or generally, then he will take into account in his formulation that the hearer takes into account in his interpretation that the speaker has taken into account in his formulation the convictions of the hearer. Thus in apprehending an utterance the hearer has different options, and the decision for one or the other will lead to different interpretations, in some cases; and a hearer who is conscious of possible communication failures caused by this, will ask questions with the purpose of getting information that helps to decide between those possible interpretations. But this strategy is limited by the energy and time available to speaker and hearer. The problem is overcome in a general way if the speech community, or at least the pair 'speaker–hearer' does substantially agree in convictions, *ie* is a semantically very homogeneous speech community.

The chance of communication failure is diminished by linguistic and paralinguistic means that can be used to indicate that certain presuppositions of interpretation pertain. The speaker can hint at these presuppositions or make them explicit and thus diminish the chance of incorrect interpretation of his utterance. The constellations and presuppositions for the interpretation often depend very much on specific speaker–hearer relationships, and thus may hardly be penetrated by an observer.

Furthermore, certain indicators for considerateness can be deceiving: there are speakers who use a style of communication that is saturated with indicators of considerateness, without actually being considerate on the level where it really matters, namely the level of convictions of the other. Relying on the indicators, the hearer might reconstruct an incorrect speaker intention; and he is right in doing that, even when the speaker later opposes it.

The question of whether a certain hearer is right to claim a certain interpretation of the utterance against that of the speaker, can, sometimes, barely be decided by an observer; and providing an objective reconstruction of the speech situation, especially with respect to communicative indicators for certain presuppositions of interpretation, cannot be expected either from the speaker or hearer. Claimability, and with that the chance for a just observer decision, rises with the degree to which the presuppositions of correctness are made explicit in the context. These are the presuppositions under which an expression is correct as an expression of a certain intention; and at the same time they are the conditions under which an interpretation of the expression as expressing a certain intention is correct in this or that context. This kind of correctness of an expression will be called *contextual intention correctness*. It means that the expression is adequate as an expression of a certain intention within a certain contextual (including situational) constellation. A hearer interprets an utterance under the presupposition that it is correct in this way. High claimability, however, does not exist with respect to insider communication, but rather with respect to communication with an outsider against whom the speaker behaves considerately by making much more information explicit than he would do with regard to an insider.

An expression can be used perfectly correctly in an insider communication, *ie* be suitable for expressing the speaker's intention such that it can be grasped by the hearer, while it would be incorrect as an expression of this same intention with a stranger. The boundaries between insider and outsider communication with respect to a certain topic are vague, and they are an obstacle to determining what is a correct expression for an intention in a situation. Correctness concepts for communication with insiders and for communication with outsiders, partially, do not coincide. Rationality and cooperation have to be realized differently in different situations. We can say that they are formal concepts that acquire a different content according to the kind of situations in which they are realized. These different contents are different norms. Behaviour that is adequate in communication with strangers (within the same speech community) under the goal of achieving understanding leads to the formation of correctness concepts that are characteristic for unrestricted communication within the whole speech community, such as linguistic explicitness about introduced referents in assertions by descriptions, explicit predication and expression of relationships, and explicit presuppositions. They guarantee information transfer in a somewhat reliable way in situations with little common background between speaker and hearer. This explicitness is not required for insider communication; any insider communication that would take place according to the norms typical of outsider communication would be pragmatically incorrect.

The notions of correctness that regulate unrestricted communication among members of a speech community are based on rationality and cooperation as universal principles of human interaction, and on particular conventions of the speech community. Both the general and the conventional norms of interaction in a speech community determine what is a claimable interpretation of a certain utterance in that speech community. Generally speaking, claimability is relative to the standards of a group. Such a group can be the whole speech community, but it can also be a certain subgroup. Thus there is also claimability with respect to an in-group situation that goes beyond claimability with respect to the speech community. Every piece of information that, according to the correctness notions holding in that group, can be derived from an utterance that appears to be sincere is claimable in that group. Franck (1980) pointed out that this realm is delimitable by the following questions: 'Which conclusions has the speaker or hearer rightfully drawn from this utterance?', 'To which conclusions drawn from the utterance are we justified?', and 'For which conclusions drawn from the utterance is it not possible or permitted for the speaker to disclaim them?'. According to Franck, this is what the utterance says; and besides this, there is something the utterance conveys; and this can be something the speaker intends, but also something which the utterance betrays. For that which is only betrayed by the utterance, claimability does not hold; and for something the utterance conveys, but does not say, claimability is restricted. Depending on whether or not the interpretation rests on generally accepted convictions, it is, or is not, claimable.

This concept of claimability is very doubtful with respect to its applicability, since it is difficult to judge whether a certain conviction is generally accepted or not; and even if it is, we must take into account whether the speaker was not justified in assuming that the hearer does not adhere to these convictions, and that therefore it could not be expected that the hearer would interpret the utterance in the light of these generally accepted convictions. And even then, the hearer can reply that the utterance really was to be apprehended as being intended for a broader public and that therefore it had to be interpreted under the assumption of those general convictions in question, although he would have interpreted the utterance differently if he had apprehended it as a strictly private utterance in an insider situation. Within this constellation, it has to be proven that the situation was such that the utterance could not be apprehended as an insider utterance. We can easily imagine a situation of offence or one of request in which things become that complicated. At any rate, the speaker is not freed from his responsibility by stating that he did not mean it in that way; this means that the speaker's intention was different from the result of the hearer's interpretation. The speaker has the moral responsibility to take into account convictions and norms of others, and he has further to take into account the hearer's knowledge of the situation. The speaker, generally, is not so much responsible for the intention he *has* in communication, but for the intention which, on the basis of his communicational behaviour, others *must attribute to him*, although he may not have it. His utterance ought to be a semantically and pragmatically correct expression of his intentions with regard to the assumptions of his public that play a role in interpreting his utterance.

This problem has moral, juridical, and political consequences with respect to the requirement that a general freedom of expression in communication should exist such that everybody should be free to say and to publish what he wants, and that everybody should be free to hear and read what he wants. This requirement, however, is by no means unproblematic. The analysis of communication and communication failure given above, based on Allwood (1976) and Quine (1964), makes it clear that the linguistic expression used is only one of the factors on the basis of which the hearer finds out the communicative intention of the speaker or writer. The other factors are convictions, knowledge, accepted norms. And these may be quite heterogeneously distributed over the speech community. Therefore it is not far-fetched to draw patronizing (*ie* protecting) conclusions that have politically dangerous aspects: the alternative 'Either heterogeneity of convictions and norms within a speech community, or unrestricted, free communication' is implied. More homogeneity, indeed, makes free expression in communication less risky in the sense that it diminishes the danger of interpretations that were not intended and for which the speaker or writer does not want to accept responsibility. Luckily, restrictions of free communication would only seem necessary if people were to act directly on the basis of interpretations and failures of interpretations, without first evaluating what they think they have discerned as the speaker's or writer's intention, according to generally accepted moral measures. If one wants free communication together with a certain plurality of convictions in the population, one has to take care that almost every member of the speech community is able to perform such a critical evaluation for which at least generally accepted moral measures are necessary.

As far as school and other agencies of socialization counteract the heterogeneity of convictions and semantic and pragmatic correctness notions in a speech community, they are busy creating the basis for free expression in communication. But then, in doing that, they are politically active in favour of certain norms and convictions. This is a dilemma between trying to achieve homogeneity or restricting free expression in communication. Both solutions diminish the risk of wrong interpretations for which nobody wants to claim responsibility, but both are totalitarian. The politically preferable solution seems to be not to do one or the other, but a little bit of both and taking the risk of heterogeneity and free communication, in order not to become a totalitarian society.

Also, if one rejects governmental censure, it remains a fact that speakers and writers are responsible for what they say, as well as for how they say it. There exists for a speaker or writer the moral obligation to express himself in such a way that his audience or public can understand what he says in the way that he intends. Only then is the public not deceived about the speaker-writer's intentions, whether deliberately, by negligence, or by inability. If a speaker or writer does not heed this obligation, then his freedom to express himself in front of a broad public, and the freedom of others to hear or read him, will be restricted or completely negated by as many censure agencies of private or semi-governmental character as there are groups, unions, clubs, societies, publishers and newspaper editors, mass media editors, and scientific editors. Likewise, appointment committees at schools, universities, and broadcasting institutions play a role in censuring. This means that even in Western democracies there exists, rightly so, a net of censure and sanctions that restrict the freedom of communication for the members of a speech community and, in this way, filter out the risks of free communication.

A huge problem that lurks behind this kind of censure is that opinions themselves will often be censured under the cover of censure with respect to proper expression of opinion. According to the position advocated here, censure should only apply to utterances (spoken or written) for the interpretation of which the author does not want to take responsibility or is not able to take responsibility by claiming that interpretation by his audience or public does not coincide with what he intended to express.

The answer to the question under which conditions censure of opinions would be justified will vary with the political stand one takes, although it is common opinion that public utterances ought to be semantically correct: untrue statements have to be withdrawn and corrected. This is part of the responsibility which every author or speaker has to accept. But even this is very problematic across different groups with heterogeneous backgrounds of convictions and norms: the notions of semantic and pragmatic correctness are dependent on these backgrounds.

1.2.6(3) Definitions and examples of pragmatic correctness

There are several factors with respect to which *utterances* are pragmatically correct or incorrect:

(a) Appropriateness with respect to social parameters that determine whether and in what way somebody can perform certain speech acts in interaction with other persons. For example, for a person A to give an order to a person B, A must have authority with respect to B.

(b) Appropriateness of the illocutionary goal with respect to preparatory conditions: for example, to request that someone close a door, the door must be open to begin with. Or, to request that someone carry a heavy load, one must be able to assume that he is strong enough.

(c) Appropriateness with respect to a perlocutionary goal: for example, an authority gives an order to somebody who generally reacts badly to orders. This hinders reaching the goal, namely that the other person perform the action ordered. Here, a friendly request might be more efficacious with respect to reaching the goal.

Structurally pragmatically incorrect utterances contain expressions that make evident a violation of the correctness conditions of their speech-act type. Here the speaker says something that makes it impossible to reach the illocutionary goal in question and is therefore irrational. Examples are:

- *It is raining in Vienna; but I don't know whether it is raining there.* (explicit violation of the sincerity condition)
- *It is raining in Vienna; but I don't want you to know that.* (explicit violation of the essential condition)
- *The door is closed; but, close the door!* (explicit violation of a preparatory condition)
- *I know you don't know English; but, translate this into English, please!* (explicit violation of a preparatory condition)
- *You have not heard about Fred for years; nevertheless, tell me how he is doing!* (explicit violation of a preparatory condition)

Similar examples are considered by Groenendijk and Stokhof (1975, 1978) to illustrate their notion of *epistemic pragmatic correctness*, *ie* correctness of expression with respect to information the speaker has:

- *It isn't raining in Chicago; but it may be raining there now.*

In opposition to the correct:

- *It isn't raining in Chicago; but it might have been raining there now.*

And:

- *The cat is on the mat; but I don't believe it.*

In opposition to the correct:

- *The cat is on the mat; but John doesn't believe it.*

And:

• *John knows that it is raining; but it isn't.*

The structurally incorrect sentences contain an expression that implies that one of the conditions of epistemic correctness is violated. These sentences therefore can never be used pragmatically correctly.

In the next paragraphs, the notions *pragmatically meaningful* and *pragmatically correct* shall be defined *vis-à-vis* the notions 'semantically meaningful' and 'semantically correct'.

The notions of meaningfulness have to be defined with respect to the goals for which language is used as a means. Therefore these notions, in the first place, have to be defined with regard to sentence *utterances* and not with respect to sentences themselves; since only in an utterance does an expression become a means to a goal.

An *utterance* is *pragmatically meaningful*, if as an action it is goal directed and goal adequate. It is then a rational action. This can be the case in a non-conventional way. An utterance is conventionally pragmatically meaningful, if it constitutes a valid speech act in a conventional way. Such an utterance I call a *pragmatically correct utterance*, and the *expression* used in it is, then, *used pragmatically correctly*. An *expression is structurally pragmatically correct*, if it can be used pragmatically correctly, *ie* if there is a possible situation in which it can be uttered pragmatically correctly. Structurally pragmatically correct expressions are also called simply *pragmatically correct expressions*, like structurally semantically correct expressions, which are simply called *semantically correct expressions*.

According to these notions the example sentences above are examples of pragmatically meaningless utterances and pragmatically incorrect expressions. They contain a pragmatic contradiction. If, instead of negating a correctness condition, we were to state a correctness condition explicitly in the above sentences, they would contain a pragmatic tautology, as in:

It is raining in Chicago; and I believe it is raining there.

Or in:

The door is open; please close the door!

Semantic tautologies are semantically correct, but they are pragmatically incorrect, *ie* they cannot be stated meaningfully: the goal of informing the other is violated in principle and obviously.

They can be pragmatically meaningful on a meta-level as semantic explications for language learners, though. Semantic contradictions are semantically incorrect, and they are also pragmatically incorrect, because they obviously violate the sincerity condition.

If a speaker utters a pragmatically incorrect sentence or makes a pragmatically incorrect utterance, the hearer generally is prepared to apply the so-called 'principle of charity', that means he assumes that, nevertheless, the speaker acts rationally, which implies that the speaker acts in a goal-directed way and does not contradict himself. According to this assumption about the rationality of the partner in communication, the hearer searches for a meaningful intention behind the utterance that would be pragmatically meaningless if taken literally. This search procedure follows more or less established strategies, which guide the hearer to interpretations of the utterance as an indirect speech act, as irony, as intended exaggeration, etc. These strategies of interpreting indirectly are the basis of Grice's (1975) non-conventional but conversational implicatures. The principle of charity is employed by the hearer when he assumes that the speaker behaves rationally with respect to the goal and other conditions of conversation, although it seems otherwise.

Note that the principle of charity is not always employed symmetrically: relations of social dominance and presumed asymmetry in knowledge and intellectual capacity between partners influence whether and to what extent the principle has to be applied, by whom, and in what kind of situations. If, for example, a foreigner tries to make a pun in the language of his host country, he is usually not understood, because his utterance will not be interpreted under the assumption that he is a competent speaker, and that therefore his somehow deviant or funny utterance has to be interpreted indirectly, but rather the hearer will assume that he has made a linguistic mistake.

For conversation, the principle of rationality amounts to Grice's 'principle of cooperation' in information transfer, as Kasher (1976a) has pointed out. This principle and its consequences have become the basis of most work in pragmatics, especially in formal pragmatics, *cf* Gazdar (1979), and it has been aided by Goffman's principle of cooperation in image support in interaction (Goffman 1967), also called 'principle of politeness' (*cf* Franck 1975, 1980; Boeren 1982; Goody 1978; Leech 1983).

According to Grice's principle, the speaker should try to be cooperative in the sense that he tries to make his contribution adequate to the goal of conversation and the stage it is in. The adequacy is specified under the aspects of quantity, quality, relevance, and manner of the utterance. The hearer assumes that the speaker behaves correctly from these points of view, *ie*: *conversationally correctly*. He also employs the principle of charity in semantic interpretation of an utterance, which plays a role in accepting semantically incorrect utterances as at least semantically meaningful. If, for example, someone uses a definite description in a semantically inadequate manner, then it does not denote in accordance with its conventional meaning; nevertheless, the hearer may be prepared to try to determine the referent meant by the speaker on the basis of other information in the sentence or demonstrative gestures. To employ charity is cooperation from the hearer's side. Under the assumption of such a principle of cooperation, which coincides with that of Allwood (1976), we can characterize utterances as indirectly semantically meaningful and indirectly pragmatically meaningful.

The utterance of a sentence is *indirectly semantically meaningful* if the hearer who is prepared to cooperate can, on the basis of situational information (including further linguistic, paralinguistic and extralinguistic information), relate the utterance to the domain of discourse such that it can be judged whether or not the predication made in the utterance is fulfilled by the referents in question. This means, for example, that the sentence 'The King of France is bald' can, with respect to the president of France, be interpreted in an indirectly meaningful way.

The utterance of a sentence is *indirectly semantically correct* if the hearer who is prepared to cooperate can, on the basis of situational information (including information mentioned above), conclude that the sentence can count as true to some degree. This means that the sentence is not true without any reservation, but that it is evident which property the speaker wants to attribute to the referent in question and that the referent has this property. This case often occurs when words do not fully fit that which the speaker wants to express. Thus, the utterance 'Giscard is bald and Giscard is not bald' is, in this sense, indirectly semantically correct if Giscard has sparse hair. Accordingly, the utterance 'The king of France is bald, and the king of France is not bald' is, related to former president Giscard, indirectly meaningful and indirectly semantically correct.

We can speak of *indirectly pragmatically meaningful* and *indirectly pragmatically correct* utterances in the case of non-direct, and especially indirect speech acts, *cf* Ehrich and Saile (1972) and Searle (1975). The notion of indirect pragmatic correctness presupposes the notion of pragmatic correctness as well as the notions of conversational correctness, which means that in conversation one employs the principle of cooperation in information exchange, and the principle of cooperation in image support, which means that one respects and supports one's partner's and one's own image. *ie* observes the principle of politeness. These principles, comprised in the general principle of cooperation, supersede the specific norms of pragmatic correctness, as they occur in the correctness conditions of speech acts. The latter are derived by application of the principle of rationality to the illocutionary goals of speech acts. If a pragmatic correctness condition of a speech act that is conventionally tied to a certain type of expression is not fulfilled, the principle of charity requires the assumption that the speaker nevertheless behaves rationally; therefore the hearer assumes that the speaker must have another illocutionary goal than the one conventionally connected with the expression used, and that this goal is not expressed directly because the speaker wants to be cooperative, for example with respect to supporting the image of the hearer, or because the speaker has to attend to several goals at the same time and therefore cannot directly push the illocutionary goal he has. What is adequate behaviour with respect to a goal depends very much on the conditions that pertain in the special situation; and if there are several goals that have to be taken into account, goal-directedness with respect to each single goal is only relative, in accordance with one's preference ranking among the goals. Therefore, rationality with respect to a whole cluster of goals requires choosing less goal-directedness and less goal adequacy with respect to some of the individual goals, *ie* behaviour with respect to a certain goal cannot be the same as it would be if that goal were the only one. Thus, for example, instead of stating a request directly by using the performative verb or the imperative form conventionally tied to this type of request, the speaker rather will give hints to the hearer such that the hearer can determine by himself what the speaker wants him to do. This can be done, for example, by merely making explicit one or more of the correctness conditions of the speech act intended.

We distinguish between two kinds of non-direct speech acts, namely implicit speech acts and indirect speech acts. In *implicit* speech acts the literal interpretation of the utterance is pragmatically correct because all the correctness conditions with regard to the illocutionary goal that is conventionally connected with the utterance type seem to be satisfied. Still the hearer is not expected to rest with the literal interpretation but should ask himself 'why does the speaker tell me that?', *ie* look for the purpose the speaker has in making the utterance. If, for example, the speaker tells him that his suitcase is heavy, he has to consider this in the light of his knowledge about the speaker's strength and general social norms about assistance that people ought to give to each other. In the light of these considerations, *ie* by practical reasoning, the hearer determines that the speaker implicitly makes the request to help him by just making a statement about the weight of his suitcase. In indirect speech acts, on the other hand, the utterance is pragmatically incorrect in its literal interpretation, because one or more correctness conditions with regard to the illocutionary goal that is conventionally connected with the utterance type are obviously not satisfied. Thus, if *A* asks *B* at the dinner table whether *B* can hand him the salt, while the salt is right in front of *B*, *B* can certainly reach it, and *A* is obviously close enough for *B* to hand something over, then the utterance cannot be meant as a question, since the answer is obvious to both speaker and hearer. As a question, the utterance would not be rational, and therefore the hearer will assume that the illocutionary goal the speaker has in mind is something else. The interpretation of this utterance type as a request is already conventionalized, though it depends very much on the situation, whether it is a question or not. In a test about motorial ability of the hearer, where the speaker certainly is not in need of the salt, the question is meant as a question, and nothing else. At the dinner table it can also be understood as a question in case it is not so obvious that the salt is in reach of the hearer. But there it is also necessary to consider the purpose of this question and thus derive the implicit request. It thus depends on situational factors whether the pragmatic correctness conditions of an utterance are fulfilled or not, and with that the distinction between implicit and indirect speech acts is not tied to utterance types or expressions but to utterances.

The distinction between implicit and indirect speech acts plays a role with respect to claimability. The implicit speech act, as it is defined here, is not claimable on the basis of linguistic conventions and the principle of rational use of linguistic means, but merely on the basis of social norms. As far as the use of linguistic means goes, the speaker can insist that he just meant what he said and nothing more, and the hearer can claim that he understood the speaker to have performed the speech act that is conventionally expressed by the type of utterance under consideration, and nothing more. The indirect speech act, even if it is not already conventionalized, is claimable on the basis of conventional linguistic means and the principle of their rational use: the obvious violation of the pragmatic correctness conditions forces another interpretation than the literal one. Indirect speech-act interpretations are conventionalized to some degree; it is not the case that the expression itself has to be interpreted as an idiom (rather it is fully productive in the linguistic sense, such that the meaning of the whole is calculated from its parts), but the use of the expression in certain types of situations, though not in all its possible situations of use, receives a certain conventionalized interpretation: certain expressions used in certain situations just count as polite formulations of a request. Their literal interpretation in these situations would not be pragmatically correct, because correctness conditions for such interpretations are obviously not satisfied. These utterances are then indirectly pragmatically correct, often in a conventionalized manner, but sometimes not. The last mainly holds for implicit speech acts. A statement, for example, can be an insult or a request in a conventionalized manner, or in a very individual and subtle manner that is not conventionalized at all, as far as its use for making an insult or a request is concerned.

1.2.6(4) Conversational and contextual correctness

The notion of conversational correctness is based on Grice's principle of cooperation in information exchange. A speaker can behave conversationally correctly, and that means that his utterance is conversationally correct, with respect to the categories of quantity, quality, relevance (relation to the context), and modality.

The principle of cooperation with respect to the quantity of a contribution to a conversation says that one should not give more nor less information than is required in the context with respect to the goal of the conversation. For deviation from this maxim, one has to apologize and to give an explanation. An acceptable excuse is that one cannot tell more than one knows, *ie* that one values the maxim of quality higher than the maxim of quantity. Pointing to a higher norm generally is an excuse for violating a lower norm, if the two are in conflict with each other. If one gives too much information one marks this additional information as exceeding the information asked for, by certain expressions, such as *und zwar* or *übrigens* in German. They indicate that the speaker, on his own initiative, wants to add something that is not strictly necessary as far as the request for information is concerned. If, for example, someone asks *Was macht Hans eigentlich?* ('What is John doing?'), the quantitatively correct answer can be *Er liest* ('He is reading'). But if the speaker wants to add something more, for example to indicate that he thinks that John does not want to be disturbed, he can add *übrigens mit großer Konzentration* ('furthermore with much concentration'). The answer *Er liest mit großer Konzentration* ('He is reading with much concentration') would be conversationally incorrect under the aspect of quantity, since that would be an appropriate answer to the question in what manner John is reading. In such a case the hearer would look for an explanation for such a deviation and probably conclude that the speaker has an extra goal in mind, namely to let him know that he does not want John to be disturbed.

Another example for correctness with respect to quantity is the use of the connective *or*. It is incorrect to say *p or q* if one is sure that *p* is true, or if one is sure that *q* is true, or if one is sure that both are true. In these cases one would have to say, according to the maxim of quantity, either *p*, or *q*, or the conjunction *p and q*. If in these cases the speaker were to say *p or q* he would behave, hiddenly, incorrectly, because the hearer would have the right to assume that the speaker does not know which of the alternatives is true. The hearer does so rightfully, because it is generally accepted that the maxim of quality overrules the maxim of quantity; this means that the hearer, when he hears *p or q*, has to assume that the speaker cannot give more information in a responsible manner because he does not know which of the alternatives is true. Secret non-correct behaviour is insincere or dishonest behaviour: others are deceived because they rightly presuppose that the speaker behaves correctly, especially cooperatively. They have the right to such a presupposition because all linguistic means in communication only function under this general assumption of correctness of their use.

Correctness with respect to quality of an utterance requires that one only asserts something which one believes and for which one has sufficient evidence. This was also an aspect of pragmatic correctness of statements generally. Concerning pragmatic correctness, the point was that an utterance was invalid as such and such a speech act, *ie* did not count as that speech act, if sincerity was evidently violated. Concerning conversational correctness, the point is that conversational correctness seems indeed to be violated if sincerity is evidently violated; but because of the openness of this violation, the hearer, presupposing rationality and especially cooperation, can look for justification of this flaw on behalf of the speaker, and this in two directions: either (1), the speaker behaves adequately with respect to another aspect of conversational correctness, and the fulfilment of the norms of this latter aspect conflicts with the fulfilment of the norm violated; thus the speaker can tell a fantastic story, fulfilling the maxims of quantity and of manner, as long as he gives hints about the quality of his story in order not to deceive the hearer; or (2), the speaker refuses, for some reason, to cooperate at this stage in the conversation with the partner with respect to the goal in question, possibly in consideration of other commitments and goals. Such refusal breaks up conversation. The hearer can draw conclusions from this behaviour in the way that he takes the utterance of the speaker to be an indirect speech act; and in doing this he assumes that the speaker has intended an indirect interpretation. For example, the speaker can give an answer to a question of the hearer that is evidently wrong or absurd. Implicitly, the speaker shows the hearer in this way that he does not want to answer. Thus, children often answer the question *Why do you want to do that?* by simply saying *Because*, and in doing so they flout the maxim of quantity. Or they answer the question *What occupation does your father have?* by *German Kaiser* or *President of America*, violating the maxim of quality. In these cases, speakers refuse to cooperate. The hearer can, depending on what he thinks about the rationality of the speaker, understand this behaviour as rational and thus look for reasons for the speaker's being uncooperative on this point. These examples show that cooperative behaviour and rational behaviour do not simply coincide; they coincide only if the partners strive for a common goal in communication as, for example, exchange of information about a certain topic. Grice's principle of cooperation is a special kind of application of the principle of rationality, namely rational behaviour with respect to a commonly accepted goal of information exchange. Rationality with respect to other goals asks for other strategies in communication, and for other maxims, such as the maxim of politeness. Only if speaker and hearer have common goals will there be cooperation principles with respect to these goals. In all communicational situations in which the conventional meaning of linguistic expressions plays a role, speaker and hearer have at least a minimal common goal, namely literal understanding of the linguistic expressions, although perhaps not their acceptance. Therefore a minimal cooperation has to be achieved in speaking clearly, listening carefully, and using a language and style known to the respective hearer.

Grice's maxims of conversation pertain to cooperation in a conversation that is oriented towards exchange of information about a topic. Other forms of communication than conversation with this purpose require other kinds of cooperation; and other forms of conversation that have other purposes than exchange of information also require other kinds of cooperation, especially other maxims; examples are party conversation, which serves to establish or reinforce contacts, public discussions, especially panel discussions, in which Gricean cooperation very often has to recede in favour of showing off, or story-telling. In these activities, entertaining and boasting are the central aims. The form which the respective cooperation principles will take depends on at least two factors: (1) what is the goal of communication?; and (2) what are the situational circumstances and what is the form of communication: conversation, interview, monologue with or without the possibility of perceiving reactions of the hearers, or even different audiences with different requirements at the same time?

Secret violation of sincerity does not impair communication and does not terminate it; conversation remains meaningful conversation. Only because of this is the speaker able to deceive his partner. Deceiving is possible only in functioning communication. Sincerity is not a condition for communication or conversation to function properly; rather it is the assumption of the hearer that the speaker is sincere in what he says. Of course, such an assumption only makes sense if one is justified, in some way or other, in counting on sincerity in general. Such an assumption is justified to a high degree if sincerity is a communicational norm.

Up to now sincerity in a restricted sense was the topic, namely sincerity with respect to making assertions. But there is a communicative sincerity in a much broader sense, of which the first is only a special case. Sincerity in the broad sense is the topic of the following paragraphs.

Norms introduce correctness concepts: 'Something is correct with respect to this or that norm.' It is important to realize that this relationship between norms and correctness is mediated by our cognitive ability: the fulfilment of a norm, and thereby, correctness must be generally recognizable. Yet, this recognizability is poor when we need to recognize the intentions of other people. This means that in these situations we cannot easily control whether such norms for the performance of actions are fulfilled that imply that in this or that situation of interaction somebody ought to have intentions of a certain kind. The same holds true of any other norm of correctness the fulfilment of which is not easily recognizable by the hearer but is suggested by the speaker by using linguistic expressions the correct use of which requires that these correctness conditions be satisfied. Therefore, we all need to assume that norms of action and inter-action are fulfilled by all our partners in interaction, as long as the opposite is not revealed in the situation of communication. To have strong doubts about somebody in this respect disqualifies him as a partner in interaction and communication.

Sincerity in the broad sense is a formal norm of interaction and in being applied it is filled content-wise with respect to the different aspects of correctness, *ie* it becomes specified in different norms of correctness. This broad norm of sincerity is: 'Do not breach the norms of communicaton (and other norms with which your partner in interaction reckons) in a way not recognizable by the hearer!' This means, do not behave secretly incorrectly. This is an ethical norm, that could be called *norm of honesty*, in distinction to the norm 'Do not violate correctness norms in such a way that communication (interaction) becomes impossible when you want to communicate!' This last norm is not a categorical but a hypothetical norm, namely: 'If you want to communicate and if that will be endangered by violation of norms, *ie* by incorrectness, then conform to the norms!' This is not a moral norm, but just a norm of prudence, required simply by rationality. It can be formulated as a minimal principle of correctness:

(PC) Try to conform to the norms of communication (interaction) to such a degree that communication (interaction) is possible when you want it!

This principle is much broader than Lewis's (1969) 'convention of truthfulness' or Searle's sincerity conditions for the different speech acts which contain only a requirement of subjective correctness, namely to have the intention or attitude that is typical for each class of speech acts, such as to believe the prop-osition p, when you make the statement that p. The principle is also broader than Grice's maxim of quality which, for making the statement that p, requires next to believing that p also that p be warranted.

PC implies that besides trying to behave correctly in all the aspects mentioned so far, one should behave structurally correctly with respect to these semantic and pragmatic aspects. This is obviously so, since structural incorrectness implies incor-rectness, whatever the communicational situation is like, except if it occurs in quotation. However, structural incorrectness is permitted by ethical norms, like all kinds of evident incorrect-ness, since it is easily recognizable by a competent partner in interaction, who thus is not deceived or misled. For ethical reasons, evident incorrectness is not permitted in interaction with partners incompetent to some relevant degree, for example with children who still have to learn language and interaction, and whose language acquisition would be impaired by behaviour of this kind.

The principle **PC** is not an ethically founded norm but rather a so-called *Klugheitsnorm* ('prudential norm') or a technical hypothetical norm of interaction: it is not clever to utter too many obviously incorrect utterances, since, in serious communication, the hearer observes limits of cooperation in being ready to interpret indirectly and in being tolerant of behaviour that appears irrational. This means that application of the principle of charity has its limits. A speaker can disqualify himself as a partner in communication or interaction generally, although as a *Büttenredner* ('witty fellow'), clown, or as a poet, he would make an excellent figure, given the appropriate situations, where quite different expectations and limits of tolerance obtain.

The categorical sincerity norm, *ie* the norm of honesty, is:

> (**NC**) Conform to the norms of communication (interaction) as long as you must assume that the hearer (partner) cannot directly recognize the breaching of the norms!

The ethical norm **NC** has the form 'It is obligatory: if the interaction partner . . ., then . . .'; its *must* is not conditional, as it is in **PC**, where only if you want communication to function *must* you conform to the norms of communication to a sufficient degree.

Returning to the Gricean maxims, we recollect that correctness with respect to the category *relation* means that an utterance has to be relevant within the conversation with respect to the stage the conversation has reached. This relationship of relevance refers to the content of what is said and what is understood to be the common goal at a certain point in a conversation, and therefore can be judged by the partner in conversation. This means that the contribution relevance makes to conversational correctness is evident to the hearer. If the contribution of the speaker obviously appears to violate the requirement of relevance, then the hearer, complying with the principle of charity, and by that assuming the speaker to be cooperative nevertheless, will try a conversational implicature, and thus indirectly interpret the speaker's contribution as a relevant one, in the sense that he assumes that the speaker feels compelled not to formulate a contribution that would be directly relevant. What that means in special cases depends on what the hearer knows or believes about the situation the speaker is in.

If the speaker wants to give some information that does not appear relevant in the context, without intending an indirect interpretation, then he has to mark this information. This can be the case if he wants to change the topic, or if he wants to introduce new points of view. In marking his information, the speaker shows that he is aware of the fact that he is violating immediate relevance, but that he does so in the light of other goals he is pursuing in the conversation, which might not be goals of the hearer at the same time. Thus, in German, non-restrictive relative clauses are often marked by the particles *ja* or *übrigens*, if they give additional information that would be incorrect according to the maxims of quantity or relevance with respect to the goal of conversation common to speaker and hearer, and therefore would be valued negatively if the speaker did not mark his utterance in such a way that he shows that he is aware of this. By this indication of awareness on the side of the speaker, his deviation does not count as a fault, rather it takes on weight. In the moment that the speaker indicates that he consciously flouts a conversational norm, the hearer must assume that the speaker has other goals according to which his utterances are pragmatically meaningful. This again is an application of the principle of rationality, which does not coincide with the application of the principle of cooperation in conversation. For example, it often happens that by uttering a non-restrictive relative clause marked by the particles mentioned above, the speaker pursues the goal of building up a certain image of a third person or of getting across some of his opinions, although this is not relevant to the topic of conversation. Therefore, opinions communicated in such a manner do not very likely invite the hearer to react explicitly by opposing them, since that would change the topic of the conversation (for these particles, *cf* Bartsch 1978, 1979c; Hartmann 1977). Since what has not been rejected by the hearer counts as accepted, the speaker here ventilates opinions without making them an object of discussion. In such a manner he can get away more easily with half-truths and with casting suspicions that are not discussed.

Correctness with respect to *modality* concerns the manner of expression. Norms of traditional stylistics, which specify how one would express oneself in certain communicational situations, have their place here. This is, among others, true of norms that specify how one should express oneself in such a way that the partner in communication can apprehend one's contribution effectively. Some of these norms are norms of *contextual-pragmatic correctness*, that, with the help of special linguistic means, regulate the process of interpretation of utterances in a context.

The speaker regulates the interpretation process of the hearer not only by linguistic expression of the literal content of his utterance, but also by linguistic means that do not contribute to the semantics of the expression, but rather regulate the process of interpretation in a broader sense by embedding the information given in the utterance into a background of other information in a certain way. There are linguistic means that mark some information as asserted, or presupposed, or recollected, or unexpected, or implying something favourable or unfavourable, or hint about some information that is provided in the context or situation, or that is otherwise presupposed. In doing this the speaker opens or shuts off certain directions of reaction to the information provided in the semantic content of the utterance. Thus, for example, the hearer can oppose asserted information simply by asking '*Really?*' or by simple negation by just saying '*No*' or '*That is not true*'. But the same is not possible with respect to information that is marked as presupposed. Linguistic means for organizing linguistic interaction are certain syntactic construction types, intonation patterns, and the so-called particles, which are used a lot in German and Dutch.

If the hearer wants to oppose information that is marked as not asserted, he must use for that purpose specially marked ways of speaking in which he has to mention specifically the information he wants to negate or doubt. One of these means is contrastive stress. Furthermore, there are special intonation patterns and speech formulae for that purpose. Using these means causes a break in the course of conversation, because they rearrange the constellation in the conversation that has been created by the speaker: they reverse the presupposition–assertion structure presented by the previous speaker, and often also the topic–focus structure. The latter will be changed by means of contrastive stress in the hearer's objection. By placing contrastive stress on elements of the presented topic information, the hearer, in his reaction, makes this the focus of his negation or doubt. Presupposed information has to be mentioned explicitly if it is to be negated. Thus, if the sentence *The archbishop of Scotland visited Brighton Cathedral* is negated or doubted by simply saying *No* or *Really?*, what is negated is that the visit took place, and it remains presupposed that there is an archbishop and that there is a Brighton cathedral. If some of the presupposed information is to be negated the negated information has to be made more explicit, as in the objection *No, he did not, as there is no cathedral in Brighton*, or in the objection *That is not true, since there is no such man (and there is no such cathedral)*. (The example is from Allwood 1977.) Definite descriptions and proper names, wherever they occur in a sentence, are presupposed to refer to an entity as long as this is not explicitly negated or doubted. Therefore simple negation of a sentence is always negation of the whole sentence, and that the negation in fact applies to the asserted information only is a result of the fact that the presupposed information of the sentence is not touched by simple negation or doubt, as long as it is not explicitly mentioned as the scope of negation.

The concept of *contextual-pragmatic correctness* is based on the use of certain linguistic means with respect to information in the context or the situation including assumptions about expectations and valuations of the hearer. Here, too, it is not the actual fulfilment of these conditions of use of certain linguistic means that makes their use acceptable in a certain context, rather it is assumed that these means are used correctly as long as there is no evidence against their conditions of use being fulfilled. Under this assumption they provide information about properties of the context, namely that the context has properties that satisfy the conditions of their correct use.

The use of an expression in a context is contextually pragmatically incorrect, if properties of the context are counter-evidence against the assumption that the conditions of use of the expression are fulfilled in this context. Such contextual properties are the topic–focus structure of preceding sentences, presupposed, and, especially, previously given information, and properties of the text-type, as for example story-telling. These contextual properties influence the distribution of asserted and presupposed information of following sentences, as well as their topic–focus distribution, and with that the use of pronouns and definite or indefinite articles, and the use of certain particles, intonation patterns, subordinate clause constructions, and word order. The linguistic means whose conditions of use are discussed here are: (1) the choice from a set of semantically equivalent alternative syntactic constructions; (2) intonation; and (3) particles. (A more extensive elaboration of these points can be found in Bartsch 1975, 1976, 1978, 1979c.)

The context regulates the choice of syntactic constructions from a set of constructions that are alternatives for expressing a single semantic content. This relationship is not simply 'If these context properties, then this construction'. Rather, certain context properties allow for a subset of the alternative constructions and exclude others. The speaker chooses one of the constructions permitted by the evident context properties, depending on whether, by choosing a certain construction, say C, he wants to indicate that he makes further assumptions above those that are already evident from the context. If these assumptions were also evident from the context, then he would be forced to use construction C, if that was the only construction adequate to all the contextually evident assumptions. This means that what he could choose in the first case, he has to choose in the second case, since otherwise contextual-pragmatic incorrectness would arise. The hearer realizes from the construction used by the speaker that the speaker is making certain assumptions. He is justified in doing that since he has to assume that the speaker uses syntactic constructions according to their conditions of use. These are of the kind detailed in the following paragraphs.

If a speaker makes assumption A, he must indicate that by choosing construction types $C(A)$. As long as there is no evidence to the opposite, the hearer presumes that, since the speaker uses one of the construction types $C(A)$, he assumes A. The freedom of the speaker to choose among semantically equivalent syntactic constructions is delimited by context properties to a certain set of constructions and consists of the possibility that he can, by choosing a certain construction type out of this set, indicate further assumptions that are not included in the context, but that are compatible with it. It is to be expected that there are construction types that are neutral with respect to assumptions that can be made over and above, and compatible with, the context properties correlated with the chosen construction type, and that there are others that are not neutral in this sense.

Adverbial constructions, with an adverbial phrase or an adverbial subordinate clause, are an example of alternative syntactic constructions that are semantically equivalent generally, or at least in certain contexts. In English and German, we may put the adverbial clause in front of, behind, or somewhere inside the main clause. Besides these hypotactical constructions, it is possible to extend main clauses (and others) by adverbial phrases, and this in at least three positions: in front, behind, and inside, separated by pauses or commas from the main clause. Furthermore we can use a nominalization, or a pronoun that refers back to the last sentence, and connect that with a neutral verb, like *happen*, *be*, or *do*, as the head of the adverbial modifier. And, finally, we can also use two main clauses in parataxis, with or without a connective carrying part of the adverbial information.

An example of a construction type $C(A)$ is 'adverbial information in front, together with standard intonation'. Roughly, standard intonation means that the intonation peak lies on the last constituent of the sentence. This construction type can be realized by three different, more specifically characterized construction types, all compatible with the assumption A, namely that the information given by the adverbial phrase is presupposed. If A is the presupposition that John had a headache, the following constructions are compatible with it: *Because John had a headache, he went to the doctor*, or *Because of his headache, John went to the doctor*, or *Because of this (therefore) he went to the doctor*. The full parataxis *John had a headache. Therefore he went to the doctor* cannot be used under the presupposition that John had a headache; the same holds true for the parataxis *John went to the doctor. He had a headache* and for sentences with the adverbial clause or the adverbial prepositional phrase at the end of the sentence together with standard intonation. Which of the alternatives among $C(A)$ we choose depends on further assumptions (*cf* Bartsch 1978). If $C(B)$ is the construction type 'adverbial phrase', $C(D)$ is 'adverbial clause', and $C(E)$ is 'pronoun referring back to the last sentence', then B, D, and E are the types of assumptions under which these construction types can be used. Under the assumptions A and B, for example, one has to choose among the construction types that have the properties $C(A)$ and $C(B)$. If, for example, we presuppose the information that John had a headache, we use a construction of the type 'adverbial in front, with standard intonation'; if, furthermore, the information that he had a headache has been been given in the previous sentence, we use $C(E)$, *ie* a pronoun referring to that sentence. Both restrictions together make us use the construction *Therefore (because of this) he went to the doctor*.

The different ways of expressing a single semantic content are tied by conditions of contextually correct use to assumptions that are made about whether the hearer has certain information already directly available, or whether he has to be made to recollect it from his memory, or whether it must be given to him as new information.

The speaker can introduce information which he wants the hearer to consider in the interpretation of his utterance, which includes the hearer's implications of what is said in conjunction with other information or valuations of it. In introducing such information, the speaker may use different syntactic forms, side remarks, or particles, directing the use he wants the hearer to make of this information. By these means he indicates whether he wants to assert the information, to put it to discussion, to introduce it as new without making it a point of discussion, or whether he only wants to remind the hearer of this information. Particles are important linguistic means for these purposes.

Some particles have semantic components of meaning, *ie* components that contribute something to the truth conditions of sentences in which they occur; and they have at the same time other components that do not add to the semantic content of an utterance. These last are conditions of use that refer to certain assumptions that the speaker makes. These assumptions can be about the world and are, then, supposed by the speaker to be true when he makes his utterance correctly. But these assumptions can also be about beliefs and expectations of the hearer and other people. All these assumptions can previously be fixed by the context, or the speaker is free to make them as long as they are compatible with the context. In the case of incompatibility with the linguistic context the whole text becomes a structurally contextually pragmatically incorrect text. If they are not compatible with other situational information, as, especially, the actual belief of the hearer or speaker's own assumptions, then the utterance that contains indicators for these assumptions is contextually (situationally) pragmatically incorrect in this situation. As with respect to other concepts of correctness, here, too, structural incorrectness implies incorrectness in every possible situation.

Now a few examples: the German sentence connective *aber*, 'but', has the truth functional value of *and*, and thereby has the same semantics as *and*. The expression *p, aber q* has the semantics of *p and q*, and the contextual-pragmatic condition that the speaker, considering that *p* and, maybe, further premises, assumes that one would expect but *not q*. The speaker hints at this assumption by using *aber* in German, and *but* or *nevertheless* in English in contrast to a mere *und* and *and*, respectively.

Another example is the use of German *beide* and English *both*, in opposition to German *die zwei*, and English *the two*. Consider the following text:

> *Two men entered the bank. Both took position in front of the counter.*

The second sentence has the same truth conditions as *The two took position in front of the counter*. This means that the semantics of *both* and *the two* is the same. But the use of *both*, in opposition to that of *the two*, suggests that the speaker assumes that it would be more likely that only one of them will stand in front of the counter, and the other will be somewhere else, for example next to the exit. The same holds for *all six* in opposition to *the six*, and other numbers accordingly. *All six* means that one would assume that some of the six would do something else than what is predicated.

There are other particles without any semantics, *ie* with no contributions to the truth conditions; rather they only have non-semantic conditions of use. Examples are German *selbst*, '. . . self', and *selbst* (or *sogar*), 'even', as in the following sentences:

Sogar/selbst der Präsident öffnete die Tür.
'Even the president opened the door.'

Der Präsident selbst öffnete die Tür.
'The president himself opened the door.'

These sentences have the same truth conditions as the sentence without the particles:

Der Präsident öffnete die Tür.
'The president opened the door.'

In the first example, *selbst/sogar* is used if the speaker assumes that (1) others opened the door, and that (2) it was not to be expected that the president would open the door. The information asserted in the constituent marked by *selbst/sogar*, *ie* in its scope, is indicated as somewhat unexpected. In the second example, *selbst* follows the phrase that is in its scope; it is the so-called intensifying *selbst*. It has as its condition of use the assumption (2) in conjunction with the expectation that someone other than the president would open the door for him. Condition (1) does not belong to its conditions of use.

The connectives *auch*, 'also', and *und*, 'and', do not differ with respect to the contribution they make to the truth conditions. But in contrasts to *und*, *auch* separates the second conjunct from the first in such a way that in conversation the second is primarily the target of negation or questioning by the hearer.

The role of particles in linguistic interaction has been described by Franck (1980) within a theory of conversation about how a speaker uses particles to steer the interpretation of his utterances in interaction (*cf* also Weydt 1977, 1979; Hartmann 1977). The speaker indicates by using certain particles that he makes certain assumptions and presupposes certain information and valuations with respect to the state of affairs he is talking about; and it is possible that he himself does not really presuppose all that he indicates, but rather suggests this to the hearer. In doing this, the speaker takes advantage of the fact that the hearer assumes that the speaker behaves linguistically correctly, *ie* that he uses linguistic expressions according to their conditions of use. In this kind of hidden insincerity, it is important for the further course of interaction that such information and valuation hinted at by particles are only indicated by the speaker and not asserted; therefore he can hardly be called upon to justify his giving of that information. This is typical of suggestive and insinuating talk. Part of the information transferred in such talk is out of the conversational control of the hearer in the sense that he can hardly object to this information except by changing the topic and the course of the conversation and, in doing that, being uncooperative with respect to the goal of the conversation that has been openly agreed upon by speaker and hearer.

One aspect of certain kinds of interaction that is widely used (or misused) is that the speaker indicates that he takes into account the state of information and the position the hearer is in; for example, the speaker indicates what he assumes to be the valuations of actions the hearer adheres to, and what he assumes to be his social position. This can help to steer the hearer's apprehension of the speaker's utterance into a certain direction, and can help to avoid misunderstanding in sincere communication. But it can also be used to suggest to the hearer a certain stand that in fact is not his own and by which he is forced to draw conclusions from what has been said which he otherwise never would have drawn. The point is that linguistic means which have other than truth-conditional conditions of use – as is typical for stylistic means generally and particles especially – indicate all kinds of assumptions and expectations that are not uttered with a truth claim, *ie* are not asserted, and are therefore not introduced as topics of discussion, but as a background which can only be pulled to the foreground of conversation and discussion by being uncooperative.

Another point is that contextual-pragmatic hints and especially the use of particles play a role in building up or in suggesting a certain self-image of speaker and hearer, which mainly consists of being characterized as someone who holds certain convictions; this indirect kind of self-characterization also narrows down the range of possible interpretations of utterances. Self-characterization and characterization of the other serve as a means for steering interaction, and this goal is easier to achieve indirectly than directly, because it is difficult to oppose an indirect characterization brought about by using linguistic means with certain

conditions of use that do not primarily serve to bring about a
certain image of speaker or hearer.

Concluding this section on pragmatic correctness, I want to
stress that conditions of correct use of linguistic means are
necessary for the functioning of these means in sincere communication; but at the same time they are also what makes possible
all kinds of insincerity. There are not only lies, which come about
by hidden semantic incorrectness, but also other kinds of dis-
honesty which come about by hidden pragmatic incorrectness. Next
to these there are all kinds of wrong information in communication which come about by unintended semantic or pragmatic
incorrectness, mainly due to an insufficient understanding and
analysis of the situations spoken about and spoken in, *ie* the
reference situations and the speech situations. And finally, there
are all the misunderstandings which come about by differences
in understanding of situations by communicational partners and
by differences between their semantic and pragmatic notions of
correctness, *ie* by semantic and pragmatic heterogeneity within
a broader speech community.

1.3 The relation between notions of correctness and norms

Notions of correctness and norms are intimately related. We
could embed the conjunction of all correctness notions for utterances into one norm, which then would not need to say more
than 'Speak correctly, as specified by the whole set of correctness
notions!' This would be too crude though, because different
notions of correctness are associated with different normative
forces, often conditionally, relative to certain types of situations
and groups within the population. Different notions of correctness are the content of different norms. The norms can be organized in subsets, according to certain properties which they have.

How are norms related to the corresponding notions of
correctness? The norms are the constellations in social reality
that create, delimit, and secure the notions of correctness. These
norms consist of relationships between people, in which it is
determined what the models or standards which have to be
followed are, who has to follow which models, who provides
models, and who enforces, if necessary, adherence to the models.
There are central models and less central models; by the same
social relationships it is also determined which people provide the
central models, which ones have to follow the central models
within acceptable margins of deviation and are then secondary

models for other people who then follow the secondary models within acceptable margins of deviation. These, further, may be tertiary models for still other people. Since people have to be acquainted with the models relevant for them, the hierarchy of models roughly corresponds to social hierarchies between groups: availability of contact with models that are more central in the hierarchy diminishes with social distance. The availability of written models to broad groups of the population after cheap printing techniques were developed and the availability, via radio and television, of models specially trained in correct speech have led to a general availability of the central models. Even so, models which are closer to one's own speech and therefore seem more familiar can be followed more easily and provide a more realistic motivation for following them: they are not strange, because they are to a great extent compatible with one's own notions of correctness, which have been built up by means of primary socialization in one's local and familiar surroundings, including linguistic surroundings.

The hierarchy of models is a social fact, which is evident in the different degrees of acceptability of speech which is incorrect when measured against the central models: the further away a person is socially from the central models, the more acceptable it is when he produces incorrect speech. Generally speech is judged as correct or incorrect relative to the models that are supposed to be the models of the speaker. These are the village teachers for village populations, or local officials and merchants. The teachers are the officially provided models, who for a long time have been local people with better education and teacher training. Now, more and more primary teachers are not local people, and this makes a difference in the role they play as models: bigger steps are required of local people when the model they have to follow is a stranger. On the other hand, radio, television, and newspapers provide so much additional input into the process of acquiring varieties of the standard that this difficulty is less severe.

In spite of all the changes in the last seventy years in the patterns and media of communication, there is still a hierarchy in the orientation towards central models. The educated people follow the central models, provided by (high) literature, handbooks, and personal models. People with less education follow the more educated ones: their teachers or civil servants; the least educated ones follow, often enough, not their schoolteachers, if they have any, but those people who are one step higher on the social ladder – if they have a chance of upward social mobility

– or they follow subgroup leaders who have enough prestige to compete with those models who are socially and economically better off. This whole construction, consisting of a centre, a graded range around it, vague boundaries, and an area outside the standard, which is represented by the models with their different degrees of centrality, is an idealized structure of social relationships that exists with regard to the task of securing and reinforcing the notions of correctness of speech (cf 6.1.2 for an extensive discussion of this topic). This construction of orientation and order in the social background that carries and supports the standard is modified in reality by additional factors. In a society, an economically and politically strong group can be a stronger model than educated people, but this makes a difference only if such a group is not itself oriented towards educated models. Or people may have reasons to follow local leaders or subgroup leaders with prestige and this, too, makes a difference if these leaders do not orient their speech towards the standard provided by interregional, educated, or otherwise influential speakers.

Generally, the social reality of a norm consists of relationships between norm authorities, norm enforcers, norm codifiers, and norm subjects, any of whom, in the case of linguistic norms, can in principle also fulfil the other roles. The force of a norm is built up in these relations by providing models and correcting speech behaviour with respect to them. Acts of correction are aided by rewards or penalties. The other part of the norm, besides normative force and possible conditions restricting application, is the norm content. This consists of a notion of correctness, or a whole set of such notions, which can be spelled out explicitly or be exemplified by models. If only examples are provided as models, speakers construct a concept or a complex of concepts, using their normal capacity of concept formation to abstract the relevant features from the exemplifying situations (cf 1.2.5 and 5.2). In this way they construct semantic concepts, concepts of sound, and concepts of syntactic patterns as well as concepts of the semantic functions of these patterns. The boundaries of these concepts are provided by the relevance of certain features and by acts of correction applied to over-generalization. Especially by acts of authorized correction, the degree of deviance from the models is limited.

All these correctness concepts are constructed on the first level of concept formation, on which the concepts are not yet systematized in relationships of higher order, ie according to relationships that can be established between them. They are mostly still polystructures: polysemic complexes in word semantics; poly-functional complexes in the semantics and pragmatics of certain syntactic forms, as for example the set of functions of the imperative form, or the set of functions of the present tense form; and poly-'phonic' complexes as sets of perceptional qualities of sounds, as described in 1.2.1. All these complexes are structured according to typical contexts or surroundings in which the linguistic form in question is used. These concepts of the first level are built on the basis of perception of speech and its use, *ie* the linguistic means, consisting mainly of linguistic forms, are perceived in their use. Correctness notions are constructed under both these aspects: the perceptions of the linguistic means, as they are used in communication, are structured in subsets according to typical contexts such that concepts of their correct forms, including aspects of their quality in these contexts, are achieved; the concepts of the functions of these means are constructed likewise according to typical contexts of use. Because oppositions between them have to be taken into account for delimitation of the concepts, the cognitive operation of substitution has to be used, as well as the operation of class formation from the point of view of similarity under a certain aspect. Logically, substitution is also based on class formation: the point of view is identity of the surroundings; all those expressions are classified as belonging to one class that appear in the same linguistic surroundings, or in linguistic surroundings of the same type. The recognition of syntactic form involves the recognition of patterns; the construction of concepts of these patterns requires the employment of the operation of substitution for forming equivalence classes of expressions with respect to linguistic distribution, *ie* with respect to occurrence in identical or equivalent linguistic surroundings. At least the two cognitive operations of class formation are necessary on the first level of concept formation: equivalence on the basis of similarity of the items themselves under certain points of view, and equivalence on the basis of occurrence in identical or equivalent surroundings.

The second level of concept formation consists of systematizations of the concepts of the first level. These systematizations can take place from different points of view and can thus lead to extensions beyond what is learned in primary concept formation. Order and other relationships among constructed concepts of basic items and patterns of the first level are established – for example, the formation of recursive rules on the basis of observed patterns and relationships among them, especially as there is substitution of patterns into other patterns or even into the same ones. And there are still higher-order rules that refer to the categorial structures constructable by the recursive set of categorial rules, or phrase structure rules; an example of this kind of rules are rules that describe the (theoretical) linguistic relationships between patterns of coreference in sentences. Likewise, different kinds of relationships between the meanings of words are constructed, for example taxonomies, which are based on inferences. These second-order networks of syntactic as well as semantic relationships play a role in guiding the introduction and change of first-order linguistic concepts, namely of the concepts of linguistic correctness (*cf* Ch. 7).

In this way, a whole network of semantic, syntactic, morphological, and phonological relationships is constructed among the respective kinds of concepts formed on the first level of concept formation, and can then, furthermore, be constructed among constructs of the second level to yield a tertiary level of rule schemata, which are generalizations over systematizations and especially rules of the second level.

The concepts of the first level are the content of linguistic norms; they are directly delineated by normative linguistic behaviour in the linguistic community and in this way are intersubjective, public entities: objective notions of correctness, so to speak. They are the objective social base for the corresponding subjective notions of correctness in the heads of the individual members of the speech community, which are more or less adjusted towards the socially recognized objective notions of correctness established and employed by the community as a whole.

The systematizations of the concepts of the first level, *ie* the concepts of the second and higher levels, are of a different kind: in so far as they are real, they can be mapped homomorphically (*ie* preserving structure) on relationships and operations in the heads of the speakers. In this case they are formulations by linguists of systematizations that supposedly can be found in the heads of the speakers as systematizations of their correctness concepts. They are not constituted by public actions as were the first, which therefore are norm contents, but they are constituted by systematization activities that go on in the heads of the speakers. They are thus psychic entities, the public formulation of which is part of the theoretical work of linguists. These formulations have an objectivity as far as they are based on data that conform to the public correctness standards of a language. But by this they are not social entities, nor are they reconstructions of social entities. They are part of theories about the linguistic capacity in the heads of speakers, or, if a theoretician does not want to commit himself to this view, part of theories about possible systematizations of the contents of linguistic norms under several points of view.

The connection between linguistic norms and (theoretical) linguistic rules and systematizations exists via the norm contents which are concepts constructed by individual speakers, the formation of which is restricted by human cognitive abilities, by states, events, and things in reality, and by social control exerted by providing models and correcting deviance outside the accepted margins, which vary with different conditions of language use. The intersubjectivity of these concepts is only secured by these restricting factors: the restrictions on the possibilities of human perception and cognition together with the outside reality of the world, give the objective restrictions, and the social control provides the social or intersubjective restrictions. These objective and inter-subjective restrictions together, apparently, are sufficient to secure formation of concepts and systematizations of concepts by individuals such that they are similar enough to make possible both communication and the coordination of people's knowledge.

In conclusion, we can state that linguistic norms are the social reality of concepts of linguistic correctness; this social reality secures the coordination concerning form and use of linguistic means in a speech community.

Chapter 2

The theory of norms with respect to law and language

2.1 Theories about existence and validity of norms

According to Hart (1961), who argues against the imperative theory of norms, norms are not orders or prescriptions which are issued by a superior to a subordinate. The characterization as prescriptions only applies to some norms and even then it characterizes them only partially, because a general prescription is understood as a norm only if people measure behaviour against it and, accordingly, judge this behaviour as correct or incorrect. Prescriptions and orders are only followed so long as not complying with them is sanctioned negatively, especially by punishment. Norms, on the other hand, are considered to be a guideline for action, even in situations with no threat of punishment. Only general prescriptions which are accepted by the subjects are norms for them. But not all norms are accepted general prescriptions. Raz (1975) does not give arguments against the imperative theory of norms, but refers to Hart (1961), who is a representative of the practice theory of norms.

The practice theory claims that a norm or rule that x ought to do H under condition C in society S exists if and only if the following conditions are satisfied (*cf* Raz 1975:53):

1. Most members of S regularly do H under C.
2. If somebody does not comply with the rule, he or she will be criticized by members of S and such criticism will be looked on as justified by other members of S, such that this criticism is not criticized by them.
3. Members of S refer to the rule by expressions like 'An x ought to do H when C' or 'It is a rule that x ought to do H when C' in order to justify their actions, or demands made of others, or criticism of behaviour.

This definition of a norm or a mandatory rule as practice has been attacked by Raz, who argues that a rule or norm need not be a practice; *ie* there are cases in which one believes that something is a rule or a norm without believing that it is widely complied with in *S*. We can say, for example, 'This rule is not often complied with any more', or 'This rule should be complied with by everybody, although hardly anybody follows it.' This points to the necessity of a distinction between a norm as practice and the validity of a norm, and it means that the notion of 'norm' or 'rule' is not simply defined by the notion of 'practice'. Likewise, not every practice, *ie* the fact that people in *S* do *H* in situations of type *C*, is a rule or norm. Raz points out habits which are not a rule or norm. Also not every accepted reason by which one does *H* in *S* under condition *C* is a rule, although a mandatory rule is a reason for a certain action. Not every practice is a reason for certain actions, but it is possible that in *S* everybody adjusts to the practice of the others. In this way conventions arise in *S*, *ie* one can expect that others shall behave in a certain way, and one believes that others expect that one act in that way, too. But according to Raz, conventions are not norms as long as they do not have a normative character. They would have a normative character if they could be formulated only in a normative terminology. This is not generally the case with respect to conventions. They can be described completely as regularities to which everybody is expected to conform and expects the same of others, as long as almost everybody does conform to them. This is basically the definition of conventions given by Lewis (1969), in which no normative terminology is used.

Raz (1975) argues that mandatory rules or norms are 'exclusionary reasons for action'. But he is aware of the fact that not all exclusionary reasons for action are norms, because not all such reasons are general with respect to situations of a certain type and with respect to persons, as norms are.

In what way, for example, are rules of thumb exclusionary reasons for certain actions? They are devices which make it possible for us to act in standard situations (to which these rules apply) quickly and effectively. These rules save time and labour which otherwise would have to be invested in continually new analyses of situations, considerations of reasons for decisions, negotiations, and final decisions.

> Rules are thus justified as time-saving devices and as devices to reduce risk of error in deciding what ought to be done. We may add to these features the related justification as labour-saving devices. . . . When a situation to which it applies actually occurs the norm subjects can

rely on the rule, thus saving much time and labour and reducing the risk of a mistaken calculation which is involved in examining afresh every situation on its merits.' (Raz 1975:59)

The action then takes place exclusively on the reason given by the existence of the rule; other reasons are not considered, because the function of the rule is exactly to make this unnecessary. The rule is the exclusionary reason for performing the action only in a situation of a certain type C. This, of course, does not exclude the fact that the situation being of type C is also a reason for the action. This initial condition is the first, and the rule is the second premiss of the conclusion that says that a certain action has to be taken.

The situation is similar with respect to norms that are issued by an authority. If a person is accepted as an authority on the basis of her knowledge and experience, this means that someone is likely to substitute her judgement for his own judgement, because there are reasons to trust her judgement more than his. If authority is based on the fact that it is necessary for securing coordination and cooperation between the members of a society, then utterances performed in her role as authority are the exclusionary reason for a certain action, because otherwise coordination would be threatened. This is an important aspect in the functioning of norms of language, where certain models, especially great authors and teachers, are the authorities, supported by official institutions.

> To say that a person is an authority is to say that his word is taken as an exclusionary reason. (Raz 1975:65)
> To regard a person as having authority is to regard at least some of his orders or other expressions of views as to what is to be done (eg his advice) as authoritative instructions, and therefore as exclusionary reasons. (Raz 1975:63)

Note that rules of thumb and authoritatively issued rules have the same function as general decisions, ie decisions that hold for all cases of a certain kind: one has decided in advance how one shall act in certain cases.

Raz points out that not all exclusionary reasons for actions are valid reasons; but following a rule or norm includes believing that the reasons are valid. This means that a norm is understood by an individual to be valid. One believes that one has to comply with a valid norm even in those situations in which this is not an advantage. This attitude points to the fact that one understands the reason for action as a rule or norm, ie as an exclusionary reason for action and not just as one reason among several others

against which this reason is weighed.

Raz introduces the following important distinctions. To say of a mandatory norm that it *exists* can mean three things (1975:80):
1. The norm is valid;
2. The norm is a practice;
3. The norm is prescribed by a certain person or institution.

The norm is valid if the norm subjects, by this norm, are justified in exhibiting behaviour conforming to it. It is another question whether the norm itself is justified, *ie* whether the norm subjects really should be guided by such a norm (*cf* 1975:81).

Non-valid norms can be practised, and it is also possible that valid norms are not practised. Raz (1975), unlike Hart (1961), takes validity and practice of norms to be, in principle, independent from each other. But there are social rules which are only complied with because they are in fact practised, and because a deviation from this practice would cause confusion. In this way, being practised can cause an invalid norm to become a valid one; one case in question is rights founded upon custom. The same is also the case with conventional rules: they are only valid if they are really complied with. This is especially the case with conventions which serve for solving problems of coordination: only as long as the regularity is conformed to in the overwhelming number of cases is the goal, namely coordination, reached. When the goal, because of too many deviations from the regularity, cannot be reached any more, then it does not make sense to follow the convention further on, and then the convention ceases to exist (*cf* Lewis 1969).

Next to norms that are based on a convention there are prescribed norms. In this case, the norms have been set by a speech act in which the one who issues the norm intends the norm subjects to take this act as an exclusionary reason for certain actions (Raz 1975:82).

There are norms that give permission to perform a certain action. Such a permissive norm is an exclusionary reason for the justification of the permitted action, though not for its performance. If something is permitted, one also has the right to do it. This claim by Raz can, in fact, only be argued for, if one assumes that a complete characterization of the situation of action is given in condition *C*. This, I think, is not possible: there can arise intervening points of view and facts which have to play a role in the decision for or against action *H*, which are not anticipated in the characterization of type *C*. This can lead to the situation that in certain situations one cannot make use of one's rights, or does not even have the right to use one's rights. An example is that one does not have the right to enforce one's right of way. The goal of preventing an accident in a situation is higher than the subordinated rule, which, in normal cases, contributes to reaching this goal; but in special cases, in which this right has been neglected by somebody else, an accident may ensue if the other enforces his right. Note that a similar problem arises with respect to mandatory norms which are, according to Raz, exclusionary reasons for performing certain actions; if there are norm conflicts in a situation, one can have several obligations that cannot be realized at the same time, or even sequentially. (For examples, see 7.2.)

Along with mandatory and permissive norms, Hart (1961) and Raz (1975) also discuss power-conferring norms. These norms give certain rights to certain persons to set certain norms themselves or to establish certain institutional facts: the right to make certain contracts, to make testaments, to sell property, to vote in elections, etc. This means that normative power is, by certain norms of higher order, transferred to people; in a certain range of situations they can then set mandatory or permissive norms or can abolish or suspend them. This we also find in language cultivation or language planning generally, where the state has transferred power to certain agencies and institutions to issue, promulgate, or to enforce certain norms.

Power-conferring norms are a special kind of permissive norm which regulates the procedure of norm-setting itself. With respect to the norms which are issued or enforced according to them, they are norms of a higher order. They determine the validity of the norms of lower order.

Rules of chess are, according to Raz (1975), permissive rules, which are aided by one mandatory rule, namely that one has to make a move within a certain stretch of time. To think of rules of chess as permissive rules is, actually, only correct if one assumes that everything that is not allowed is forbidden. Different from rules of chess, the strategies of chess are summary rules in the sense of Rawls (1968), which are directed towards a value or goal that is presupposed, namely to win. With respect to this goal, they determine what a good move is, though there might be better moves, but they do not determine what a correct move is. Strategies do not determine correctness, but promote quality (*cf* Diggs 1968).

Raz's considerations about systems and, especially, institutionalized systems of norms are of special interest for the questions of to what extent and in which way regularities of language and language use can be understood as norms, and how language can be understood as a normative system of norms, *ie* a system consisting of norms.

Groups of norms form a system from the point of view of normativity if the fact that these norms form a group is normatively relevant, *ie* has normative consequences (Raz 1975:107). Is something like this the case for a group of rules of language? The set of norm sentences that formulate these norms has to be consistent, because a system as a whole can only be normative if it does not have arbitrary normative consequences (and this is only secured if it does not contain contradictions). A system of norms is only valid if the norms that are its members are valid together.

Language is not a unified system, but rather a system of systems of rules. Language is systematic from phonological, morphological, syntactic, semantic and pragmatic points of view. As will be discussed later, these different systems can conflict with each other: phonological systematization can destroy morphological systematization when laws of phonetic assimilation and other tendencies of phonetic economy get their way. Simplification of morphology, especially loss of case-endings, causes changes in the syntax, etc. And also within one single component, some rules stand in conflict with each other such that one diminishes the input of the other; therefore rules cannot be fully general; special conditions and exceptions delimit their domains. Over-generalization is a permanent tendency of linguistic systematization, and often it is a question of norms and not of points of view of linguistic systematization that determine the boundaries of the domains of linguistic rules. The linguistic system itself is very unstable because of the tendency to generalize one rule at the cost of the domain of application of another rule, for which, then, compensation by further changes in the set of systematizations might be necessary to keep up effectiveness of the language as a means of communication. The balance of the system at a certain moment is set by the norms of language: they prevent contradictions between linguistic rules of the system by providing more or less deliberate fixations of the domains of application of certain ways of systematization, such that there is no, or less, insecurity about the question to which cases a certain systematization applies. These limitations result in linguistic rules with often, from a systematic point of view, deliberate limits for their domains, expressed in the conditions of rule applications, which in theoretical linguistics are considered to be part of the rules themselves. To claim normativity for a whole linguistic system requires that the conflicts between systematizations of language phenomena be solved in some way or other, as they are by the validity of certain norms of language. But even then, as I shall argue later in Chapter 4, the rules of linguistic system-atization cannot as a whole be taken to be norms. Whether a linguistic rule can be a norm or not depends very much on the kind of linguistic theory the rule is part of. There are linguistic theories that are formulated under certain empirical assumptions which make it impossible that they are systems of norms in the sense of being normative themselves. Nevertheless, they can by systematizations of the set of norms, or systematizations 'behind' the set of norms, from quite different points of view, but not from the point of view of normativity. The inherent instability of linguistic systems of natural languages leads to many violations of linguistic norms, especially by language learners, who are known to over-generalize. Considering the character of this kind of system, some tolerance of violations of norms of language is in order. In the following paragraphs we will not discuss linguistic systems but normative systems and apply this notion to norms of language.

Raz describes some features of institutions under the title 'institutionalized systems' which are not only typical for legal systems but also for a language as a system of norms from the normative point of view. He draws attention not so much towards institutions that are established by norms, but rather towards institutions whose function is to create norms and to apply norms. He analyses the conditions under which the existence of a norm-creating and norm-applying institution makes a set of norms a normative system, and he reviews their normative impact on the relations between norms of the system and between those norms and others (cf 1975:124).

The rules of the system are seen in relation to the society in which they have a social reality of some kind. There are always rules of some kind Y, for example the legal rules of the society S. Likewise there are the linguistic rules of the society S, which make S a speech community. The language $L(S)$ is the system of linguistic norms that is practised in S. Just as with respect to the legal system, it is an idealization to assume that the system of linguistic norms (which has to be distinguished from the linguistic system considered in theoretical linguistics) is practised completely by all members of the speech community, or is completely accepted by all of them. With respect to the legal system, Raz states that in some cases some members of S conform to the law, but without accepting the law as a norm. They then follow the law under the threat of punishment. That people generally behave so as to conform to the law is a necessary condition for the legal system to be in force, but it is not a sufficient condition (1975:125). This, and the fact stated next, is also true about a system of linguistic norms:

It should be remembered that the degree of conformity required is not very high. A legal system may be in force in a country suffering from a crime wave, many of the laws can be generally disregarded, some of the regions may have a particularly bad record in law observance, etc. (Raz 1975:125)

This, to a great degree, is also true of a language which, in its standard form, is spoken correctly only by a part of the speech community, or of a national language that is only spoken by a small part of the population, for example the Irish language as a national language of Ireland, or, with a relatively broad spread, Hindi in India (cf Macnamara 1971; Srivastava 1979). The same can also be true of an official language of a nation or state that serves for technical, administrative, and scientific communication, but is not mastered by the masses of the people. What counts as the national language of a nation X, or what counts as an official language of the nation or state X, is not determined by whether it is spoken by all members of X. Rather, this is decided by state authority, usually the parliament, and it is fixed in the constitution, for example in the constitution of India, art. 343 (1) and the 8th schedule, where in addition to Hindi as the national language, and Hindi and English as the two official languages, another fifteen regional official languages are recognized.

Following Hart (1961:109–14), Raz uses as a further necessary criterion for a legal system to be *valid* in S, that at least the official representatives of the legal system accept the norms of this system, endorse them, and comply with these norms at least in public. The two criteria for validity of a legal system are formulated as follows:

A legal system is the law of a community if, and only if, it is generally conformed to by the norm subjects of the laws, and the officials set up by the laws of the system endorse them and follow them. (Raz 1975:126)

The first of the criteria is also true about a language $L(S)$ of a linguistic community S, but it is not always true with respect to the national language or with respect to an official language of a nation or state. The second criterion is true in cases in which institutions of language planning and language cultivation exist in a country; and this is the case if there is a school system that promotes and cultivates the language $L(S)$. A case in which the first and second criteria are not fulfilled is classical Sinhala, which was declared to be a valid official language of Sri Lanka, but the implementation of which did not succeed (see 6.1). A second case of this kind is Irish, which is, according to the Irish constitution, the national language of Ireland, and in this way it is valid; but both criteria are not sufficiently fulfilled; even the officials of the country hardly speak Irish, although they accept it officially. According to the criteria given by Raz, the Irish language cannot be called a valid system of linguistic norms with respect to the Irish population.

Much of what Raz writes about the institutions supporting the legal system is, to some degree, also true about schools, language academies, and other language-cultivating institutions of a country with regard to the respective language that is valid as a national or official language. Raz writes about the legal system:

> The first major trait of institutionalized systems is that they have a criterion for being practised or in force which is not identical with all their norms being practised, and which assigns considerable weight to the activities of officials and institutions. (1975:126)

In this way officials play a role in deciding whether a norm formulation expresses a norm of the system or not, *ie* whether it is a valid norm. This means that they identify norms as valid or invalid. They also create norms and enforce them among the norm subjects.

According to Raz, a norm is *systematically valid* if and only if the fact that it belongs to a system is reason for its validity (1975:128). This is also true of norms of language. Norms of language are systematically valid if the institution in question decides that a certain norm formulation expresses a norm of the language in question by incorporating this formulation into the codification of the language. This applies to the syntactic patterns and to lexical items as well as to standards of pronunciation. Thus, German words that have been incorporated into *der große Duden* and sentence patterns that have been incorporated into the *Grammatik-Duden* are accepted by German schools, which are the institutions that primarily apply and enforce the norms of German language.

Primary organs of institutionalized norm systems have the power to make decisions about the application of norms:

> Of course, people do evaluate behaviour on the basis of norms of other types of normative systems as well, but only institutionalized systems provide for primary organs the function of which is to evaluate

behaviour authoritatively on the basis of norms of the systems. (1975:142)

The primary organs themselves comply with the norm system which is to regulate individual behaviour of the norm subjects. In this way the behaviour of these organs themselves supplies a criterion for recognizing a norm as valid.

> Hence if the primary organs do not regard themselves as bound to apply a certain norm it does not belong to the system. Thus the introduction of primary organs affects the criterion for membership in the system: if the system's guidance and evaluation are to coincide it must be regarded as containing only those norms which its primary organs are bound to apply. (1975:142)

This characterization, which is tailored to fit a valid legal system, also fits those organs which normalize, plan, and cultivate a system of linguistic norms to perform the role of a standard language. These organs are orientated towards the norms which are practised by the linguistic community, but at the same time they also determine by their normative decisions in the production of dictionaries, grammar books, and style manuals, and by acts of correction in schools in accordance with these codifications, what has to be treated as a valid linguistic norm.

How far these organs can make their decisions dependent on practice in a speech community differs widely with respect to the kind of linguistic norms and the historical situation. In developing a written language, for example, the decision as to which script shall be used (Roman, Gothic, Greek, Cyrillic, Devanagari, Arabic, Irano-Arabic, etc.) has to be decided from political and practical points of view, and which orthography will be devised has to be decided from phonetic, morphological, and etymological points of view, which stand in conflict with one another. In such a situation one cannot fall back on practised norms, but the decision, whatever it will be, will be taken authoritatively. Somewhat different is the situation in which competing systems of a written language have developed and unification is desired. Also in decisions on word meaning or syntactic patterns, established linguistic usage plays an important role, as well as points of view of linguistic systematics. In larger speech communities with some variation, oral language use of an élite is the orientation point in literalization of a language, and if there is already an accepted written language, the oral language use of the élite is influenced by the written language. Codification of linguistic norms in non-homogeneous speech communities, and along with this validity of linguistic norms, is determined by the language use that is most relevant in this community; and this is the language use of those who, in one or more senses, are the models for others. It has been pointed out that in codification of linguistic norms, the linguistic intuition (German: *Sprachgefühl*) of the officials of the institutions of language codification and cultivation is the main criterion. This does not contradict what has been pointed out above, because the officials are members of the same élite whose linguistic usage provides the model. Linguistic intuition is only an internalization of the norms that regulate accepted linguistic usage, *ie* the linguistic usage of this group.

In a certain respect the authority of the linguistic institutions is stronger than that of the legal institutions with regard to their respective norm systems; lawcourts are clearly bound by decisions of the legislature, although there is some latitude with respect to problems for which there is not yet a regulation by law, or with respect to cases in which there is a clash between positive law and natural law. In these cases decisions by lawcourts become models for further decisions and in this way establish norms. The linguistic institutions cannot fall back on such a clearly defined lawmaker as, for example, a parliament. Their agents rely on their own linguistic usage, that of their social class; and in doing this, they rely less on their everyday language use and more on their linguistic intuition about what constituites good language use, which is based on formal style and literature. In this way they arrive at formulations and applications of linguistic norms which may collide with norm practice and intuition of people of other regions and social classes. As far as regional forms have entered into the speech of the educated people of a region, they are noted as alternative regional forms in the codifications of the language in question.

The problem of injustice which arises when, on the one hand, it is necessary to provide coordination in transregional and transsocial communication by a national or official language for the whole political community, and, on the other, the definition of a standard happens on the basis of the linguistic usage of a subgroup of the political and linguistic community, has been discussed for more than ten years (*cf* for example Gloy (1975)). An additional difficulty is that the standard is primarily oriented on a special language use, namely the use of language in writing; nevertheless it is also supposed to be valid for spoken language. It is certainly not self-evident that this has to be so, since spoken and written language are two different, though related, codes. The differences are due to different functions which the two codes fulfil, to the difference of the medium that plays a different role with respect to parsing complex expressions in short term memory, and to the difference between the situations of emitting and receiving a message in written language. But, on the other hand, the orientation towards written language guarantees transregionality for the spoken standard as well.

In non-literalized linguistic communities we find a kind of natural state of language use which is not regulated by a codified, and thus institutionalized, system of linguistic norms. This state is comparable with the one described by Hart for pre-legal societies, which are 'primitive societies where no distinction between moral and legal norms is made'; in this state there are only primary rules, namely 'uncodified rules of obligatory conduct' (Hart 1961:56). These are rules of obligation, ie the majority of the members of the society comply with them from the internal point of view, which means that for them the rule is reason for exhibiting the desired behaviour (cf Hart 1961:56); the members exert social pressure on each other to behave in accordance with the rules, ie there are acts of correction performed by elders who teach the rules to the young and newcomers. The same is true of small linguistic communities, dialects, and non-literalized languages in general. The valuation of utterances as correct or incorrect is necessary to keep intact a system of communication. At the same time, this valuation is a matter of social control in the way that the population understands its language as a symbol of group identity by which it defines inclusion or exclusion of people with respect to the community. This is one of the reasons for the emergence of group languages within a larger speech community, for example for the creation of slang and fashionable vocabulary by which youths mark their distinction and dissociation from the established world of the elders.

From the point of view of group identity, adherence to the norms is watched closely, much more than would be necessary for the mere functioning of a language as a means of communication. This is especially true of acts of correction that apply to those linguistic forms that symbolize the internal social order of a group or society: special morphological and syntactic forms, as well as vocabulary and styles that are connected to roles, positions, and social status (cf Neustupný 1974b for Japanese, Hartmann 1973 for German, and Ervin-Tripp 1972 generally). These linguistic forms with 'social meaning' are enforced as norms; they not only symbolize the social order within a group, but strengthen this social order and the control exerted on its members, and in this way help to perpetuate the status quo. In as far as these norm concepts are not codified, they are customs, but they are stronger because they are treated as obligatory norms which are enforced with normative power. In the terminology used here, customs or conventions which are enforced with normative power are norms. For being called 'norms' it does not matter whether these norms are in a natural state or whether there are institutions responsible for enforcing and conserving them and thereby making them part of a normative system. This means that norms can have a normative force in an institutionalized way, as well as in a non-institutionalized way.

With respect to law, a state of living together regulated merely by primary rules is only possible in small communities.

> It is plain that only a small community closely knit by ties of kinship, common sentiment, and belief, and placed in a stable environment, could live successfully by such a regime of unofficial rules. In many other conditions such a simple form of social control must prove defective and will require supplementation in different ways. (Hart 1961:89)

The same is true with respect to linguistic communities. Only small regional linguistic communities (dialects, tribe languages) can do without official organs of regulation. As soon as the groups become large and are spread over a wide territory, especially with natural barriers in between, they get divided into smaller speech communities, and thus different languages come about. On the other hand, official regulation steers language change, which always happens anyway, by restraining or promoting a new variant in such a way that it will be acceptable to the whole speech community within a span of time in which for all speakers the old variant is still common. Thus a communication gap is prevented, not just between neighbours, but between the outer ends of the linguistic community. In this way falling apart of the linguistic community is prevented.

According to Hart (1961), the weaknesses of legal norms as merely primary rules are the following:

1. The insecurity about whether something or some behaviour came about by following these rules, or whether it is only in an accidental accordance with the rules; or whether some regularity is a mere regularity or whether it is there because of a rule; this is the problem of identification of rules;
2. The static character of these rules: they cannot be changed deliberately by better judgement of the society, but only in a slow process of coming into being and and passing away;
3. The missing efficiency of the diffuse social pressure in favour of these rules.

With regard to the second deficiency of primary rules, we can state that this is in principle an advantage in the case of natural languages, which can only be effective as a means of communication when they are basically conservative. It has been mentioned above that changes which add up over generations lead to a split of speech communities, and that institutionalization and transregional mass communication restrain this process. But it is true that the processes of language change cannot be controlled by people without an institutionalization. Institutionalization makes possible some control of the otherwise uncontrollable. Also, the relatively conservative character of language compared with economic and social change due to scientific and technical innovations can lead to problems of communication. It is just this area where language planning by official institutions becomes necessary. Especially in African and South-east Asian countries, but also in Israel, there are language committees at work to modernize languages; and there are committees for developing and standardizing scientific and technical terminology within European languages, even on an international level. These are institutions that devise and regulate primary norms of language.

To provide for necessary and coordinated language change, especially elaboration, institutions are set up which work according to secondary rules to decide which primary rules, in our case norms of language, should be valid in which regions and in which areas of life. These secondary rules are the guidelines for the work of the institutions of language planning and language cultivation, which work on the implementation and codification of (new) primary norms. Research in language planning describes the secondary rules and considers the justification of these secondary rules and recommends that new secondary rules be set up.

The first and third weaknesses of 'primary rules only', namely the uncertainty in the identification of the rules and their missing efficiency, are amended in the step from a natural linguistic state to institutionalization; national language institutes and academies, for example the Institut für deutsche Sprache in Mannheim or the Deutsche Akademie für Sprache und Dichtung in Darmstadt, editorial offices for dictionaries, grammars, and style manuals, like the "*Duden*-Redaktion", and schools which refer to the institutions just mentioned, the language departments of the universities, the societies of established literature, and literature itself fulfil the tasks of identification of linguistic norms and promote efficiency of linguistic communication over broad areas.

Hart's characterization of secondary rules with respect to the legal system also applies, as has just been pointed out, to the rules of language cultivation and elaboration: the secondary rules have the purpose of eliminating the deficiencies of the primary rules by regulating the formulation, codification, and application of the primary rules. They are thus not obligatory rules of behaviour of the subjects of the primary norms, but they are norms or strategic rules regulating the existence of the primary norms.

> They specify the ways in which the primary rules may be conclusively ascertained, introduced, eliminated, varied, and the fact of their violation conclusively determined. (Hart 1961:92)

The three deficiencies of primary rules are taken care of by three kinds of secondary rules.

The uncertainty of the identification of rules is compensated for by a 'rule of recognition'. This rule gives criteria for recognizing the valid primary rules:

> The existence of such a rule of recognition may take any of a huge variety of forms, simple or complex. It may, as in the early law of many societies, be no more than that an authoritative list or text of the rules is to be found in a written document or carved in some public monument. . . . What is crucial is the acknowledgement of reference to the writing or inscription as *authoritative, ie* as the *proper* way of disposing of doubts as to the existence of the rule. Where there is such an acknowledgement there is a very simple form of secondary rule: a rule for conclusive identification of the primary rules of obligation. (Hart 1961:92)

A dictionary, a grammar, and a style manual of a national language institute or academy has, for schoolteachers, for editors, and for secretaries, the function of a 'rule of recognition'. For the language institute itself, the situation is more complicated: it has to have criteria for deciding which primary rules practised by some people in the speech community shall be incorporated into the dictionary or grammar and thus can be considered valid for the whole community. The institute cannot just pick deliberately whatever norm of whatever part of the population and declare it valid, or simply make up norms. The parallel problem will be easier for a legal system, if there is a clearly defined organ that provides legislation. Positive law is then what is proposed by this organ in accordance with the procedure designed for making law. But the decision becomes complicated even in the area of law if this criterion is not the only one. Then a hierarchy of criteria of recognition of primary rules has to be defined which decides in cases of conflict which is the higher source of law. Problems of recognition exist with respect to natural law and law of custom. These are not legislated by the organ of legislation, and therefore they are not simply positive law. The sources of law are different in these cases, and in weighing natural law against positive law in a situation in which they clash, the two sources of law have to be differently valued. A hierarchy of the sources with natural law on top, then positive law and finally law of custom at the bottom seems to be generally accepted.

The linguists who work at language institutes and academies on the identification of norms of language refer to different sources:

1. Literary corpora of the last 100 years; here the 'great' authors are a central source (*cf* von Polenz 1970). These are then models, sometimes with the precaution *Quod licet Jovi non licet bovi* ('what is allowed to Jupiter is not allowed to the ox'), as we find in Reiners's style manual (Reiners 1963/1969:29), which is widely used in West Germany.

2. Enquiries among members of the speech community; here the selection of the ones to be consulted poses a problem, because the linguistic usage and judgement of certain social and cultural groups are recognized as more relevant than the language use and judgement of others; also a certain region can be considered to be more relevant than another, for example Paris compared to other French regions, Oxford compared to other English regions, and Haarlem compared to other Dutch regions. It is necessary to make such a selection because otherwise the high linguistic diversity would cause too many variants in the language which would not be understood by linguistically relevant groups in all regions, not to speak of all members of all regions and classes.

3. The linguistic intuition of the codifiers themselves; this intuition is more how they think they speak, or should speak, then about how they in fact speak. In their judgement about what is correct they adjust themselves to great models. This is an advantage, because it makes this source for delivery of data identical with the results of the other sources.

As a whole all three sources provide a fairly homogenous output, the reason being that they are not independent of each other. Really, the linguistic intuition of the educational élite enters three times into the data that form the basis for the decisions of the standardizing and codifying institutions.

This procedure is typical for stating norms: one has to take certain judgements, here cases of language usage and judgements about correctness, as the standard or model cases, on the basis of which one formulates the norms. In case of doubt, one has to decide in favour of the unity of the system, *ie* one will avoid *ad hoc* adjustments of the system, which are not extensions or analogies of rules or norms that are already taken to be part of the system. But difficulties can arise in two ways: firstly, the selection and boundary of standard cases is not always self-evident; and secondly, the notion 'unity of the system' is double-edged: what is a simplification or systematization from phonological points of view can cause an exception and complication from morphological points of view, and a morphological simplification can cause a syntactic complication (*cf* Ch. 5). Furthermore, the decision in cases of doubt can work out too conservative, in the sense that the standard language is protected from the development of the vernaculars to such a degree that language barriers arise between the standard language and the linguistic usage of the speech community that ought to carry it. If the cleavage between the standard language and linguistic usage and intuition of the educated middle class, which is supposed to be the substratum of the standard, becomes too broad, then the standard language cannot fulfil its very purpose; its normalizing and unifying force with respect to linguistic usage diminishes, because it is no longer accepted by the (relevant parts of) the population: the standard language is then felt to be too rigid, too antiquated, and too strange. Instead of being a norm which coincides at least with the linguistic intuition of the educated class, thus being a real norm for them from the internal point of view, it would become a mere prescription, *ie* a norm content that has been imposed on them.

It should be mentioned here that large groups of the population have always found themselves in this position anyway; but they have not had to codetermine what the standard language should be and what it should look like. They are expected to accept it as a norm, even without being able to comply with it, and to make it a practice of their own if they want to participate in higher education and the job privileges bound up with this kind of education. The educated class itself, except in case of foreign domination, does not need to accept a strange norm; rather, it is presupposed by them that the selection and codification of linguistic norms have to be adjusted to the models they themselves provide. In this way the educated have great power in determining the standard language, comparable with the parliament in legislation, with the sole but important difference that they have not been elected to perform this task. Rather they have the status of specialists in a presupposed division of labour, the ones who create the written products of a nation or society.

The point of view of a desirable linguistic systematization of a standard language makes it necessary to take a fairly homogeneous linguistic usage as a substratum, *ie* to prefer one single dialect as a basis rather than a great number of dialects. Such a diversity provides a very heterogeneous material on the basis of which it would not be possible to formulate a somewhat orderly grammatical system, not even in the form of sentence patterns, as is done, for example, in the *Duden* grammar of German. A set of rules that provides for all the admitted alternatives is then not conceivable in a conclusive grammatical system. German, and also every other standard language, is not construable as the intersection of all dialects of the language area. Such an intersection that could be called a language is not defined (*cf* Bartsch and Vennemann 1982:18). The superstratum is not an intersection or average of the substrata. The point of view of systematization of the standard language, and along with that the point of view of its learnability, forces us to take a fairly homogeneous linguistic usage as the substratum, and this is the language usage of a certain social group that is transregionally movable, communicates transregionally, and thus is a linguistic group the members of which are spread over the different regions. This group is the group that has to provide the standard.

If one extends the domain of norm subjects beyond this standard-devising group, if others have to use this standard language – and doing this belongs to the essence of a standard – then one should be aware of the fact that such an extension can be an unnecessary burden and restriction for some people in some functions of language use, compared to their communicative needs which can be fulfilled by regional languages or dialects and their modifications, which are formed in boundary regions between different dialects. But the remedy of linguistic injustice cannot be to dispense with standard language altogether in favour of a heterogeneous set of languages, subsets of which are compatible interregionally in neighbouring regions; rather it is necessary not to strain the situational domain of the standard language, *ie* its domain of use for different functions, and not to require its use where it is not really necessary.

As has been pointed out, the linguists at language institutes and the teachers in schools take their own linguistic intuition as the basis of what they consider obligatory and according to which they judge, criticize, and correct linguistic usage of others. Correspondingly, we find that Hart draws attention to a juridical intuition of the officials of the legal system:

The use of unstated rules of recognition, by courts and others, in identifying particular rules of the system is characteristic of the internal point of view. Those who use them in this way thereby manifest their own acceptance of them as guiding rules and with this attitude there goes a characteristic vocabulary different from the natural expressions of the external point of view. (Hart 1961:99)

If, in a language area, the heterogeneity of linguistic usage is great, then what is self-evidently a norm for one ('internal point of view') might be a prescribed foreign norm, ie a prescription, for the other, which he might not even accept, although he possibly adjusts his speech behaviour to the strange norm, if this is of advantage for him and he is capable of doing so. Something like this can be the case with speakers of other sociolects or dialects with respect to the standard language. In the most favourable case, they learn it as a second language to be used in certain situations. They can then accept the standard language as a set of norms specific to certain situations. This context-dependence of the use of different sets of norms is not accounted for in Hart's opposition between 'internal' and 'external' points of view; but it is important for the working of linguistic norms.

Hart distinguishes the 'external point of view', according to which behaviour is predictable in certain situations, from the 'internal point of view', according to which the rule is reason for certain behaviour. From the external point of view, a person expects negative sanctions if he does not show a certain behaviour, and therefore exhibits this behaviour. Fear of punishment of disadvantage is the reason for this behaviour, and not the rule itself.

The external point of view may very nearly reproduce the way in which the rules function in the lives of certain members of the group, namely those who reject its rules and are only concerned with them when and because they judge that unpleasant consequences are likely to follow violation. Their point of view will need for its expression, 'I was obliged to do it', 'I am likely to suffer for it if . . .', 'You will probably suffer for it if . . .'. But they will not need forms of expression 'I had an obligation' or 'You have an obligation'; for these are required only by those who see their own and other persons' conduct from the internal point of view. What the external point of view, which limits itself to the observable regularities of behaviour, cannot reproduce is the way in which the rules function in the lives of those who normally are the majority of society. (Hart 1961:88)

For this majority the rules function as 'guides to conduct of social life'. With respect to the standard language, this majority is not the majority in a numerical sense, but the educated class.

Only in the natural state of a speech community is a numerical majority, for which the linguistic norms exist from the internal point of view, guaranteed. Hart writes about the majority which is the pillar of a valid norm system:

> For them the violation of a rule is not merely a basis for prediction that a hostile reaction will follow but a *reason for hostility*. (1961:88)

What are, according to Hart, the norms of the majority can in some cases be merely the norms of a dominating élite. Gloy (1975) and others draw attention to the fact that the norms of the German standard language are felt to be one's own norms and are complied with only by a minority of the German population. This, I think, is an over-simplification; we should make some finer distinctions: something that is not an accepted norm can very well be complied with because of fear of disadvantage; and something that is not felt to be one's own norm for all one's linguistic usage can very well be accepted as a norm that applies in certain situations only, for example in writing, or in formal interaction in public or in business. There is thus no reason to expect that someone who manages the standard language will use it in all situations; and those situations in which it is not required cannot count as situations in which the standard language is not mastered. The question of whether people master and use the standard language cannot be answered by just looking around and realizing that apparently in most situations most people do not exhibit a correct standard use.

People use different languages and varieties as different codes which are connected to different types of situations. People can use two languages with a different stylistic value in different functions, and in a manner that is absolutely natural to them, as has been found by Gumperz (1971) and Blom and Gumperz (1972) for different Indian and Norwegian villages.

Acceptance of the standard language is often found even with people who speak this language insufficiently or incompletely and who therefore do not dare to communicate by means of the standard language in those situations which require standard usage. They either avoid active language use in these situations and mainly listen and answer with utterances as short as possible, or they manage some compromise between the standard and their own dialect. They would understand it as an offence if, in these situations, they were not spoken to in the standard language. Dialect speakers speak, in formal situations or with strangers, a form of dialect that is adjusted to the standard language; and in doing this, they show that they think that in these situations the use of the standard is appropriate; they would judge the use of their dialect to be inappropriate in such a case; and it would, of course, be less functional in such a situation, compared with the standard that is provided just for situations of this kind.

There are in-between forms of norm adoption and compromises which show that the speaker accepts the standard norms to be valid in certain situations, even for himself, and that he has, as far as these situations go, the internal view with respect to the standard norms, although his linguistic behaviour is only partly adjusted to these norms. Acceptance of the standard can also be indicated symbolically by using a few indicators of the standard while at the same time retaining those indicative of his regional and social identity. The use of indicators of the standard expresses that one also accepts the larger community and its institutions, *ie* the nation or state, for which the standard can be an expression of identity.

This attitude of different loyalties which often need to be expressed in a single situation gives rise to compromises between standard language, dialects, and sociolects, which make communication between speakers of the standard and speakers of other varieties easy. Also the in-between forms of the so-called creole continuum with a growing orientation towards the matrix language, the use of which counts as educated speech, rest on social loyalties: it is not true that creole speakers do not manage to learn the matrix language right away; rather they have to show solidarity with their group of origin on the one hand, and on the other hand they have to take into account occupational mobility and prestige, if these goals are within reach for them (*cf* 5.1).

Another kind of compromise is known from India: in a census people claimed to be speakers of Hindi although they spoke not Hindi but related languages or dialects, some of which were more similar to Urdu than to Hindi. Hindi and Urdu are basically identical, but because of the different religious backgrounds they have a partly different vocabulary, and they have a different script (Devanagari for Hindi, and the Arabic–Iranian script for Urdu). Depending on religion, either Hindi or Urdu is the norm with which people identify, even without really being able to speak Hindi or Urdu. Although this situation is confusing for the census, one cannot blame those people of intended deceit. They do not lie, rather express their acceptance of Hindi–Urdu as a norm without practising it (*cf* Khubchandani 1976, 1978).

In cases like those described here, I speak of acceptance of a norm by people without it being practised by them. Their factual behaviour is not guided by this norm except in language attitude tests, in which they express their acceptance of the norm in question. In many cases, for example those in which the relation dialect–standard or creole–matrilect play a role, people adjust their practice more or less, depending on ability and attitude, to the accepted norm in accordance with situational requirements.

The extreme opposition which Hart proposes between the external and internal point of view will be found with regard to norms of language only in situations of conflict and fighting between a minority and the majority, or between a majority or minority and the élite or the governmental and economic power. Thus, in the New York ghettos especially, male Black youths have a strong negative attitude towards Whites and their language, which makes them reject standard American English (*cf* Labov 1972b). We also find a non-acceptance of a language in the history of the language conflict between the Walloons and the Flemings in Belgium (*cf* Lorwin 1972), and in the attitude of creole-speakers towards French, the matrilect, in Mauritius (*cf* Hookoomsing 1986). In the last case, the motive is the opposition to the French-speaking élite, who are more regarded as suppressors than as models of normative orientation. In this case and in the case of Black youths, the following remark applies:

> At any given moment the life of any society which lives by the rules, legal or not, is likely to consist in a tension between those who, on the one hand, accept and voluntarily cooperate in maintaining the rules, and so see their own and other persons' behaviour in terms of these rules, and those who, on the other hand, reject the rules and attend to them only from the external point of view as a sign of possible punishment. (Hart 1961:88)

With respect to the standard language, to see one's own and others' behaviour in the light of these norms does not mean that one speaks the standard language extensively or perfectly. Acceptance of the standard norms admits taking into account at the same time norms of subgroups, for example dialects, or even personal standards, like a personal speech style used in some situations. Taking these into account, people develop dialectal, sociolectal, and personal modifications of the standard language, or develop a modification of their dialect by taking up standard features. The use of these 'mixed' languages points to loyalty and solidarity with respect to different norm systems; one accepts both or all, often as stylistic devices used according to the situation: for different situations different competing norm systems are relevant to a different degree. Because of this, stylistic registers are created as mixed forms the use of which carries social and personal connotations. Mixed forms are not necessarily signs of linguistic incompetence or unintended interference between two linguistic systems in the speaker's mind. The positive valuation of certain kinds of mixed forms or mixed speech follows from the analysis of norm conflicts and strategies for their solutions (see 7.2).

From the above considerations we can conclude that Hart's explanation of what it means to accept a rule seems too strict, *ie* excludes too much, at least as far as the norms of standard language are concerned. To accept a norm and to treat it as valid ('internal view') is, in the context of language, under one aspect more, and under another less, than being guided by the norm and following it. Hart's definition of acceptance includes criticizing those who do not behave according to the norm. But this is too strong with regard to linguistic norms. Here, to behave according to the norms means in many situations only a gradual but clearly recognizable adjustment of one's own linguistic usage to these norms. This, provided understandability is still guaranteed, can be reduced so much that the acceptance of these norms will be expressed in a symbolic way by using a few forms typical for the norm system as an indicator of the fact that one accepts the validity of it for the present situation. By indicating this, one prevents criticism. Acts of correction are then not appropriate, except if the situation is one of strictly formal language use, or a teaching situation. Only in written communication, especially in formal situations, are the norms required to be followed strictly; if a situation is less formal, the norms of the standard need not be applied strictly. The degrees of adjustment that are required in the different situations for different kinds of persons determine to what extent criticism for not following the rules is justified, and on this depends whether acts of correction are appropriate.

It is important to point out that strict adjustment to the standard language in informal situations can be experienced as unpleasant, and that, the other way around, dialect speakers do not like it when strangers or newcomers try to speak the local dialect. But the adoption of a few features of the dialect, especially intonation patterns, into the everyday language of the newcomer is felt to be pleasant. I experienced this when I lived in two different villages in different regions of Germany. A balance has to be found between adaptation and the stranger's own identity; and the group wants the boundary between itself and the stranger to be accepted, even in linguistic usage. The dialect speakers speak in the standard or an adjusted variant of the dialect with the newcomer, or when she is present in a conversation even though they know that she has come to understand the dialect. This behaviour can be understood as a tribute paid to the linguistic norms of the stranger or to the norms that are common between both parties (and on this broader level an identity between both parties is recognized). However, the more specific identities of both parties need to be respected, and a stranger who does not try to imitate the dialect shows that he has no intention to intrude; and by taking up only a few dialectal features he shows his acceptance of the norms of the group. This is a weaker form of acceptance, which does not mean to make the norms one has accepted to be the guidelines of one's own behaviour. There are degrees of acceptance; the lowest degree is to comply with a norm because of its being valid, and at the same time to work at having it declared invalid.

People, generally, do not feel hostile towards others just because they do not speak their language properly, but they sometimes display hostility with respect to other norms of communication and interaction. So people of northern European countries feel offended and threatened in their personal integrity when people, as is common in the south of Europe, talk to them quickly, wildly gesticulating, and without keeping a proper distance. In general, hostility against a norm breaker arises more easily if he is a member of one's own community, which defines itself, among other ways, by adhering to the norms broken. This behaviour will be understood as an attack on the community and its norms and values from the inside. A stranger is not expected to behave according to the norms of language and custom, as long as he does not become a burden; but he is expected at least to respect these norms and to indicate his respect. Therefore his deviation from one's own norms will not so easily be understood as an attack.

After this excursion about the notion of acceptance of a norm, the question is whether Hart's characterization of the rule of recognition as a mere fact fits the activity of the language institutes and their products. The decisions of the language institutes can be criticized, even by their own members. But this possibility is negated by Hart for legal systems; the validity of the 'ultimate rule of recognition' can itself not be questioned; this rule exists as a fact,

> as a complex, but normally concordant, practice of the courts, officials and private persons in identifying the law by reference to certain

criteria. Its existence is a matter of fact. . . . By using it, those who use it consider it valid. (Hart 1961:107).

This also holds for the seemingly somewhat naive attitude towards the products and the activities of the language institutes: for many it is unquestionable that the German language is such as the *Duden* has stated. But in this attitude there is a deep truth: the German (or any other) standard language does not exist as a linguistic system given by God or grown naturally. Rather the standard language is what, among others, the language institutes have laid down as the German language and what is enforced by teachers in schools. Another seemingly naive attitude is that of the linguists at the language institutes when they take their own linguistic judgement as the last criterion in the identification of what the norms of the German language are. Their linguistic intuition is indeed a pure fact. In the meantime, this naive attitude has been officially overcome, because one is aware of the heterogeneity of the German language, regionally, socially, and functionally. But the decision about how, from such a diversity, called 'the German language', some system can be attained, also called 'the German language', has been made less consciously and has as a result the very same fact, namely linguistic usage and intuition of a certain group, as a rule of recognition. But, how can it be otherwise? Let us consider again the whole situation.

It has already been pointed out that what is common to all German dialects does not form a language; no language can be an intersection or average of the common properties of all its dialects because these notions are undefined. And even if they were, the result would not be a language because hardly any linguistic rule would be within this result. There is only a family resemblance between the different dialects; there is no fixed set of common internal lingustic properties by which they are all identifiable as dialects of German; there is certainly one external relational property, namely that they are all members of a complex of means of communication that are related to each other and that carry, for historical reasons, a common name, namely 'German dialects'. This name is not the name of a concept but the proper name of a collection; as far as its contents go, it can also be characterized as a complex concept (*cf* Bartsch 1984c), with the additional restriction of being causally connected to a historical entity.

Theoretically, it would have been possible to construct as a German standard language an Esperanto based on all varieties of German. But one has chosen the written variant of the language of the educational élite, with some variants as stylistic alternatives. Some regional variants with broader regional domains of use and some variants from prestigious registers have been included, in some cases marked as such. Doing this, it was possible to codify the language somewhat systematically, though it is already a conglomerate of forms that are parts of different varieties which are the regionally and functionally coined linguistic varieties of the educational élite (*bildungstragende Schicht*, *cf* Riesel 1970:10; Gloy 1975:84).

I mentioned above that I think that this procedure of orientation on the linguistic usage and linguistic intuition of the educational élite is justified and thus legitimate, although it is undemocratic. But this does not free us from, in fact places upon us, the obligation to be conscious of what one does, hereby, and what one inflicts upon other groups of the population; one therefore has the obligation to mitigate the adverse consequences this has for them, as well as take credit for the general advantages a standard language provides for everybody.

With respect to the role the educational élite and its agents (officials, teachers, editors, etc.) fulfil with regard to a standard language we can use Putnam's (1975) notion of 'division of linguistic labour', although he only seems to have taken into account the lexical aspects of language. The subgroups of a population do not to the same extent have at their disposal the standard language in all its elaborations specific to particular fields. The educational élite makes the most extended use of the standard language and, as a whole, works on its development in oral and written use; but there is one group of people who, by occupation, work on the elaboration, conservation, and availability of the standard language. The division of linguistic labour has been institutionalized to overcome the deficiencies of a natural linguistic state with only primary norms.

The second weakness of 'primary rules only', *ie* rules in a natural state without being formulated, has been their static character: they cannot be changed in a deliberate and controlled way. This is the case because, without being formulated, they cannot be made the object of discussion and consideration. This deficiency, according to Hart, is overcome in the legal system by a second kind of secondary rules, namely 'rules of change' or rules of legislation which regulate how the legal system can be changed by an organ of legislation. In this way a juridical system can be adjusted to changing custom and changing conception of right and wrong. Similarly, language institutes and committees prepare and promote the implementation of new norms and try to keep a balance between conservatism and change, by admitting old and new linguistic forms as variants, and by guiding language development and modernization (*cf*, *eg*, Jernudd 1977 and Fishman 1974b).

The third weakness of 'primary rules only' has been the failing efficiency of social pressure. This deficiency has been overcome by creating institutions that monitor compliance with the primary rules and that can take measures against rule breakers. These rules of second order are the rules of jurisdiction by lawcourts and the rules of police and penalty institutions. The rules of jurisdiction are not independent of the 'rules of recognition', since the courts have to refer to them. On the other hand, important decisions of lawcourts also fix primary rules by applying certain interpretations of these primary rules; and by its decisions and the argumentation with regard to them, jurisdiction adds to the specification of the 'rules of recognition'. Next to the interpretation of positive law, this also applies to the directions provided by decisions which refer to laws of custom and natural law.

> These [the decisions and determinations of the courts] cannot avoid being taken as authoritative determinations of what the rules are. So the rule which confers jurisdiction will also be a rule of recognition, identifying the primary rules through the judgements of courts, and these judgements will become a source of law. (Hart 1961:94)

The role of the judges with respect to the legal system can be compared with the roles of the teachers at schools and the editors in publishing houses. Through acts of correction by these agents, especially by teachers, linguistic norms are declared valid according to the linguistic intuition of the teachers and their social class. These conceptions of correctness can be enforced in teaching and in writing teaching material. Something similar is true of editorial work done with respect to newspapers, journals, books, radio, and television. (For research about acts of correction *cf* Jernudd and Thuan 1983.)

The last question addressed in this section refers to Hart's remarks about the breakdown of a legal system:

> A legal system breaks down if the congruence of rules which are obeyed (by society) and rules which are considered valid (by officials) is distorted. (1961:107)

The question is whether a system of linguistic norms, for example the German standard language, that has been fixed and codified by language specialists and writers, can collapse when it does not conform with the linguistic norms that are followed by the population. Such a collapse would only occur if the majority, which according to Gloy (1975) does not speak Standard German, were to try to effect a competing standard language. But this is not possible because of three reasons: first, the majority which follows other rules than those of the valid standard language is split up; the majority has no common linguistic norm system, but rather many different language varieties. Second, a standard language will fulfil the cultural, administrative, and economic needs of a modern society only when it is a written language. But, as far as this example goes, there is no other written form of German. Such a language cannot be pulled out of a hat, but has to have a tradition, if it is to be a serious competitor to the existing standard. Both arguments, of course, presuppose that a lingua franca is absolutely required for the German language area. Third, the existing standard language is not an insurmountable problem for the majority of the population. And it certainly is not a problem for people who are not in a position to use this language at work and in public anyway. With the advance of technology and with the growth of bureaucracy, even instruction and training for lower jobs and understanding of conditions and safety instructions at work require a certain degree of at least passive knowledge of standard usage. But a full command of the standard language is not required. Tolerance with respect to deviation from the norm system may thus be much greater with respect to language than with respect to law.

Reaching occupational positions which require the use of the standard language is, as is well known, difficult for non-standard speakers; on the other hand, strong motivation is developed if, together with upward mobility with regard to occupations, entrance into the middle class is also aimed for – and membership of this class is indicated by the use of the standard language. This motivation can only be resisted by convinced proletarians whose feeling of solidarity with their group prevents adaptation. Generally, along with achieving a higher position, the language typical for people in such a position will be valued positively, and there is thus motivation for learning the language variety in question.

The standard language creates a real problem for people with difficulties in learning languages, but who nevertheless fulfil other requirements of social mobility. If someone like this who is otherwise qualified, for example, for the position of an engineer or physician, wants to fulfil such a position, this should not be prevented by poor performance in the standard language if this does not form a serious obstacle for performing his tasks. (This point of view has been stressed in the last decade, but has become discredited in the meantime because it was exercised by progressive teachers in connection with lowering pretensions and expectations in many other fields of knowledge.)

These considerations show that although for society as a whole there is no congruency between the set of valid norms and existing linguistic norms, this will not lead to a collapse of the norm system of a standard language. There will be no linguistic revolutions.

It would be quite another case if, as has been mentioned above, the language institutes were not oriented towards the linguistic norms of today's educational élite and middle class, but towards, for example, the German language of the time of Goethe (eighteenth to nineteenth century). In fact, there was such an orientation towards literary texts from the nineteenth century twenty to thirty years ago, and it was criticized (*cf* von Polenz 1970). Fortunately, the difference from modern educated German was only minimal, because educated speech still was orientated towards nineteenth-century models. In the meantime the editors of the codifications of German have taken into account modern literary, scientific, and political texts when collecting their corpora for standard German. These corpora include written texts of the cultural élite, which can be used as a standard that does not lead to conflicts with the linguistic usage of the middle class a long as existing variants and linguistic changes carried by this class are taken into account, as they are by the language specialists, who have the cultural and linguistic background of this class.

2.2 Theories about emergence and functions of norms

2.2.1 Ullmann-Margalit (1977)

Edna Ullmann-Margalit, in her book *The Emergence of Norms* (1977), does not address the question 'Under what conditions do we say that a norm x exists?', which is central in Hart (1961) and Raz (1975); rather she wants to answer the question why a norm of type y exists (1977:8). She focuses on the conditions under which norms arise. Norms come about when certain recurrent problems of adjusting actions between partners in interaction emerge. Norms provide solutions to these problems.

> My basic argument is that certain types of norms are solutions to problems posed by certain interaction situations. (1977:9)

She investigates three different kinds of social norms which solve three different kinds of interaction problems. A preliminary definition of social norm for her is:

> A social norm is a prescribed guide for conduct or action which is generally complied with by the members of a society. (1977:12)

Within this class of norms the class of obligatory norms is investigated as defined by Hart's characterization of 'rules of obligation':

1. [Norms] are conceived and spoken of as imposing obligations when the general demand for conformity is insistent and the social pressure brought to bear upon those who deviate or threaten to deviate is great.
2. The [norms] supported by [a] serious pressure are thought important because they are believed to be necessary to the maintenance of social life or some highly prized feature of it.
3. It is generally recognized that the conduct required by these [norms] may, while benefiting others, conflict with what the person who owes the duty may wish to do. (1977:12, 13)

The first class of norms which serve for solving the 'prisoners' dilemma' exhibit all three of the characteristics. Since these norms do not exist as linguistic norms, as shall be argued below, they will not be treated here extensively.

The second class of norms serve for the solution of problems of coordination; they are, according to Ullmann-Margalit, not all norms of obligation; they are characterized by another set of features, which are formulated in Lewis's book *Convention* (1969), and which apply to norms of language.

The third class of norms, called 'partial norms', serve to keep up a certain status quo which is in the interest of a group or party; they fulfil conditions (1) and (3), and only sometimes condition (2). This kind of norm has to be discussed in our context, because in the literature about norms of language (*cf* Gloy 1975) it has been argued that the norms of standard language serve to keep up the status quo by holding people from lower classes, who do not speak the standard language at home, in their position of disadvantage. Furthermore, literature in anthropological linguistics points out that in many communities forms of language and style serve to symbolize and reinforce the social structure and hierarchies in a society. Examples are the different language- and style-variants in Indian villages (*cf* Gumperz 1971), the use of Bokmål and Ramamål in Norwegian villages (*cf* Blom and Gumperz 1972), the use of different morphological forms in the language of men and women in several languages (*cf* the survey of Bodine 1975), forms of deference and politeness, for example, in Japanese (*cf* Neustupný 1974b) and forms of address, for example, in German (*cf* Hartmann 1973).

I shall now present a review of the three different types of norms treated by Ullmann-Margalit.

2.2.1(1) Prisoners' dilemma norms

The general structure of the prisoners' dilemma (PD) is the following. Two persons, *x* and *y*, may perform two alternative acts, *A* and *B*, with the following results: if *x* and *y* both do *A*, then the result for both is moderately favourable (*eg*, both have a chance to win). If only one of them does *B* and the other *A*, then the result for the one who does *B* is particularly favourable (he will win) and for the other very bad (he will lose). If *x* and *y* both do *B*, then the result for both is fairly bad (both will very likely lose). Of course, both have a tendency to do *B*; but if both do *B* the result for both is fairly bad. Further, knowing from each other that the other has the tendency to do *B* makes it completely unrewarding to do *A*. What the PD-norms do under such a constellation is to secure that the unstable situation is achieved in which both do *A*, and which is moderately favourable to both.

The name of the dilemma is due to the example of the two prisoners *x* and *y*, whereby *A* is the act not to confess, and *B* is the act to confess to a certain crime which they had committed together. If only one confesses, he will get freedom and the other ten years in prison; if both confess, each will get five years in prison, and if neither confesses they can only be proven guilty of a minor crime for which each will go to jail for one year. The last situation is the best for both of them, though none has 100 per cent success in this case. To achieve this situation, each has to be sure that the other will not confess to get 100 per cent advantage over the other. Here, an agreement not to confess, will help. If such an agreement is a general agreement that holds for all constellations of this kind, we can speak of a norm, by which prisoners solve this kind of problems.

> The problem is that of protecting an unstable yet jointly beneficial state of affairs from deteriorating, so to speak, into a stable yet jointly destructive one. (1977:22)

It is characteristic for this kind of interaction problem and norm that it is of advantage to do *A* in case the other does not also do *A*; this means it is of advantage to break the norm only if one is sure that the other complies with it. To prevent this, such breaking of the norm is threatened by punishment. A generalized form of the PD-problem for a whole society is exemplified by the paying of taxes: as long as only a few people evade taxes they have a big advantage, but if most people do this the whole order collapses; and this is to great disadvantage of everyone. The relatively most beneficial situation for all is if taxes are not evaded; but this situation is unstable because individuals can evade taxes to their own advantage as long as not too many people do this. To make people pay their taxes threat by punishment is necessary.

Linguistic norms are not of this kind, because it can never be of great advantage to break the norms. (A similar case is only the norm of sincerity, but it does not show the full structure of the prisoners' dilemma norms.) Generally, a parner in communication has no advantage in breaking the linguistic norms, for example by using words in deviation from their meaning, or using strings of words which are not grammatical. He then, of course, will not be understood. In deviating, and being the only one to do this, he can never reach his goal, as long as this goal includes being understood. This goal can only be reached in cooperation, *ie* if both partners follow the norms of communication.

Also PD-norms are norms of coordination of actions of people. But by them, people can only achieve the second-best result, not the personally best one; but at least they preclude the worst result. Because they only help to achieve the second-best result, they have to be aided by sanctions which make it unattractive to try to reach the best result.

Prisoners' dilemma norms are not norms that solve problems in which coordination is itself the goal, which would mean that by reaching coordination for both parties the best result has been achieved. Rather PD-norms solve interaction problems in which there is at least one situation in which both parties taken together reach a relatively optimal goal, which is only the second best compared to what one person alone could achieve for himself. The point is to secure the solution that is the second best for each party by herself in order to avoid a risk that is too great. Another example of such norms are 'Anti-Trust Laws', which are favourable for a whole industry together, though they are not optimal compared to what a single group could achieve.

2.2.1.(2) Norms of coordination
The main difference between PD-norms and norms of coordination lies in their function:

> A coordination norm helps those involved 'meet' each other; a PD-norm helps those involved protect themselves from damaging, even ruining, each other. (1977:119)

That in the case of coordination norms it is not necessary to threaten with sanctions is due to the fact that each party is interested in the coordination because this is the best situation that can be reached by him.

> Conformity to coordination norms is in the best interest of those concerned, whereas compliance with PD-norms serves only their 'second best' interest; sanctions play a primary role in the case of PD-norms, but only a secondary one in coordination norms. (1977:77)

With respect to norms of language, we also notice that at least first-language acquisition takes place without evident negative sanctions, because the normal child has a need to communicate, whereby learning a first language takes place in situations which satisfy this need and, at the same time, promote the ability to communicate. There are no severe negative sanctions necessary, though correction and praise are favourable to language learning.

In second-language acquisition, or in the special case of acquiring the standard language by a dialect speaker, negative sanctions could also be dispensed with if it were evident to the learners that coordination in communication with strangers is a problem that is relevant for them, at least in so far as it provides enough motivation to overcome the problems and troubles that accompany learning a second language. But neither are these problems of coordination relevant to everyone to the same degree, nor are they sensible for everybody. We therefore have to state that sanctions have to play a role in the acquisition of a language, even though these sanctions are only in order in second-language acquisition. But since most people are in this situation with respect to their own official or national language, not to mention other foreign languages for international communication, this problem is worth considering.

The need for direct sanctions and for praise comes about because in learning situations for foreign languages and the standard language, problems of coordination are not apparent in their generality, or they are not apparent at all; teachers can only point out that there are situations that require coordination by means of these languages, or they can try artificially to create situations in which these means of communication have to be used. But in such artificial situations, usually, there is no real communicative need. To this, further difficulties are added, namely that children already have communicative means functioning well enough for their purposes, and that they have to learn strange sounds and structures, though they are already conditioned to another set of sounds and structures.

Even though problems of coordination solved by the standard language are not urgent for individual people to the same degree, they are problems of the whole social–political community in which the individual lives in our culture. It is the task of a whole society to solve the problems of transregional communication; and this problem is solved in a division of labour. Not every member in a community has to have the same ability to solve these problems of communication. With more division of labour in this area, it becomes less urgent that everybody learn a foreign language, or even the standard language. But an extensive division of labour in mastering linguistic and communicational means and skills leads to dependence on those who are linguistically better trained. Deficient acquisition of means of communication leads to helplessness.

The point in coordination problems is that one or more persons have to choose one possibility out of a set of possibilities for action, depending on what the others choose. As long as one does not know what the others will do, one has to try to make a good guess. With regard to communication this means that one has to choose signs which the others will understand in the way one intends. A good guess about which sign the others most probably will understand in the intended sense can be based on very different and very idiosyncratic reasons. For example, if a sign has been used once for the same purpose and both partners know about this and know that the other knows about this, then it is handy to use this sign again; in this way, regularities of the use of signs emerge, and with the expectation that people will continue this regularity in almost all cases in which the same has to be communicated, conventions arise (cf Lewis 1969).

In communication it is not necessary that one use the same expression that the partner would use for the intended message. It is sufficient that the partner can understand the expression, even if he would not, or could not, use this expression actively himself. This can be the case if people of two different groups in a village speak with each other, who can understand each other but are not allowed to use the language of the other actively (for examples cf Gumperz 1971), or when men and women talk with each other in two very different language varieties, whereby social rules forbid members of one group to use the variant assigned to members of the other group. The solution of communication problems thus does not require that both partners use the same language, and certainly not that both use the same language variety. But, it is obvious that the use of the same communicational means is a good way to achieve coordination in communication.

According to Ullmann-Margalit (1977:83), norms that secure the solution of coordination problems emerge in two ways: by convention and by decree.

If a coordination problem recurs, the solution that has once been successful will be repeated and thus becomes a convention (Lewis 1969) and may become a norm. In special cases an explicit agreement can be made to install as a norm the solutions already applied. A recurrent pattern of behaviour or action by itself is not normative, though those who recurrently have had positive experiences with these solutions expect that the successful strategy will be repeated. To expect this, and also to do this, is simply clever. But how does it become a norm? Ullmann-Margalit points out that the repeated solution is only obvious to those who had already taken part in the coordination problem and its solution. Newcomers, especially children of the community, threaten to destroy the established regularity because they have other knowledge or other standards, which can lead to different decisions in situations in which coordination is required. On the other hand, those who are already used to an established pattern of action cannot expect newcomers to follow it.

> Newcomers to the community, or in general people concerning whom there can be no definite expectations, pose a problem, if not a threat, to the continuing existence of this type of regularity. But once future behaviour in accordance with the established pattern is prescribed, anonymity can be accommodated. (1977:86)

With regard to norms of language this means that they are conventions in the sense of Lewis (1969) as far as their origin is concerned, but for every new generation, and every newcomer, they are norms. We can say: they are conventions from a phylogenetic point of view; but from the ontogenetic point of view, *ie* relative to the individual who has been born into a speech community, they are norms. Norms of language are typically more than just Lewis's conventions. But some are also regularities in communication that are merely conventions, which are not obligatory, and which are usually not complied with by strangers: these are customs more than norms, or are conventions which are not strictly necessary for solving the coordination problem in understanding, but which regulate the use of social

indicators. These rules or aspects do not solve coordination problems and thus do not belong to the class of coordination norms
but to the third group of norms, the norms of partiality, which
will be treated later.

For coordination norms the following holds:

> The existence of a norm, rather than merely of a discernible regu-
> larity, will alleviate the burden of searching for specific clues in the
> specific context of each instance of the coordination problem; it will
> prescribe – and hence provide – a uniform solution to a problem-type,
> thus circumventing the difficulties of solving anew, and possibly with
> strangers, the varying problem tokens. (1977:86)

In this way every occurring problematic situation ('problem
token') obtains the solution which already exists for this type of
situation ('problem type').

In certain newly arising coordination problems it is probable
that a norm for the solution of such a problem will be set by an
authority, specifically for this purpose. These norms, for example
traffic rules, are called 'decrees' (1977:83). Ullmann-Margalit
points out that this second kind of rule can be expected especially
in situations where different communities, small groups as well
as whole nations, come into contact with each other:

> Very generally, where communities which have their own ways of
> going about things – their own arrangements, regularities, conventions
> – come into contact, and where the situation demands that barriers
> between them be dropped, or that one – any one – of them absorbs
> the other, various coordination problems are likely to crop up and to
> call for these decree-type coordination norms to solve them. (1977:92)

This applies to the problems of communication which are
solved by institutions of language planning in African and South-
east Asian countries: the introduction of scientific and technical
terminology into languages which are not developed in this direction happens by decree. This has also been the case with respect
to Hebrew, a language formed by an ancient culture, that
suddenly had to function as a language of modern civilization.
The task of language-planning agencies in Israel is to unify and
Hebraize the terminology that has been spontaneously developed
or adopted from English by the different scientific and techno-
logical institutes (cf Fellman 1977; Fellman and Fishman 1977).
The choice and implementation of national or official languages
in newly founded nations, resulting from colonization and
comprising many different nationalities and tribes, also happen
by decree (cf 6.2).

Besides the advantages of norms compared with mere regularities which are mentioned above, Ullmann-Margalit addresses the following three advantages:

> 1. The regularity's assuming the status of a norm entails its being taught to the young and told to newcomers, and hence its being more widely known and adhered to, and more securely perpetuated.
> 2. While a regularity extracted from past events might sometimes be continued in more than one way, a norm will provide the principle of continuation which will resolve potential ambiguities in future events. (1977:87)

If one considers a few antecedent cases, but in principle also when a long row of cases antecede, an ambiguity can arise because one does not know which of the observed regularities are the ones which one can expect will be continued by others (cf also Wittgenstein 1960: nos 199–242). The third advantage of norms is also due to the ambiguity and difficulty in determining the regularity in a series of cases:

> 3. There is a higher degree of articulation and explicitness associated with a norm than with a mere regularity of behaviour. In this respect a norm is closer to an agreement than a regularity, and an explicit agreement affords the best and safest solution to any coordination problem. (1977:87)

Such explicit agreements have, for example, been reached in international biological nomenclature. At the same time, it can be observed in other areas of language planning that terminological fixations are achieved only with difficulty, or not at all; even small groups of scientists prefer to use the terminology they themselves have developed, even when a unifying terminology has been proposed. This partly has to do with science policy, because giving up one's own terminology in favour of another one can be understood as becoming adapted to the scientific or cultural position of a dominating competitor. In addition to this emotional problem, there is a theoretical and also practical problem: it is not at all obvious that the translation of a terminology that has been used in certain scientific or cultural contexts will be possible without loss of part of its meaning and without acquiring new aspects of meaning. As soon as terminologies have been developed in different contexts, for example the names for fish in biology, fishery, trade and the consumption industry, a translation between these terminologies is problematic. By being used in different practical and theoretical contexts, the names are part of differently structured semantic fields (semantic nets, and especially taxonomies), in which their meaning is determined alongside causal or historical restrictions of their use (cf Jernudd and Thuan 1980 for naming fish, and *cf* further Ch. 6 for problems with decreed norms of language).

Beyond these advantages of norms above mere regularities, Ullmann-Margalit mentions another point that plays a role in the area of linguistic norm:

> The fact that a norm is taught and told, and its being supported by social pressure, enhance the salience of the particular coordination equilibrium it points to; in a sense it even slightly changes the corresponding pay-off matrix so as to make this particular coordination equilibrium a somewhat more worthwhile outcome to be aimed at than it otherwise would have been. (1977:87)

This phenomenon can be observed in the higher valuation of the standard language compared with its local alternatives, namely the dialects. People also seem to evaluate their own dialect higher than neighbouring ones, which might be due to the social pressure during its acquisition, though its norms are not taught and told, as are those of the standard language at school.

On the other hand, some norm that has been enforced with social pressure and social esteem can be stigmatized by those who deliberately dissociate themselves from the society that carries this norm. In this way Black English, peer languages, and other sociolects and variants of public language arise, which provide alternative solutions of the coordination problem that language has to resolve, namely to make communication possible. The officially supported coordination equilibria and their positive valuation are opposed, although one needs to adjust to them outside in-group or subgroup communication if one wants to communicate more than simply the fact that one does not want to communicate.

Ullmann-Margalit shows how mutual expectations about regularities of behaviour, which are built up in an inductive and empirical manner, achieve a normative character 'by themselves', so to speak. Her argumentation (1977:89) comes down to the following: because an action that conforms to a regularity which has already solved a recurrent coordination problem meets the interests of all those involved, and because, from an ethical point of view, one expects others not to harm either themselves or others, one must expect the others to follow this regularity as well. In this way a moral obligation to comply with this regularity arises because otherwise one would do harm to others and to oneself. The harm would be disorientation, which would be caused by disappointed (and repeatedly disappointed) expectation, such that action would be troublesome or even impossible.

The strict division between conventions and decrees within the class of coordination norms applies to linguistic norms only in extreme cases. The features presented by Ullmann-Margalit as typical for conventions apply to linguistic norms only in their 'natural state', *ie* for dialects and languages without a writing system, in communities without educational institutions that promote language cultivation. In addition we find the typical features of conventions in new conventions arising by spontaneous language change (*cf* Ch. 5). Standard languages and literary languages generally have features of decrees, which have their origin in the activities of language institutes, editorial offices, and schools.

Conventions are, in opposition to decrees, characterized as follows:

> Conventions are, typically:
> (1) Non-statutory norms, which need not be enacted, formulated, and promulgated.
> (2) They are neither issued nor promulgated by any identifiable authority, and are hence what is usually called impersonal, or anonymous norms.
> (3) They involve in the main non-institutionalized, non-organized, and informal sanctions (*ie* punishments and rewards). (1977:97)

All three properties, in their exclusiveness, are only applicable to languages in a 'natural state', *ie* in a state with only primary rules − in Hart's terminology. They do not apply to languages which are cultivated, promoted, and planned. But this is precisely the case with all languages which are supported by an educational system and which have been developed such that they are written and include registers for broad domains of public life. They share properties with decrees.

> Decrees, in contrast, are typically:
> (1) Statutory;
> (2) Issued and promulgated by some appropriately endowed authority (not necessarily on the level of state);
> (3) The sanctions they involve might be organized, institutionalized, and formal, even physical. (1977:97)

These three properties apply to norms of standard languages, with the provision that these usually have a history as conventions of subcommunities, in which they can still be experienced as such by those who have learned the norms in primary socialization. But even there, they are norms, not conventions in their pre-normative phase of emergence. In socialization at school, norms of standard language certainly have all three properties of decrees, even if they originate as conventions of certain subgroups. Parts of standard language, for example specialist terminology for products and processes in new economic and technical developments, are by origin decrees and not conventions. This also holds for names of states: for example, according to West German language regulation, the East German state had first been called *Ostzone*, an expression which negated its statehood; after a while the name *DDR* (German Democratic Republic) that the '*Ostzone*' had given to itself was used more and more, and in following this development the official regulation in West Germany was such that *DDR* was to be used in quotes and in quotes only, as a variant for *Ostzone*. In the meantime, in 1985, West German language regulation is such that *DDR* may be used without quotes; and only a few people of the older generation still speak of the '*Ostzone*'. In the GDR (German: *DDR*) the language regulation is such that, parallel with *DDR*, West Germany is called *BRD*. This expression, which puts West Germany on a line with East Germany, must, according to West German language regulation, not be used. Until very recently, if somebody used this abbreviation *BRD* for *Bundesrepublik Deutschland* (Federal German Republic) instead of the simple *D* as abbreviation for *Deutschland* (Germany), he would be classified as a communist or friend of communists, with all the consequences this can still have for his career in several of the West German states. This possible consequence may be 'Berufsverbot' as far as employment in the Civil Service is concerned: school, postal services, and public traffic systems. The word *Berufsverbot* is another example of a word which must not be used, and the use of it is threatened with punishment by the very same sanction expressed by it. The official name for these sanctions is *Wehrung von Radikalen aus dem öffentlichen Dienst* (*ie* banning of radicals from the Civil Service). Decrees in the area of linguistic norms are generally all norms of the use of expressions, which are the product of official or half-official regulations of language.

Because norms of coordination are useful for all who follow them, Ullmann-Margalit suggests that it is better to say that people use these norms rather than that they follow them (1977:98). The reward for behaviour conforming to these norms consists of this behaviour itself (1977:99). This also applies to norms of language and communication: behaviour that conforms to linguistic norms establishes communication, and this is the general goal of the use of linguistic norms.

One might well ask in whose interest norms of coordination

are. These norms are in the interest of all who are concerned with the kind of coordination which is achieved by conformity to these norms. With respect to the goal of making communication possible, all people who live in a certain regional and social domain are concerned with these norms when they show behaviour conforming to them and in this way form a speech community.

It has been pointed out above that the interest among people in communicating with each other has its limits, which differ according to social, occupational, and regional circumstances, and goals with respect to which communication is necessary or useful. When the use of a standard language is enforced against the use of dialects, or a national or official language as a lingua franca in a multi-tribal state is chosen over tribal languages, many people get into a difficult situation: if they do not benefit from broad transregional communication, conformity to the prescribed official language does not do them any good, at least according to their preferences or possibilities. In this case, the answer to the question of whom conformity serves, cannot simply be 'everyone'. It serves the unification of state power and economy, as well as the mobility of the population for economic and military purposes and purposes that strengthen governmental power. If the development of the greater unit (nation, state) is favourable to a group and is experienced by this group as such, then conformity to the norms that serve unification is useful for this group, and this group will support the norms in question. In addition to group interest, a personal interest in conformity can be induced by officially binding occupations, especially in the area of the Civil Service, to the standard or official or national language. This way, people with a drive towards upward mobility are motivated to conform linguistically. Such an interest can be induced within a population which initially would not be interested in a common transregional language. In such a case, linguistic conformity serves those most who are interested in promoting unification and controllability of the population in the development of a transregional national state. It might be the whole population, or only a subgroup, who has an advantage from linguistic conformity. This depends very much on the political situation.

Norms of coordination, which in principle are supposed to be useful for everyone who conforms to them, are experienced by people as a value; this is especially true of a national language in its unifying function. In situations in which a nation or the unity of a nation is felt to be threatened, adherence to the national language is an important ideological weapon. Ullmann-Margalit addresses this aspect of the function of norms in her discussion about the social role of coordination norms, which is their integrative function, expressed by the terms 'consensus', 'cohesion', 'social control', 'group solidarity'. They contribute to social integration, support and enforce conformity so that reciprocal expectations of members of a society are satisfied. It has to be added here that justification of such expectations, and their satisfaction, forms the precondition for every act of meaningful planning and previewing of actions in society, and thus is the basis for human action generally. (This is the reason that every revolutionary, inevitably, becomes a conservative as soon as he has achieved his goal.) Although the functioning of coordination norms is unproblematic within a community which defines itself by these norms, it becomes a problem as soon as the borders of the community are defined within which one has to get along by complying with these norms. This problem has been illustrated above with regard to people and tribes of whom it is required to integrate into a larger unit.

There is one more aspect to be stressed: coordination norms can serve social change. By introducing new norms of coordination, or by discouraging the use of existing ones, the behaviour of groups can be changed. They can serve the conservation of traditional structures, but they can also serve to change these.

Before moving on to the third type of norms, a short excursus about coordination and cooperation is in order. Ullmann-Margalit defines cooperation as a special kind of coordination, namely coordinating the actions of several people with respect to a common goal that cannot be reached alone, or that is difficult to reach alone. Thus cooperation norms are a special kind of coordination norm, namely that which serves a cooperative goal, for example traffic safety.

In as far as successful communication is a goal that can only be reached together, norms of language are norms of cooperation. But this does not mean that in communicating one has to cooperate in every respect. In complying with norms of communication, one is cooperative only with regard to achieving understanding; at the same time the aim of communication can be something other than cooperation, for example, fighting, competition, or scolding.

Understanding, as the general goal of communication, is a purely formal goal, which is not identical with a consensus about some matter that might be the topic of discussion. Habermas's (1976) elaboration of the general preconditions of the possibility of communication goes astray due to an equivocation of the word *Verständigung* (understanding) between understanding of intentions of speakers and retrieving information on the basis of the linguistic means that express these on the one hand, and consensus about opinions and normative judgements about special matters on the other. This equivocation of *Verständigung* (1976:177/8) leads to a confusion of technical and moral preconditions for a language to function as a means of communication. Understanding of utterances is something other than consensus about what one understands in the first place. Only from the first can one hope to derive universal preconditions for the functioning of language. The second notion of understanding as consensus is culturally bound: relevancy of a real consensus and communicative strategies that can lead to it, namely a dialogue which is not influenced by one-sided power ('herrschaftsfreier Dialog'), can exist or play a normative role only in communities of equals. The definition of equality is that those are equal with respect to certain matters who are accepted or allowed to engage in a dialogue that is consensus-oriented. Under this definition the idea of a universal dialogue is equivalent with the idea of a universal equality of all people. This is a normative idea, or moral principle, that certainly is not the precondition for communication or the functioning of language generally. Of course, communication and any language whatever is only possible if there is a conformity in judgements of correctness, especially in judgements about truth (*cf* Ch. 1, and also Quine 1964 and Wittgenstein 1960, nos 241/2); but this does not mean that this agreement has to be due to real consensus. Agreement on the basis of authority and power is sufficient as far as the fixation of notions of linguistic correctness goes: whether the coordination problem is solved by a norm based on convention, or by a norm based on decree, does not matter as long as it is complied with.

Ullmann-Margalit points out that coordination norms are technical norms:

> Norms of coordination, then, are norms concerning means to certain ends, whether the ends be the achievement of a distinct cooperative goal, or the mere achievement of the particular sort of harmony and accord concurrent with a state of coordination equilibrium. (1977:133)

Although these norms are technical norms with respect to the goal 'coordination', they often define certain forms of life, practices, and actions; this means that they are constitutive for these. Being a constitutive norm and being a technical norm are not contradictory. A rule can be constitutive with respect to goal A (which then is defined as the result of applying this rule), and can be technical, *ie* regulative, with respect to goal B (*cf* also Raz 1975:108). In cases like this, achieving A, for example performing a certain action, like giving a promise, serves for achieving B; in the example this is: being in a state in which others can count on certain preconditions for further action and being aware of one's obligation to fulfil these preconditions.

2.2.1(3) *Norms of partiality*
The third type of norms treated by Ullmann-Margalit are what she calls 'norms of partiality'. They serve to preserve a status quo in which the one party has advantages over the other. The disadvantaged party strives to improve its position, while the privileged party tries to prevent this in protecting its own interest. Just to use force in these situations is detrimental; it is more effective to protect the status quo by means of norms. An example of such norms are those regulating the security of private property.

While brute force clearly discriminates a certain group or person, norms are not discriminatory, at least not according to their form which is typically general: they apply anonymously to all groups and persons in a society. The privileged group is not exempted. But it will not mind this too much, because its members have little reason to disregard norms which support the status quo. A poor man is more likely to violate the norm 'Thou shalt not steal!' than a rich man. There are the well-known exceptions of people of privileged classes who steal in department stores, or people who withhold taxes or commit other white-collar crimes; the privileged class has to see to it that these members are punished in order to keep the whole system intact. As has been pointed out above, norms are considered to be values, and because of this, violating them will be judged as morally evil. This would not be the case if people were able to fight for the betterment of their position without breaking such norms, just by pitting force against the force which suppresses them. According to Ullmann-Margalit, one has to have norms which make it impossible to fight without violating norms, *ie* to fight without a moral stigma. Furthermore, people consider punishment of a norm breaker to be morally justified as a defence of the norms and common basic beliefs of the community; the justification of punishment would not seem so obvious if someone who fights for betterment of his position gets punished just because of this. So much for the comparison that

Ulmann-Margalit makes between the effect of norms, on the one hand, and simple force on the other (cf 1977:170–4). In this way, norms of partiality help preserve social inequality and injustice.

> But generally speaking, and that is the main point, my contention is that the character of some of the possible defence mechanisms of the institution of private property and of inheritance is that of norms of partiality. (1977:174)

Ullmann-Margalit adds to this that the Marxists' claim reaches much further than hers:

> Let me add that the Marxists' claim is in fact a much stronger one: it is that the very institution of the state, and all the social systems and institutions that support it, inevitably represent norms of partiality. In particular, it might be said that according to them a state's legal code is a cluster of partiality norms: they regard it as being oriented towards the protection of the positions and the property of the strong. (1977:174)

(This position is typical for Marxists who are anarchists, but not for Leninists.)

Norms of partiality play a role which is claimed to be that of norms generally in the conflict model of society. In this model, norms and social institutions are described as the general means of power and rule. (Ullmann-Margalit also refers to Dahrendorf's relationships of authority as universal principles according to which human societies are organized.) In the type of Marxism sketched above, they are at the same time a means of exploiting the underprivileged (cf 1977:183).

Norms are especially effective in protecting the status quo, because they are internalized by most of the members of a society, which is to say that these people make these norms their own in the sense that they will fight for them. Norms, including norms of partiality, serve people as a means of orientation in their social environment and in society as a whole; this is why even the members of the privileged groups do not recognize the true character of norms of partiality.

> Indeed, it might be the case that to a large extent there is a conviction, ideological or otherwise, on the part of the beneficiary party, that the prevailing norms, say, the regulation of office, private property, and the like, are beneficial to the *entire* society. Moreover, the effectiveness of these norms would quite likely have been hampered had they been consciously conceived as explicit restrictions imposed by the beneficiary on the deprived. (1977:181)

The anonymity of norms, *ie* that they apply to everybody and are obviously not installed by anybody in particular, helps hide the true function of norms of partiality, namely preserving power (*cf* 1977:189). The effect of these rules is to preclude a range of alternatives for actions and strategies which, at the cost of the privileged group, would be useful to the underprivileged group. By seeing to it that these alternative actions and strategies become violations of norms, the privileged party prevents the other party from using these strategies.

German linguists, for example Gloy (1975), Gloy and Presch (1976), Küchler and Jäger (1976), von Polenz (1982), have made claims about the effect and the role of linguistic norms that agree with the characterization of norms of partiality presented above. They have claimed that the norms of standard language and the institutions supporting these have the status which, according to the position called 'Marxist' by Ullmann-Margalit, is the status of all social institutions implemented and promoted by state government.

These linguists' arguments will be discussed in the following paragraphs. In this discussion I shall presuppose that the norms of standard language are norms of coordination, as are the norms of dialects and other sociolects. The question is then: How can such norms, or at least some of them, at the same time be norms of partiality?

At first sight one is inclined to doubt that they can, because norms of coordination, by definition, serve to achieve a state that is beneficial to all participants: the coordination itself implies a common advantage. Norms of partiality, on the other hand, serve the interests of only one party, and this in an open or latent conflict. How can a single norm serve both? The answer is that the conditions under which coordination is strived for, are different from the conditions under which the conflict arises. In principle the situation has to be such that something that is good for all from one point of view is, from another point of view, beneficial to only one group, and maleficial to another, and so far not in its interest.

The difficulty of determining the preference for coordination by means of standard language has been pointed out in the above discussion about the advantage of broad communication for different people. It is especially difficult to estimate to what extent this coordination is in the interest of non-standard speakers, compared with the labour they have to invest in learning the standard, and what the consequences are for them if they do not learn this language to a sufficient degree.

The norms of standard language discriminate in favour of

those who need not learn these norms as a second language. These are the members of the cultural and social élites, who have the privilege not only to invest less energy and labour in the acquisition of the standard and written language, but who are also positively discriminated with regard to conditions of work, income, and use they can make of the economic and bureaucratic system. I have already pointed out that the norms of standard language are less in the interest of the non-standard speakers than of the standard speakers, and that learning them is only reasonable for those who want to move upwards socially, or who want to leave their regional or social environment. With respect to these goals, we should distinguish the extent to which standard language is really necessary as a means of solving problems of coordination, and the extent to which the interest in mastering these norms is induced artificially by requiring people to master them for positions or occupations which could also be filled without a perfect command of standard language. Obviously, for many occupational functions fluency in standard language is not necessary.

Careful enquiry into every position for which command of standard language is required could result in proposing degrees of mastering this language. But even if one would be willing to do this, there remains the basic question of whether the standard language is necessary just to profit from teaching in special fields. To be sure, all school books, all tests, and teaching itself are in standard language. Does it make any sense to change all that? Would this be good for backward children only, or for all who do not speak standard as their mother tongue? And if a deviation from standard language use in special subjects would make sense, would this then be advisable for the first grades, or for all grades, and would it be advisable for all schools, or only for certain types of schools? Would it be at all financially possible to produce alternative teaching materials?

Only if it were to turn out that we could dispense with standard language to some extent in certain public types of situations of use could we infer that the enforcement of the norms of standard language with regard to these situations would not be justified by real problems of coordination, and that these norms, to the same extent, would be norms of partiality. It would be a second step to argue from this that they are norms of partiality which serve to protect the whole status quo.

Unfortunately, it can very well be that a norm that is perfectly justified as a norm of coordination is at the same time a norm of partiality: even if it could be proven conclusively, as

I am inclined to think it can, that a fairly broad implementation of standard language, especially in its written form, is necessary, this still means a situation in which non-standard speakers and standard speakers have unequal chances, and in which social mobility and even careers in trade unions and in left-wing parties depend, among other things, on the command of standard language. If in addition to this we realize that upward mobility is bound to having acquired knowledge, which can be acquired by reading, writing, and communicating in standard language, then we cannot but notice that language barriers are barriers of social mobility. In this way, the norms of standard language discriminate socially, so long as there are people who have difficulty in complying with them. But do these norms, because of this, serve for a privileged group to protect the status quo?

The answer to this question is this: the norms of standard language do not serve primarily to keep intact the status quo in favour of a privileged group, but they help to do so. They are norms of coordination whose existence and validity are justified because they solve coordination problems, the solution of which is more in some people's interest than in others'. At the same time, the norms of standard language accidentally have the effect of norms of partiality in favour of one group. From a relevant point of view their discriminating effect is not accidental, but necessary: for many positions and functions in society the command of the standard language is necessary to some degree. But it is accidental with respect to these norms that the positions and functions are connected with economic privileges for those who perform them.

If one wants to prevent norms of standard language from working as norms of partiality, it is not wise to propose dispensing with these norms altogether, since they are necessary for every large, transregional, technically organized, and scientifically and culturally oriented society. One can, of course, enquire whether some of these norms can be simplified or liberalized or even dispensed with in order to make learning the standard language easier. But the suggestions made so far only hit very marginal norms, like the unimportant orthographical, stylistic, or grammatical ones discussed in von Polenz (1982) and Jäger (1971), for example whether the popular variant *der einzigste* (lit. the onliest one) should be allowed next to the standard *der einzige* (the only one). One also can enquire, as pointed out above, whether for some occupations one could dispense with a perfect active command of the standard, and only require a good passive command.

The requirement of command of standard language for certain occupations cannot and should not be dispensed with, but in some cases it can and should be loosened. If one does not want norms of standard language to have a socially discriminatory effect, then one has to cut the connection between occupations and economic privileges. From the point of view of the discussion about the 'partiality' of norms of language this last connection is the cardinal point to work on, if one wants to eliminate the discriminating role of linguistic norms. It might be that the elimination of this connection is very counter-productive and thus is precluded, not just by certain political systems, but also by the very nature of human beings, as conservatives never fail to point out. In that case, the only possible strategy is to enforce the norms of standard language more strongly in schools, so that all children that are able to do so learn the standard language. This way, the distinction between privileged and underprivileged, as far as it is reinforced by the norms of standard language, runs along the line between people who are gifted to learn standard language and other technics of modern society and who have the mental strength and will-power to take pains to do so, and those who have not been fortunate to have been provided with these gifts by nature. Our modern societies, be it in the West or in the East, already show clear signs of this basic division.

Linguists like the ones mentioned have not only criticized certain norms of standard language, but have also criticized strict enforcement of the whole set of norms of standard language by schools. This seems to be very commendable, but in the meantime, after more than ten years of being more liberal with respect to the enforcement of these norms, there are strong tendencies to reverse this movement. The conservative argument mentioned above has recently won ground, and this, in fact, is to the advantage of those with abilities relevant for modern societies, but it leaves behind a fairly large minority which cannot keep pace.

2.2.2 Luhmann (1972)
Luhmann (1972), in his sociology of law, has developed a theory about the emergence and functions of norms in the chapter about the creation of law. This chapter has been discussed with reference to norms of language by Gloy (1975). Since several aspects of this topic have already been treated in 2.1 and 2.2.1, I shall only stress those points about the functions of norms which contribute to their institutionalization. The main subject here is what Luhmann has to say about the disappointment of expectations which results from the violation of norms.

People live in a complexity and multitude of impressions caused by their environment. Among these they make a selection:

1. A selection of regularities from biologically and socially relevant points of view, *ie* they select mainly those properties and relationships that are important for survival. These regularities are the same for people who live in a comparable environment. The selection is not uniquely determined by the organism but is complemented by a selection on the basis of norms. In this way our perception and experience are socially coordinated. The perceptions and experiences of people who live in a single community and who exert on each other a pressure towards adaptation do not differ much from each other;

2. A selection of regularities which are culturally and socially relevant for building up and supporting social bounds within the community.

According to Luhmann, norms regulate both these selections (1972:31). To this it should be added that selections can only be made from existing sets of alternatives. It is therefore more appropriate to speak of a constitution of culturally and socially relevant regularities, than of a selection. There is no selection to be made from a set of existing forms of life because they do not exist before they are constituted. If one wants to refer to a set of real and possible forms of life (to select from), one first needs a notion of possible forms of life, and a criterion for distinguishing possible ones from impossible ones. This is, of course, different with respect to regularities within the natural environment, which exist by themselves, independently of the epistemic activity of people; out of these regularities a selection can be made.

In a certain situation people have certain preferences and a variety of options for action with regard to these. They can make a choice out of these, if they have

(a) expectations about experiences of others;

(b) analysis and valuation of possible actions with regard to their consequences; and

(c) expectations about expectations of others with respect to their own choice of action.

For controlling a social interaction, or at least for steering it somewhat, it is not only necessary that each experiences what the other expects of him, but also that each can expect what the other expects of him (*cf* 1972:33). These expectations of expectations are needed because the reactions and actions of the other depend on what he has expected of the partner in interaction, and whether his expectations have been satisfied or disappointed.

Norms regulate the choice of actions; *ie* they restrict the freedom of action and, hereby, make them predictable. They give some security about what to expect. This security in expectation is security of one's own behaviour and the calculability of others' behaviour (Gloy 1975:43).

This assurance with respect to expectations of expectations is, according to Luhmann (1972:39), a necessary foundation for all interaction, and it is much more important than the assurance of satisfaction of expectations.

Norms reduce the complexity and contingency in the natural and social environment. This is their major function (1972:39).

Norms make possible an orientation in the natural and social surroundings that agrees with the orientation of other people. They legitimate certain expectations about others, as well as expectations about which actions, attitudes, and orientations others expect of oneself. This legitimation is based on the validity of the respective norms, which remain in power even when they are not complied with. Luhmann captures this aspect by the phrase 'norms are counterfactually stabilized patterns of behaviour'. He continues: 'Their meaning implies absolute validity in as far as their validity is experienced and institutionalized independently of their factual satisfaction or non-satisfaction' (1972:43).

By way of an excursus, I shall point out, as Gloy (1975:43) has also done, that it is not just the situation that determines which norms have to be applied, but also the other way around: the norms that, in fact, have been applied also determine how the situation has to be understood. This is the case, because generally behaviour is presupposed to conform to the norms in question and to their conditions of application. This way, norm application can define situations, or redefine situations in cases where the behaviour seems to be inadequate to the situation in the first place, but, since correctness is presupposed, the interpretation of the situation is adjusted to the norm if this is at all possible (*cf* also 7.2). In this way, social relationships can also be defined among partners in interaction by behaving according to certain norms which presuppose the social relationship in question.

Norms relieve people from repeated attempts at orientation: they need not again and again try to find out what the expectations of the others are, or how they interpret the situation, *ie* which they consider to be the relevant features of the situation. Nor need they negotiate with the others over and over again about which course of action should be taken. People would be overburdened by negotiating without being able to take effective action in time. The relief consists in the fact that one has the right to have certain expectations with respect to the other. Even if these are not fulfilled one does not need to be totally disoriented but can be sure that one was right and that the other is to be blamed. In this way, one can protect one's normative orientation from facts which seem to call it into question. Orientation according to a rule makes superfluous any specific orientation on expectations. It diminishes the chance of making mistakes, since because of the rule we can find fault with those who deviated from it. By relying on norms, people become more independent from complexity and contingency (cf Luhmann 1972:39; Gloy 1975:43/4).

Gloy, additionally, draws attention to the fact that the reverse of this unburdening is that, by sticking to norms, one loses sensibility for the other and his specific motives and expectations. People lose flexibility in their reactions and actions with respect to particular features of situations. Gloy remarks that the binding of the other to the rule demolishes, if we look at it this way, his importance for constituting one's own self. In place of creating concrete social ties, this way we easily come to live in anonymous relationships defined by social pressure (Gloy 1975:44). We can add to this that the same holds for the relationship between people and nature: standard patterns of orientation tend to block new or original ways of dealing with nature.

The advantage of the restriction of the possibilities of selecting experiences and actions is combined with the danger of an overly strict selection and fixation, and a lack of sensibility for the unexpected, which sometimes can be important. Since von Humboldt, Cassirer, Sapir, Whorf, and Quine we know that the norms of language are dependent on basic beliefs of a society and socially induced restrictions in perception and experience, and that, on the other hand, language guides our ways of perceiving and thinking such that it is difficult to avoid these roads, and that new roads, if they are to be permanent enough to be recognizable, can only be taken by changing to alternative forms of language. And then these forms will become fixed and restrictive, too. The same can be said with respect to what Wittgenstein calls 'forms of life' or 'language games'. They define situations and reactions to these situations; they are complexes of rules. They define boundaries of our world, of which we can free ourselves only by, together, creating new boundaries. With respect to norms of language, this means language change (cf 5.2), especially semantic change.

Luhmann (1972) explains *institutionalization* of norms in the following way: institutionalization comes about as a reaction, or as an anticipated reaction, to real or possible disappointment caused by norm violation. When a norm is broken, the one whose expectation based on that norm is disappointed has two alternatives:

1. He can ignore the norm violation and uphold the norm, or he can reprimand the other for wrong behaviour and in this way censure the norm violation, or at least draw attention to it. In doing this he contributes to keeping the norm intact. Punishing a norm breaker is a way to compensate that disappointment and to make it worth while complying with the norm in the future.
2. He can correct his expectation, in this way adjust to the behaviour of the other, and thereby give up the norm.

The first attitude Luhmann calls 'normative', and the second 'cognitive'. According to the first attitude, people keep up their norms and their orientation; according to the second, they learn something new and abandon what they were accustomed to. The first attitude is necessary for enforcing norm systems. And since these are in principle necessary for the orientation of people, this attitude is justified. Gloy (1975:45, note 7) points out that Luhmann, in calling this attitude justified, does not only describe a factual tendency for norms to be preserved, but at the same time claims that it is necessary because of the biological constitution of humans and in order to keep social systems balanced; this would justify preserving any social order. I think this need not be the case: Luhmann's stress on the necessity of norms and norm systems does not mean that just this or that system has to be valid. As far as orientation is concerned, it can be achieved by different norm systems. There has to be one, but not necessarily any particular one. The same is true of language: communication is not just possible by one language, but by many alternative ones. The point is not to keep up a certain norm system, but one out of alternatives that guarantee some coordination and order in the area in question. Because of this, Luhmann's alternative of reactions on norm violations is not complete. We have to add two possibilities of reaction which are adequate in the following situations:

3. The norm system is in itself heterogeneous, *ie* it consists of several norm systems, which are not compatible in all cases. Depending on which point of view one takes to be relevant, one will follow norm *A* or norm *B*. One of the interaction

partners interprets the situation in such a way that only norm
A is appropriate, the second such that only norm B is appropriate, or that A and B are both appropriate, but he opts for
B. In such a case, the first partner, who is disappointed, can
accept the second one's interpretation of the situation, and
thus accept behaviour according to norm B. Norm A remains
intact, or, after this experience, norm A might be restricted
in its range of application to certain types of situations. Likewise it is possible to negotiate about restricting the range of
application of norm B.

4. Norm A is valid for the first partner. The second lives in
   another culturally different subcommunity in which norm B
   is valid. The second may know that the first has expectations
   according to A, but he wants to express his solidarity with his
   subcommunity and therefore opts for B. Here, the first
   partner does not need to abolish norm A, since he may realize
   that A is valid uncontroversially only for a certain group of
   people. In dealing with a certain other group he has to expect
   B, or he has to negotiate with members of the other group
   about which norm should be followed in certain inter-group
   situations.

In the first case, ie case (3), there is a conflict between the
situation domains of validity of two norms; in the second case,
ie case (4), there is a conflict between the population domains
of two norms (cf 7.1).

The alternative discussed by Luhmann, ie the cases (1) and
(2) above, presupposes an integral or homogeneous norm system,
which is determined uniquely and in the same way with respect
to all its situations of application and for all the members of a
population; it does not contain any conflicting norms.

Luhmann's homogeneous norm system is a fiction, especially
with respect to the heterogeneity of the systems of linguistic
norms and linguistic means in a speech community, such as standard language, dialects, sociolects, and also stylistic variants and
different stylistic registers for different areas of knowledge and
interaction. The alternative with regard to violations of norms of
language is not, on the one hand, blaming the violator or any
other form of norm-enforcing reaction, and, on the other, adjustment through abolishing the norm. Rather, in between there is
a spectrum of reactions of tolerance with respect to the variety
of norm systems that are effective. The limits of this variety are
certainly to be found where the goals of communication, to which
these norm systems serve, cannot be reached any more. The

outermost borders are those that are determined by the possibility of understanding each other in the whole speech community. Since in a larger speech community not all the dialects are mutually understandable, there has to be a lingua franca. The standard language serves as such a common language; and this common language is, necessarily, institutionalized. Since certain types of mistakes with respect to the standard are probable in certain regions, institutions of language codification and language teaching pay special attention to these real and possible 'disappointments' that a well-educated standard speaker will have when communicating with common people from the different regions. But with respect to linguistic norms, disappointments are not so severe because one does not expect everybody to speak perfectly according to the standard in any case. Disappointment only plays a role with respect to people of one's own group when they deviate more from the standard than the other members of the group do. With respect to the speech community as a whole, expectations never have been high.

Institutionalization of norms presupposes a consensus about the general validity of the norms in question. But with respect to language, the consensus about the general acceptance of, and compliance with, its norms is not as broad as it is often thought to be, as Gloy (1975:56) points out. Overrating the consensus about compliance with the norms is part of the mechanism by which institutions are kept in force. According to Gloy, the agents of these institutions do not enquire whether all members of the community indeed accept the norms, or at least follow them, but they 'nourish the overestimation of the factual consensus' (1975:56).

Against Gloy, I would argue that the institutions have the quite proper task of creating such a consensus. Saying that this consensus exists is part of this task.

Luhmann also calls an institutionalized norm system simply 'an institution'. Its continuation is guaranteed as long as nearly all assume that nearly all agree, or even if nearly all assume that nearly all assume that nearly all agree. Therefore institutions do not rest on factual agreement, but on successful overestimation of agreement (cf Luhmann 1972:71).

With respect to language as an institution, this overestimation is not only carried by the linguistic agencies, but by all members of the speech community that are the carriers of this institution and see themselves as such, whether they really follow the norms or only think they do.

According to Gloy (1975) this assumption of agreement is, with respect to language, a deceiving confidence, which negates the problems in communication that actually arise, and causes misapprehension of situations of mutual misunderstanding as being caused by indignation, malice, neglect, or incapability, instead of realizing that they are caused by discrepancies between the norm systems of different speakers.

The assumption of general agreement about norms leads to fast and selective communication, which is necessary because of man's limited attention span (Luhmann 1972:68). But according to Gloy, Luhmann's claim that it also leads to more precise communication is wrong, because the assumption hides unsuccessful communication. I think that this criticism is true, but it does not refute that the above assumption of agreement about norms indirectly leads to more precise communication, as every normalization does, because it helps to interpret behaviour in an unambiguous way according to certain norms. We can state that making precise by normalization is successful only if the norms are actually accepted and complied with; and because of this, propagandizing the norms in question is a goal of the institutions or agencies that are concerned with these norms.

Successful communication is only possible when people agree in means of communication and their use. Presupposing that all members of a linguistic community always agree in this way is a simplification which leads us to 'mis-take' reality. This much I agree with Gloy. But even though Luhmann's point of view is right, communication can function relatively smoothly only if we presuppose agreement in communicational means. Without this we could not interpret utterances and behaviour of others, and we could not expect that they can understand our utterances. Gloy, on the other hand, directs attention to the fact that to presuppose agreement in norms implies to presuppose that smooth and precise communication is guaranteed. He speaks about a naive confidence in 'communicative achievements' (1975:60) of language, and especially of educated or standard language; this leads to an attitude that views the institution of language itself as something sacred that cannot be touched.

Arguing against this negative attitude towards norms of language I want to point out that it is essential for norms to achieve the primary goals they are made for; just by keeping up their partly fictional reality we achieve their validity and existence. These fictional presuppositions, namely that we agree in our norms of communication and language, are the precondition for reaching such an agreement, which is our aim if we want communication to be possible. This does not mean that we should disregard the many cases in which this agreement is not achieved; rather we have to work on it and to negotiate about it, always being aware of communicational failure. For people who want to be integrated in a broad speech community a fully functioning standard language is a necessary regulative ideal, but not a simple reality.

Chapter 3

Validity and justification of linguistic norms

3.1 Conditions for issuing and validating linguistic norms

Gloy (1975), following Kutschera (1973), distinguishes between issuing a norm (*eine Norm setzen*) and validating a norm (*eine Norm in Geltung setzen*): A norm is issued once somebody states a normative sentence expressing the norm in question, even if he is not authorized to do so (Gloy 1975: 17). A norm is posited validly if the one who posits it is authorized to do so. This condition, I claim, is not sufficient for the norm's being valid.

We can treat the act of issuing a norm as a speech act in the sense of Searle (1969) and look into the conditions for its correctness and for its validity. An institutional fact is created by a speech act of this kind; this institutional fact is, in our case, a norm or a norm system (as an institution). I distinguish between the correctness and the validity of speech acts. Even a non-correctly performed speech act can be valid, if it is not evident that the conditions of correctness are violated, *ie* if the hearer believes (and is justified by the available evidence in his belief) that the conditions of correctness are fulfilled. This can be the case when non-satisfaction is hidden in such a way that the hearer cannot realize it.

The utterance of a norm sentence is a correct act of issuing a norm if and only if the following conditions are fulfilled:

(a) the utterance of the norm sentence is understandable by the addressees;

(b) the utterer is accepted as a norm (sub-)authority in the area in question, *ie* he is authorized;

(c) the addressees are possible norm subjects with respect to the area in question and with respect to the norm authority;

(d) the norm content is realizable, *ie* the norm can be complied with;

(e) the norm content is not already implied by existing and valid norms;

[(f) the norm content does not contradict other norms that are valid for the norm subjects;)]

(g) the norm authority wants the norm to be followed (sincerity condition);

(h) the norm authority intends its utterance of the norm sentence to count as a requirement that the norm subjects act according to the norm content and accept this requirement (essential condition).

If the act of issuing a norm sentence seems to be correct, it is valid. That is, issuing a norm is valid if no violation of the above conditions is evident. An invalid positing of a norm I would not call issuing a norm, but rather count as a mere utterance of a norm sentence. Such an utterance is by itself not issuing a norm. If all conditions except (b) are fulfilled, we can speak of an attempt to issue a norm. If all conditions except (e), or (b) and (e), are fulfilled, we speak of a norm explication or codification. Norm explication can be an attempt by the utterer of the norm sentence to establish himself as a norm authority with respect to the norms in question and the norm subjects; it can also teach somebody a norm or correct his behaviour, or just strengthen the norm and call its content into consideration.

To incorporate condition (f) among the correctness conditions is problematic because we have to reckon with possible norm conflicts, without being able always to avoid them. A conflict can arise between existing norms, or between an existing norm and a posited norm: if the existing norm and the posited norm have the same norm authority, this norm authority is contradicting itself. In such a case the norm authority does not behave correctly; it should withdraw either the existing norm or the norm just posited. Thus condition (f) certainly holds if the norm authority of the conflicting norm contents is identical. If there are two different norm authorities involved, the norm conflict is ultimately one between the two authorities, which very likely will be acted out over the norm subjects. A conflict like this exists, for example, between the Christian norm 'Thou shalt not kill' and the norm requiring soldiers to kill enemies in war. This conflict is solved in the way that the Christian norm authority (*ie* the church) subordinates itself under the state authority by blessing the battle. Since the church authority is not autonomous but sees itself as an executor of God's will and is, in this way, a sub-authority under the authority of God, the norm subjects can refer directly to God's word and refuse armed service. In doing this, they do not recognize church authority as an autonomous norm authority, but rather as a sub-authority which is mistaken as far as this question goes.

If one norm authority is dependent on the other, solving the conflict consists in declaring the act of issuing the norm performed by the dependent authority invalid, because this sub-authority has to adjust to the higher authority. In such a case the sub-authority has surpassed its competence, *ie* (b) is not satisfied; with this, the act has not been correct and is therefore invalid. As long as this incorrectness is not recognized the act is valid. If the incorrectness is recognized we speak of an infelicitous attempt to posit a norm.

If norm authorities are independent of each other, the act of issuing a norm is correct even in case of a violation of condition (f). But the norm subjects, who, so to speak, have to serve two masters, find themselves in a conflict in which they have to reckon with negative sanctions by one or other norm authority. The norm subjects cannot accept both norms; they are the victims of the conflict. Such conflicts regularly arise in multicultural and multilingual societies (*cf* Ch. 7).

Taking into account that, according to Hart (1961) and Raz (1975), norm acceptance is a necessary condition for the existence of a norm for a population, the norm conflict that arises with violation of condition (f) can vanish to some degree: if the content of the issued norm contradicts a norm that already exists for them, this will be a reason for the norm subjects not to accept the content of the norm sentence issued as a norm. They will see it as a mere prescription. The conflict is then not between two norms, but between a norm and a a prescription. Only if the population accepts the prescription as something which guides its behaviour, even where there is no threat of sanctions, will it become a norm. Then a real norm conflict arises which, for the norm subjects, means a severe insecurity in their orientation in action. In case of a conflict between a prescription and a norm, or between two prescriptions, people will keep the damage minimal by avoiding complying with the prescription as much as possible. If that is not possible because of sanctions and if the norm is of high value to those people, serious suffering cannot be avoided.

This discussion shows that even issuing a norm validly does not automatically result in a norm that exists for the population; this requires their acceptance and adoption of the norm content as a norm as well. Without acceptance and adoption the result of a valid act of norm issuing is not more than a valid prescription. For an act of norm issuing to be successful such that the posited norm comes to exist for the norm subjects, conditions of acceptance must be fulfilled and the norm content must be adopted as a practice. A posited norm is thus not simply an existing norm, and on the other hand, there are existing norms which have not been posited. These are norms that are not valid because there was no valid act of issuing them. But in such a case, according to Raz (1975), norm subjects at least believe that their norms are valid, though not because of an identifiable act of norm issuing. A norm is valid for norm subjects if they justify behaviour conforming to this norm by just referring to it. The primary notions are the relationships 'exist for' and 'being valid for', *ie* norms exist and are valid for certain people. Secondarily we can also speak of existing or valid norms if there are norm subjects for whom they exist or are valid. With respect to norms of language this means the following.

Norms of language exist for a community, are justified for them, and are valid for them by the very fact that nearly everyone complies with them (or at least believes that nearly everyone complies with them) and also believes that nearly everyone complies with them. They are valid linguistic norms for the speech community if speech behaviour that conforms to them is regarded as legitimate because of them, and if linguistic behaviour that is deviant with respect to these norms may be criticized by referring to them. It is in such criticism that these norms are explicated. Only when the norms are explicated can we speak of 'norms explicitly recognized as valid'. Such norm explications are performed by linguists in norm codification, and by teachers and educators in teaching language to children and others. Note that explication of linguistic norms becomes necessary and comes about with literacy, when linguistic products acquire a permanence as physical objects which can be considered and analysed with scrutiny, or in second-language acquisition where learning the correctness notions of a new language is experienced as a problem and can be stated in a language already available to teacher and learner.

An act that for one group is an act of explication can be an act of norm issuing for other groups of a population. Only if the latter accept the strange norm will this become a norm for them, and at the same time, be a norm that is valid for them. If they do not accept the norm it remains for them a prescription, though a valid one if the above conditions are fulfilled. As far as norms of standard language are concerned, often a conflict arises with other norms that exist for these subgroups; for example, the norms of received pronunciation are in conflict with the norms of pronunciation in several dialects. This is a conflict between transregionally valid prescriptions and norms that are valid within a subgroup. A real norm conflict arises only if these groups identify with the prescriptions by accepting them as norms which are valid for them.

A consequence of these considerations is that, for standard language, we often do not have norms being explicated or posited but rather just prescriptions being given. A dialect-speaking pupil's reaction to standard language will be one of conflict between norm and prescription. This situation is comparably transparent for him. Only if he accepts the prescription as his own norm does he get into a real norm conflict. If he cannot comply with one of the conflicting norms satisfactorily, he is in a situation in which he blames himself for not living up to his own norm. If there is a strong subgroup solidarity on which the identity of the individual is partly based, then this difficult norm–norm conflict can be avoided in favour of the easier norm–prescription conflict. An example are the Black male youths in New York City described in Labov (1972b), who adhere to their Black English against school, which requires Standard English. Dialect speakers in Europe find themselves more in a norm–conflict, because the group solidarity which supports dialects is generally not a strong force against the wish to integrate into the national community, which is tied to standard language as the means of communication and as a national symbol. The Black youths mentioned above do not want to integrate; therefore for them Black English is norm, and Standard English is just prescribed.

A partial solution of the norm conflict in which pupils speaking dialect find themselves is to abandon the old norms that are in conflict with the new norms. But this is unsatisfactory as long as one is not able to adjust perfectly to the new norm. Then one has to live with the idea that one behaves deviantly, ie incorrectly with respect to the measure one has accepted for oneself.

In this situation it is helpful to specify the different norms with respect to situations of application in such a way that the situational domains of validity of both norms overlap as little as possible: dialect norms are applied and cultivated in certain (mainly informal) situations, and standard language norms in formal situations. With this division explicitly stated, these norms are not categorical any more, they are hypothetical norms. In linguistics one calls these conditionally applicable norms 'styles' or 'registers': for different situations and purposes one uses different registers. If a pupil understands this division, then the whole situation is not one in which he speaks incorrectly any more; it becomes a situation in which he has not mastered a certain register, though he may well have mastered another.

In case of a prescription–norm conflict, as in the case of a norm–norm conflict, the members of the groups that conform to the standard norms, especially teachers, suppose that the nonconforming groups are also a part of the (German) linguistic community, and therefore are a part of the population domain for which the standard norms are valid. Hereby, they presuppose that the (German) linguistic community is defined as the validity domain of the norms of standard language, and not as a union of the existence domains of the norms of different, though related, varieties. This second definition would indeed be insufficient, since it is not only vague, but would possibly also count Dutch and other foreign language areas as part of the domain of German language. The first definition is in fact more adequate, but one should realize that this definition does not state a natural fact, but a normative delimitation resting on historical, cultural, and political facts.

Members of the (German) linguistic community are at least all people of whom *it is expected* that they understand and speak German as their first language. The (German) language is understood to be the standard language, including its regional variants which are also considered to be standard. But not all those of whom this is expected really understand and speak the language. What one expects is therefore less, namely that at least they *accept* the language as their standard, that is, want to adjust as far as their capacities permit. Teachers and language cultivators thus presuppose more than actually is the case, namely that everybody accepts the standard language norms as his own norms, and not just as prescriptions and compulsions, or as norms that are only valid in special situations. On the basis of this position those who fail with respect to standard norms will not merely be taught that they *deviate* from strange standards, but also that they *fail* in the light of their own and everybody's standards. Strange norms are presented to them as if they were their own. This happens implicitly; it is explicated in the following chain of argumentation, which can be generalized to other nationalities.

'You are part of the German linguistic community.' Every German will agree to this, because it is good to belong to a large group and, as a German, one is even born into this group. 'Therefore, these linguistic norms are for you, too; *ie* you naturally accept them as guidelines to your linguistic activity and action. But you have not complied with these norms. Thus you have failed.' And maybe even: 'Regret your failure and promise improvement; only then can you really belong to our German community.'

The mistake in this chain of arguments lies right in the beginning, namely with the notion of what it means to belong to a linguistic community. The members of the German linguistic community are not born into it, unless they are born into the fairly standard-conforming subgroup. They do not simply and in a natural manner belong to the German speech community, as narrowly defined by the standard norms. Only the standard-conforming subgroups experience them as existing and being valid for them, since their linguistic practice is governed by them. For the non-standard groups these norms do not exist in this way, other norms do. And with this, standard norms are not their norms in that they are not experienced as valid and existent for them. They are seen primarily as prescriptions, if anything.

On the other hand those subgroups are treated as if the standard norms were also their norms, and they become persuaded that these are their norms, and that they fail with respect to them, be it because of missing capacity, be it because of lacking eagerness to learn. This is a moralizing criticism, namely that they do not live up to their own and others' norms. It is not taken into account that these norms are not norms for those people but rather prescriptions, and that the domain of validity of norms that are strange to them is extended to include them.

One should be aware that the way in which offences against prescriptions and regulations are negatively sanctioned cannot in general be a moral one; it depends rather on the kind of regulations, the difficulty of complying with them under individual circumstances, and the will to do so. As far as regulations about the use of the linguistic standard are concerned, non-compliance requires a fairly differentiated reaction: convincing the non-conformers of the importance of mastering the standard in certain situations, tolerance and practice.

If one extends the definition of the '(German) linguistic community' such that the primary norm subjects are those that are born into it, including the prescription subjects of the standard that are norm subjects of related dialects who have to learn the standard language as a second language, then the second step of the above argument does not hold any more, namely the claim that the standard norms exist for and are felt to be valid by every member of the (German) speech community.

It becomes clear that the sociolect–dialect of the culturally, economically and politically active élite is imposed on the other members of the socio-political unit. This happens because the élite and middle class organize and administrate all official and public situations, and everybody who wants to take part in this has to adjust to the linguistic usage of this group.

In the light of these considerations and according to our convictions about justice, the necessity for broadest linguistic tolerance becomes evident. This does not mean that mistakes are not to be corrected in school, but it does mean that the sanctions connected with them should be as mild as possible. The standard language requirement for several occupations should be loosened, while the use of dialects together with standard language in official situations, eg in schools or in courts, should be encouraged at least orally. Understanding of regional dialects by administrators and civil servants should be promoted; and dialects should be accepted as regionally valid means of communication next to standard language.

By such measures the one-sided prestige of standard language would become a merely relative one, the prestige of dialects would be enhanced. Communicational means used in dialects can be incorporated into the standard language, or at least into its variants, more easily.

It is not the case that dialects are in principle unsuited to express and manage the occupational and cultural specializations of institutions. But it would be very ineffective and senseless to reconstruct everything that is expressible in standard language and its specializations in dialect. This would require a lot of linguistic inventivity and codification, and unnecessary labour and energy, and it would not help anybody much. Mainly transregional activities are performed in standard language, and they have to be performed in a transregional understandable communicational means, if one does not want to rely on such translation procedures as are common internationally, with all the troublesome apparatus and costs.

Likewise it would be senseless to extend the use of standard language on to regional activities and local contacts which are performed by means of dialects. These would be changed by the use of standard language towards more formality and transregional openness, which would run counter to their character of local secludedness and familiarity. It is just the possibility of change of registers or styles – and the use of standard language or dialect is a stylistic means if the choice exists between these two – which differentiates between kinds of situations of communication and purposes, and which is, in this way, also constitutive for the existence of certain forms of life.

3.2 About justification and change of linguistic norms

The basic justification of linguistic norms in general is that without them communication and understanding would not be possible at all. This includes socially coordinated perception and experience. According to their origin and function they are conventions that solve coordination problems (*cf* Lewis 1969): in order to inform somebody about something, one has to agree in communicational means used for that. From the set of potential communicational means, which is in principle unlimited, a selection has to be made which is common for all members of a community. The most important feature of linguistic conventions, and all other conventions, is the expectation of expectation pointed out by Lewis (1969) and Luhmann (1972): one expects that all members of the validity domain of the convention exhibit the regularity that is the content of the convention, and that they in turn expect the same of others. Above Lewis's notion of convention, the conceptualization of this expectation–expectation as a norm takes into account that it is not a mere probability that holds for nearly all members of its domain, but that this reciprocal expectation of expectations is a normative expectation which every member rightfully has with respect to every other member. This aspect has been stressed by Luhmann, Hart, Raz, and Ullmann-Margalit.

In fact, there are deviations from the norm, and this is not surprising if one takes into account that the norm can come into conflict with competing norms of other sociolects, dialects, and other registers of style, and if one takes into account that these norms are learned in processes of socialization and teaching which can run rather differently for different members of a society. These differences are caused not only by different private, social, regional, and cultural surroundings in which somebody is formed as a social being, but also by the fact that these norms are not in general explicitly formulated, but have to be learned from examples and models, which leave different generalizations and interpretations open. For the different members of a speech community, the abstractions of norm contents from a collection of examples will agree to the extent that there is a common realm of experiences. In spite of possible differences, and because of these, the members of a speech community have to strive to adjust their communicational means to each other, for the sake of a reasonably functioning communication and interaction. A deliberate private deviance from these norms contradicts the goal to make communication possible, and therefore is meaningless. Since the goal, smoothly functioning communication, is in the interest of all members, a deliberate divergence is considered to be counter-rational. The supposition of agreement, though not an empirically given fact of a 100 per cent agreement, is normatively justified on the basis of the principle of rationality, applied to 'functioning communication' as a presupposed goal of the community.

This basic justification of linguistic norms does not mean that any particular linguistic norms are to be preferred: the question of which norms does not play a role, as long as they fulfil their purpose. But they can fulfil their purpose only if they are common to all. Naturally, it is the case that those linguistic norms that exist at a given moment in a speech community deserve the preference compared with possible alternatives, if the purposes have remained the same. It would be a meaningless effort and waste of mental energy and time to introduce new norms which are not better than the old ones. But despite this trivial fact, linguistic norms change in history. Those changes are an adjustment to new economic, social, and institutional facts. They serve living in these new circumstances, and thus serve new purposes, and are justified because of this. This is the case, for example, for the immense linguistic changes that came with the introduction of writing as a useful tool in the change from domestic economies to trading economies and large-scale administration and transmission of information across space and time (*cf* Slaughter 1985).

But there are also many linguistic changes which cannot be explained and justified by the new purposes which the linguistic means have to serve. It is well known that some of such linguistic changes are simplifications under certain aspects of linguistic systems. Often, at the same time, they lead to complications in other parts of the system: because of physiological reasons there are changes in the sound system of languages (simplifications such as assimilations and neutralizations) that cause changes in the morphology such as the loss of case discriminations and other discriminations in unstressed final syllables. These are unjustified changes, due to natural causes. To prevent too many ambiguities and homonyms, new distinctions and new rules are added to the grammar; for example, word order rules concerning the position of the noun phrases with respect to the verb, as in English, which has a fairly fixed word order in comparison with languages which still have a richer morphology of inflection and conjugation, like German or Russian. Here, one language change is justified by another language change as a way of compensating its bad side-effects.

Certain changes in pronunciation are often orginated by individual persons who hold esteem in a group and to whom other members adjust in order to show their solidarity with the prestigious person. In this way, certain phonetic changes can arise in a short time and be a social marker of a group. They can even lead to phonological changes, if loss of phonological oppositions or shifts in the phoneme inventory occur due to the primary phonetic changes and compensations they might require. If such a group has some prestige, these forms can also be adopted by other members of the speech community as a way of showing solidarity with that group (cf Labov 1972a). Slang expressions and other fashionable words also enter into common language, and sometimes even intrude into standard language, depending on the usefulness of these words, be it as markers of being up to date – and as such they can only last some short time – or as expressions that also serve a primary function of language. Norms regulating the form and the use of these expressions have as their origin the need for prestige, identification with leaders or leading groups, psychic relief, or, simply, creatively playing around with language. Changes due to these causes are justified by fulfilling these needs, as long as no ethically doubtful goals are connected with satisfying them. The extent to which these kinds of linguistic changes remain short-term stylistic alternatives in common language, or acquire a more permanent status even in standard language, depends on factors that are not understood well enough today, and might, to a large extent, be just accidental. It does not make much sense to claim that it is good or bad for a language if such developments persist and become part of it. But when they have become part of the language, ie are understood by the linguistic community as being a practice justified by the community's norms, then they are as good as the other existing norms are in as far as they serve as a means of communication. If they are unfortunate in terms of linguistic systematization, changes in the realm of systematizations can be developed that compensate the disadvantage of the new forms. Such changes in the set of systematizations can lead to further changes of linguistic norms.

It is counter-rational to stick to old norms under all conditions.

Of course, it is not necessary that everyone adjusts his old way of speaking to new norms, and especially for elderly people there are limits for doing so. But a speaker who himself has been socialized in the old norms, cannot expect all others not to adjust to new developments in language. In such cases, the right attitude is one of tolerance. As long as necessary, different forms and speech styles should be accepted as variants. The older forms will generally lose ground, and adjustment towards the norms that will be taken up by the new generation is reasonable. In such situations, a lot of conflicts arise: in newspapers, citizens caring about their language write columns about the dissolution of 'our language', and about 'spoiled' language causing 'spoiled' thinking; politicians give directions of how to use which expressions. The president of the Dutch parliament, for example, decreed recently that the word *afbouwen* should not be used any more to express cutting down with respect to expenditures on social security, because this word in this meaning is a germanism, while the word in Dutch traditionally has been used for finishing off something, especially construction works. Under the presidency of this Dutch politician, social security will not be *afgebouwd* but *gekort*, 'cut short', or *afgebroken*, 'demolished'. These conflicts are not of great practical importance because communication is not hindered much by existing alternatives; at least people are able to learn alternatives well enough to use them passively, and they can rely on context to disambiguate if a word becomes a homonym because it acquires a second meaning. Thus they can understand each other all right through at least three generations, but with larger time periods most alternatives have to be cancelled out because otherwise, in the course of time, memory would be overburdened by learning a language with too many alternatives.

More problematic is the question whether linguistic change should be hindered or at least slowed down in order to keep alive the traditional cultural heritage from past generations, transmitted in written documents. A certain conservativity, at least in spelling, is to be recommended for this reason. But there will come a time when translations are necessary anyway, like those from Old English, or Middle English, into modern English.

That existence of norms as a practice justifies these norms is true of linguistic norms in their natural domain of validity, *ie* for a range of people for whom they are the primary norms of the group one is born into. For these people, and for norms that are 'natural' for them, existence and validity collapse. Each member has internalized these norms and has experienced them as being valid. This means that these norms for these people exist as their own norms and not as strange norms or prescriptions, and that they suppose their behaviour to be legitimated by these norms. It is a general property of norms of coordination that their existing practice as functioning norms justifies their validity, and this is also true of linguistic norms that are primary norms of a population.

The justification of the validity of norms of standard language, though, is more difficult. In this case a claim of validity is at issue that extends their natural domain of validity, which is their domain of existence as the linguistic practice of a cultural and economic élite, on to the whole population of a nation or state. Here we have a discrepancy between natural validity for a smaller domain of people, and a claim to a much larger domain of validity, the domain of claimed or assumed validity. The problems concerning this validity claim, that is carried out via schools and examination boards, appear in the criticism and the discussion pertaining to it (cf Moser 1967; Grebe 1968; Steger 1968; von Polenz 1968, 1970; Jäger 1971; Küchler and Jäger 1976; Bahrdt 1973; Gloy 1975; Lo Cascio 1978; Al 1977; Hartveldt 1978).

The norms of standard language seem justified if the manifold linguistic variants and varieties in a community become a burden to the language users. Variety becomes problematic if there appears a rising number of situations in which communication and the production of linguistic products, as well as their distribution, become difficult because of the many different alternative means of communication, which at the worst cannot be understood and used by all participants in communicational processes, for example by people who do not understand far-away local varieties, but who nevertheless need to have contact with speakers of these varieties. In these cases of transregional coordination, especially in communication, there needs to be a transregionally functioning means of coordination, a lingua franca. The development of a standard language, and the promotion of its use by declaring it valid transregionally, is the best method of solving existing problems of transregional coordination in communication.

In principle the justification of a standard language is the same as for languages generally. However, the situation is a special one, because there is already a number of communicational means in the form of linguistic varieties. But it is precisely the manifold nature of these and the divergence between them which destroy the functioning of these means in contact situations:

people have to learn too many varieties or variants, and the cost becomes too high, if they want to be able to communicate successfully in such situations. The alternative for learning and writing a standard language would be to learn and to write a potentially unlimited number of varieties, which would all count as languages in their own right.

Since the domain of existence and the domain of validity of the norms of standard language do not coincide (the validity domain is larger than the existence domain) the question whether these norms are justified amounts to whether it is justified to define such a large domain of validity for them. This question has two facets, namely, whether norms with such a large validity domain are really necessary, and whether these particular norms and not the norms of another variety should play the role of a standard language.

Since linguistic norms are the social reality of linguistic correctness notions, the question as to whether linguistic norms are, at least in principle, justified amounts to the question whether or not linguistic correctness notions are necessary. This question trivially has to be answered by 'yes', because only correctness notions constitute linguistic means and their use, and with this, make possible recognition and interpretation of these means. It is another question, whether we need just these or any other linguistic means and semantic and pragmatic correctness conditions. This last question addresses the justification of special linguistic norms, and it is equivalent to the question whether we should have this or that language and not another one, or whether the language in question should not, in certain respects, be different from what it is now. Such a question is by no means always trivial. It does, for example, have a trivial answer when it is instantiated as the question 'Should all English people speak English?', or 'Is the validity of the norms of English justified for the English people?' But the corresponding question with respect to the Irish people is quite sensible, namely, 'Is the validity of the norms of Irish justified for the Irish people?' It has to be answered negatively for the present situation, because nowadays the norms of English are justified for the Irish people, and they identify with their variant of English, Irish English. Likewise, it is meaningful to ask whether the validity of norms of a standard language is justified for a population with a broad linguistic variety, and it is meaningful to ask whether the norms of Standard English pronunciation should be valid for the Irish, instead of their own Irish English norms of pronunciation.

A special instantiation of the question raised in the last paragraph about the justification of specific correctness notions is whether certain semantic and pragmatic norms are justified, *ie* whether their validity is justified. It might be that the semantic correctness notions fixed by these norms give a misleading picture and orientation about reality, such that certain facets of it cannot be trusted. It might be that certain semantic correctness notions contain unjustified stereotypes and prejudices about certain groups of the population. It might be that certain pragmatic notions of correctness are such that certain groups of the population are disadvantaged in interaction, and that they serve to uphold and establish power of certain persons above others, as, for example, power of parents and adults over children, and men over women. Why, for example, had all Dutch adults, up to about 1950, the right to address children with *jij/je*, but the children had to address the adults with *U*? Questions of this kind are not meaningless: they are questions about the justification of patterns of orientation in our natural and social surroundings, which have been preset for each of us by the language we had to learn. To ask whether specific patterns are justified is, at the same time, to ask whether the validity of certain semantic or pragmatic norms is justified. Should these norm contents, *ie* these correctness notions, be perpetuated and reinforced, or should they be changed? Human action preserves them, and it is also human action which can change or abolish them. To understand that the reality of linguistic correctness notions consists in people performing certain actions which constitute the existence and validity of these norm contents, is also to understand that by appropriate actions their existence and validity can be cancelled. Language not only serves human action and interaction, but it is also subjected to human action and control, as far as specific linguistic norms are concerned. To this extent, language is manageable. This insight is the basis for all language planning, be it controlled language change, or controlled language conservation. For language planning the question as to which specific linguistic norms are justified is central.

Often there are different points of view from which a certain linguistic change can be more or less justified, and usually it is decided by the masses of the speakers and by influential models which road will be taken. Thus, Baron (1982: 229) can state that the history of American language planning is a history of failure, 'of overwhelming lack of success', and that this does not deter current language cultivators from continuing. A problem with Baron's statement is that success can hardly be identified because it is in agreement with the overall convergence of American

English as a very well-justified lingua franca for all those who originally spoke different varieties of English or totally different languages, and who had to deal with each other and to live together. Only the failures become evident, and they are in focus, rightfully enough, since it is interesting to look into their causes, one of the causes certainly being poor understanding of important aspects of linguistic systematizations and linguistic usage by those (partly self-)appointed individuals or committees like the Harper dictionary panel, the flaws of which are described by Baron (1982: 233f). But here, too, it is evident that many of the panel's rulings were not contested. Since they agreed with what historically survived, or what was incorporated into language by influential American speakers, they proved to be unproblematic and thus became not apparent. That 'language makers' or language planners who address themselves to certain tasks of transregional language planning, especially language cultivation, very often do not succeed, is due to the fact that there are always many other language makers who, in their smaller speech communities, by certain actions influence the course of language development in competing directions. Furthermore, most people like to take up new forms of expression, especially if they fit in an evident manner into easily recognizable linguistic systematizations and prove to be a useful means of communication. Here, validity and existence of certain linguistic norms arise in a 'natural' way, certain linguistic means acquiring broad currency because they are felt to be useful or because they fit nicely into evident linguistic systematizations, certain paradigms and analogies. But we should be aware that in a strict sense the way these linguistic norms arise is not natural at all, but rather is established by a whole set of human actions for which there is justification rather than natural cause. Also from this point of view, language is made by people in certain kinds of interactions and established social relationships, it is not a naturally developing organism.

At the end of this chapter, I want again to point out explicitly that *justification* and *validity* of norms have to be distinguished from each other. Norms can be justified on the basis of other norms and values, in so far as they contribute to their realization. From this point of view, there are *hierarchies of norms on the basis of justification*: norms that can be derived from other norms as justified are relatively *lower norms*, and those from which they are derived are *higher norms*.

On the other hand there is a hierarchy of quite a different kind, namely between *norms of lower order* and *norms of higher order*. The norms of higher order are those norms that regulate the validity of norms of lower order. For example, norms of second-order state how a legislative body is constituted and which procedures it has to follow in legislation in which it devises norms of first order. Norms of $(n + 1)$th order determine the validity of laws of nth order. Whether the norms of nth order are also justified is another question. But it can be ruled by norms of the $(n + 1)$th order that in validating norms of nth order at least a procedure has to be followed which will guarantee that questions of justification are discussed. They can require, for example, that before a law is legislated by parliament a discussion has to take place. Parallel procedures are possible for meta-linguistic discussions in linguistic institutes that have a function in planning the status of a language or language variety, or in language codification and cultivation.

Chapter 4

Norms and rules in linguistics

In this chapter I shall sketch the use of the notions 'norm' and 'rule' in linguistics, define the central notions of a theory of linguistic norms, and discuss the difference between linguistic norms, *ie* norms of language, and the linguistic rules formulated in theoretical linguistics.

4.1 'Norm' in traditional, structural, and functional linguistics

Hartung (1977) has treated this topic, and I shall partly follow his presentation with regard to H. Paul, F. de Saussure, L. Hjelmslev, E. Coseriu, B. Havrànek, M. Dokulil, and F. Danes, but I shall be more elaborate with respect to Paul, Saussure, Coseriu, and Havrànek, and I shall treat extensively Schnelle (1976), who discusses the relation between norms of language and their systematizations in the linguistic competences of language users.

Paul (1880) distinguishes between *individual speech, usage* ('usus') as an average among the individual utterances, and the *norm* as the standard language in two forms, namely as the norm of spoken language and the norm of written language. The different speakers or linguistic competences are called *Sprachorganismen*, and in comparing these an average can be distilled which determines what is normal in language, *ie* what the 'Sprachusus' is (1880/1970:29). The competences cannot be observed directly; rather their linguistic activity, in which they express themselves. The average can be determined with more certainty if more individuals and more of their utterances can be observed. The less complete the observation is, the more doubts remain about what is an individual peculiarity and what is common to all or to most of the speakers. The 'usus', which is the object of the grammarian, governs the language of the individual speaker only to some degree, in addition to a lot of features which are not determined by the usus but even contradict it (1880/1970:29). A change of the 'usus' is, ultimately, caused by the individual linguistic activity: although it is taken to be the norm, the 'usus' always leaves some freedom for the individual linguistic activity to vary; and the activities which deviate from the norm influence the linguistic competences. The shifts in the individuals' competences add up if they have the same direction; the result then is a shift of the usus (1880/1970:32). In this way a new opinion about what is normal is built up, and the old norm is superseded. Linguistic usage influences the individual linguistic activity, and the individual linguistic activities *en masse* determine linguistic usage.

These remarks about language change show that Paul had an empirical notion of *usus* as a set of regularities which are somehow mapped on the individual competences and are thereby concentrated as psychic entities. These are the mediators between individual linguistic activity and linguistic usage. These psychic entities are not the object of linguistic research. As far as the empirical content goes, norms are the average of all or most linguistic activity, *ie* the 'usus'; but at the same time this *usus* sets borderlines for accepted language activity and is, under this point of view, a norm. The normative character of the *usus* is implicitly referred to in Paul's remark that the *usus* permits some degree of individual freedom for linguistic activity to vary. The empirical content of the norm, or the *usus*, is problematic in as much as the notion of the 'average' of observed linguistic activity is unclear.

For Saussure likewise, language was 'a kind of average' of the individual speech productions. This average, at the same time, is the norm of all utterances. He distinguishes between *langage*, *parole*, and *langue*. These are the whole of linguistic behaviour in a speech community, individual speech, and language, respectively. Language, 'langue', is two things together, namely the norm for all utterances within 'langage', and with that also the norm of individual speech; but as the second it is at the same time the linguistic system which is stored in the heads of the speakers. Thus, language is a social entity, or institution, as well as a psychic entity, an internally built-up system. It is structured according to syntagmatic and paradigmatic relationships. Language as a system in the heads of different speakers emerges by collective adaptation between language users. In this process of adaptation the structural associations which as a whole form the language are approved of (1916/1967:18). The individual receives a lot of linguistic impressions from which an average, or product, is formed in the individual, which in this process is passive. In none of the individuals is there a complete grammatical system. The grammatical system is merely a virtual system that exists in a complete fashion only in the mass of people (1916/1967:16).

'Langue' is the social part of the whole of 'langage' and it is independent of the individual; it exists only by virtue of a certain kind of contact between the members of the speech community. On the other hand, the individual has first to learn it to get to know how its rules are (structurally) connected with each other (1916/1967:17). Apparently, the rules are the rules of language as a social entity, *ie* the conventions, which together form the norm, while the structural connections between these rules are established on the basis of the paradigmatic and syntagmatic relationships. This means that these structural connections form the system. Implicitly, Saussure seems to have made a distinction between norm and system, at least as two aspects of a whole which he calls *langue*. But since he has only one term that comprises both, the distinction has not been much examined, even by Saussure himself. Saussure assumes that applying the method of classification by the two kinds of relationships will result in one language system with only small deviances between language users. This is an assumption the truth of which is by no means obvious. A unified norm and a unified system for a language presuppose a homogeneous speech community, which is an idealization that is not justified for natural languages because of the local, social, and functional varieties that are comprised in a single natural language. The main cause of language change as change of norms and as change in systematizations is the diversity within natural language, on the normative level as well as on the systematic level. The possibility of one unified norm is not compatible with the assumption that this norm should be the average of the language behaviour of the whole speech community. The existence of such an average is very doubtful *vis-à-vis* the factual heterogeneity of a speech community; and it is also not at all clear how such an average should be constructed. The notion of 'average' with respect to the whole of linguistic usage is a metaphor that resists any close understanding.

Hjelmslev (1942) distinguishes the language *system*, or

schema, as a pure form from its material realization, which comes in three steps:

1. The *norm* as realization of the schema in a certain social reality, abstracting from details of its realization;
2. The *usus* as the set of speech habits in a social group; and
3. The *observable manifestation* in speech activity.

Here, *usus* and *norm* are abstractions on different levels. While *usus* is the set of expressions from which one chooses in a certain utterance act, *norm* is an abstraction from the *usus*. Although the hierarchy of *schema–norm–usus–utterance*, in which the lower concept is a realization of the higher, certainly is suggestive, it leaves open the question what 'realization' means in this context. We understand that an utterance is the realization of an expression; but how can something abstract, like a norm, be a realization of something even more abstract, namely a schema? If we were just to assume that the schema, as a structure, is embedded in the norm, as a structure with some additional more specific properties, we would not take into account that in the norm some of the properties of the schema can be distorted; we would only state that the norm has more characteristics than the schema, which have to be compatible with the schema, in the case of an embedding. The problem repeats itself when we want to know what is meant by the statement that the *usus* is a realization of the norm. The more specific properties of the instantiating level would merely be specifications of parameters that are left open on the more abstract level.

The tripartition *System–Norm–Sprechen*, 'system–norm–speech', proposed by Coseriu (1970) is organized in the same way: the norm is a realization of the system. The structures that constitute the system of a language restrict what the possible ways of expression are. The *patterns and structures of normal speech* in a speech community, constituting the norm, are a selection from the possible ones. Thus, the norm is a choice from systemically permitted patterns. In other words, the norm is **one** realization of the system among several possible ones which are permitted by the properties of the system. This selection, the norm, is a historically developed restriction on the possibilities which the system of a language permits. Different variants that are equivalent from a functional point of view are identified in the system, because they do not form oppositions from this point of view, like the variants [b] and [β] of the phoneme /b/ in Spanish (Coseriu 1970:78). Systemically equivalent linguistic items are identified. This identification is a mapping of the norm, including sets of admitted variants, on to the system, by which whole classes of variants within the norm correspond with single elements in the system.

Speech, in turn, is a realization of the norm. The individual linguistic norm lies in between the social norm and speech, and seems to be a particular realization of the social norm. This individual norm seems just to be the individual speech habits. But since these habits have no normative force, I would not call them 'norm' at all. The language system, on the other hand, is a realization of the language type (1970:80). And since there are also several language types, we could extend Coseriu's hierarchy of realization by putting at the top of the hierarchy the set of universals of human language, which are realized in different ways in the different language types.

This whole hierarchy of realizations, or of levels of abstraction, is hardly compatible with the fact that a norm can be a rather imperfect realization of the system, or even a distortion of it, and with the fact that types are not easily defined, because many languages do not fit into one type but have properties of several types (assuming that linguists have come up with clear definitions of types). Coseriu's view on language as a whole looks to me rather metaphysical: the system seems to be the essence of a language which seems to exert some force on its realization in the norm, and the norm does the same with respect to actual speech. And the same can be said with respect to the force that the type exerts on the system.

The mode of existence of the type, the system, and the norm remains unclear, as does the notion of realization which connects the abstract levels of type, system, and norm, and the level of norm with concrete speech. All language change, which is change of the norm, is based on properties of the system; it is just realization of the system in a language (1970:81). How, then, can there be change of a language system itself? According to the hierarchy, such a change of a system, if it could take place at all, would take place within the restriction given by the type, and thus not be a change of type. And the same question repeats itself: how can the type of a language change?

Coseriu claims that the system has no existence by itself but is just a systematization of properties of concrete speech. But how is this claim compatible with talking about **the** system of a language, as Coseriu always does? The notion of a system as just a systematization of properties of concrete speech allows for several systems of a language as the result of different systematizations. What could provide for a unique system? Does the type exert a force on the systematization to that effect? But then, how is that possible if the type itself has no existence by itself but is no more than an abstraction?

And, finally, how homogeneous has a language community to be to give rise to **the** norm, if this norm is just what is 'normally spoken' in the speech community? This seems to be a statistical notion, but then there might not be any 'normal speech' as long as we take into consideration speech of the whole speech community. Coseriu also writes that the norm carries with it 'obligation', but he does not pay attention to the possible conflict between obligation and what is mostly, or normally, done.

It is obvious that the notions 'system of a language L' as used by Hjelmslev and also by Coseriu are not identical, or somehow equivalent, with the notion 'competence of L'. A speaker who 'knows' only the system of a language, but not the norm, would not be able to speak correctly. To be competent in a language L is to 'know', or at least to be able to comply with, the norm of L. In this respect Coseriu's notion of 'the system' is similar to the notion of 'the core-grammar' of a specific language in the current developments of Chomskyan grammar. But in addition to the core-grammar, the linguistic competence in a specific language comprises all kinds of peripheral linguistic knowledge which does not need to be systematic from grammatical points of view. The relationship between 'universal grammar' and the core-grammar of a specific language is viewed like Coseriu's and Hjelmslev's instantiation, or realization: parameters of universal grammar are specified in each particular natural language. A natural language thus is an instantiation of universal grammar.

To speak of **the** system and **the** norm presupposes one single system and one single homogeneous norm of a language. I shall not adopt these notions; I shall speak of 'norms of a language' rather than of '**the** norm of a language'; and what is usually referred to as a deviation from the norm, I will, in many cases, treat as conflict between different norms.

Hartung points out that linguists from the Prague School (Havrànek 1964, 1971; Dokulil 1971; Danes 1968) did not share the essentialistic and genetic view presented above, but have focused on the function of norms and their diversity; not only the standard language has its norm comprising what is accepted as obligatory in language use, but also dialects and registers have their norm, which is the whole of accepted linguistic means, schemata, and principles in a speech community (Hartung 1977:57).

According to Vachek (1964a), a standard language exists in two forms, a spoken and a written language. Thus there are two different, though related, norms: the norm of the spoken language and the norm of the written language. The difference between them is due to the different functions that are performed by spoken language on the one hand and written language on the other. Vachek even claims that there is no common norm that comprises the two norms of a language. He does not employ the notion of 'system' as different from 'norm'. He uses the Saussurian term *langue* for what he calls the 'sum' of the norm of written language and the norm of spoken language.

Havrànek (1964) distinguishes codification of the norm of a language from the norm of the language itself. Whether codified or not, every socially or geographically defined linguistic community has its own linguistic norm. The linguistic norm consists of what is obligatory in language usage. There is an additional norm of written language, which is distinguished from the norm of spoken language by a higher degree of functional differentiation (*Schichtung*), a more strongly developed consciousness of the norm, and a stricter notion of obligatoriness. This higher degree of strictness is due to the strong requirement of stability (*Stabilitätstendenz*) of the norm of written language. Written language is differentiated according to its communicative function, practical function in a field of knowledge and activity, its theoretical function in such a field, and its aesthetic function. In other words, the norm is differentiated according to registers.

The norm of a written language undergoes changes by incorporating new terminology and by being taught to ever larger populations who tend to influence the norm of written language through the norms of their various dialects and sociolects. This latter influence is counteracted by strongly protecting the norm of written language against regional and social peculiarities. The conservation of the norm of written language should not go so far as to save archaic features in written language if these are antisystematic, *ie* contrary to the current system of the language. Written language should not be burdened with antistructural elements, because that would damage the 'rational clarity of linguistic structure' (1964:419). According to Havrànek, linguists perform two different activities, namely, on the one hand revealing the structure that exists within the linguistic norm ('die Enthüllung der tatsächlich in der Sprachnorm gegebenen Struktur', 1964:419), and on the other codifying the linguistic norm. Decisions to be made in the process of codification can profit from taking into account structural properties of the language.

Havrànek employs a notion of 'the structure' of a language, comparable with 'the system' of Hjelmslev and Coseriu. And likewise, its ontological status remains unclear: 'Language should be conceived as an abstract system of norms, it is a necessary prerequisite of mutual understanding, but has no independent form of existence and can be recognized only from concrete utterances' (Havrànek 1964:466).

The Prague School's notion of norm is such that they speak of the norm. Coseriu uses the term 'the norm of a language'; but in the Prague School there is nothing like 'the norm of a language'; rather they speak of the norm of a dialect, of a sociolect, of a functionally defined register, of the written or of the spoken language. Thus, there are different 'strata', which each have their own norm. That this stratification can give rise to a differentiation on the systematic level is a consequence that needs to be drawn, but is not. The notion of 'the system' or 'the structure' appears to be obsolete.

The notion of a different norm for each dialect, sociolect, or register is not yet the notion of norm I am going to develop and analyse in this book. What structuralists, including the Prague School, have called 'the norm of . . .' is, in the terminology used in this book, a set of norms. It is necessary to make this further differentiation, if one wants to be able to analyse norm conflicts. Schwarze (1980), for example, points out that according to the different functions a language fulfils, there are different norms that might be in conflict with each other. In order to be able to point out such a conflict in detail, we have to be able to cite those specific norms which are required to, but cannot, be satisfied simultaneously.

Hartung (1977) points out that a theory of linguistic norms has to be a dynamic theory which treats norms within their social relationships and which pays attention to the difference in the relation between a language user and a norm, and between an observer and a norm (Hartung 1977:63). Additionally, the different forms of existence of a language have to be taken into account, as there are common language (*Umgangssprache*), formal language (*gehobene Sprache*), written language, regional and other special varieties; the order and manner of their acquisition by different groups of speakers has to be studied. Because of the different order and manner of acquisition for different groups of speakers, the norms influence each other in different ways, and this can cause norm change.

A theoretical treatment of the aspects just mentioned is given by Schnelle (1976), based on the assumption of an inhomogeneous speech community and on a broad notion of human language competence:

> People are not only able to develop a language such that, by a finite set of means, they structurally manage an infinite set of expressions – call this *structure-creativity* – but besides this, they are able to acquire, develop, and manage several essentially different language varieties, and thereby to comply with a plurality of norms and a plurality of purposes of language use; of course, this multi-normativity and multi-functionality is often achieved by paying the price of a mutual accommodation of the respective competences of the different language varieties in order to achieve a better organization of the whole.
>
> The plurality **together** with the requirement of its organizability causes language communities to be inhomogeneous; this means that its members do not have an identical linguistic competence (translated from Schnelle 1976:401–2).

According to Schnelle, somebody counts as a competent speaker of a language if he manages some essential varieties. He calls the competence of a speaker in one variety *eine Sprachausprägung*, 'a linguistic print' or 'coinage', so to speak. The totality of a speaker's 'Sprachausprägungen' in their systematic, structurally characterizable connectedness is called *die Sprachbeherrschung*, the linguistic competence, of a speaker.

Different language varieties, and with that different linguistic prints in the individual speakers, come about because a language has to be functional from different points of view. Schnelle calls the ability to manage a great number of 'linguistic prints', or Sprachausprägungen, and the tendency to introduce new 'linguistic prints' *creativity of the second order or system-creativity* (1976:410).

The speaker construes a structure for each 'Sprachausprägung' which he acquires or develops. The construction of a 'Sprachausprägung' is not only subjected to optimal adaptation to the linguistic data provided by other partners in communication, but also to adaptation to the other 'Sprachausprägungen' which the speaker commands (1976:415). Thereby the different 'Sprachausprägungen' of the speaker influence each other such that also the structure of each 'Sprachausprägung' is influenced by his other 'Sprachausprägungen' and their structures. In this way, a system of structures emerges which are connected with each other and which are accommodated to each other. This is the system of the linguistic competence of the speaker.

Since even speakers of dialects command several 'Sprachausprägungen', there is a heterogeneity even in dialectal communities, compare also Gumperz (1971). From this it follows that the idea of a common language as the general and obligatory model is a fiction rather than reality: we have an intuition that one speaks such and such. But this does not necessarily mean that we all refer to a single common language system that comprises all the rules which are intersubjectively valid and which we follow. Schnelle suggests that we understand the intuition about valid norms as a fictive assumption of the existence of a model which commands the intersubjectively valid system of rules and complies with them strictly:

> Such a conception, to me, seems to be characteristic of this kind of norm. Because the individual speaker is not himself the model he only needs to adapt to it as much as (a), it is possible for him, and – this is important – as much as (b), it is compatible with other relevant behaviour that he has chosen and that is typical of a subgroup of the speech community (*eg* logic and scientific language, poetry, etc.), and as much as (c), it is compatible with his legitimate and special interests and aims. (1976:412)

This position is supported by the fact that norms need not be followed so rigidly as they would if the reservations (a), (b), and (c) did not hold. Different language varieties are not important in the same way and to the same degree for different groups in a population. Generally, those speakers are taken to be closest to the model assumed for the respective variety who are specialized in this variety because for them it is the most important one. These people themselves are then taken to be the model for the respective variety. In cases of doubt one refers to their judgement of what is correct in the variety in question. Schnelle mentions that in normative contexts there may arise a reciprocal effect between several competencies: somebody may be taken as a model of language usage because he is very competent in another non-linguistic area.

Schnelle's remarks about linguistic norms are summarized in the following statement:

> Generally people are able to comply with more than one norm steered by a model. They can comply with the standards or models of several dialects, and often several languages. In addition, they are able, on the basis of situational indicators, to command the norm that is appropriate for a communicational situation, and this at least as a point of reference in situations of doubt, but often also as active ability in the respective 'Sprachausprägung. (1976:412–13)

Schnelle's remarks on norms and the relationship between

norms and systems are the most clearly thought through in the linguistic literature on this problem. To be sure, the relationship between norms and systematizations is not a topic that has been dealt with by theoretical linguists, with the exception of Schnelle. This seems to be the reason why theoretical linguists usually have a very naive notion of what a grammar must look like, namely a nice, elegant, and coherent system. This optimistic view makes them invest lots of time in inventing involved systems of rules to integrate what does not fit with the rules they have devised in the first place. But the notion of norm has played a role in the theory of language change since Paul (1880), and it is furthermore an important notion in boundary areas of linguistics, such as ethno-linguistics, socio-linguistics, and stylistics. In these fields, language usage is investigated rather than the language system; or, more adequately, language systematizations of a grammatical kind.

In this book it will be repeatedly argued that the grammatical rules of theoretical linguistics are not norms. Therefore I now insert a section about the kinds of rules in theoretical linguistics.

4.2 'Rule' in structural and theoretical linguistics

The notion of 'rule' is widely used in theoretical linguistics. American structuralists preferred the concept of 'regularity' when talking about language behaviour, and the concept of 'pattern' or 'form' when talking about linguistic structures. Instead of rules they presented patterns of expressions and relationships between patterns with certain structural properties.

Since Chomsky (1957), linguists have become used to speaking about 'rules'. The notion of 'rule' comprises more than the notion of 'pattern' or 'form' because by it we can formulate recursive-ness. The notions 'pattern' or 'form' are not sufficient for that, since one has to say how one can substitute patterns into other patterns and can in this way expand them. To do this means to formulate a rule. The patterns of the structuralists were always conceived of like this: expansion of constituents was possible by substituting forms into other forms. Thus, implicitly, they used rules in managing the forms or patterns.

For about thirty years the concept of 'rule' has been used in theoretical linguistics, and much longer in logic. In *logic*, there are traditionally two kinds of rules: *formation rules* according to which logical formulas are built up from basic expressions, and *rules of inference or deduction* (sometimes also called *transform-ation rules*), which say what is a permitted step in a deduction of one formula from another such that if the first is true then the second is true as well, and which generally lead the way from true premisses to true conclusions. That they do this had been taken for granted on the basis of intuition, but since the development of model theory it has been proven by correctness proofs with respect to certain types of models in model-theoretic semantics.

Formation rules are *constructive* rules; they can be stated in an algorithm, that is, a set of rules that uniquely determines every step and that, in this case intrinsically, determines the order of the steps which are necessary and sufficient for building up a formula. The rules of inference are *restrictive* rules; they restrict the method of deduction to permitted steps, and they can be proven to be valid in the sense that they guarantee that the deduction leads from true formulas to true formulas. The inference rules, except for those of propositional logic, cannot be formulated as an algorithm. This means that they do not provide a uniquely determined procedure for deduction. Rather, they only restrict procedures. Both kinds of rules are *methodical* rules. Methodical rules define borders for permitted actions or operations in a certain field. Those actions that are not permitted by the rules are prohibited, at least within the field in question.

Formation rules are also *constitutive* rules, since they define the notion 'formula of *L*'. Only expressions that are structured according to these rules are formulas, *ie* expressions that are well formed in *L*, and which we deal with in *L*. In other words, the formation rules define the notion of *correct expression in L*. Inference rules define the notion of *correct inference* only in a secondary way: they are not pure conventions, since only those steps that preserve truth from one or more formulas to another formula are valid. Only those schemas that are valid in the sense that they preserve truth can be inference rules. They are not constitutive in the sense that they would define the notion of a valid step. They may be called *instrumental* rules – in the sense of Diggs (1968) – with respect to a semantic goal, namely the preservation of truth in deduction, defined independently of them. But within the syntax of *L* they define a notion of correctness, namely inferential correctness. It is a matter of convention, guided by the aim of completeness (if it is possible), which of the valid schemas are chosen as the basic inference rules in a logical syntax. And these, then, might be said to be constitutive for what in this syntax is a correct step of deduction.

Besides methodical rules that define notions of a correct expression and a correct inference step, there are methodical rules that do not define a notion of correctness, but rather provide 'good' methods for reaching a certain goal. These rules give criteria as to what is a good method for reaching the goal, without guaranteeing generally that the goal actually will be reached by the proposed method applied in similar cases. These rules are the so-called *strategic* rules, or strategies; we find them in logic books as strategies of deduction, for example in Quine's *Methods of Logic*. They are not constitutive for the notion of deduction. Often, strategic rules are not stated explicitly: one has to make them up, learning from experience by going through the examples given and the exercises required. In this sense, they are *summary* rules (Rawls 1968), or *practical* maxims (Diggs 1968). They are a second class of instrumental rules, next to those that are *legislated* rules, which constitute the correctness or incorrectness of inference steps. For both kinds of rules, as for instrumental rules generally, the goal can be formulated independently of the rules serving this goal. In this summary rules are different from constitutive rules, or 'rules of game' that define institutions, 'forms of life', and certain aims, procedures and products.

When we speak of rules in theoretical linguistics, we primarily think of methodical rules, like the two types of non-strategic rules mentioned above. Syntactic rules of a language *L* are thought of as defining the notion 'sentence in *L*'. Since the notion 'sentence in *L*' is a pre-theoretic notion, the system of rules can only be understood as a reconstruction of that notion in a certain linguistic theory. Therefore, these rules are only constitutive within the language reconstruction system, where they define the notion 'expression', or 'sentence', in that system. These expressions, constructed by the system, correspond to expressions of the language outside the reconstruction system. In this way, they can be called reconstructions of expressions, and especially sentences, of the language in question.

An important feature of all grammars as sets of rules for the formation and interpretation of expressions is recursiveness. It can be achieved by having recursive rules among the formation rules and by recursiveness within subsets of the formation rules, or by so-called 'generalized transformations', as in Chomsky (1957), which put pairs of structured sentences together to form new structured sentences on which further transformations apply to achieve the structured sentences of the respective natural language. In the so-called Standard Theory (Chomsky 1965) of Transformational Grammar, recursiveness was achieved in the formation rules for basic phrase structures by embedding structured sentences into other structured expressions and sentences, and thus having a categorially restricted recursiveness in the phrase structure component. Transformations that were meaning preserving transformed these structured strings into the structured sentences of the respective language. Later versions of Transformational Grammar restricted transformations to those that are structure preserving (*eg* Chomsky 1980) and also permitted recursiveness for other categories than the category of sentences, as other grammatical theories that were oriented towards a grammar of surface structure have always done – for example, categorial grammar, especially Montague Grammar and Generalized Phrase Structure Grammar (GPSG, *cf* Gazdar *et al.* 1985). In recent versions of Transformational Grammar (*eg* Chomsky 1981) the only transformations employed are those of *wh*-movement in question formation and NP-movement generally in topicalization.

Instead of this kind of transformation, versions of Montague Grammar which generate expressions structured by labelled bracketings (*eg* Landman and Moerdijk 1983) use substitution rules which obey the principle of semantic compositionality and are also structure preserving because the substituted phrases just fill in a position of an abstract pronoun in a syntactic structure. These substitution rules belong to the formation rules. In GPSG the SLASH-device does the same work by providing within a phrase an empty place which is categorially labelled, and which can be bound by a dislocated expression of this category. In GPSG, transformations as well as abstract pronouns are avoided in order to obtain a surface-like syntax. To achieve this and, at the same time, assign different interpretations in the case of *de re* and *de dicto* readings and regulate certain cases of coreference, the principle of semantic compositionality has been weakened.

The *rules of interpretation* in Montague Grammar, and in GPSG, parallel the syntactic rules. Since in GPSG they are all rules of functional application, they need not be spelled out next to the assignment of the proper semantic types to the syntactic categories. Rules of interpretation are methodical rules; but they are not conventional and not constitutive, because they are a consequence of the principle of semantic compositionality and its expression in syntactic rules. They say what the correct interpretation is of an expression of L in a model.

Strategic rules have never played any role in theoretical linguistics. They have figured, however, in stylistics and sociolinguistics, including ethno-linguistics, when it is said that under certain contextual and situational conditions certain linguistic forms are chosen rather than others, or are more adequate than others.

In traditional prescriptive linguistics, sentence patterns, noun phrase patterns, verb phrase patterns, and word paradigms were presented and illustrated by examples in order to provide a method that says which expressions are correct sentences of a language L. And, apart from that, some rules were stated, sometimes in readily memorizable verse forms, that say, for example, which prepositions take which cases, which verbs or nouns follow certain paradigms, etc. Furthermore, traditional grammars generally are functional grammars: they say, in an informal way, which parts of speech fulfil which functions or roles in expressing meaning. They also present practical maxims or strategies for constructing sentences and, especially, for placing or locating the parts of speech in a sentence with respect to the verb.

It is typical of non-generative and non-prescriptive structural linguists (for example, Joos 1957; Harris 1970; Hjelmslev 1943) that they did not use the notion of 'rule', although they presented linguistic structures in the form of patterns or axioms that are not essentially different from formation rules and transformation rules. Their patterns were not an algorithm for the production of sentences. They could, however, serve as generalizations over examples of linguistic products, and thus for judging for a great many cases whether a phrase is an expression of language L and for predicting what would be acceptable utterances. According to certain methods – cf Joos (1957) – they tried to make explicit *the* or *a* system of the language as manifested in a corpus. The corpus used was based on judgements about the correctness of expressions, given by native speakers. Structuralists' grammars were thought of as 'linguistic grammars' only, presenting a systematic account of a language L (cf Harris 1970; Hockett 1954; though Hockett 1948 claims that linguistic structure, as stated by the linguist, ultimately must be thought of as existing 'in the central nervous system' of the speaker). They were not primarily thought of as competence grammars. Therefore, the notion of 'rule' is not used in these positions. In theoretical linguistics, the notion of 'rule' seems to be linked up with the view that a grammar is a system of rules which make up the linguistic *competence* of speakers of L, *ie* the view of a grammar being a competence grammar, and that an automaton can serve as a model of linguistic competence. Such competence, which is a mental property, is thought to regulate linguistic performance in important respects. At least in judgements about grammatical acceptability this competence has been thought to express itself without much interference by other components of the mind.

In mainly syntactically oriented grammatical theories,

linguistic behaviour in which grammatical competence expresses itself most clearly are judgements of grammatical acceptability. In semantically oriented grammatical theories, for example in Montague Grammar, relevant linguistic behaviour consists in judging both grammatical acceptability and implicational relationships or truth. It is not at all clear whether the constructed rule systems are also thought of as being reconstructions of those devices that regulate production, perception, and interpretation of speech. Chomsky has been more or less careful about this matter, though he claims a biological reality for grammar, Gazdar *et al.* (1985) refrain from this issue, Thomason (1974) negates such a view and sees Montague Grammar as part of mathematics, Bresnan (1978) takes psychological reality as a means for deciding between different grammatical theories.

Certainly traditional structuralists did not think of patterns and axioms as rules that regulate linguistic production as a process. Rather, these patterns and axioms only restrict the forms of products. They do not restrict or regulate the process of production itself. The same is true with respect to logic: the non-strategic rules are in fact formulated as axioms or schemas that say what the permitted products are, they do not say how to produce them. Although at least the formation rules can be formulated as an algorithm for a production process, they are generally not thus formulated, but rather as a set of axioms describing the forms of the admitted products. Here, the difference between norms of products and methodical rules is not essential, but rather appears when looking at the same thing from different aspects. The formation rules are norms of product: they state what the products should look like. Because of recursiveness, the products cannot be represented simply by patterns. There have to be operations over patterns by which they can be inserted into each other. This is formulated by recursive rule systems. In other words: although the purpose of the rule system is merely to describe all possible products, this can apparently not be done without referring to some methodological aspect of constructing the products; apart from patterns, an operation has to be formulated as an optional rule, namely that a pattern may be inserted into another pattern (including itself) at a place with the same category label as the category of the first, *ie* the inserted pattern. It is then just a matter of economy to get along with the smallest number of patterns, the 'axioms', to form all other admitted patterns. It is another question whether this is also most economical from other points of view.

We shall come back to the notion of 'rule' in grammatical

theories in our discussion about the difference between rules of theoretical linguistics and linguistic norms (*cf* 4.4.).

4.3 Definitions and classifications of norms

The first section presents a short survey of the notion of 'norm' in comparison with related notions, such as 'regularity', 'usage', 'habit', 'convention', 'prescription', 'regulation', 'order', and 'rule'. Definitions of the main notions of the theory of norms will be provided. After that, norms of language and communication will be embedded into the general theory of norms and delineated from linguistic rules. In that discussion, learnability and systematization will be central topics.

4.3.1 Delineation of the concept 'norm'

Norm and *regularity* are related because a norm implies the expectation of a regularity, though the existence of a norm does not depend on whether the expected regularity is completely realized. But deviation from a regularity does destroy the regularity such that in the strict sense there is nothing left of the regularity. Deviation of a norm, *ie* not realizing the expected regularity, does not abolish or abrogate the norm as long as such deviation is subject to criticism, correction, and sanction, or is admitted as an exception in special cases. In this way, a norm is also more than a mere *expectation of a regularity*. Such an expectation, to be sure, would be suspended as soon as the expectation has been disappointed several times. In this, a norm is also distinguished from a *custom* or *usage*, which also imply the expectation of a regularity, namely that under certain circumstances certain behaviour will be shown. If this regularity is broken often enough the expectation of this regularity vanishes and with that the custom or usage. A norm, on the other hand, is enforced even then, as long as there is criticism, correction, and sanction in its favour. This aspect of criticism, correction, or sanction constitutes the *normative force* of a norm, by which a norm is distinguished from a mere custom, usage, or convention. A *habit* is distinguished from a norm in that the norm is a sufficient reason for certain behaviour: this behaviour is produced because the norm is the reason for it. But a habit may be a cause for certain behaviour, not a reason. For example, a habit to get up at seven in the morning is not a reason to get up at seven after a short night; rather this habit can be the cause for waking up at seven again and getting up. There are also bad habits. A habit, therefore, cannot be a sufficient reason for behaviour.

A *convention* is a social habit which is established as a solution of a recurring coordination problem (*cf* Lewis 1969). A convention fulfils its purpose as a means of coordination as long as the expected regularity of behaviour, *ie* the solution, is kept up. It can be replaced by another regularity without problems if this also serves as a solution to the coordination problem. A convention is only good as long as nearly everybody behaves according to it, otherwise it does not serve its purpose of coordination. To add a normative force to a convention, *ie* to make it a norm, is a means to save the convention from deteriorating or being abolished in favour of an alternative convention. Like customs and habits, conventions can be made norms if people are interested in keeping them, as often is the case.

Like norms, *prescriptions, regulations*, and *orders* also have a normative force, constituted by acts of criticism, correction, and sanction. The difference is that in the case of regulations and orders there is a clear personal distinction between those who make the regulation or give the order, and those who follow it. Orders usually refer only to a single case, but a regulation or prescription covers a whole series of cases of application which are of a certain kind and is in this respect general like a norm. Orders are only valid for the subjects and not for the authorities that give them. With regard to regulations and prescriptions this can be the case, too, but need not be. Here the domain of subjects can also include the authorities themselves, as is generally the case with respect to norms. A norm applies to all alike, the authorities and the norm subjects to whom the norm is issued.

The subjects follow regulations, prescriptions, and orders only as long as there exists an authority that controls how they are complied with and threatens sanctions if people do not comply. But in the case of a norm, the norm subjects identify with the norm authority; they even take over functions of the norm authority themselves and not only regulate their own behaviour in accordance with the norm, but also correct and criticize their own and others' deviations from the norm, and even threaten those who do not comply with the norm. Norm subjects have accepted the norm and *internalized* it in the way that they have made it their guideline of action. Since the norm authorities subject themselves under the norm, too, norms are valid for everybody who belongs to a community (which is actually defined as a community by having a common set of norms), and they are

therefore more easily accepted by those they are meant for
in the first place than in the case of a prescription, regulation,
or order.

The notions *rule* and *norm* are closely related, and in linguistic
usage they are often not differentiated. But in a theoretical treatise about norms it is useful to stress the distinctions between
these two concepts. A large subclass of rules are norms, namely
social rules. Some rules which regulate interaction among people
and institutions are prescriptions, or regulations, that can hardly
be called norms. Thus, a rule that regulates the visiting hours of
a hospital is not a norm, but a regulation. It is a regulation within
an institutional order that might be called an 'institutional rule'
but certainly not a 'norm'. I prefer to call rules that regulate
interaction in institutions not 'social rules' but just 'social regulations', in distinction to technical regulations. This way I reserve
the notion 'social rule' for informal interaction between people
and groups of people. Law belongs partly to the set of social
rules, and partly to the set of regulations. If we counted social
regulations as a part of social rules, then not all social rules would
be social norms.

Several subclasses of rules are not norms, for example rules
of game. The rules of a game, except those that regulate time
for making moves in a game, and those that are mere strategies,
constitute the game. You cannot play the game, except by the
rules. But they are not norms, because to play a game is not
obligatory. A game is not an indispensable form of public life,
like, for example, communication generally, and many special
forms of communication. But a game might be a form of life for
some people, for some time in their lives, and then the rules of
the game can be norms for them for some time in some situations. These are people who have an obligation to play the
game, be it by contract or other arrangements. In a very limited
sense the rules of the game in question are then felt by them to
be their norms that govern large parts of their life. But still, as
long as these people are not expected by the community to lead
that life (but rather by certain private agencies), what they might
feel to be their norms are not really norms of the community,
and are thus a private matter. Norms are social rules that hold
to the whole community or are at least accepted by the whole
community as in principle holding for everybody who wants to
live in this community. Rules of games are a private matter, they
are only valid for those who want to take part in the game. If
there were something like a community of football players, then
indeed relative to that community, the rules of the game would

be norms, and not a private matter. The so-called 'private norms' are not counted as norms in this treatise, because they do not have a public normative force. The same holds for the rules that define rituals; they are norms only if there is a community that as a whole performs the ritual.

Besides the rules of a game, algorithmic rules are also not norms, except relatively to the performance of a certain task. But only if this technical task is a task of the whole community, like, for example, coordination by means of communication is, can these technical rules then be called technical norms, and this only if they are not mere technical regulations, but are internalized as a guide for performing the technical task by those who perform it, and are accepted by those who consider the performance of this task as an objective of the community, and this has to be the whole community in the case of technical norms. Therefore, much of what is called 'technical norm' in common language will be called 'technical regulation' in this treatise; the notion 'technical rule' comprises 'technical norms' as well as 'technical regulations'. Also rules which are assumed to describe psychical processes are not norms. They represent internal mechanisms which are not a matter of social attention and which have no social reality. Psychical reality and social reality are of totally different categories.

Not all norms are social rules. Norms which regulate the form, quantity, measure, and quality of certain products are not social rules. But they are norms of a community as far as they are accepted by, or are valid for, the whole community, which, under division of labour, makes these products and deals with them. These norms are not social rules, because they refer to the product or the method of production, but not to social interaction.

We summarize: not all rules are norms. Social rules with a normative force which are not prescriptions or regulations are norms. Social rules without normative force are social habits and customs, or usages. Not all norms are social rules. All norms are rules, namely rules which have a normative force and which are accepted by the whole community and are internalized by at least the relevant part of a community. The possible restriction to a relevant part is due to the division of labour in a community. Each norm content is a rule which conceptualizes a regularity. If a community has the obligation to realize the regularity that is conceptualized in the rule, then the rule is the norm content which together with the normative force constitutes the norm. Most technical norms are based on regulations which become norms if they are generally accepted and are 'internalized' by those who directly work with them in the sense that they keep to the rule without pressure from the outside and identify with the rule such that they correct and criticize behaviour in production processes that does not conform to the rule.

Since language in one of its essential aspects is a means for representing possible and real states of affairs, norms that regulate this function of language are primarily *technical norms*, namely norms about the appearance and the use of the linguistic means. Also social and ethical norms play a role in communication because it is always embedded in social interaction.

In the area of *technical rules* we distinguish the following kinds (these distinctions hold for *technical regulations* as well as *technical norms*):

1. Rules that define the notion of 'correct product of kind X'. These are *restrictive* rules which define the boundaries for what can count as a correct product of kind X. The norms of this type we call 'norms of product' or, shorter, *product norms*.

2. Rules that regulate the production. The norms of this type are called 'norms of production', or, shorter, *production norms*. They are distinguished into *methodical norms*, which say what the correct method is, and *strategical norms*, which say what a good method is. The norms that define the correct method are to be distinguished into those that define a unique method step by step, and those that merely give restrictions as to what is a correct step. The following schema presents these distinctions:

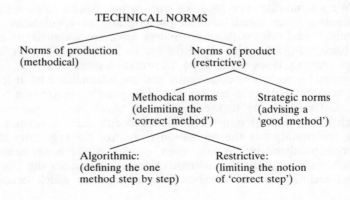

TECHNICAL NORMS

Norms of production
(methodical)

Norms of product
(restrictive)

Methodical norms
(delimiting the
'correct method')

Strategic norms
(advising a
'good method')

Algorithmic:
(defining the one
method step by step)

Restrictive:
(limiting the notion
of 'correct step')

Basically, there are two kinds of *norms of communication*. They are technical norms that coordinate the appearance and the use of communicative means, respectively.

1. *Norms of communicative products*: These norms regulate the appearance, *ie* the form and also the substance of the means used for communication. They can be classified as normalizing phonemic, graphemic, morphemic, syntactic, gestural, and intonational properties of expressions. They are the social reality of the correctness notions of these kinds (*cf* Ch. 1).

2. *Norms of use of communicative means*: These are rules of the use of instruments, the communicative means being the instruments to perform certain acts and to reach certain aims. They are semantic, pragmatic, and stylistic norms. They are the social reality of the correctness notions of these kinds (*cf* Ch. 1). These norms regulate the interpretation of expressions in situations of use. They can be codified in the lexicons of a language, in stylistic books, and even in books of etiquette, in order to achieve a normalizing effect within the language use of a population.

Pragmatic norms regulate the use of linguistic means in the performance of actions, while semantic norms regulate the use of linguistic means as far as they represent real and possible states of affairs. Stylistic norms are pragmatic norms which, traditionally, regulate the constitution of the different kinds of text, and the use of different registers, generally.

Recognizability of communicational means is guaranteed by the norms of product which delimit the appearance of these means. The interpretability of communicational means is guaranteed by the norms that delimit their use. Speaker and hearer are wise to stick to these norms. Since, to begin with, the hearer does not know what the speaker wants to tell him, he can best achieve the aim of communication, namely understanding the message of the other, in identifying and interpreting the utterance by making use of the same patterns and designations that the speaker uses in his utterance. And also for the speaker the safest way to be understood is to use those patterns of appearance and use of communicational means that are fixed in the language that is the common language of speaker and hearer.

The validity of linguistic norms makes it possible for the speaker to insist rightly on his utterance being understood in a certain way, *ie* as regulated by these linguistic norms. Likewise, according to these norms, the hearer can rightly insist on his interpretation being what the speaker is committed to by his utterance. These rights and duties exist because of the validity of the linguistic norms. They exist in all cases in which neither the situational properties nor the speaker or hearer provide any indication that the linguistic norms, or some of them, are put out of operation. Such indications for specific linguistic norms being inoperative can be linked to whole registers or kinds of text and genres. For example, if the text is proclaimed to be a poem, other normative expectations become valid than those valid for a report or a scientific text. It is even possible that the aim is to fulfil communicative needs which cannot be satisfied by use of normal language but require the invention of new forms of expression and try to establish intersubjective rules for their use; in this way one tries to make them understandable as means to communicate about and in a new area of experience. This, actually, means to work at creating a 'new' language. Normative expectations are also put out of operation when people indicate that they will not communicate seriously, or when they openly give the impression of irresponsibility.

Acceptability of an utterance is not in all cases identical with linguistic correctness or grammaticality of an utterance, *ie* correctness with respect to established linguistic norms of appearance and use of expressions. In standard cases acceptability (*ie* correctness with respect to the highest norm of communication: achieving understanding) is achieved by compliance with established linguistic norms, *ie* by linguistic correctness. But situations in which this is not the case justify deviation from specific linguistic norms and can lead to change of linguistic norms, or new linguistic norms, when these situations recur (*cf* Ch. 6 about linguistic change). Contact situations between speakers of different languages are such situations, in which speakers and hearers need to be inventive in how to achieve understanding, and here language change, new registers, and even whole sets of new means of communication, *ie* new languages, like pidgins and creoles, are created.

4.3.2 The analysis of the concept of 'norm'
First I shall summarize some essential properties of norms, that have been extensively dealt with in previous sections, then I shall discuss the question whether the concept of 'norm' is itself an institution, and finally I shall distinguish the components a norm consists of and define the different ways in which a norm exists.

Norms define a practice in a population, *ie* they define socially relevant activities and actions in a population. As such, they are constitutive for the social order in a population and make the population a 'community', and in special cases a 'speech community'. On the basis of the norms of a population P, behaviour in P is interpreted as activity, actions, and acts. Norms reduce the complexity of perceiving and evaluating states of affairs and behaviour and thus make effective action possible; but they also keep features out of sight and may so lead to rigidity.

Successful ways of perceiving and acting become persistent and thus 'frozen patterns' of orientation. They are more than social habits as they acquire a normative force in the population. As norm kernels, the regularities in these patterns provide the individuals in P with an orientation towards reality (facts, possible states of affairs) and action; this orientation is coordinated for the members of P. It consists basically of expectations about socially relevant things and events, of expectations about the behaviour and intentions of others, and of expectations about others' expectations about one's own behaviour and intentions.

A member of P is justified in adhering to his expectations and expectations of expectations if they are based on norms holding in P. Norms count as reason for certain behaviour and as reason for criticism and correction of other behaviour.

In principle, norms are conservative: individuals persist in their adherence to their norms, because otherwise they lose their orientation and become incapable of effective action or of any socially relevant action at all; especially, without common norms, they would not be able to interpret the behaviour of others as actions, nor could they rely on others interpreting their behaviour as they intend it to be interpreted.

This is the reason for *ethnocentricity*: the value of one's own norms is over-generalized to the extent that one wants these norms also to be valued highly by other people, and the domains of existence and validity of these norms are over-extended. People cling to their own norm system because it provides and reinforces their orientation within their group. At the same time this clinging to one's own norms causes disorientation with respect to foreign cultures, and instead of taking into account their norms one wants them to adapt to one's own norms. *Culture shock*, on the other hand, is the momentary loss of orientation due to a conflict between one's own norms and foreign norms, and to a loss of functioning norms generally. A person experiences a loss of norms when others do not adhere to the norms. This is one of the reasons why many men, as well as many women, are afraid of women's liberation.

Secondary functions of norms are *stabilizing the status quo*, which often means securing privileges for those who mostly profit from the norms against those who mostly suffer from them. And further, norms define group identity: people feel that they belong to a group when it makes them feel secure in orientation and expectation.

Additionally to providing socially coordinated orientation for individuals and reducing complexity, thus securing effective action in standard situations, norms serve to solve coordination problems, because they guarantee the solutions to be common solutions in the population. Norms of form and use of communicative means are norms of coordination.

Coordination norms evolve out of conventions when the latter achieve a normative force in a population. This means that they become an obligatory guideline for certain kinds of behaviour and a basis for judgements about behaviour as being correct or incorrect, right or wrong. Especially when conventions are adopted from the older generation they are learned as norms. Coordination norms can also be based on prescriptions that are general with respect to situations and subjects. A prescription that has been accepted and internalized by a population as a standard guiding one's behaviour, and as a measure of judgement of behaviour as right or wrong, is a norm. That is, norms can arise from conventions or from prescriptions.

Institutions are possible because people have a notion of 'norm'. An *institution* is a whole of rights and duties established between persons. This whole of connections can be explicated by a set of rules, or a concept of an institution, in short: an 'institutional concept'. An institution is valid, if the realization of the respective concept, *ie* the creation of the respective institutional fact, is permitted. A certain class of norms, the civil code, make it possible for people to involve themselves in a situation of rights and duties that hold between them. Some speech acts, especially declarations, but also promises (according to Searle 1969), are institutions in this sense. Other well-known institutions are marriage and the relationship between tenant and landlord.

Institutions are defined by rules. These rules are constitutive for these institutions in the sense that they define the institutions and that there is no definition of the institutions that is independent of the rules. All these rules are not categorical but hypothetical: 'If you want to get into a marriage, then the procedure *A* has to be followed.' Only if *A* has been followed is the relationship a marriage and not some other relation. Generally, the creation of an institutional fact by a group of people is a voluntary affair. Therefore the norms regulating this act are not categorical. But if one wants to create the institutional fact in question, following these norms is obligatory; otherwise the fact does not come into existence. The possibility for norms to exist is a precondition for any institution.

Is the notion of 'norm' itself an institutional concept? If this were the case, an institution of higher order, the norm *überhaupt*, would constitute the possibility of all other institutions of lower order. I think that this view is not quite correct: the norm *überhaupt* cannot be an institution, of whatever order, because we are not in the position to involve ourselves in this 'institution' voluntarily. We cannot generally abstain from being involved in realization of norms, we are born into a situation that requires us to employ norms, and we must stay within it, if we want to be a member of any community whatsoever. A human community is always a 'community in norms and institutions' which provide their members with a common natural and social orientation and with the social possibilities, *ie* 'forms of life', in which they can live and act. Without norms, people could not understand human behaviour as action, and thus there could not be any action.

A society built on instinct would be an alternative, where instinct would make possible a kind of prestabilized harmony in natural and social orientation. But it is an empirical fact that such an orientation by instinct is, to a large extent, not available for humans; this is the reason for the great variety of forms of societies and cultures.

But apart from the involuntariness of becoming involved in it, the 'norm *überhaupt*' has several properties that are characteristic for any institution: people stand in relationships of duties and rights to each other; there are norm authorities, norm subjects, norm promoters, norm watchers, norm codifiers, etc. All these persons perform certain roles with regard to the realization of a norm concept. We can call this whole scenario an 'institution of higher order' if there are norms of higher order that regulate these roles with respect to norm concepts of certain kinds. For these kinds of norm, we then speak of an 'institutionalization' of norm legislation, norm implementation, and norm conservation and reinforcement. For a norm, or norm system, to be an institution it is required that there are rules or norms of higher order that regulate this institution. The possibility of institutionalized norms thus presupposes the notion of a 'norm *überhaupt*', which itself is not an institution. Constitutional law, for example, is itself an institution of third order, which regulates the creation of civil law, an institution of second order, which regulates contracts like marriage, buying and selling, leasing, etc., which are institutions of first order. But constitutional law presupposes a non-institutional notion of 'norm', although we can imagine that constitutional law would be regulated by an international law, which then would be of fourth order; and this then would presuppose a 'natural' notion of norm.

The notion of a 'norm *überhaupt*' and its realization as the most comprehensive form of life for humans can, ultimately, not be an institution, because it would have to presuppose itself. Therefore the realization of the notion of 'norm' is ultimately a natural fact. It makes all institutions possible.

A norm consists of a *norm content*, which states a regularity, and the *norm character* which is one of the two characteristics 'obligatory' or 'optional'. Norm content and norm character together form the *norm kernel* (Von Wright 1963). This norm kernel is associated with a *normative force* that is exerted by norm authorities, and other agencies involved, towards the norm subjects, and it is also exerted by the norm subjects among themselves by corrections, criticism, and sanctions. This is particularly so with norms of communication where norm subjects feel they are norm enforcers when they correct the speech of others, especially of foreigners and of children. The reason for this is that everyone feels responsible for ensuring that the means of communication are common to all involved in communication, since only then are they effective as solutions to the problem of coordination in communication.

Apart from *norm authorities* and *norm subjects*, there are also other roles fulfilled by persons or agencies that are involved in establishing the social reality of a norm: *norm promulgators, norm promoters, norm enforcers, norm beneficiaries, norm victims*, and maybe others. All members of a speech community are supposed to be norm beneficiaries, but often those who cannot quite live up to the norms of the prestigious dialect or standard become norm victims with regard to their career and the manner in which they are not accepted in situations in which they would have to use the standard linguistic forms to make themselves sufficiently understood and be taken seriously.

Also the kinds of *sanctions* available against norm breakers belong to the social reality of a norm: with respect to norms of communication, and of language in particular, they range from correction and criticism to bad school grades and their consequences, neglect, ridicule, and exclusion from interaction.

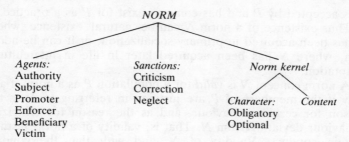

With regard to the ways in which norms exist there are important notions which should be distinguished; they play a role in the later chapters of this book.

1. Norm concept vs. norm formulation vs. norm codification vs. norm promulgation:

A *norm concept* is a norm content which conceptualizes an expected regularity, together with the character of the norm. It is thus the concept of the norm kernel.

A *norm formulation* is a formulation of the norm concept.

A *norm codification* is an official formulation of a norm concept with the purpose of providing a guideline for realizing the norm concept as a norm.

Norm promulgation is the activity of introducing a norm as valid for a population.

2. Norm existence vs. norm acceptance vs. norm adoption vs. norm validity vs. norm justification:

All these concepts are relative concepts with respect to a population. They play an important role in the analysis of norm conflicts.

A norm concept *N exists* for a population *P* as a norm if *N* regulates behaviour in *P*, *ie* if it is a *practice* in *P*. Existence of *N* as a praxis is 'existence of *N* in a narrow sense'. If the population has an external attitude towards the norm concept, *ie* follows it only under pressure, it exists for them merely as a prescription. If the population has internalized the norm concept, *ie* uses it without external pressure as a guide for behaviour and correction, it exists for them as a real norm.

A norm concept *N* is *accepted* by a population *P* as a norm if it is accepted as a guide for behaviour, *ie* if correction in favour of *N* is welcome or at least accepted in *P*.

A norm concept *N* is *adopted* by a population *P* as a norm if

N is accepted by *P* and has come to exist for *P* as a practice.

Thus existence of a norm *N* can be 'natural' existence, where *N* has been acquired in primary socialization, or it can be adoption, where *N* has been acquired later in life in intercultural adaptation.

A norm concept *N* is *valid* for a population *P* as a norm if and only if the members of *P* are justified in referring to *N* as the reason for certain behaviour, and as the reason for criticizing behaviour deviating from *N*. That is, validity of a norm justifies certain conduct. Validity of *N*, and with that the conduct according to *N*, is backed up by norm authorities and norm enforcers.

A norm concept *N* is *justified* in a population *P* as a norm if behaviour according to *N* is rational, *ie* goal directed and goal adequate, with regard to a higher norm or value *V* of *P* and does not conflict with another norm or value of *P*. In the case of conflict between favouring some higher value or norm and hindering another value or norm, *N* is only justified to some degree.

I call the group of people for whom a norm *N* exists as a practice the *existence domain* of *N*, the group of people by whom *N* is accepted the *acceptance domain* of *N*, the group of people who have adopted *N* the *adoption domain* of *N*, the group of people for whom *N* is valid the *validity domain* of *N*, and the group of people for whom *N* is justified the *justification domain* of *N*.

Apart from these population domains with respect to a norm *N* there are the *situation domains* of *N*. These are the sets of situations in which *N* is a practice, for which *N* is accepted, is valid, is adopted, and is justified in *P*. We can call these, respectively, the situational existence, acceptance, adoption, validity, and justification domains.

Norm conflicts will be analysed with respect to population domains and situation domains (*cf* Ch. 7). Likewise language-planning processes and language change will be analysed in terms of these kinds of domains (*cf* Ch. 6).

4.4 Learnability and systematization of linguistic norms

An important property of norms is that they have to be learned. They must be learned by prescription or from observable regularities in linguistic usage within frameworks that provide relevance and salience to these regularities. This means that the norm content cannot be some abstract rule connected with observable regularities only via a rather complicated theoretical system. Therefore many rules proposed in theoretical linguistics cannot be norm kernels and thus cannot be realized as norms.

The phrase structure rules that build up the non-observable deep phrase structures, and likewise the transformational rules of the so-called Standard Theory of *Transformational Grammar* (*cf* Chomsky 1965) cannot be norm kernels. The Extended Standard Theory (*cf* Chomsky 1977) could be a more likely candidate for a theory that describes linguistic norms because there transformations are structure preserving. This means that phrase structure rules produce syntactic structures that do not differ from structures obtained after a *move-NP* transformation, which moves an NP into a COMP-position. But these structures contain non-realized elements, namely traces and abstract pronouns, or NP-marked places within the COMP-position which cannot be observed in each individual example structure, though they are in principle observable as syntactic positions, because in other examples noun phrases or pronouns can be found in these positions. The later development of transformational theory (*cf* Chomsky 1981), the so-called Government-Binding Theory, assigns an important role to the level of so-called 'logical form', on which structures that are not sentence structures but are the result of over-generation are filtered out. These somewhat dubious 'logical forms' are not observable and thus are an obstacle to learning the grammatical rules, except if one assumes this level to be innate. In any case, 'logical forms' cannot be norms, and with that the whole system of linguistic rules, in which they play an indispensable role, cannot be a system of norms.

Lexical Functional Grammar (*cf* Bresnan 1978) makes strong claims of being psychologically real, *ie* in the heads of language users. These claims are based on the use of phrase structure rules that generate surface structures directly, and the broad use of lexical functional information in deriving some kind of 'logical forms'. With respect to the question at issue here, we can state that there are two obstacles to considering these grammars as sets of norms: first, the phrase structure rules over-generate and the reverse question- or *wh*- transformation is needed as a filter to throw out unacceptable syntactic structures, and second, a level of a kind of 'logical forms' is essential for interpretation of linguistic structures.

The rules of *Generalized Phrase Structure Grammar* (*cf* Gazdar *et al.* 1985), a kind of generative grammar that is not transformational, are in principle surface structure rules. To avoid transformations, there are formation rules for incomplete structures with empty places of certain categories that can be bound to phrases of the respective categories outside the incomplete structures. These empty places are not directly observable, but they can be figured out by comparing complete structures with incomplete structures, as in the case of hidden traces and abstract pronouns. This theory of grammar is thus pretty close to providing grammars that are fairly direct descriptions of syntactic norms. Since scope ambiguities are not treated in syntax, these grammars cannot be fully compositional as far as the relation of interpretation to syntax goes, especially since proponents of this kind of grammar want to avoid assuming an indispensable level of logical form. If translation of syntactic structures into logical forms were not fully compositional, then at least the interpretations of the logical forms could be compositional; but then the level of logical form would be essential for grammar, which, according to this school, should not be the case.

Montague Grammars (*cf* Thomason 1974), at least those that strictly adhere to the principle of compositionality, use abstract pronouns in the course of syntactic derivation to make possible a syntactic counterpart of strict semantic compositionality such that scope ambiguities, and with that *de re/de dicto* distinctions in interpretation, can be based on differences in syntactic derivations. This great semantic expressibility of syntax makes a level of logical form superfluous. Translations into logical form are only used for convenience to simplify the formulation of rules of interpretation in semantic models. Thus, in this kind of grammatical theory the level of logical form is not an obstacle to the possibility of the linguistic rules being linguistic norms. The existence of abstract pronouns, though, and with these the differences in syntactic derivations without corresponding differences in syntactic structures (presented by labelled bracketings) make the syntactic rules bad candidates for being linguistic norms.

It is difficult to give a firm answer to the question as to how much a learner can be expected to construct and how much must be observable, considering his general learning capacity as a human being. The postulate of a special linguistic learning ability should be argued for independently of specific grammatical theories: it does not suffice to develop a grammatical theory and then to answer the question as to how somebody could learn grammars built according to this theory, by postulating an innate framework necessary for learning this specifically designed grammar, thus tailoring the innate framework in such a way that the special grammar readily falls into slots.

The question of how somebody can learn the rules of a certain linguistic theory is not a meaningful one. These rules are not what has to be learned; they are at most certain forms of organization and systematization of what has been learned, namely the linguistic norms. The question which of the possible forms of organization of linguistic norms can be imagined and which of them could be real, taking into account results of psychological and physiological research, is an important interdisciplinary question. But this question should not be understood in such a way that one considers a construct of theoretical linguistics as that what has to be learned by a language learner. It is only a systematization of the norms of language and communication, which have to be learned.

In teaching norms it should, in principle, be possible for teachers to indicate which norm content has been violated. If it is necessary to refer to hidden abstract pronouns or traces, or to hidden 'logical forms', or to non-observable transformations to show which rule has been violated such that a deviant product, *ie* a deviant linguistic form, was produced, then the system of rules referred to cannot be a system of norms.

Even the kinds of rules employed in the Amsterdam version of *Functional Grammar* (*cf* Dik 1978, 1980), though they are called 'social rules', are not norms. They seem to be rules by which a language production ability is reconstructed, and they can therefore be considered methodical rules representing a psychical mechanism. They cannot be used in language teaching. This is a point of difference between this kind of functional grammar and traditional functional grammar. Dik's grammar is a competence grammar, including semantic and pragmatic competence. Probably Dik calls his rules 'social rules', because they are supposed to be the same for every speaker of a language and in this sense shared by a speech community. But under this criterion all abilities that people have in common could be called 'social'. This is clearly not what is meant by 'social' in this book. Here we speak of '*social* rules' if they can be formulated and referred to by the members of a community in correcting and teaching socially accepted behaviour, and if they are actively reinforced or changed by the community. The content of a social rule, like any norm content, must be a regularity of behaviour or of products that can be specified, usually in situations that are created especially for this purpose, namely teaching situations. And further, the regularity can be specified and pointed at in all situations in which the fulfilment of a special norm can be judged.

The rules of so-called *competence grammars*, even if they include semantic or pragmatic competence, cannot be called 'social rules' only by reason of their being the same for all members of the linguistic community. Firstly, this sameness has neither been proven for any of the existing competence grammars, nor is it obvious. Secondly, it is very probable that language learners build up their linguistic competence in different ways, depending on the different prerequisites from which they start out to learn the language (*cf* 5.1). Schnelle (1976) presents a view on competence in which the acquisition of languages or varieties of one language leads to different systematizations by different language learners. Different language learners acquire different language 'prints' (*Sprachausprägungen*), and they construct relations between these. Language 'prints' and the organization among them constitute the total competence of a language user, including several variants.

We have, at least presently, no method to decide whether two speakers of a language have the same linguistic competence, in the sense that they have reconstructed the same competence grammar. But we know what it means that a social rule or norm is the same for two or more speakers. For this, we do not need to look into their heads. We merely have to study their practice from the following points of view:

1. Do they have the same practice in actual speech behaviour as far as this norm is concerned? If 'yes', the norm *exists* for both.

2. Do they accept correction in favour of the norm, or do they answer positively when we present a norm formulation to them and ask whether they expect of themselves that they comply with this norm? If 'yes', the norm is accepted by both.

3. Is there an institution or agency that has the right to require them to comply with the norm, and does it do this? Or, are both justified in referring to the norm as a reason for behaviour? If 'yes', the norm is valid for both.

4. Is there a higher norm or value for both that is promoted by complying with the norm? If 'yes', then the norm is, at least to some degree, justified for both.

From these points of view we can decide whether a certain norm is the same for two or more speakers. What is common to a speech community can only be defined by making use of these notions with regard to linguistic norms; it cannot mean that all members of the speech community have the same competence grammar in their heads. The reason is that we do not have a criterion for psychic commonality of rules, but we do have one for social commonality. We only call those rules 'norms' or 'social rules' that are recognizable as common in the community under the criteria mentioned above. These rules can meaningfully be called '*common* rules', or 'norms'.

Also the so-called *variable rules* of Labov (1972a) are not norms or social rules, but rather statistical descriptions of empirical facts concerning the distribution of speech forms, according to social parameters. It is doubtful whether a statistically based notion of 'variable rule competence' makes any sense if understood as a system of rules regulating the production of speech in individuals, although there is, of course, an awareness of the social distribution of speech forms among the speech community.

From the point of view of learnability and citability in situations of correction and language teaching, pure surface structure rules will be likely candidates for norm contents. The patterns formulated in grammars of *descriptive structuralism* are usable in formulating norms, presuming that the grammatical categories have been introduced to the learner by operational procedures (substitution, movement of phrases, and deletion tests). The same is true of the rules, patterns, and descriptions of functions of linguistic phrases that are given in *traditional school grammar*.

Norms can be formulated in varying degrees of generality: from citing examples or persons who produce the examples to formulating norm contents by means of patterns or rules, making use of theoretical notions, such as categories. Compare the formulations:

> We say *the apple* and not *apple the*.
> *The* is placed before the noun and not after it.
> The determiner is placed before the noun and not after it.

These are norm formulations in which different norm concepts are formulated that, from the point of view of validity of the norms, stand in an implicational relationship, under the additional premisses that *the* is a determiner and *apple* is a noun.

These *implicational relationships* between norm contents determine a hierarchy among norms on the basis of validity: that is, if a norm with the content p is valid, and p implies the content q, then a norm with the content q is valid. By means of these logical relationships between norm contents, sets of norms can be systematized to become a *norm system*, or a system of norm systems. So far, all the contents of rules formulated or formulatable in the system are norm contents. This is another aspect under which a systematization of norms is possible, besides the one that defines a norm system by the way of a hierarchy of norms of different order, which is typical for institutionalized norm systems (*cf* 2.1). This latter kind of systematization is not at issue in the present chapter.

Systematization of norms is not only possible on the basis of logical relationships, but also on the basis of other relationships between norm contents. Statements or linguistic rules expressing these relationships are **not** themselves linguistic norms. They nevertheless may be important for the organization of the vast mass of linguistic norms. In principle this is also true of, for example, transformational relationships between syntactic structures, such as relationships between the structures of declarative sentences, *wh*-sentences, especially question sentences, declarative sentences with marked topicalization, imperative sentences, etc. Such transformational relationships are not norm contents. Only the different sentence patterns themselves are norm contents. They are learned from examples and explicitly cited patterns. They can also be constructed by generalizations over learned patterns; but because of possible over-generalization these patterns can only count as conforming to the norms if no correction is applied to them. But there is no norm, guiding our speech activity, with the content 'In order to make a *wh*-question take the standard declarative pattern, select the phrase that should be questioned, make it into a *wh*-phrase and put it in front of the sentence', or something like that. This could be a strategic rule in a 'teaching English as a second language' class, possibly serving certain purposes. But a speaker of English is merely required to make *wh*-sentences of the appropriate form, he is never required to make them in a certain way or according to a certain method.

Thus, linguistic norms are norms of the product, but they are not norms of production or generation, *ie* they are not methodical rules of how to make the product. Norms of linguistic form are non-methodical technical norms. This means that all methodical linguistic rules we have discussed under the heading 'linguistic rules' are not norm kernels: rather they are rules formulating a method for constructing products that ultimately conform to the norms. But somebody who speaks English does not need to proceed according to these methodical rules, as long as he comes up with the required products.

What is the use of grammatical systematizations with respect to grammatical norms, *ie* with respect to the norms of linguistic products?

In the above example of the three syntactical norms which stand in an implicational relationship with respect to each other, the use of the theoretical terms *determiner* and *noun*, and a list of *m* basic nouns and *n* basic determiners saves us the formulation of *n times m* special norms; or, let us say, the set of a list of *n* basic determiners and *m* basic nouns and the norm formulation *the determiner is placed before the noun* comprises *n times m* possible norm formulations. If in our grammatical theory we also have recursive rules for producing derived nouns, like ADJ + NOUN = NOUN, and NOUN + REL-CLAUSE = $NOUN_{rel}$, we comprise infinitely many special norms. Instead of having a great number of special norm concepts, we can have more general norm concepts in which categories figure as theoretical terms, and we can have lists of basic lexical items of these categories, and formation rules for derived expressions.

With respect to all the sentence and phrase patterns we want to generate or to represent, we can choose the most efficient set of formation rules or axioms. This set is equivalent to the most economical selection of a minimal number of patterns, like $[_S NP\ VP_S]$, $[_{NP} DET\ N_{NP}]$ $[_N ADJ\ N_N]$, etc. with permitted substitution according to category label. This set of patterns is an axiomatization of the set of surface patterns, with substitution. From the axiomatic patterns all others are derivable by substitution.

In the hierarchy of implicational relationships among contents of norms of linguistic products, *ie* among forms or expressions and patterns of expressions, the axioms for the formation of the expression patterns together with the lexicon of categorized basic expressions are the most general norm formulations, as far as syntactic form goes. They comprise all the others by derivation, based on the substitution operation, which preserves the validity of the norms. Actually, morphological restrictions of congruency in case, number, and gender have to be incorporated into these patterns.

We see that in linguistics the norms of product, *ie* the norms limiting the notion of 'correct product', can best be presented in an organized fashion by rules of production of a certain kind, namely methodical rules, like formation rules or an axiomatic system. Athough these methodical rules are not the norms an individual must employ in his linguistic behaviour, they are structurally equivalent to a distinct organization of norms; and apart from this they can, in the form of patterns, be viewed as norm kernels themselves, namely kernels of the highest norms in the hierarchy of valid syntactic norms of linguistic expressions.

Not every grammatical system, though being an organization of the linguistic norms exemplified by correctness judgements, is by itself part of the hierarchy of norms or structurally equivalent to such a part. If it contains rules that are not structurally equivalent to norm kernels, as, for example, transformational rules are not, this grammatical system is not part of the implicationally defined system of norms; it may still be an organization or systematization of the set of norms under certain other respects. Thus, for example, the Extended Standard Theory of Transformational Grammar certainly can be looked at as an organization or systematization behind the set of linguistic norms, but not all of its rules belong to, or are structurally equivalent to, a subset of the set of norms themselves.

When a language is learned, the norms of the language have to be learned, not the systematizations behind them. These systematizations may be constructed in the mind of the language learner in order to facilitate learning and predicting, with a good chance, what the patterns, *ie* the possible norm contents, are that have not yet been learned by exemplification or explicit statement. But it seems to be impossible to produce speech by using, rule by rule, the mechanisms theoretical grammars present. It has been argued that in order to be able to adjust one's linguistic activity to them one would have to know these rules. But how can that be the case with regard to grammars that have been worked out only partially and tentatively by theoretical linguists, even after so much effort has been invested into linguistic science?

Chomsky (1980) discusses some of the criticism on his notion 'knowledge of grammar', which, according to him, may be knowledge that is 'unconscious and not accessible to consciousness' (1980:128). He refers to criticism by John Searle and Steven Davis who claim that speakers should, at least in principle, be able to become aware of the rules they adhere to. Speakers should be able to recognize that they have used these rules when this is pointed out to them. To claim that a speaker knows certain rules means that he should be able to refer to them in some way or other; otherwise one could say at most that the speaker's behaviour is describable as being in accordance with certain rules. Chomsky agrees with the claim that the rules proposed in Transformational Grammar are 'abstract and complicated' and 'a long way from having the intuitive plausibility that ordinary grammar book rules have' (1980:132), but he does not consider this fact an argument against his kind of rules. I think Chomsky is right in not accepting this as a valid criticism of the kind of grammatical theory he advocates.

Both Chomsky and his critics are right and wrong at the same time. They do not really contradict each other, because they are talking about different kinds of rules. The kinds of rules

Chomsky has in mind are rules that are not norms of language, but rather systematizations of and behind these norms; and he would be more consistent if he did not claim that the rules proposed in grammatical theory are learned. To some extent, he seems to be aware of this consequence when he writes about the development of the 'knowledge' of grammar in a child:

> Informally we speak of this process as 'language learning'. But it makes sense to ask whether we misdescribe the process when we call it 'learning'. The question merits some thought, I believe. Without attempting to inquire into many subleties or to settle the question, I would like to suggest that in certain fundamental respects we do not really learn language; rather grammar grows in the mind. (1980:134)

On the other hand, Searle and Davis are right, considering that they discuss rules that are norms of language and not rules in the sense of theoretical linguistics. The rules we find in ordinary grammar books are norms of a language; they are not only the linguistic idiosyncrasies which Chomsky assumes such books to consist of, but also regular sentence- and phrase patterns. These norms are learned by the language learner. Which and how many of the regularities have to be included in a grammar book depends on the kind of language learner the book is geared to.

As soon as we realize that 'rule' and 'rule' are not the same, but that some kinds of rules are norms and others not, we may conclude that the whole discussion between Chomsky and Searle about the unconscious knowledge of linguistic rules is pointless.

According to Chomsky's theory of grammar, the rules of a grammar are not knowledge in the normal sense of 'knowledge'; they are rather a biologically based mechanism that is automatically filled in and completed in language learning to become the grammar of the language that is learned. These rules are, by no means, norms. In my view, the rules of these grammars can only be (biologically restricted) systematizations of sets of norms. These systematizations are not norms themselves but they make it possible to store the systematic aspects of norm contents in such a way that a fairly regular part of a system of linguistic norms can be derived from it in an effective manner. Such a grammar does not describe norms nor *the* norm system in a direct way. Since there are several points of view according to which systematization is possible it does not seem meaningful to speak of *the* grammar of a language. There seems to be not *the* grammar of a language, but different grammatical systematizations of a norm system. A norm system is an ordering of the set of norms from certain points of view in which the elements of the system are norms. In grammatical systematizations the elements, or rules, need not be norms; but norm contents can be derived from thse systematizations.

To my knowledge, Itkonen (1974) was the first to make a distinction between linguistic norms, or pre-theoretical 'rules of language', and 'linguistic rules' of scientific grammar which, according to him, is a theoretical 'explication' or 'reconstruction' of the pre-theoretical linguistic intuition that is expressed in the rules of language. I do not fully agree with Itkonen because it is necessary to distinguish 'explication' from 'reconstruction'.

An explication of linguistic intuition results in more or less general formulations of norms; it is just an explication of norms that can reveal implicational relationships among norms from the points of view of validity and of justification; it thus can take into account relations between higher and lower norms, and between norms of higher and lower order.

A reconstruction of linguistic intuition, on the other hand, can be done from quite different points of view: for example, from the empirical point of view of innate biological foundations of language generally. In this manner one tries to construct, like Chomsky, an empirical theory of language, no matter how hypothetical and speculative it may be.

Itkonen, on this point, reprimands Chomsky for trying to construct an empirical theory of language based on linguistic intuitions (*ie* correctness judgements) as data, although such data, according to Itkonen, only permit a hermeneutic approach to language that will never result in an empirical theory. This reprimand is based on the fact that Chomsky does not distinguish between explication and reconstruction from a certain point of view. Itkonen refers to Chomsky (1957:13):

> For the purpose of this discussion, however, we assume intuitive knowledge of the grammatical sentences of English and ask what sort of grammar will be able to do the job of producing these in some effective and illuminating way. We thus face a familiar task of explication of some intuitive concept – in this case, the concept 'grammatical in English', and more generally, the concept 'grammatical'.

Itkonen, rightly so, points out that 'explication' and 'empirical explanation' are notions of quite different order (Itkonen 1974:274):

> But since the difference between empirical hypothesis and explicatum is irreducible, Chomsky is here contradicting his own standard position.

Indeed, Chomsky has shown a lack of methodological reflection, although that became apparent only in Chomsky (1965, 1966), where the empirical claim of the existence of a language acquisition device in humans is introduced and where the notion of 'linguistic intuition' is used not only for conscious judgements of grammatical correctness, but also for internal linguistic rules that establish linguistic competence and that are assumed neither to be conscious (Chomsky 1966:11), nor to be be made conscious easily. Itkonen is right in pointing out that an explication of linguistic intuitions is something quite different from an empirical theory with the aim of showing how these intuitions can be explained on the basis of biological restrictions and the processing of linguistic input by an innate language acquisition device.

But against Itkonen, I shall maintain that linguistic intuitions about grammaticality and ungrammaticality of sentences and other expressions permit not only explication but also reconstruction from different points of view and, among others, from empirical points of view. Further, I would not restrict 'explication' to the hermeneutical method, but rather speak about explication in the sense of making explicit linguistic norms in formulating them and in making explicit the implicational relationships between them under the respects of validity and justification. And further, the term 'reconstruction' refers to all kinds of systematization of norm contents, achieved from different points of view. These points of view can be nonempirical ones, like the aim of achieving the most elegant and economical systematization, or they can be empirical ones, like the goal of achieving a systematization that is best suited to accommodate language change as a change of the system, and to 'explain' it in this way, or the goal of achieving systematizations that take into account biological explanations. 'Explication', then, is a special kind of reconstruction, next to other kinds.

Concluding the discussion about learnability and systematization we summarize the results in the following paragraphs.

Not every grammatical system, even if it is an organization of the contents of linguistic norms exemplified by correctness judgements, is itself part of a system of norms. What has to be learned by the language learner are the norms of the respective language. The question whether and how somebody learns the linguistic rules proposed by a linguistic theory is not meaningful. Such rules are not learned; they can only be thought of as an organization of what has to be learned, namely the linguistic norms. Nevertheless, it is a meaningful question of what such an organization looks like and how it is built up in the heads of language users, and what function it serves in learning and storing language.

It has been pointed out above that in the present stage of scientific development we do not have a method to decide whether two speakers have the same linguistic competence in the sense that they have constructed in their heads the same competence grammar. We can only test for some separate systematizations whether speakers have made them; this can be done by observing over-generalizations and other mistakes in speaking (*cf* Fromkin 1973, 1980; Bierwisch 1970). The interpretation of the empirical data can be theory dependent such that they can be fitted into different grammatical theories and thus cannot provide a basis for judging which grammar 'is in the head'.

Empirical data are compatible with different competence grammars. This is just a special case of the general empirical under-determinateness of scientific theories (*cf* Quine 1963), which in grammar construction can only be bypassed if one puts strong restrictions on what possible competence grammars are. Attempts to do this have either been quite arbitrary, or they have been trivial universality assumptions that also hold for other non-linguistic cognitive activities or are of such weak restrictive power that they do not fulfil their purpose. No proof has been given for the existence of a restriction on human languages that has as a consequence the uniqueness of a construction or reconstruction of a grammar of some language. But even if there were such a restriction, the arguments by Schnelle (1976) would still hold: the heterogeneity of the speech community and with this the different inputs and the different orders of inputs which different language learners experience would result in different grammatical constructs, even if the same restrictions on grammar reconstruction hold for different learners.

Finally, I want to make a few remarks about the lack of consistency in systematizations which prevents the construction of a nice linguistic system. Such inconsistencies come about because of different points of view according to which systematizations take place; the different respects of systematization bring about systematizations for which compatibility is not guaranteed in all cases of application. In mathematics, for example, the ordering structure, the topological structure, and the algebraic structure on the set of real numbers are compatible, *ie* do not destroy each other; in other words, they obey compatibility conditions. But the same is not true for the different structures we can discover in a natural language.

The norms of a language can be ordered into components. We have phonetical, phonological, morphological, syntactic, semantic, and pragmatic norms. Within each component, different systematizations are possible depending on the aspects of the systematization we consider and the methods we use. They also depend on which interactions between the components we take into account. For example, a grammar that treats paraphrase relationships and ambiguities on the syntactic level differs from a grammar that treats these relationships by considering semantics and even pragmatics.

Further, one should notice that some feature that is systematic from one point of view can give rise to unsystematicity ('exceptions') from another point of view. Often, phonological systematicity gives rise to morphological exception and vice versa. For example, one single (abstract) morpheme can be realized quite differently because of phonological rules; it is then no longer a single morpheme but a whole class of morphemes that are equivalent from morphologically relevant points of view. A simple example is the phonological rule of final devoicing in German and Dutch. It causes different morphological forms for Dutch *hand* ('hand'), such as / *hant* / and / *handen*/, and German / *hant*/ and / *hände* /, with the additional irregularity caused by 'Umlaut', which historically was caused by a phonological rule of 'vowel-assimilation' by which a low vowel is heightened by a high vowel in the following syllable. The single semantic unit 'hand' is thus represented by two different morphemes. The wish to represent the semantic–morphological unity gave rise to the notion of an abstract morpheme that can be realized in Dutch and also in German by two different concrete morphemes in the singular and in the plural. This is, of course, quite a complication of morphology, compared to English morphology where a single morpheme / *händ* / occurs in singular and plural forms. On the other hand, morphological systematization can cause distortions in the phonological component; there are cases where the so-called 'Humboldt principle', according to which there is precisely one form for one meaning, distorts a phonological regularity (for examples see Vennemann 1972). From a purely phonological point of view, linguists took these cases as examples of a newly invented phenomenon, namely a change from one extrinsic rule order to another. If one takes the morphological component into consideration, the exceptions from a phonological rule are explained by the intervention of the Humboldt principle. This principle gives a motivation for breaking a phonological rule, without making it necessary to use extrinsic rule order among phonological rules and invent a new kind of change in rule order, namely 'out of bleeding order', for which no phonetic or general motivation is apparent. This is different for the change into 'feeding order', which just means to abolish extrinsic rule order in favour of the natural intrinsic rule order (*cf* Vennemann 1972; Bartsch 1973).

But even within one component different systematizations can conflict with each other: what appears regular under one generalization or systematization leads to distortions under another. Historically, of course, relicts of formerly systematic relationships now appear as exceptions under a new regularity; for example the strong verbs of the Germanic languages are relicts of old systematic paradigms. Such relicts are stabilized by norms; otherwise they would disappear faster, as is evident from speech of young children who tend to over-generalize the paradigm of the weak verbs and are corrected on that. Norms have systematic properties, but also unsystematic ones. The latter are mainly relicts of formerly systematic properties, or are caused by conflicts between systematizations from different points of view.

The fact that different systematizations counteract each other causes the set of systematizations to be unstable. In other words, rules become extended in application while others become more restricted because of this. That is, one systematization can become more general while another may just be distorted by this process. Reanalysis, or restructuring, of syntactic and morphological structures is a well-known phenomenon in this area (*cf* 5.1). This happens because systematization, including rule formation, under different aspects is a never-ending activity of language learners and language users. In this light the notion of '*the* system' of a language does not seem very usable nor realistic.

There are consequences to be drawn with respect to linguistic methodology, namely a heuristic strategy of the following kind: do not try to incorporate every phenomenon of irregularity into *one* system, or into one component of a system or systems by just making this system or component more and more sophisticated. Rather, take an irregularity for what it is and try to find out why it arises by taking into account other aspects of systematization through which the apparent irregularity becomes part of a pattern, or look into the history of a language for explanation of the irregularity. Note that different systematizations can be in conflict with each other, such that they distort each other to some extent. This is as it is, and there is no reason to expect that it should be otherwise. In language we not only experience conflicts between norms but also between systematizations of the whole body of norms. This situation of systematic instability is one major cause of linguistic change.

Chapter 5

Linguistic change in the light of the theory of norms

5.1 Norms of language and types of linguistic change

There are changeable and unchangeable norms. The non-changeable ones, ie the necessary ones, are called *principles*. Principles are a precondition for action generally, and especially for inter-action, communication, and socially coordinated experience. They are not conventions because one does not have the choice between them and alternatives serving the same purpose.

A central principle, and at the same time the most important one, is the principle of rationality, which says the action has to be goal directed and goal adequate. For interpreting behaviour as action, the goals of the behaviour need not be rational with respect to other goals; interpretation is already possible on the basis of the rationality principle if it is known what the goal or motive is to which the behaviour can be assumed to be directed. If the goal is not evident, then it is necessary that it can be derived from a higher goal or value as rational with respect to these; otherwise the behaviour shown cannot be understood as an action.

Depending on which goal is relevant and what the initial conditions are under which the goal is to be pursued, different specific norms and strategies are derivable by applying the ration-ality principle to the pair '(goal, initial conditions)'. A central aim is, for example, optimal orientation in our natural and social surroundings, with the purpose of being able to act in a control-lable manner. It is reached by researching the surroundings, building up contacts, securing one's position, creating personality images of oneself and others and supporting these in order to give them some permanency. To reach all these goals, which

provide orientation, interaction between people is an indispensable further goal, which is reached in an efficient manner by
communication. Orientation about the natural surroundings has
to be socially coordinated by way of communication, initially in
the process of language learning, especially in concept formation.

The highest norm of communication, a principle, is derived
by applying the principle of rationality to the overall goal of
communication, understanding. This principle requires us to use
means of communication which are known to others in the way
that they recognize and interpret them in the same way as we do.
Recognizing and understanding utterances presupposes coordination of communicational means. This coordination arises in
speech communities in the way that people adjust their
communicational means and their usage to the communicational
means of those who 'have the saying': children adjust their
speech to that of their parents, strangers adjust their speech to
the indigenous, and the powerless adjust their speech to those
with power if that is of any advantage to them, as usually is the
case.

In order to achieve an agreement about the use of linguistic
means a consensus about the syntax and semantics of expressions
has to be created. This consensus is not a matter of negotiation,
but occurs by adjustment, stipulation, and tradition. Only after
such a consensus is negotiation about other things, for example
about supplementing linguistic means, possible.

The highest norm of communication, ie the principle of
communication, is not changeable or negotiable since it follows
from the application of the rationality principle to goals that are
central to human life and is a prerequisite for all negotiating, and
also for understanding language change.

Specific linguistic norms, which regulate specific communicational means and specific ways of using them, are changeable
and in principle negotiable. There are limits to such changes,
which are set by the goal of optimal orientation on the one hand,
and the properties of the world and of human perception and
thinking on the other, which are the initial conditions for
pursuing that goal. We distinguish natural change from planned
or controlled change. Usually they occur together, and change
appears 'natural', if the separate actions and their interrelations
that caused the change can no longer be identified in the course
of history.

Linguistic change can be called forth by changes in the natural
and social surroundings: language has to fulfil new functions, for
example, to make new areas of science terminologically access-

ible, or to define and describe new social, administrative, and political relationships.

Language change can also be called forth by new power structures, for example by dominance of certain groups, tribes, or people in economic, political, or military respects. These situations are typical for linguistic borrowings in contact situations, like in the history of English: this language originated from Anglo-Saxon, with strong Norman influence since the middle of the eleventh century (in 1066 was the victory of William the Conqueror in the Battle of Hastings over the Anglo-Saxons), by which French words entered the language in the areas of administration, politics, the military, and jurisdiction, as well as in the lexicon of the elevated style of cooking.

Both 'natural' and planned linguistic change originate under these two conditions, change of natural and social surroundings and change in power relationships. They are, to some extent, reflected by language.

Much has been written about linguistic change with respect to its principles, as well as about its details. Therefore only two aspects are treated here that play a role in linguistic change, namely basic reasons for the change of norms in general, and changes in the area of linguistic systematizations that are called forth by these. Crucial for changes of norms is heterogeneity under different aspects. It is the reason for all kinds of tensions and conflicts, which are compensated or smoothened by linguistic changes, but always with the risk that the cure is worse than the pain, ie that the remedy shows side-effects which also have to be treated, with the effect of further changes, and so on.

There are three major kinds of heterogeneity, which again and again cause linguistic change.

(1) Heterogeneity in a speech community

The speech community is not homogeneous, but there are regionally and socially different language varieties. People borrow expressions from other varieties and thus become members of the existence domains of norms from several varieties. In systematizing their linguistic experiences, which are linguistic input from different varieties, they create adjustments and systematic connections, which have effects on their language behaviour in the way that they produce a new kind of linguistic output. If the combination of varieties is approximately the same for different speakers, these can come to approximately the same systematizations, which show an approximately identical effect on their speech behaviour. If these speakers become a model for other people – and they often do, just because transregionally and transsocially mobile persons have prestige and are accepted as a model by others – their linguistic innovations become accepted: they become a model for further linguistic usage.

An extreme form of this heterogeneity is the one between different languages, which in contact situations can lead to creating new expressions and even new languages. This reaches from language change through borrowing and the integration of the loans into one of the languages, to the creation of pidgin- and creole-languages.

In terms of the theory of norms, this first type of heterogeneity can be described as a discrepancy between the ways of existence of norms in a population: for the norms of each of the different varieties, the population domains of practice, validity, acceptance, and justification of these norms show discrepancies; and they also overlap between different varieties.

(2) Heterogeneity between different styles or registers

This heterogeneity can be found within a language or within a set of linguistic means which, in special cases, consists of two languages, used in different registers and having different stylistic values. Also in this case we speak of 'borrowing'. Furthermore, expressions and ways of speaking are borrowed from technical languages and other registers and styles into the common language. What happens here is that a speaker of several registers – and most people are competent in more than one register – systematizes his linguistic experiences by partly adjusting these to each other and creating connections and orderings between his linguistic data that come from different registers. Also in this case speakers who manage approximately the same set of registers can come up with approximately the same set of linguistic systematizations. The innovations in their linguistic behaviour due to these systematizations are also similar, or can at least be recognized as systematic among these speakers. Also here, speakers with a broader competence in registers and styles are usually those with some prestige, just because of their skills to which these registers are related. They are therefore likely to be linguistic models for other people. Their innovations thus have a good chance of being accepted and adopted by others, and thereby they have initiated language change by creating new linguistic norms.

An example is semantic systematization in polysemic complexes: a speaker can build up a polysemic complex for a word by integrating the different uses the word has in different registers. Such a complex of concepts related to one single word can provide possibilities for the extension to the use of the word in new types of contexts and situations (*cf* Bartsch 1984b). This way concepts can either be extended or new concepts can be created.

Another kind of semantic systematization, namely the development of conceptual networks and especially taxonomies in several technical and scientific languages, can likewise lead to semantic change by incorporating definitions of concepts based on these semantic networks into the lexicon of standard language.

With respect to the second type of heterogeneity there is an extreme case, too: there have been linguistic communities in which a certain register, for example, the juridical or administrative or military register, was not formulated in their own but in a foreign language. This has happened because of political dominance by a foreign power. In this situation the foreign technical vocabulary of the respective areas of activity is borrowed into the language, like the French vocabulary of certain registers into English, or the English administrative and juridical vocabulary into the languages of the people under British rule during the last few centuries. Even foreign syntactic constructions can be incorporated into a language, like for example the passive construction from English into Marathi (*cf* Subbayya 1980), in the course of translating English literature from technical and other fields. This happened when India was ruled by the British.

In terms of the theory of norms, this second kind of heterogeneity can be described as a differentiation of the situational domains of linguistic norms.

(3) Heterogeneity in the linguistic system

As has been pointed out in previous chapters, we can hardly speak of *a* or of *the* linguistic system of a language. Very likely, there is no closed system, but rather a set of systematizations, which sometimes even overlap each other in such a way that one linguistic phenomenon can be integrated into two or more systematic connections and be analysed in terms of these. Likewise, what appears systematic from one point of view and therefore can give rise to rule extension, can be an exception to a rule from another point of view, *ie* break up a systematization. This can lead to rule loss or to new embedding into systematizations, *ie* to creation of new rules.

Tensions and conflicts not only exist between the systematizations of the different components, like syntax, morphology, phonology, semantics, and pragmatics, but even within one single component there can be tensions between systematizations: competing systematizations can be laid out, which pick up partly the same linguistic data: integrated into one systematization, this is extended (rule extension or generalization), at the same time, the competing systematization loses this instance (rule narrowing or specialization, or even rule loss). These processes are the result of ongoing human activity of systematizing data in our heads, during language acquisition, but also in later life. This kind of change is known in linguistics as 'reanalysis' or 'restructuring' (for examples see *p* 206).

In fact, it is this competition between systematizations, *ie* the variety of possible systematizations of linguistic phenomena, that makes it necessary to delimit the domains of application of linguistic rules conventionally by holding intact norms of form and use of expressions. If the limits of these domains are deliberate, as far as systematicity goes, then they can, in principle, be shifted.

In what follows, I shall distinguish three types of linguistic change. The first one is related to the first and second kind of heterogeneity, and the third is related to the third kind of heterogeneity. The second type of language change is something separate, that neither is called forth by relationships between the norms of a language nor by relationships within the set of linguistic systematizations, but rather has more of a natural cause.

1. Changes that are based on discrepancies between justification, validity, acceptance, and existence of linguistic norms;
2. Changes that are based on natural causes, supported by social processes;
3. Changes that are based on mental processes of systematization of linguistic material.

These three kinds of linguistic change can be distinguished in theory, but in fact they occur together, influence each other, or even cause each other.

5.1.1 Discrepancies between justification, validity, and existence of norms

5.1.1(1) *In the cause of constant goals*
Suppose a certain goal G can be reached by means of various norms; for example, an equilibrium solving a certain coordination problem can be reached by different norms $N_1, N_2, \ldots, N_n$.

Assume that N_2 exists, *ie* is a practice in a population. Although with respect to the coordination problem all norms N_i are equally suited, there can be different circumstances under which the different norms are not realizable with the same ease. For example, N_1 is favourable in circumstances U_1, *ie* can easily be realized then, while N_2 and N_3 are unfavourable from this point of view with respect to U_r. Let us assume that the circumstances under which N_r had been favourable until now have changed in such a way that it is now less favourable compared with, for example, N_5, which is better realizable under these new circumstances, while serving the goal G equally well. Then N_5 is justified, but does not yet exist, at least not for the population in question, and N_r exists for them, but is comparably less justified. To skip N_r and issue N_5 as a valid norm is justified under these new circumstances.

What kind of circumstances can be relevant?

(a) *Social circumstances*. In the cases considered here, the goal G persists, but other goals, values, and norms change. It is then possible that the compatibility of N_r with the new norms is bad and conflicts arise. Then it might be better to introduce an alternative norm, for example, N_3. This can happen slowly, as if it emerges 'naturally', *ie* first this norm is adopted by some, and then it is accepted and adopted by many. The other possibility is that the new norm can be introduced in a planned and controlled way.

(b) *Systematization*. Part of the set of linguistic norms and their realizations might become systematized differently, for example, by reanalysis of certain data, possibly induced by change of some other norms, for example, relaxation of pronunciation of certain morphemes in certain linguistic surroundings. N_r is now an exception in the kind of systematization in which it had its place up to then. N_7 fits better into the new systematization, and thus it is more justified within this frame than N_r and can therefore be introduced instead of it.

An example for cases of kind (a) are the changes of pragmatic norms, for example, norms of politeness and tact. They change when a society develops from hierarchical to more democratic relationships. The goal served by these norms remains the same, namely showing the partner in interaction that one accepts him and is willing to protect and reinforce his image. The forms in which this is done have changed quite a lot within the last century.

Cases of kind (b) are the processes of reanalysis and restructuring, for example, the origin of the English progressive from prepositional gerund constructions. Here the relaxation of the norm of the pronunciation of the preposition in a certain type of linguistic surrounding led to its disappearance in this context type and gave rise to construction pattern *be X-ing*, which did not fit well with the nominal interpretation of the *-ing* form as a gerund, but rather with the adjectival interpretation of this form as a present participle (*cf p* 206).

An example of cases that belong to both (a) and to (b) is decreolization: a creole language is adjusted to the respective matrix language in a pidgin–creole chain of developing varieties with growing systematization. This so-called 'post-creole continuum' is oriented towards what is the language of the ruling class, be it English, French, Portuguese, or Arabic (*cf* DeCamp 1971; Bailey 1973, 1974; Day 1974; Bickerton 1975).

On the one hand, the speakers, and especially the language learners, regularize the creole by an internal process of systematization: the conglomerate of basilects and matrilect with all its irregularities is under the pressure of a process of formation of linguistic rules, *ie* the development goes from marked to unmarked, *ie* regular, structures (Bailey 1973). Accompanying this tendency towards greater regularity, *ie* towards generalizing the relationships between linguistic forms and the relationships between forms and meanings, there is an orientation of socially mobile speakers towards the matrilect (DeCamp 1971).

For socially mobile speakers the point is, on the one hand, to avoid the basilect, since it is stigmatized, and on the other, not to move away too far from one's own group in order to avoid ridicule and to be able to fall back on group solidarity, if necessary (Washabough 1977). Further, these mobile speakers are under the pressure of schools and job-training institutions, where corrections take place in favour of the matrilect. In this way, an intermediate language is formed between basilect and matrilect, the so-called 'mesolect', and the 'acrolect' that is even closer to the matrilect. Stigmatized forms of the basilect are avoided in the mesolect and are replaced by features of the acrolect, if models of this 'higher' level of language are readily available. This development of a creole towards the respective matrilect is repeatedly drawn back, when new speakers from rural areas come into the cities and start at the bottom of the social ladder, speaking the basilect, as in the example of Juba-Arabic in Sudan, which is a system of pidgin- and creole stadia existing in parallel, with Arabic as the matrilect (*cf* Mahmud 1979). Speakers of a creole who are directed towards upward mobility firstly change their speech habits on the basis of new social circumstances (which originate for them by their striving to move up the social ladder) and, secondly, at the same time change their speech habits under the pressure of systematization, under which a young creole language always stands. Primarily the children regularize their language, the creole, when they acquire it, and adults follow new systematizations they find in the language of the youngsters, especially if these agree with features of a 'higher' level of language. This process is strengthened by parents who come from different linguistic backgrounds, and who learn from their children a common language that is influenced by the pidgin and creole varieties in the streets and the matrilect taught at school, for example Arabic in the Juba area (*cf* Mahmud 1979).

5.1.1(2) *In the case of changing goals*

Goals can change or become unimportant. With this, norms that serve reaching these goals become superfluous. They are then abolished, or sometimes persist because of their secondary function as markers of group solidarity (and hereby acquire a kind of a ritual character). New goals may become important and require new norms to be introduced. Well-known examples are the following:

1. Words denoting appliances and techniques of old crafts disappear with these; sometimes they survive in old sayings.
2. Words denoting institutions that are no longer realized vanish.
3. Words change their meaning with the change of customs and cultural activities.
4. Stylistic norms, for example letter styles, vanish with the disappearance of certain social relationships: changes in form of address, loss of morphological markers which, in some languages, distinctively mark the speech style of men and women, or of speaking about either men or women (*cf* Bodine 1975), and loss of markers which distinguish speaking about authorities from speaking about other persons (*cf* Neustupný 1974b, 1978).
5. With the development of new political, juridical, administrative, or technical relationships, new registers and styles are developed, the technical languages of the various fields of activities. From these registers borrowing takes place into the standard common language.

A discrepancy between validity and existence of norms gives rise to language change, especially if the validity of certain norms is justified, and these therefore can be implemented. In this way, dialects vanish or change in the direction of the standard language since standard norms are valid in those domains that are important for the social and local mobility of people, for example in the area of schooling and training.

A discrepancy between justification and validity leads to changes: if certain norms are valid without their existence being justified, acceptability of these norms in the population is low. Therefore these norms cannot be implemented or enforced successfully. Despite their validity they lose ground. Classical Sinhala, for example, could not be carried through as the standard language of Sri Lanka. It had been valid for all official purposes after independence, but it was too old-fashioned and too strange really to be justified as a standard language in comparison with the Sinhalese common language (cf 6.1.2(5)).

5.1.2 Changes by deviation on the basis of natural and social processes

Generally, in standard language there is quite a lot of tolerance with respect to small deviations. These can add up to notable deviations, which are registered as changes in linguistic usage and then in language, as soon as they are adopted by people with enough prestige to count as models for other speakers. The following schema is an example of a shift of a phoneme, cited from Bartsch and Vennemann (1982).

The norm of the children deviates within a range of tolerance from the norm of the parents. This deviation can add up, such that there is a noticeable difference in the pronunciation between grandparents and grandchildren, as in Fig. 1.

Here, the pronunciation of the grandparents lies just outside the tolerance range of the grandchildren; these experience the pronunciation of the grandparents as old-fashioned. Likewise, in

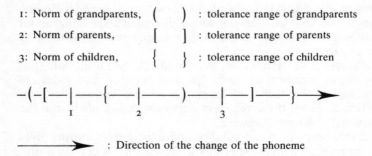

1: Norm of grandparents, (   ) : tolerance range of grandparents

2: Norm of parents,   [   ] : tolerance range of parents

3: Norm of children,   {   } : tolerance range of children

————→ : Direction of the change of the phoneme

the envisaged situation, the pronunciation of the grandchildren lies outside the tolerance range of the grandparents; they find the pronunciation of their grandchildren careless, or 'slang'. It is a question of phonetics and physiology of articulation, in which direction the shift naturally develops. Conditions of articulation and of auditive perception play a role in these matters.

The direction of the shift of a sound can be dependent on its typical phonetic surroundings, in which its change may start, for example by assimilation. Let us assume a mental image of this sound that is typical for these surroundings; this typical image, a kind of 'stereotype' of the sound, is of influence for the whole mental image of the sound, if surroundings of this type are very frequent. The articulatory feeling of pronouncing this sound will be coordinated with this prominent sound image by adjusting the sound image of one's own pronunciation of this phoneme to the prominent sound image. This way, the prominent sound image is also reinforced by the quality of the input of the learner's own production of the sound. In comparing the image of the child's own input of the sound with the image of the input of the parents and others, a sufficiently close similarity is established by adjusting to these, at least in the prominent cases of phonetic surroundings, on which the child and its models concentrate primarily. Because new input, anyway, is compared with a complex of images of the sound in question, the measure of comparison (which is just this complex) is vague for the child as well as for the parents, who, because of this vagueness, have a natural range of tolerance. This range of tolerance has a weakening effect with respect to possible correction, *ie* they will more likely tend to tolerate than to correct deviancies. The schema in Fig. 2 is meant to represent this constellation more clearly.

The input is ordered as a complex of typical sound realizations I_1, I_2 of I in typical surroundings c_1, c_2 etc. The image i_1 of I_1 is

Input: Space of images: Output/own input:

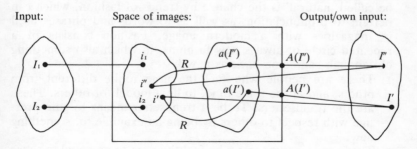

compared with the image of the self-produced sound I', ie with i'. At the same time there is a correspondence R between i' and the image $a(I')$ of the articulatory feeling $A(I')$ when producing I'. Via $a(I')$, new realizations of the sound are produced, for example, I'', whereby $A(I'')$, the articulatory feeling when producing I'', is adjusted to $a(I')$, if i_1 and i' were found to be sufficiently close; $a(I')$ and $a(I'')$ are compared for equality, as is i'', the image of I'', and i_1 and i'. In all these comparisons between images of perceptions of the sound and between images of the articulatory feeling when producing this sound, there are ranges of tolerance in recognizing identity. If similarity is sufficient, identity is stated. This way we get complexes of closely related images, with which every new input can be compared. As a whole, in these processes comparison remains vague, ie small deviancies are not recognized.

When, in this way, a recognizable deviancy has come up by addition of small deviancies between speakers, then the phoneme receives a new quality; and eventually the whole phoneme system may be shifted in such a manner that the distances between separate phonemes remain big enough to save their function in semantic discrimination. This can lead to changing the qualities of the whole basic sound inventory, but as long as the oppositions remain unchanged the systematic value of the phonemes remains constant. However, without a compensation in the realm of the other members of the phonetic inventory, a reconstruction of the whole phonemic system will take place, and we thus have a linguistic change that influences morphology and lexicon in the way that words and affixes collapse, ultimately causing even syntactic changes. These natural processes of deviation and addition of deviations had already been formulated by Paul (1880, cf 1970:32).

Quite a different kind of change that, in some sense, can also be called 'natural' is the change by trends of fashion, which can pertain to pronunciation, as well as to words and phrases used in magazines with a modern image. Fashion consists of a repeated circle of always new fashions, in which also something old enough can come back as new:

1. There are people who feel the urge to be different from others, and at the same time, to be a model for others. These are the trendsetters. To be a trendsetter means to gain prestige with respect to others by being an example for something new.

2. There are many people who feel the urge to be equal to those who have prestige; they want, for example, to be like the

trendsetters, and they therefore imitate the trend, *ie* adopt the innovation.

3. There are many people who want to belong to the large group (2.); they do not want to stay back. They follow those who follow the trendsetters.

4. Because of this process, the fashion or innovation is spread over broad populations and therefore no longer has the function referred to under step (1), namely of being different. It has acquired the function of making every follower equal with the broad masses. Therefore the trendsetters have to introduce something new, and the circle begins again with the first step. Thus, fashion is a self-regulating system built on basic human desires. Economic interests take advantage of this process.

Fashionable words and phrases may become the content of linguistic norms, if they are also justified by other reasons than just by being modern. Such innovations can, for example, be useful for representing a part of reality in a relevant way, or they can acquire a function of structuring discourse. For example, in the Netherlands the phrase *en fin/en. fijn* has been fashionable for some years; it appears in the beginning of sentences at all places in a conversation. (Some years ago the same was true of the word *dus*, which really means 'therefore', and which in the meantime, possibly due to lots of criticism in newspaper columns, has regained its old, fairly constrained use.) If this phrase should acquire a clear use, for example, of announcing the end, or a conclusion, or a summary of a piece of discourse, and this would be strengthened by correctness judgements, then this phrase could become a permanent member of the Dutch particle system, with its function of discourse organization. At the moment this fashion already seems to be fading away.

5.1.3 Changes in systematizations

Firstly, changes of this kind can be initiated by norm changes, as has already been mentioned: new norms have to be integrated into the set of systematizations, or at least, there exists a natural trend to do this. If that is not easily possible, a norm content can remain an exception from the point of view of linguistic systematization; but it is also possible that new systematizations are added which partly take away material from old systematizations, whereby these are abolished or, at least, diminished in their area of application. Also old systematizations can be extended over the new norm contents and so become more general and more prominent in such a manner that they even might withdraw material from other systematizations by partly restructuring and changing it. In this way, a norm change causes a change in the systematization of a language, and this change appears in the linguistic products that are formed on the basis of the systematizations. Any change of linguistic product is, of course, also a change of linguistic norms if it becomes accepted by the population. An example is the slurring of the preposition in the prepositional gerund construction that lead to the progressive form of modern English.

The English progressive form has originated from a prepositional gerund construction (*cf* the records in Visser 1973). Like the German nominal construction *Hans ist am Schlafen*, English had *John is on sleep(i)n(g)*; the English form becomes *John is sleep(i)n(g)*, analogically to *John is happy* and other constructions with a predicative adjective, by which *sleeping* is classified, *ie* systematized, as an adjective (especially a present participle). Hereby the rule for building verb phrases according to the schema '*be* ADJ' is extended in its domain of application. This syntactic reanalysis was made possible, because in this context-type the preposition *on* had no semantic opposition: there was no opposition by sentences like *John was in sleeping* or *John was at sleeping* with a meaning different from *John was on sleeping*. Not hindered by any semantic opposition in this context-type, the preposition *on* could slur by a natural phonetic process and finally fade away. At that point, there was nothing that resisted the reanalysis of the gerund as a present participle.

In this example, one component, namely the phonetic one, had an influence on another, namely the morphological component: the preposition *on* in the particular context-type was reduced to '*n*, and finally was lost altogether. The morphological change then made the syntactic change possible. Other examples of the influence of grammatical components on each other are the following.

From syntactic–semantic points of view, a fixed word order of the adverbials and the complements of the verb in a sentence would be systematically very simple, *ie* regular. On the other hand, in a language with clearly distinct case markings, a totally free order of the noun phrases with respect to the verb would be very simple, because all sentences, as far as the position of the terms with respect to the verb goes, could be generated by one very simple rule schema. Since the syntactic form of a sentence (aided by intonation markers) also has to carry out a pragmatic function, it is necessary to have a word order that is unmarked from pragmatic points of view (namely the actor as topic), while the other word orders are pragmatically marked to fulfil certain pragmatic functions that differ from the unmarked pragmatic standard function. Because of pragmatic functions, the syntax becomes more complicated than it would be by itself (*cf* the serialization patterns in the expression rules of Functional Grammar in Dik 1978, 1980).

Another example is the influence of phonetic simplifications on the system of case morphology: the simple one-to-one relationship between the semantic functions and the morphological expressions of the cases is destroyed. This means that phonetic processes make morphology more complicated or, in other words, greater phonological regularity with respect to noun-endings hinders morphological–semantic regularity, *ie* makes it more complex. At the same time we can say that in a certain way morphology becomes simpler, too, because there are fewer noun-endings: just two noun-endings for singular and plural, and may be a third one for the genitive, or just one suffix for the plural, or even none at all. With such a reduction, morphology loses expressive power, and another component, namely syntax, has to compensate this either by strict word order rules, or by new prepositions or postpositions instead of the old case-endings. Thus, language as a whole does not seem to become simpler in such a process: if it becomes simpler under one aspect, it often, by way of compensation, must become more complicated under another, in order not to lose expressive power (*cf* also Bartsch 1973).

Secondly, there is the internal diversity of the system, or the set of systematizations, that has also been mentioned before. This diversity is repeatedly a cause of conflicts in the structuring of linguistic material, which are solved in one way or another by rule extension or by rule restriction. In this process, remnants of old systematizations, *ie* of old rules, can persist as exceptions of new rules. Thus the forms of the strong Germanic verbs are remainders of former systematizations (*cf* Bynon 1977:20); they have been superseded by the new weak *-ed* forms for past tense, which are formed on the basis of old forms of the auxiliary verb which is today 'do, did, done'. Language learners generalized this analytic way of forming past tense, and by phonetic processes the auxiliary verb in this linguistic context-type was reduced to the past tense morpheme *-ed* in English, and *-t(. . .)* in German.

To summarize, generalization or systematicity under one aspect can give rise to complication, *ie* weakening of systematicity, under another. This change for the worse can be compensated by further changes in the system. But such a compensation can again call forth a deterioration in another area of the system, and so forth. In other words, the linguistic system is an unbalanced system, actually a complex of systematizations that get in each others' way. Because of this, language change keeps going for ever. It is slowed down, however, by the development of written language and by the persistence of written products. Therefore natural phonetic changes and, with these, changes in the norms of pronunciation, can only have slow consequences within the grammatical components. Written language, at least partly, has an existence independent of speech. Since written language also conserves correctness notions for formal speech, it usually influences the change of spoken standard language by hindering it. The broad spread of standard models of spoken language by radio and television supports conservation of language. Since the spoken products, like the written ones, are in the meantime also conserved and can be repeated, this effect of conservation is strengthened. Via the register of formal spoken language, the norms of written language provide the highest model for the whole of language and in this way extend their conservative influence beyond their own domain, especially because the written and the formal register play the most extensive transregional role in communication, education, and occupational opportunities. On the other hand, by the mass media linguistic innovations are spread faster than in former times, and therefore are accepted faster and can be adopted faster into the standard and the common language. Thus, the mass media support acceptable linguistic change. But as a whole, the conserving influence on the standard language seems to be greater. This influence has to be evaluated positively, taking into account the accessibility and the conservation of linguistically expressed cultural values and goods. The fact that the linguistic system or, better, the set of linguistic systematizations is unstable, places the main burden of achieving a desirable degree of stability of communicational means on the linguistic society, which creates, accepts, and reinforces linguistic norms.

5.2 The change of semantic norms

The application of the theory of norms on language change will now be illustrated by a more concrete case, namely semantic change, which is taken from Bartsch (1984b) (partly published also in Bartsch 1981 and Bartsch and Vennemann 1982), where we also find documentation for the examples treated.

Semantic norms are norms of coordination that regulate the

use of expressions, especially of words, with respect to natural and social states of affairs.

5.2.1 The dialectic of norm and tolerance, and of stability and change

Jespersen writes in his book *Language*:

> It is a natural consequence of the essence of human speech and the way it is transmitted from generation to generation that we have everywhere to recognize a certain latitude of correctness, alike in the significations in which the word may be used, in syntax and in pronunciation. The nearer a speaker keeps to the centre of what is established or usual, the easier it will be to understand him. If he is 'eccentric' on one point or another, the result may not always be that he conveys no idea at all, or that he is misunderstood, but often merely that he is understood with some little difficulty, or that his hearers have a momentary feeling of something odd in his choice of words, or expressions or pronunciations. (Jespersen 1922: Ch. XV, para. 5)

Essentially, people are conservative with respect to their norms. They care about keeping to the forms and patterns of linguistic means and their use, and they correct deviancies. But the conservatism of linguistic norms, which guarantees unproblematic functioning of communication in most cases, and certainly in standard cases, is only one side of the dialectical relationship. At a closer look, we see that what is required for the norms of communication to fulfil their function is not so much stability of the solutions of the coordination problems that have to be solved in order for communication to be possible. Merely the solutions have to be common ones: everybody has to know, which solutions the others expect, and that the others know about this expectation. This expectation is best secured if one has to have certain expectations about which expectations the others *must* have. In this way, a normative force is connected with the expectations. Because of the weaker requirement of common expectations instead of stable expectations, we can change communicational means in a linguistic community, if we do this in such a way that the change will be adopted by the community as a whole. By the same argument, deviations are acceptable in communication under the restriction that we are able to count on the other's understanding the expressions as we do, *ie* on the other's being able to follow the deviation. This will be achieved best if the deviation or change serves the demands on communication in society, or at least serves individual, but recognizable needs in communication.

An example of the functionality of change is the following: Clark and Clark (1979) write that a noun can only be used as a verb if there is no verb with that meaning already in the language. Thus we have *milk* as a noun and *milk* in *to milk the cow* as a verb, *bottle* and *to bottle the milk, carpet* and *to carpet the house, jet* and *to jet to New York*. Not acceptable is, parallel with the noun *hospital*, a verb *to hospital*, because its meaning is already expressed by the verb *to hospitalize*. *To hospital* would be a dysfunctional innovation that could only win ground in very special situations where it would, for example, be a matter of prestige to coin new words, or where the old word had been stigmatized. It can be a certain stylistic means, and an indicator of 'being in', to coin innovations that are alternatives for already existing words; such a style is typical for Dutch disc jockeys, but also sports reporters, and some other journalists who use English words in Dutch, which they adjust to Dutch by using the typical Dutch suffix *je* with the borrowed English nouns, and the Dutch verb morphology with the English verbs. Here, the function is a social one, namely to show one's linguistic flexibility and international orientation. Generally, the principle of functionality of innovations says that new words are not used with meanings, for which there is already a word in the language, except if the new word, or the old word, acquires a meaning which is group specifically marked, be it positively, *ie* expressing prestige, or negatively, *ie* being stigmatized.

Except in situations of language planning by decree, language change happens only gradually in small steps, starting from occasional use of a word in special situations by special people to more common usage (*cf* Paul 1880/1970:75). This is also true for semantic change. Only broad use of an expression (relative to its contexts of use) is part of common language, and it becomes part of standard language if this use is adopted and promoted by the cultural and economic élite and consequently accepted by the broader middle class. Then its use enters into the codification of norms in lexicons, which are meant to be the standard of correctness and on many occasions are used in that way. But only lexicons for technical terms are intended as strict and unambiguous. For everyday language, strict norms are hardly possible or even needed.

Lexicons can be nothing more than guidelines for the use of words. They are explicit only when they express structural lexical relationships, like synonymy or context- dependent synonymy, contrast, hyponymy, and antonymy. Words can be contrasted with respect to their meanings within a field of words, such that in the field all words that belong to it are delineated from each other by being members of different classes of words by which the field is distributed, and by standing in different semantic relationships with each other. In such a case the resulting determination of meaning of a word within the field is only as fine as the distinction between words of this field with regard to their meaning requires; the meanings of the words of the field are not completely described by this method (*cf* Lutzeier 1981). By placing words into a field of concepts (not words) we can describe word meanings more closely and strictly because here also concepts that are not expressed by just a single word but by descriptions can play a role in describing the meaning of a word. Taxonomies of concepts, which also play a role in lexicon definitions, are special fields or nets of concepts. But apart from this, the examples given in a lexicon of the use of a word in different contexts, and the context-specific semantic markers abstracted from these, are a guideline rather than a codification. At least certain examples of use are approved of in a lexicon entry, which are understood to serve as models of use of the word in question; but it is left open which further use is possible, although it is understood that it should be related in a recognizable manner to the examples cited. The whole set of typical examples in a lexicon entry together with the markers abstracted from these and the context-dependent synonyms give an indication about possible extensions of the use of the word to other examples than the ones cited. This is all a lexicon is able to do, and it should not do more.

This indeterminateness of the meaning of expressions is compatible with conceiving of the content of semantic norms as consisting of a kernel with certain directions of application: the kernel consists of distinguished examples of use of the word in question, that should serve as a pattern to prevent it from being used arbitrarily, and thus from becoming unusable. The further directions of application consist in patterns of transfer of the word into other contexts than those specific for the kernel examples. In this way a certain freedom of continuation and transfer of examples into other kinds of situations of use is laid out in the formulation of the content of a semantic norm. The possibility of change is, in principle, already included in the semantic norm itself, namely in the vagueness of application of its norm content. This vagueness of the norm content means that tolerance has to be shown with respect to every application of context-specific parts of the norm content. This necessary tolerance with regard to semantic norms is based on the highest norm of communication, a principle which is derived by applying the rationality principle to the general goal of communication.

5.2.2 The highest norm of communication

Linguistic conservatism, that is, insisting on the stability of linguistic means with respect to appearance and use, and, on the other hand, linguistic change by deviating from current usage in creating new context-specific meanings, have the same reason (cf also Hertzler 1965:151–6, 168ff on conservatism and change, and Stern 1931/1974). This reason will now be explicated.

The promulgation of, and the adherence to, linguistic norms – and with this, their existence – is justified because they are essential conditions and means of communication. They make utterances recognizable as linguistic utterances, and they make them interpretable. This they do in such a way (1) that the speaker can count on and insist on his words being understood in a certain way (namely according to the linguistic conventions), and (2) that the hearer can count on and insist on his interpretation being valid as that to which the speaker has committed himself (according to the linguistic conventions). All specific linguistic norms are justified relative to the highest norm of communication, which is: 'Express yourself in such a way that what you say is recognizable and interpretable by your partner in agreement with what you intend him to understand.' And, correspondingly, for the hearer it is: 'Interpret such that the interpretation will be in agreement with what the speaker intends.'

Since the hearer does not know, to begin with, what the speaker intends by his utterance, he can follow this principle best if he takes care to identify and interpret the utterance of the speaker by making use of the same patterns and semantics the speaker uses in his utterance. Normally these are the patterns of appearance and of meaning that are fixed in the specific linguistic norms. These specific norms are not independently justified, but rather relatively via the validity of the highest norm. The general method to follow this norm in both its aspects is for partners to use the means of communication in agreement.

But, on the other hand, there are situations in which rigid application of a special norm N just hinders the satisfaction of the highest norm, or makes it difficult to conform to it. In such a case, correctness with respect to N has to be subjugated to correctness with respect to the highest norm. This follows from the dependent status of the specific norms with regard to the highest norm. It implies that norm N need not or should not be followed if this creates difficulties for satisfying the highest norm. Rigid correctness with respect to N, in such a case, would have as a consequence incorrectness with respect to the highest norm; and with that failure in communication could be the likely consequence. An example of such a failure is the 'hypercorrect' health manual, cited in 6.1.2, that was not understood by those for whom it was written.

Acceptability of appearance and use of expressions, therefore, is not simply identical with correctness with respect to valid specific linguistic norms; rather, it is correctness with respect to the highest norm. Correctness with regard to specific norms is only necessary as long as this serves correctness with respect to the principle of communication. What is correct with respect to this principle largely depends on the special demands of the particular situation of communication. In standard cases, correctness with respect to this highest norm is achieved by correctness with respect to specific linguistic norms. Cases in which this is not so justify deviance from specific linguistic norms and lead to change of linguistic norms, if these kinds of situation become important and occur regularly. In extreme cases, like those of people in contact situations who do not have the same linguistic means available, clinging to specific linguistic norms would be totally out of place. Here, only ingenuity in creating new communicational means, like pidgins, can help. For those there are no notions of correctness: what works is what is acceptable, *ie* serves the highest norm of communication. According to Bickerton (1977) there can be no question of grammaticality in such linguistic stages, though there is acceptability: what is acceptable is what works. Pidgins and creoles are created in these extreme cases of language change which require a whole new set of linguistic means, which massively violate specific linguistic norms of the languages in contact.

Other situations in which conforming to specific linguistic norms has to regress *vis-à-vis* the highest norm of communication, *ie* where deviance from specific linguistic norms is justified, are the following:

1. Situations of cognitive conception of our physical and social surroundings and transmission of this cognitive orientation to a hearer, when common linguistic means do not express what one wants to express: there are, for example, no suitable words for newly discovered phenomena or relevant features of them;

2. Situations in which the speaker wants to express a special attitude or evaluation for which there is no simple expression in the language;

3. Situations in which the speaker wants to achieve special effects in the hearer in order to influence his attitudes, values, fantasy, creativity, and, generally, his being involved in the dealings of the world.

The first case mainly occurs in new scientific and technical states of affairs. All three cases occur in everyday communication, but especially in poetry and art because of their innovative and creative character. One tries to reach the goals of communication by deviating from conditions of semantic correctness of certain words; that is, one violates norms for the sake of reaching the goals of communication. In spoken language and in poetry, we even deviate from syntactic norms to achieve certain effects. The situation, including the context, must make it possible to recognize what the specific deviation consists of. Otherwise the chance of misunderstanding is especially great, and the highest norm is violated. The deviations must be motivated and recognizable. This will be the case if there is an associative connection between usual and occasional meaning. Certain kinds of associative connections play a role in language learning, as well as in the manner in which word meanings exist (cf Bartsch 1984b). These connections are paths along which deviation has a high chance of being understood, and along which language change proceeds, when occasional deviance becomes new common usage of an expression.

Summarizing, we can state: the highest norm not only requires conforming to the subordinated norms, but also tolerance and creativity in violating these norms. The highest norm is categorical for situations of communication. The subordinated norms are hypothetical, since they are valid only in situations in which the highest norm is satisfied by satisfying the subordinate norms. In interpreting deviant utterances, the hearer assumes that the speaker is observing the highest norm, and that therefore the deviation is functional. This is analogous with Grice's (1975) principle of cooperation, though it is much more general, since it applies to all notions of correctness. The hearer entertains this assumption as long as there is no strong evidence to the effect that the speaker might not observe the highest norm, ie behaves irrationally as far as communication is concerned. Therefore the hearer tries to find the meaning of the deviant utterance. Doing this, he or she follows certain strategies that play a role in context-dependent interpretation generally (cf Bartsch 1984b, c) and in semantic change especially.

5.2.3 Semantic change and context-dependent meaning

The necessary tolerance in the application of semantic norms is the vehicle of semantic change. Semantic norms structurally carry the possibility of change with them. Because of this, we can adjust our language to change in our physical and social world. If vagueness and context-dependence of meanings were not part of the meanings of words, language would be a less efficient means of communication, as has often been pointed out. Only by using elaborate descriptions, or by introducing new terms in situations from which these terms are learnable, could we talk about phenomena that fall outside the known schemes of classification. The alternative to a rapidly growing mass of words and the efforts necessary for their introduction and acquisition would be impractical descriptions. Schaff (1968) has pointed out that the vagueness of the meanings of expressions of natural language makes it possible to prevent these inefficient situations in daily life. Exact descriptions, making precise word meanings and introducing new terminology, are only necessary in science, technology, and administration.

The limits of the acceptability of deviation from a norm in merely occasional use of an expression are set by the requirement of understandability for the hearer, which depends on what special information is provided by the situation and what the hearer's general knowledge is. For an occasional deviation to become normal use, understanding must be possible on the basis of general knowledge in the speech community about certain kinds of situations. Language change has its limits set by the possibility of understanding the first step of change, *ie* by the understandability of the deviation. Stern (1931/1974) stresses that new changes have to be formed according to old patterns, and that therefore a limited number of types of change can be distinguished.

It is known that the tropes of rhetoric are not only kinds of deviations of poetic language use from the norms of everyday language or of standard language. Rather, these tropes describé kinds of 'deviations' that are very common and that introduce semantic changes in language. Tropes are widely used means by which speakers satisfy their communicative needs. If we project the 'tropic' strategies of deviating from semantic norms on to the norm content itself, we can conceive of the polysemic structure of word meaning, which then is the norm content, as consisting of these tropic relationships.

Paul (1880/1970), in his chapter on semantic change, discriminated between types of change according to the tropes, which make it possible to describe the relationships between old and new meaning as a deviation and, consequently, as a change that follows certain patterns: change in the kinds of objects that are the denotation of a word, without changing the concept itself (for example, German *Schreibfeder*, from the feather that was used for writing to the steel pen used nowadays); change of the cognitive and evaluative connotations or stereotypical knowledge that is connected with a word and the concept it expresses (for example, German *Weib*, 'woman', which acquired a negative connotation and was therefore replaced by *Frau* in an evaluatively neutral sense); change of the conceptual content itself in broadening or narrowing the concept by taking away or adding semantic features. The main tropes with respect to semantic change are metaphor and metonymy, in their different forms. Of metonymic kind, for example, is the change in meaning from *milk* as a noun to *milk* as a verb, and likewise for *carpet*, *jet*, etc. Here we have a transfer of the word that is based on a factual connection between the denotations of the word in the first use, to its denotations in its second use; both denotations are part of a single typical situation of the use of the word. Within this situation the transfer of the word can take place.

The tropic strategies for the regular deviations from semantic norms can be considered as part of the norm content itself. This also seems to happen in the acquisition of semantics: the semantic correctness notions are learned by distinguishing and delimiting uses of the word according to different typical contexts or situations of use. Structured according to these types of situations, they have a polysemic structure of metaphorical and metonymical connections that relate these context-specific notions with each other. The norm content itself, *ie* the correctness notion, is the correspondence relationship between the word in question and its polysemic structure. The following schema (Schema 1) is meant to illustrate this. It is a schema for the formation of word meanings in language acquisition and, at the same time, a schema for semantic change in the history of language. The transfer strategies mentioned in the schema are metaphor, metonymy, concept broadening, and concept narrowing. They are optional methodical rules. Furthermore, they are rules of second order because they regulate the treatment of rules of first order, namely the formation and change of semantic norms. Apparently, they belong to the innate faculties of systematization. This assumption is supported by Jakobson's (1960/1971) statement that in some aphasics only the metaphorical and in others only the metonymical processes are destroyed.

Schema 1
Word x has learn- and verification situations (*ie* satisfaction situations) of context-type c_i: $s_{i,1}$, $s_{i,2}$, . . ., $s_{i,n}$. The learner abstracts those regularities that are salient in context-type c_i and takes these to be the content of a semantic norm, *ie* conforms to this regularity, expects others to conform to it and to expect that he himself conforms to it. The norm content N_i that has been constructed on the basis of the typical situations consists in the correspondence between word x, the typical satisfaction situations which are of context- type c_i, and the complex X of semantic features that represent the salient regularities in the typical satisfaction situations. Actually, the features are not just a heap, but rather a set of propositions the truth of which is salient in the typical satisfaction situations.

N_i : [Word x – complex of features X, in context c_i]

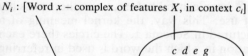

New situation e_j

X'

The highest norm of communication weakens the special norm N_i. It is therefore possible to transfer word x to the next situation e_j of context-type c_j with its set X' of salient features. The transfer takes place by means of one of the transfer strategies, which also help to single out salient features in e_j. If situation type e_j occurs repeatedly as $e_{j1}, e_{j2}, . . . e_{j,10}$, or becomes important, one abstracts the regularities that are salient in context c_j, and takes them to be a norm content:

N_j [word x. – feature complex X', *in context* c_j].

In the first analysis, two norms exist next to each other, in the second analysis they are connected in one single norm which has as its content a polysemic correctness notion. Both analyses are possible, but because of the general tendency towards systematization the second unified analysis seems to be correct.

Analysis 1 N_j : N_i :

$$\left[\begin{array}{c} word\ x \text{───── } features\ X \\ in\ context\ c_i \end{array} \right] \left[\begin{array}{c} word\ x \text{───── } features\ X' \\ in\ context\ c_j \end{array} \right]$$

Analysis 2 $N_{i,j}$

$$\left[\begin{array}{c} word\ x \end{array} \right. \begin{array}{l} X\ in\ c_i \\ X'\ in\ c_j \end{array}$$

The same relationships that we find in semantic change, we also find in the structure that relates the different context-dependent meanings of a word to each other (*cf* Bartsch 1984b, d). It is the same phenomenon; language change only goes one step further than context-dependent meaning or use of a word: the change in meaning takes place when certain contexts, and with that certain meanings of a word, become distinguished in importance that have not been central before, and others possibly vanish by going out of use. This way, the kernel meaning of a word is shifted, as is pictured in Schema 2. The circles there each stand for a type of situation in which the word is used in referring to a part of the situation, together with the regularities that have been abstracted from the use of the word in this type of situation. The overlap consists of those regularities that two such types of satisfaction situations for the word have in common. The hatched circles represent the old and the new kernel meaning. The shift from one to the other takes place via one or more types of situations of use, which in the course of history become central situations of satisfaction for the word.

Schema 2

Semantic shift

Old kernel   New kernel

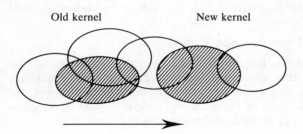

5.2.4 Illustrations of semantic change

Well-known cases of deviating use of expressions are the rhetorical tropes, and further, concept broadening and concept narrowing. Concept narrowing does not run via perspicuous deviations, since the more general concept is applicable in all cases in which the more specific concept also applies. For example, the meaning of English *deer* is a result of concept narrowing of the concept 'wild animal', while German *Tier* has a meaning that is the result of concept broadening since it means 'animal', including wild and tame animals. The deviation that is the result of concept narrowing only becomes evident when the range of application of the word is contrasted with ranges that belong to the originally broader concept. While English took over a lot of words of French origin, many English words were narrowed down in their range of application, for example, English *queen* from Germanic *quena*, 'woman'. An example of concept broadening is Middle English *dogge* (a certain race of dogs) to New English *dog*. Before, or at the same time, Old English *hund* was narrowed to a certain race of dogs for hunting, namely 'hound'. For further examples see Bloomfield (1933:426), and Ullmann (1964:228). A comparable process took place with respect to Dutch *varen*, that was narrowed to 'moving on by means of a water craft', and Dutch *rijden*, 'ride', that was broadened to 'moving by means of a land vehicle, including animals as vehicles'.

The two most important tropes that characterize relations of semantic change are metaphor and metonymy. Through metaphoric transfer we had *bit* (of a key), in German *Bart* (*eines Schlüssels*) from 'beard', *foot* (of a mountain), etc. The basis of metaphor is a similarity between the primary denotations of a word and its secondary denotations, which are of another kind or genus. Different from metaphor, the designations of a broadened concept do fall under the same genus proximum. Synaesthesis is a special kind of metaphor, where words used with respect to one area of sensation come to be used with respect to another area of sensation. For example, from hearing to seeing: German *knall rot*, lit. 'bang red', which means 'pop red', or *schreiend grün*, lit. 'shrieking green'; from touching to seeing: *warm colour*, *cold colour*; from feeling to seeing: *gay colours*, which can also be a metonymy via 'colours that make us happy', which is based on a cause–effect relationship. For further examples *cf* Schippan (1975:180*f*).

The connection between old and new meaning via metonymic transfer can be of different kinds: spatial, temporal, cause–effect, action–result, means–product, material–product, and maybe others (*cf* Schippan 1975: 184–7). Examples are Latin *lingua* from 'tongue' to 'language', *school* from the institution school to the school building, *iron* from the material to the product or instrument used for ironing, and further to the activity of ironing, German *Wache* from the activity of guarding to the ones who perform that activity and to the place where the activity is performed (English 'guard' and 'guardhouse'). Other examples of metonymy are those of Clark and Clark (1979), like *jet* from the craft to the activity, *milk* from the product to the activity that has this product as a result, or Dutch *kachel*, 'oven', in comparison to German *Kachel*, 'tile', with transfer from the tiles to the oven covered with tiles, and Dutch *bagger* 'mud' to *baggeren*, 'wade through mud', also transferred to Dutch and German *bagger* for the machine that digs and scrapes out mud and sand.

In this context, it is interesting to note that Jakobson (1960/ 1971) points out that metaphor and metonymy are characteristic for two basic processes in our linguistic activity: they can be disturbed independently in certain kinds of aphasia. Further, they are typical ways of association in poetry: some poems mainly build on metaphoric associations, others on metonymic. The last is especially true in epic poetry.

I now want to present some examples from Dutch and German, in which the difference in meaning of phonetically related words in these languages can be explained by processes of semantic change that took place via one or more context-dependent meanings within the limits of tolerance of semantic norms. These limits of tolerance are defined by semantic relationships: concept broadening, concept narrowing, and the rhetorical tropes, with special emphasis on metaphor and metonymy. The documentation of the examples presented is to be found in Bartsch (1984c), where kinds of context-dependence of meaning, kinds of vagueness of meaning, and heterogeneity of meaning in the speech community are also discussed.

Example 1

    knap (Dutch): 'able', 'fit', 'clever', 'good-looking'
    knapp (German): 'narrow', 'hardly sufficient'

The original kernel meaning, that is the proto-meaning as stated in historical dictionaries of Dutch and German, was 'fitting close, tightly'. In German the word was used as an adjective with respect to clothes and economic situations. The typical occasions of use in Dutch were also with respect to clothing, but with a positive evaluation. A *knap* piece of clothing was one that fitted well, and being dressed *knap* still means being well dressed. In this use it could also be found marginally in German up to around 1800. The typical meaning in German was negative: too tight, too narrow, too short, leaving no room for motion. This has been transferred to bad economic situations. In Dutch *knap* is further used with respect to conversational contributions: a *knap* contribution is not a very short or quite insufficient one (as it would be in German, except for the positive qualification *knapp und treffend*, 'short and to the point'); rather it is an especially well-suited, intelligent contribution. Furthermore, *knap* is used to characterize intellectual ability in the sense of 'bright' or 'intelligent'. With respect to people, *knap* means, depending on further context, 'intelligent', 'good-looking', 'fit', and all these together if the context is not further specified. The meaning 'pretty', 'handsome', 'smart', can also be found in the variety of German spoken in East Frisia, a German province on the Dutch border. Etymologically, *knap* seems to be related to *knijpen* (German *kneifen*, English 'nip', 'pinch'), like Dutch *glad* (German *glatt*, English 'slippery' or 'smooth') to *glijden* (German *gleiten*, English 'slide'). *Knijpen* in its proto-meaning, 'to press from two sides with fingers', meant 'leaving no elbow room' when used in the context of clothing, and generally 'being narrow' as, for example, in the context of sailing, where *knijpen* means 'to sail sharp at the wind, to the utmost degree'. Schema 3 shows the polysemic complex of *knap/knapp*.

Schema 3

Between the uses in the different contexts, there are metaphoric or metonymic relationships: the transfer from a neatly fitting dress to the person wearing it can be understood as metonymic, as can the transfer from a person to her intellectual capability (part–whole), or vice versa, and from her intellectual contributions to the intellectual capability behind them (cause–effect). We do not know whether the historical development occurred in this way. (It is probable that for many speakers these associations have played a role in semantic acquisition.) But even without these associations we can derive all the context-dependent meanings directly from the assumed kernel meaning, which is 'closely fitting under aspect X', with positive connotation in Dutch and negative connotation in German. For X we can substitute the specification given by the respective

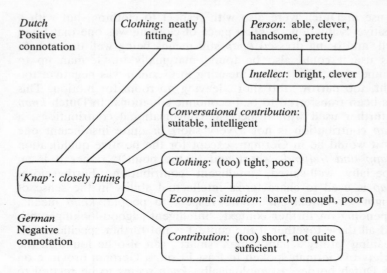

Dutch
Positive
connotation

Clothing: neatly fitting

Person: able, clever, handsome, pretty

Intellect: bright, clever

Conversational contribution: suitable, intelligent

'Knap': *closely fitting*

Clothing: (too) tight, poor

Economic situation: barely enough, poor

German
Negative
connotation

Contribution: (too) short, not quite sufficient

context of use. This assumed kernel meaning, with positive and negative connotation, respectively, still exists today. We can reconstruct the semantic complex of *knap/knapp* in such a way that one single kernel meaning can be identified. Whether the language user is aware of this kernel meaning is another question. The positive and the negative connotations are part of the respective new Dutch and German kernel meaning.

Example 2

zat (Dutch): 'drunk'
satt (German): 'be satisfied by food'

Dutch *zat* had the same meaning as German *satt*. But then it became a euphemism for 'drunk', as also happened in some substandard varieties of German. The semantic relationship is metaphoric: transfer from 'filled by food' to 'filled by alcohol'.

Example 3

flink (Dutch): 'strong', 'forceful', 'voluminous', 'courageous', 'persevering'
flink (German): 'quick', 'moving in an easy way', 'agile'

In both languages the kernel meanings no longer agree with the proto-meaning, *ie* with the former kernel meaning. For this word, the historical proto-meaning no longer exists. The semantic difference between this word in the two languages gives rise to misunderstanding: a German, listening to the Dutch weather forecast, would interpret *flinke zonnige perioden* as 'short, fast-changing periods of sunshine', thinking 'typically Dutch fickle weather', while it means the opposite, namely 'long, steady periods of sunshine'.

In Schemas 4 and 5, the paraphrases with respect to one context hold for different perspectives of judgement, *ie* for different contextual specifications of the context. In the previous example, the different meanings of *knap* with respect to persons likewise came about by different perspectives of judgement. With respect to the perspective 'character' we find at least three different meanings:

flink with respect to situations of danger: 'courageous';

with respect to resistance to short-term adversity: 'pushing through';

with respect to resistance against long-term adversity: 'steady', 'carrying through', 'persevering', 'enduring'.

Schema 4

The relationships 1–5 are metaphoric in kind: 'beaming', 'blinking' contains a component 'being distinguished', because something that beams or sparkles is, by this, distinguished from other things. One thing can distinguish itself from other things

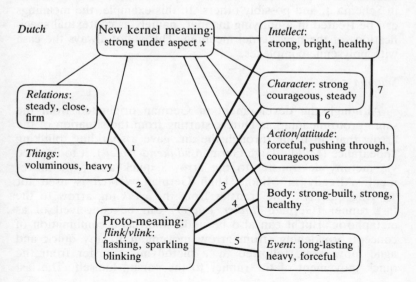

Dutch

New kernel meaning: strong under aspect *x*

Intellect: strong, bright, healthy

Relations: steady, close, firm

Character: strong courageous, steady 7

Things: voluminous, heavy

Action/attitude: forceful, pushing through, courageous

6

1

Body: strong-built, strong, healthy

2

3

4

Proto-meaning: *flink/vlink*: flashing, sparkling blinking

5

Event: long-lasting heavy, forceful

under different aspects in different situational contexts. To be distinguished under a certain aspect meant for the Dutch 'to be strong under that aspect'. Also today, they use the word *uitblinken* (lit. 'to shine out') for being distinguished positively under a certain aspect, with *blinken* as a form related to *flink* in, eg: *vlinkende pijl* in Middle Dutch, and *vlinkender pfeil* in Middle High German. Strength under an aspect X causes an individual who shows this strength, to be distinguished from others. This cause–effect relationship is the metonymic association in the transfer. The metaphorical association establishes the transfer of 'beaming', 'blinking' from the context of beaming or blinking things, to other phenomena that distinguish themselves from their surroundings. Compare English *a sparkling success, a sparkling performance, a bright boy*, and German: *ein glänzender Erfolg, eine glänzende Leistung, ein heller Knabe*, with Dutch *uitblinken*, 'to distinguish oneself', which show the same kind of metaphoric transfer. The transfer of the word *flink* as a whole is: from ['blink', or 'sparkle'] it is metaphorically transferred to ['distinguish'], and from there metonymically to ['strong under a certain aspect'].

Relations 6 and 7 are metonymic, although a metaphoric relation as in 1–5 is conceivable. From the contexts mentioned (and maybe others) we can reconstruct a new kernel meaning of *flink* for modern Dutch that can be applied in all these contexts and in others, yielding the context-dependent meanings indicated in Schema 4, and possibly others. In this example, the meanings can be treated in a unifying manner, namely as contextual specifications of the new kernel meaning. This is not always the case with polysemic complexes.

Schema 5

Although the development in German originated from the same proto-meaning as Dutch, starting from the situation of the arrow that, in flying through the air, gave a sparkling, blinking appearance (Middle High German *vlinkender pfeil*), it took place via metonymic transfer to the arrow's quick and agile movement. Already in Middle High German *vlinken* is used for 'moving quickly'. The transfer from the *vlink*-ing arrow to the fast runner (German *flinker Läufer*) can be conceived of as metaphoric. But it can also be understood as a combination of concept broadening, from arrow movement to any quick and agile movement, followed by a metonymic transfer from the quick movement of the runner to the person himself. The last

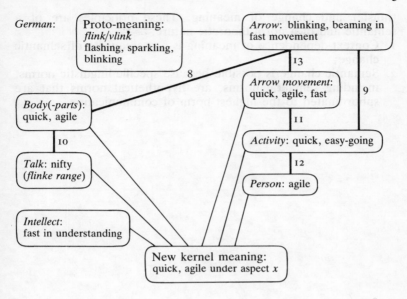

relationship we also find in German *ein flinkes Mädchen*: the girl is called *flink* by metonymical association with the agile and quick movements while performing her typical activities, in this case housekeeping. The relationships 8, 9, and 10 are metaphoric, and 11, 12, and 13 are metonymic.

From the contexts of use we can reconstruct the new kernel meaning of *flink* for modern German, that can be applied in all these and in other contexts, yielding different context-dependent meanings, which are in this case specifications of the new kernel meaning.

A problem in the reconstruction of semantic change is that, in some cases, one and the same phenomenon can be explained in several ways: for example, in one metaphoric step, or taking another road via metonymic relations and concept narrowing or concept broadening, or in combination with another metaphorical relation: in the above schemas we can at several points imagine different roads leading to the same result. But these uncertainties are not of any importance; because it is probable that different speakers took different roads in constructing the polysemic structure of the word investigated. In this chapter, the principles of semantic change are at issue, rather than the question of how every single step occurred in the context-dependent transfer and change of meaning. These principles are of a semantic and of a norm-theoretic nature:

1. Context-dependence of meaning is a prerequisite of semantic change;
2. Semantic change is possible because specific linguistic norms, including semantic norms, are hypothetical norms that are subordinated to the highest norm of communication.

Chapter 6

Linguistic norms in language planning and development

For some linguists *language planning* is almost a bad phrase, and some people involved in the field prefer the name *language development* since that leaves open how far language really can be planned. The strongest claim against language-planning activities is the title of Robert Hall Jr's book (1950) *Leave Your Language Alone!*, and Baron opens the conclusion of the book *Grammar and Good Taste*, a book about language cultivation in America, with the following remark (1982:239):

> The early planners and reformers of American English whose work has been discussed in these pages have left one common legacy for their twentieth-century counterparts to ponder: an overwhelming lack of success. The history of failure has proved to be no deterrent. Whether conservative or radical, the language planners, some ignorant of past attempts at reform, others optimistic in spite of the failure of these attempts, continue their efforts to alter our English.

Baron even blames language cultivators for causing linguistic insecurity in people (1982:228):

> Two major forces in our culture cooperate to produce linguistic insecurity: the ranking of social and geographical dialects as superior and inferior, and an educational system based on the doctrine of correctness and purity in language that invariably conflict with the observable facts of English usage.

I agree with Baron that linguistic insecurity as far as it is caused by the first factor is deplorable. However, to the extent that it is caring about correctness, it is a necessary attitude which has a positive value and is part of the human way of life, namely the wish to be in control of one's own products and actions and to secure the means that are necessary to guarantee a broad recognizability and interpretability of linguistic means of communication and interaction.

Rubin and Jernudd chose as the title of a collection of articles about language planning the question, 'Can language be planned?' (1971) and tried to argue in favour of language planning theoretically and by providing facts against the affronts directed against it.

According to the opinion of purely descriptively oriented linguists, languages and language use can only be described but cannot and should not be valued. They either think that the predicates 'good' and 'bad' cannot be applied to language; or they think that language develops like a natural organism, and then only to the good. But if the latter is doubtful, then it makes sense to interfere, and this implies that language planning is necessary or at least justified.

But as long as the implicit assumption of a kind of teleological development of language, the 'organism'-assumption of an Aristotelian tradition is held up, and the postulate of a pure descriptivism determines the only true method of the science of language, it is not surprising that linguists treat people who are concerned about correctness in language as naive and without linguistic insight. In some specific cases such a negative characterization may be in place, but it should not affect the whole endeavour of language cultivation.

On the other hand, socio-linguists and theoreticians in language planning find linguists naive that adhere to the slogan 'Leave your language alone!': language is not a socially neutral and homogeneous system; it rather is a social institution and as such object and also means of social conflicts; power determines what counts as correct language, with all the consequences that this has for the powerless; as all human works, language can be valued and criticized from functional and ethical points of view; and consequences can be drawn from these valuations. There is no doubt that language can be planned: language *has* always been planned. This planning partly consists in promoting and speeding up, or in slowing down and hindering changes that take place anyway due to several causes (*cf* Ch. 5). Language development and language planning are, like any other socio-cultural change, value laden and value directed (Fishman 1974a:26).

Also from the conservative point of view which conceives of language as a kind of organism which is organized according to a system which again is organized according to a type (*cf* Coseriu 1974, and Ch. 4), the question can arise how good change can be distinguished from less desirable change, were it not that one holds the view that the force of the internal system always directs the change of language in a good direction, *ie* towards a better realization of the internal systematic force. The mistake in this position is that it assumes a single unified force which directs the self-regulation of the system instead of realizing that there are many diverse directions of systematization enacted by the language learner and language user on the linguistic data he receives. This diversity does not add up to a single force of a single system but to an unstable set of partly conflicting system-atizations with some systematizations of second order among the systematizations of first order (*cf* Ch. 5).

Next to these believers in the internal force of a language that make a language take care of itself, there are others with basi-cally the same view who trust this force less and thus want to help language purify itself from outlandish influences and want to assist it against its growing wild due to influences from unculti-vated speakers. These purificationists are influenced by romantic views in which the old stages of a national language are taken to be purer and closer to the true 'essence' of the language; later developments tend to spoil or destroy the essential features. This traditional way of language cultivation, *eg* German *Sprachpflege* and *Sprachkritik*, rests on the conservative view of language as an organism, which has culminated in nationally oriented views according to which one has to save the 'Wesen', *ie* essence, of one's national language from being destroyed. This kind of language cultivation has met a lot of criticism by linguists, *eg* Von Polenz (1968). There is some truth behind this backward orien-tation: it is a meaningful wish that new generations should be able to understand the language of the older, and especially the cultural heritage.

On the other hand, socio-linguists, according to whom language is a social institution, are interested in questions like who determines and influences the norms of this institution in whose favour, and how one can intervene in this institution and its development, not only under systematic and functional aspects but also under ethical and social ones.

Language-planning activities are thus carried out from oppo-site points of view. They are different due to the different assumptions underlying them. Modern theoreticians of language planning, like Das Gupta, Fishman, Rubin, Jernudd, and others, start from the socio-linguistic position.

A third position is basically a technical one. The Prague position of language cultivation takes a functionalistic point of view, which stresses the functionally determined development of different sets of norms, called language varieties and registers or styles. But this perspective does not take not into account the question about how the functionally determined properties of a language relate to the language system which is still understood in the manner of traditional structuralism as one unified system, and it abstracts from the consequences of social and political interests and conflicts for the different varieties, and on the other hand, from the social consequences, which the existence of different varieties has. According to Neustupný (1974a:40), the Prague variant of language cultivation is mainly devoted to written language, *ie* to the norm of one, though distinguished, variety. A point of attention has been the instability and the stability of this norm, caused by the influence of several varieties which come about by functional differentiation according to the needs of adequacy of a language with respect to different aims. Neustupný refers to these insights of, for example Mathesius and Havrànek, with the term 'flexible stability'. Especially the various influences and the language varieties caused by these can, in combination, lead to language problems, which require language planners to intervene by way of correction. According to Neustupný, language planning therefore is part of a more comprehensive activity, namely 'language correction' in details of language use as well as with respect to languages themselves (Neustupný 1978:243*ff*, 258*ff*).

A danger in technically oriented language planning is a certain naivety, which we find, for example, in Tauli (1974) with respect to the question of what improvement of language consists of. He assumes that improvement of a language means to make it a more effective means of communication. Hereby he thinks of language as ideally a perfect and most simple system. This position is not well conceived because effectiveness and perfection are not absolute notions but acquire some content only relative to certain aims. It is absurd to assume that natural languages (could or should) form harmonic and logically perfect systems, or that every form and meaning in a language will be, or has to be, most efficient. Tauli looks at efficiency of language as a tool, without taking into account that the goals for which this tool has to be useful are different ones and therefore put different requirements on it, which can be in conflict with each other. Because of this, efficiency cannot provide a criterion about what is superfluous in language and what should be retained. Tauli is not only naive with respect to the notion of efficiency, but also with respect to systematicity when he claims that the choice of a language or variant under several possible ones can be regulated from linguistic points of view in the following way:

> From the linguistic point of view the best solution would be to choose the linguistically most efficient language, which actually is also the simplest in structure and most easy to learn by speakers of other languages. (Tauli 1974:63)

Not only efficiency, but also systematicity has to be considered from different points of view. What is systematic under one perspective may be unsystematic and even troublesome under another. For example, a language that is perfect from a logical point of view is, just because of its precision and non-ambiguity, very inconvenient and not of much use from other points of view. A natural language cannot be a unified system, nor can it be a perfect tool from one single point of view. Also Ferguson (1977:16) points out that efficiency is not a unified notion, but is determined by different aims; and this is why there have to exist different registers next to each other. Haugen writes against Tauli's conception of language as a tool:

> The ideal qualities with which our two writers wish to endow their languages could hardly be challenged, even when they are in part mutually contradictory. Ray as we have seen, wants efficiency, rationality, and commonality; for definitions of these the reader is referred to his book [ie Ray 1963]. Tauli wants clarity, economy, and beauty;. . . The qualities desired are those that good writers have long cultivated in making choices among alternate modes of expressions in their own languages. Language planning goes farther, however, in proposing the extension of these rules to established patterns and proposed innovations. The writer is not free to follow these principles in order to achieve some ideal rationality or efficiency, say, by making all the strong verbs of English regular. Aside from the fact that he would occasionally be misunderstood and often misjudged, he would be violating a basic principle of communication: the historical stability of code, which corresponds to its synchronic uniformity. Each generation wishes to be able to speak to its juniors as well as its elders. Stability is of the highest value in the written language, which in some degree speaks to eternity. (Haugen 1971:287ff)

In what follows I shall try to answer the question 'What happens to linguistic norms in language planning and language development?' Both the changes in population domains and in situational domains of norms will be considered. Before addressing this topic, the relevant notions of the theory of norms will be repeated for the convenience of the reader.

A *norm concept* is a norm content which conceptualizes the expected regularity, together with the character of the norm. A *norm formulation* is a formulation of a norm concept; a *norm codification* is an official formulation of the norm concept that exists as a norm in one of the ways defined below. Norm *promulgation* is the activity of introducing a norm as valid for a population.

A norm concept can exist in some population *P* in the following ways. It *exists in the narrower sense* as a norm for *P*, if the norm concept regulates a practice in the population. If *P* has an external attitude towards the norm concept, then it exists for *P* merely as a *prescription*. If *P* has internalized the norm concept, *ie* uses it as a guide for behaviour and correction without being forced by external pressure, then it exists for *P* as a real norm.

A norm concept is *accepted* as a norm by *P* if it is accepted as a guide of behaviour in the sense that acts of correction on behalf of it are approved of and wanted.

A norm concept is *adopted* as a norm if it has been accepted by a population and exists for them as a practice.

A norm concept is *valid* as a norm for *P* if the members of *P* are justified in referring to it as the reason for certain behaviour and as the reason for criticizing certain other behaviour. That is, the validity of a norm justifies certain behaviour in an officially accepted way.

A norm concept is *justified* as a norm for a population if it is rational (*ie* goal directed and goal adequate) with respect to a higher norm, value, or goal of the population.

With respect to a population and a norm concept we can thus speak of existence (as a practice), acceptance, adoption, validity, and justification of the norm concept as a norm. In short, we also speak of existence, acceptance, validity, adoption, and justification of a norm with respect to a population.

The domain of people for which a norm exists (as a practice) is called the *domain of existence* of the norm, or in short, *existence domain*.

Likewise, we speak of *acceptance domain, validity domain, adoption domain*, and *justification domain* of a norm in a population.

Next to these domains of people for whom a norm exists in the various ways defined above, there is another type of domain, the domain of situations of use of the norm. This domain is described by the types of situations in which the norm is applicable. It is called the *situational domain* of a norm.

Language planning and language development induce shifts or

changes in the population domains and in the situational domains of linguistic norms.

In accordance with Fishman's (1974a) and Neustupný's (1978) terminology, this chapter will be divided into a part on norms in status planning or language policy, including a part on norms in standardization and one on partial language revival, and a second part about norms in corpus planning, including language elaboration and cultivation. Language standardization and partial revival comprise several aspects of corpus planning, and are in this way bridging the two parts of this chapter.

6.1 Linguistic norms in status planning

Status planning is a part of language policy. Policy with regard to language and communication also comprises activities such as promoting a certain vocabulary that is favourable to an ideology or a political power. On the other hand, planning of the status of a language comprises more activities than merely the policy aspect of deciding which language or which variety of a language should be the national language, or the official language, or one of the official languages for the whole nation or for certain regions or states of the nation, or, generally, which language should be used for which functions. In addition to preparing and taking such political decisions, status planning also involves planning and guiding the process of implementation and planning and performing additional corpus planning, that is, codifying and elaborating the languages chosen. Neustupný's notion of 'language policy', or 'policy approach' (1978:258), also includes these aspects of planning and thus partly overlaps with Fishman's (1974a) notion of 'status planning'. Status planning always includes selecting a language for a special status by which it takes over functions and areas of application where competing languages or language varieties played their role before. These functions thereby will be closed to the competing ones.

A special kind of status planning has the aim to make a certain variety of a language the standard language in opposition to its other varieties. This process of activity is called 'standardization' or 'normalization'.

Making a clear distinction between what is a language and what is merely a language variety is not without problems as is, for example, illustrated with respect to the Chinese situation by de Francis (1972). Mandarin, Cantonese, Hakka, Amoy-Swatow, and Foochow, which are, according to de Francis, different

languages, have been considered as different dialects by patriotically minded Chinese, who applied the criterion of one single
form of writing, corresponding to the political union within one
Chinese nation. The problem in categorizing linguistic varieties
either as languages or as varieties of one language is caused by
the vagueness of the linguistic criteria used, such as common
ancestry (How far back is ancestry considered?), linguistic
analysis (Which features count, and how much are they
considered?), and mutual intelligibility (How many hours or days
or weeks has somebody to be exposed to the other variety or
language in order to, after all, find it intelligible?). Moreover, the
criteria (common ancestry, common linguistic properties, mutual
intelligibility, one single form of writing, political unity or division, and a common literary tradition) together form a cluster
concept: more or less of these criteria can be satisfied, besides
the possibility that different criteria can be fulfilled to different
degrees. Therefore the boundaries between qualifying two sets
of linguistic means as two different languages, or as varieties of
one single language, are vague. Thus, according to de Francis,
the difference between 'independent language' and 'variety or
dialect of a language' is not so much a question of linguistic properties as of recognition. For this recognition a set of linguistic
and political factors are important: they are favourable or unfavourable for the recognition of a set of linguistic means as a
language. Since in addition to their vagueness the factors are also
of different political weight, depending on the political situation,
the decision under cognitive aspects will never be a clear-cut one
in the problematic cases, though a clear political decision can be
achieved.

For our discussion about what happens with languages in
status planning, the attitudinal decision about these matters plays
an even greater role than the linguistic judgement. If a language
is chosen as an official language, this will have a different kind of
effect on the competing languages not chosen than it will if one
variety is chosen to become the standard of a language. Since all
the varieties are understood to belong to a single language, and
this language is now represented by the standard, the other
varieties will be judged as deviant or incorrect with respect to the
standard, and thus the standard will have a strong impact on the
other varieties and the way they are used and modified in the
direction of the standard. On the other hand, borrowing from
other varieties into the standard will be encouraged even by
language purists, because the varieties are native sources of
borrowing. For Hindi, for example, differences in adoption and

in adaptation have been signalled, depending on whether Hindi is used as a standard in the Hindi region itself, or whether it is used as an official language in non-Hindi regions:

> In the region where it [Hindi] spreads as a superstructure, strict adherence is kept to learning the prescribed/accepted norm as far as written form is concerned. The standard spoken form shows dialectal influences in pronunciation as well as in grammar. (Misra 1982:155)
>
> However it is well known that standard Hindi as used, spoken as well as written, in various parts of non-Hindi regions, has developed and/or is developing distinct patterns of deviations. Studies made on Kannada-Hindi, Telugu-Hindi, Tamil-Hindi, and Malayalam-Hindi reveal these patterns. (Misra 1982:156)

With respect to standardization, we shall try to answer the question of what the policy decisions and the political and administrative steps in implementation imply for the norms involved. The same question will be raised with respect to the situation in which one language out of several is chosen for certain functions. What does this decision imply for the norms of the chosen language, and what does it imply for the norms of the languages not chosen? Before that we shall discuss the aspects which play a role in making the choice.

6.1.1 The choice of official and national languages

The two most important factors that influence the choice of a language for certain functions are, among others: What are the population domains of existence of the norms of the competing languages and for which functions are they used, *ie* what are their situational domains? Both questions are specified by the following questions: Is the educational élite or a significant part of it included in the existence domain of a norm? If yes, this is a strong argument in favour of the choice of this norm or set of norms that constitute a language. The educational élite plays such an important role because it is able to provide written texts, educational resources, and carries the scientific, technical, administrative, and military knowledge of a state or nation, and furthermore performs the main functions in the area of law and religion.

Another important point is whether this élite is generally accepted by the population, since hereby also the élite's norms are accepted, so that an upward trend exists in broader domains of the population towards occupations and functions usually fulfilled by the élite. This provides an incentive to accept the language of the élite and to be eager to adopt it. The reason for this attitude is that learning the norms of the élite is justified in order to acquire functions and gain positions reserved for people with that background. Although the existence domain of these linguistic norms may be small to begin with, their justification domain, and based on this, their acceptance domain within the population, is thus fairly large. After some time the adoption of these norms by people from these broader domains will follow if assisted effectively by educational programmes.

In general, the usefulness of the official language will play an essential role for adoption. Myers Scotton (1982) answers the question. 'Why haven't more people in Africa learned the lingua franca which is their nation's official langauge?' by pointing out that the various lingua francas are only acquired by those for whom upward mobility is a real option. Whether or not acquiring a language will be a resource for people 'depends on the societal elements they already control' (1982:87). This implies that if lower-class people have no other resources that will permit them to climb the social ladder, merely acquiring the official language will not do it for them. They rather learn local lingua francas, which are not endorsed in education and which permit them to enter the job market on the lower level as a worker. As an exception she mentions Tanzania, where Swahili is successful because of the socio-economic integration of lower-class people in a socialistic state. Myers Scotton (1982:89) concludes:

> With most African societies marked by minimal socio-economic integration, learning the official languages as a lingua franca – the language of the upper strata of those societies – seems a futile task. For those African political societies depending on such official languages as a vehicle for true political integration, the prospect seems remote.

In multilingual situations where people from very different linguistic backgrounds come into contact and live together, an official language can also play the role of a lingua franca in informal situations. When that happens, spread of the official language is promoted, especially among groups where school education is offered and made use of. Thus Mahmud (1982) writes about the spread of Arabic in southern Sudan:

> Children whose parents come from different ethnolinguistic backgrounds use far more Arabic at home than children whose parents come from the same background. . . . Also their parents' use of Arabic is higher; they use it next to their respective vernaculars. (1982:177)

Also merchants, who mostly come from the north, use more Arabic than people from other occupations; and Arabic is also spoken more in urban than in rural areas. Here, certainly, Arabic performs the role of a lingua franca.

Cooper (1982a:13) points to the dynamics in the spread of a lingua franca, by citing Greenberg: 'As more people learn the language it becomes more useful as a lingua franca, thus encouraging even more people to learn it.'

Sometimes a national or official language receives an indirect support by pidginized versions of it, which serve as lingua francas in contact situations between speakers of different linguistic backgrounds. This usually happens in market-places and in slums of large cities with a linguistically mixed population, coming from different rural areas and without an educational background. Thus, Arabic-based pidgins and creoles are lingua francas in the Juba area of Sudan (Mahmud 1982).

Swahili serves in pidginized versions as a lingua franca in eastern Africa and the Muslim south of the Sahara (Cooper 1982a:22, referring to Mazrui 1971). Because English is preferred by the élite, Swahili standard was adopted only slowly, but many varieties of Swahili are spoken in a vast area of eastern Africa (Whiteley 1969).

Likewise, the lingua franca forms of Hindi have spread widely in India. In various areas we find different varieties of pidgin-Hindi (Misra 1982:156):

> The third and most important form of the language that has spread and is spreading further is the lingua franca form, which is highly contextualized, shows pidginized features, and has more or less exclusively a spoken form. It is learned informally in interpersonal interaction settings, serves the purpose of intercommunication between speakers and users of different languages in metropolitan centres, bazaars, and also industrial centers which draw Pan-Indian populations.

Because of its lingua franca function, Hindi has spread more widely in mixed urban areas than in more homogeneous rural areas. Usually, pidgins become creoles, and orientation towards the matrix or goal language, which in these cases is an official or national language endorsed by educational agencies, leads to a move towards adoption of the official or national language, along the so-called creole continuum (cf 5.1).

Complications arise if several of the competing languages have an educational and economic élite supporting them. Thus, in the 1972 Constitution of the Philippines, Tagalog could not be declared the official language of the nation. It was then the language of about 21 per cent of the population, living mostly in and around Manila. Because of strongly competing language groups, the Constitutional Convention (ConCon) could not expect to get a sufficient vote for declaring Tagalog, straight away, to be the national language. Until a Filipino common language was developed, English and Spanish should be the official languages, and further regional languages should be used in the respective areas, *cf* Sibayan (1974). As a neutral solution, speakers of the other Filipino languages rather saw two foreign languages, with even a colonial history, be the official languages than admitting to the rival Filipino language Tagalog, which should have had the best chance of being chosen. Similarly, south Indians preferred English instead of Hindi as an official language of the nation, after the colonial issue lost its urgency. To appease the competing language groups the Constitutional Convention of the Philippines in 1971 proposed something unworkable, which in fact supported the position of Tagalog:

> A common national language to be known as Filipino shall be evolved, developed and adopted, based on existing native languages and dialects without precluding the assimilation of words from foreign languages. . . . I do not know how this is to be interpreted and carried out but it seems it is the idea of the members of the ConCon that a national language is to be developed by mixing, 'amalgamating', various Philippine languages. . . . It is quite clear that the intention of the ConCon in specifying this provision is to see to it that the 'language interests' of the people speaking the various languages are protected. (Sibayan 1974:249)

This formulation by the Constitutional Convention is compatible with using Tagalog as a base and encouraging borrowing from other minority languages. In fact, Tagalog has become more and more the common language and is on its way to becoming the official language of the Philippines.

Similarly, article 351 of the Indian Constitution says that Hindi, the national language, should be enriched by borrowing from the other Indian languages. This is officially suggested by way of compromise in order to ease tensions and to make the national language more acceptable to non-Hindi speakers by incorporating features of the competing languages into the national language. Indeed, in the various regions Hindi became to some extent influenced by regional languages (see above), but these adaptations were not recognized within Standard Hindi, as the Constitution seems to suggest. These regional versions of Hindi remain non-standard varieties on the transregional level, and as such are evaluated negatively by language purists and educators of Standard Hindi outside the respective regions. From the point of view of promoting the official national language, these regional variants of the standard have a positive value since they bridge the gulf between regional languages and the official national language, making it less strange to people who are required to adopt it. In this way, its acceptability is raised and its acceptance promoted. On the other hand, a central regulation of Standard Hindi is justified to prevent the varieties of Hindi from drifting away too much from each other. What the right policy is in such a case, is not a question of principle but depends on the historical situation: in order to promote the use of Hindi one can first emphasize variation and, later, unity of the standard.

For a language to be acceptable it is very important that people with prestige use it. Haugen (1966b:177) stresses this point as a criterion for acceptability: 'A norm must be adopted or adoptable by the lead of whatever society or subsociety is involved', and he quotes Ray (1963:61): 'there is a subset of users called the *lead*, who are regarded as imitation-worthy and therefore have prestige.' This not only seems to hold for variants within a single language, but also among speakers of competing languages. For example, the adoption of Swahili and its use in culturally important functions has been hindered, among other reasons, by the fact that authors have preferred English, not only in scientific and technical writings, but also in literature:

> There is no sign of any prose literature from the younger generation to match the rise of local writers in English: anthologies of East-African writing appear in English – prose, drama, and verse – but nothing comparable is in sight for Swahili. (Whiteley 1969:126)

And Cooper notes about lingua francas:

> Nothing stops the spread of a lingua franca more surely than the existence of a rival lingua franca. (Cooper 1982a:17)

The same seems to be true of competing official languages, in particular, if the élite uses both official languages, English and the national language, even in personal communication:

> Swahili . . . tends to be used in situations in which the speaker wishes to emphasize solidarity and English in situations in which status differentials are stressed. (Cooper 1982a:17)

The linguistic usage of the élite is as important for enhancing the acceptance of an official language as it is for diminishing acceptance in the opposite type of situation: competing languages that have not received the status of official languages lose ground rapidly when the élite ceases to use them (*cf* Dua 1986; Pattanayak 1977).

The choice of a language as an official language becomes a problem if the élite of the group that speaks this language is not accepted by the population for which this official language is devised. If resistance is strong and propaganda does not work, or the politicians in charge belong to a minority of the élite that resists the élite as a whole and rather works together with the masses, language policy can lead to quite different results: a language spoken by a large portion of the population will be chosen, although the élite does not belong to this portion. This, of course, creates a host of problems, since all cultural and technical knowledge is in the hands and heads of the élite. Such a choice can only be implemented successfully if at least part of the educated élite will cooperate because of ideological reasons.

Also when a language is already chosen as an official language, the political situation may lead to a movement that wants another language to become the official language, namely a language of the masses. This has been the case in Mauritius, where a creole has been codified by its proponents and is pushed by them to become the official language next to French, and finally to replace French. The first step is to get the creole accepted as a language of instruction in primary education and to be able to print text materials and newspapers, cf Hookoomsing (1986). Whether the creole will ever replace French in Mauritius is very doubtful, especially since the development of a post-creole continuum may result in accepting French as the standard anyway. The case of Nynorsk, which will be treated in 6.2, is parallel.

What happens to the norms in the process of implementing the chosen language?

When the decision in favour of a certain language has been made, the following is going to happen:

1. The norms of this language gain validity in a broader domain of the population, competing and coming into conflict with the norms of the other languages existing there.
2. The domain of situations of use, ie the functions of the language, will be specified, depending on whether the language is to become a national language, an official language, or both, or one of the official regional languages.
3. Because it competes with other languages in some of the domains of use, its norms will be strengthened, ie the normative force will be increased by repeated acts of correction and sanctions against non-compliance, whereby these acts are justified by the validity of its norms.

This position of the official language implies that in norm

conflicts its norms come out stronger. The sanctions consist mainly in hindering people advancing socio-economically, because proficiency in the official language is required for all administrative matters and white-collar jobs. Hereby, this language clearly gains dominance.

Since the norms of the official language come to dominate in many areas of usage, the norms of the languages competing in these areas become relatively weaker and recessive. Their normative force diminishes and they gradually lose terrain from their situational domains, and since they thus become less useful, they also lose from their domain of acceptance among the population. People will get into norm conflicts when they no longer accept the norms of their old language for certain functions, and yet are not able to comply with the norms of the new language. Thus, for example, they realize in front of the lawcourt or in dealing with civil servants that the official language is considered appropriate, but, lacking proficiency in it, they have to use their own language, which very likely might affect their case. Appointing an interpreter in such cases means that it is recognized by the officials that the enforcement of justice has the precedence of the enforcement of the official language. It is a question of language policy to take into account these problems in the course of implementation of the official language and to make political decisions to the effect that human rights are not impaired in too high a degree by the enforcement of the official language.

Of course, there has to be some enforcement because otherwise the official language would not be felt to be useful enough to stimulate people to learn it. They have to need it to be willing to adopt it. Here we touch difficult, but urgent ethical problems, *cf* Cobarrubias (1983), and for situations of immigrants, Kloss (1971). Neustupný (n.d.) writes:

> The relationship between language planning and human rights has failed to establish itself as a standard component of discussion in the discipline. It is obvious that any act of language planning seriously affects language rights of members of the community concerned.

I think not only language rights are involved, but also other rights, like rights to justice, schooling, work, etc.

Norms of the official language are not learned if people need not bother about them. This is the case if they have no chance for upward mobility anyway or live in secluded groups that do not approve of contacts with the outside world. Such groups we find, for example, in the slum Dharavi in Bombay (*cf* Rajyashree

1986), where among others groups exist that are very homogeneous in terms of village origin (before they migrated to Bombay), caste, belief, and often even occupation. If an official language or a standard language is not necessary for their job, they do not bother to learn it. This is, of course, a rational attitude under these circumstances. Only people who want to move up socially send their children to school and see to it that at least one family member learns the Marathi standard language (which is the official regional language) in order to be able to keep contacts with the administration and civil servants, and to be able to fill in forms for administrative purposes (Rajyashree 1986).

A similar situation arises when immigrants live together in large numbers. To provide linguistic assistance in all their contacts with the outside world and to provide schooling in their native languages guarantees their language rights and their other basic rights, but at the same time diminishes the incentive to learn the official language of their new country. Except for the first centuries of immigration to North America (*cf* Kloss 1977), generations of immigrants to the United States had no doubt that they had to learn the dominant language, English, as fast as possible, which was usually achieved in the second generation. Due to the rising consciousness about human rights, immigrants in the United States are now in a different position. It is possible to live there in a Spanish-speaking community without any strong need to learn English. The fact that linguistic aids have been provided on a legal basis ('money of the American taxpayer' is used for this purpose) has evoked opposition of patriotically minded Americans, who have urged the government to stop these minority programmes and have introduced a resolution in Congress to the effect that English should be declared the official language of the United States by an amendment to the Constitution. The proposed resolution is S. J. Res. 167, to add the following article to the Constitution:

Article
Sec. 1. The English language shall be the official language of the United States.
Sec. 2. The Congress shall have the power to enforce this article by appropriate legislation.
(*Congressional Record*, Vol. 129, Washington, Wednesday, September 21, 1983. No. 122)

If this article is passed, it will create many conflicts with human rights. But, of course, the United States would not be unique in this. These problems exist all over the world in countries with a culturally and linguistically mixed population.

If an official language is sufficiently enforced to make a need felt to learn it, the competing languages lose more and more parts of their situational domains of use. Accordingly, they also lose part after part of their acceptance domain among the population and hereby their norms get into an accelerating retreat because these two factors increase their effectiveness in combining their momentum. The circle of 'less use causes less acceptance, and less acceptance causes less use' results in a downward spiral of retreat, whereby in the end these norms lose their domain of existence, *ie* these languages become extinguished. The old languages are finally replaced by the new language, the official one.

Intervening political movements, using the emotional adherence to the old language as a symbol of a history of independence or ethnicity, can in some cases stop this recession. If the language is only spoken at home, in in-group communication or in secluded areas, re-establishment of its functions and of use in a broader population will hardly succeed. We know from case studies about language movements that some succeeded and others did not. Misra (1979), for example, gives an analysis of reasons for success and failures of language movements trying to promote regional languages against Hindi in the Hindi region. Next to having a literary tradition and a supporting élite, political reasons are very important. This is also apparent in the way Finnish was established as the national and official language in Finland against Swedish, and it is apparent in language movements against colonial languages, which promoted re-establishing native languages in official functions like, for example, Bahasa Indonesia, Sinhala in Sri Lanka, Urdu in Pakistan, and Hindi in India.

Opposition against Russian power made the ruling Swedish class in Finland look for support from the rural Finnish population. To activate the Finnish people politically, the Finnish language was promoted for official use next to Swedish and instead of Swedish, and thus became an official language and the national language of Finland, which could serve as an official symbol of identification for the Finnish people.

Bahasa Indonesia, based on Malay tribal and bazaar languages, was promoted against Dutch, the language of the colonial power in Indonesia until 1942, which was used as the official language. Japanese occupation power supported Bahasa Indonesia. It was declared the state language of Indonesia in 1945, and English became the first foreign language; *cf* Alisjahbana (1974) and Rubin (1976) for Indonesia, and Omar (1982) for Malaysia, where English was the language of government and administration during the colonial period and until ten years after independence. It was not until 1957 that Malay was enacted and enforced as the medium of instruction and as the official language for government and administrative purposes.

Hindi was first supported as the national and as an official language all over India against English as the language of the colonial power. With the end of colonization the south lost its political motivation against English and opposition arose against Hindi in the southern states of India (*cf* Das Gupta 1976; Apte 1976b).

The same is true of Urdu, the national language of Pakistan, which was first strongly supported against English because of the colonial issue. But after the political opposition against English diminished, East Pakistan opposed Urdu and supported Bengali, which is now the national language of Bangladesh, the former East Pakistan. The language controversy in former East Pakistan became a major political issue that, among other factors, led to the division of Pakistan. Suppressing Bengali in official use, although it was the language of the people of East Pakistan with a long literary tradition and administrative function, made the Bengalis fight the official use of Urdu and caused uprising against the domination by West Pakistan. For a lively report about the issue and an analysis see Musa (1984b). The main argument for trying to implement Urdu in former East Pakistan as well was the establishment of the unity of the nation. History proved that indeed the non-acceptance of Urdu, against the general accept-ance and existence of Bengali in former East Pakistan, promoted the division of the artificial political entity Pakistan. Acceptance of a common language promotes national unity, and non-accept-ance promotes division. It is a matter of speculation whether a possible compliance by Pakistan's government with Bengali as a second national language and as the official language of former East Pakistan would have saved the unity of Pakistan, at least on a federal basis.

Likewise, Sinhala was established as the official language of Sri Lanka against English, the official language under colonial rule. After the colonial issue became irrelevant, movements for Tamil and English could again gain importance, *cf* Musa (1981). Now the government considers proposing Sinhalese, Tamil, and English as three 'national languages' instead of 'Sinhalese only', or Sinhalese and Tamil, to pacify the language controversy (Musa, in personal communication). Proposing and enforcing an official language in situations in which its use is not justified has a negative influence on its acceptability and consequently its acceptance. Musa (in personal communication) pointed out that the implementation of Sinhala as the official language of Sri Lanka could only begin to succeed, when all three languages (Sinhala, Tamil, and English) were each proposed or required only for those situations where their use was justified.

So far I have discussed languages which were re-established in official functions after a period in which they had lost these functions against another official language, the language of a colonial power. In these cases, revival of a language in these functions succeeded.

In general, people are not willing to revive a language they do not need since they have accepted and adopted a new language. Sometimes they might be willing to revive the old language to some extent for use in ritual and folklore contexts. This means for them paying tribute to old values the old language is associated with, and it is generally an expression of ethnic or national identity, especially if this identity is threatened. Mostly people who are not happy with important aspects of the situation they live in fall back on using the old language in ritual settings: turning backwards to a common past, symbolized by the old language, is a sentimental bond that strengthens the solidarity of the group.

It takes an immense effort really to revive an old language that had given way to other systems of norms that were dominant because of economic, political, and military reasons. Modern literature, mass communication, educational agencies, and administrations would have to introduce the old language again. Furthermore, people are only willing to learn this old language if it is very useful for them. (The sentimental reason is a strong enough incentive only for a few.) It could be made useful for them by taking strong measures of enforcement. But these would affect basic rights and would be, at least, troublesome enough to make people resist such a revival of the old language, even in spite of strong political motivation to begin with.

This happened, for example, in Ireland, where patriotic feelings favour the Irish language, which is the national language of the country. However, even in the few rural areas in which it is still spoken, it has lost more ground although there has been an active language movement in favour of Irish. The Irish language cannot be made useful on a broad scale, because people of all social strata resist such measures. English serves them well for all communicative purposes inside and outside the country, and they are aware of the special features of Irish English, which are a means of identification for the Irish people. Especially since Ireland is independent from Great Britain, political motives are not strong enough for replacing a language functioning well in all areas by the old language, which would even have to be reshaped and elaborated to fit modern needs (*cf* Macnamara 1971).

The case of Hebrew seems to be just the opposite of the Irish case. Israel, to my knowledge, is the only country where an old language that for centuries had been restricted to only one function, the religious one (partly including law), has successfully been revived in all other functions of daily life. But, different from the Irish case, there was no common language for all the Jewish settlers, which could function in all situations and could serve well for the whole immigrant population. A lingua franca had to be developed or chosen, and Hebrew was the only language with a history appropriate for the unity of the nation and which did not provide an advantage for any language group of settlers over the others. This language was a perfectly justified choice of language policy. Its domain of justification among the Jews, relative to the common goal of achieving a state, was perfect, *ie* everyone could not but see that the choice was justified by the aim, and was just with regard to treating all Jewish settlers equally. Because of this the people had a perfect motive for the acceptance of Hebrew as the national, and as an official language of Israel. Aided by appropriate language teaching, acceptance of the norms of a language is followed by adoption, its range of use extends, and this extension again supports adoption. In particular if there is no competing language for all purposes, the consequence is an upwards spiral, and not a downwards spiral as in some of the other cases discussed above.

Efforts to elaborate Hebrew in order to meet the needs of modern society supported its extension to new types of situations of use. However, this revival of Hebrew and its extension to new functions are accompanied by an extensive process of modernization, leading to massive loan from English, with English being the second, though unofficial, official language. Because of this, one might (as Musa pointed out in a discussion) speak of a creation of a new language rather than of the revival of an old language, whereby the old language is the basis to be enriched by a modern language, English, which is functioning in the areas of science and technology, and in types of public communication with an international orientation.

The choice and implementation of Hebrew, at first sight, seem to be an exception to the rule that the language of the established élite or educated group has most chance of becoming the official language. But this case does not really refute this generalization because there was no such homogeneous élite and no single language of a prestigious group, when the Jewish settlement in Palestine resulted in founding the state of Israel. Hebrew acquired its prestige not from being the language of a prestigious group of people, but as the language of the forefathers, and the language of God, or at least of the expression of the common faith and tradition. It is the language of the symbols of the identification as a Jew. Therefore, also in this case a prestigious language was chosen, and additionally, it could become a lingua franca that carried no unjust disadvantage or advantage for any group, because it was, with a very few exceptions, nobody's mother tongue. Thus, almost everyone was equal with respect to Hebrew, and for everyone alike it was the symbol of national identity as a Jew. We can conclude that the success of the revival of Hebrew in Israel came as no surprise.

Let us compare with the case of Hebrew the very unrealistic idea of introducing Esperanto as a common official language of the European Community: this language, theoretically, would also not be advantageous or disadvantageous to any particular language group, and it would even have common features with all the European languages. But these factors are by no means sufficient even to consider such a possibility seriously. An implementation of Esperanto will not succeed because it lacks the historical prestige and the cultural background of a supporting 'great' literature, and is no symbol of European identity. In fact, the feeling of a European identity is already lacking, and such a symbol would be without function, even if it could be provided.

Another case of introducing an official language for a whole nation is China. About three-quarters of the population of China speak Mandarin or its dialects. Further, there are the languages Wu, Cantonese, Hakka, Amoy-Swatow and Foochow, which are, according to de Francis (1972:192), as far from Mandarin as is Dutch from English, or French from Spanish or Latin. The written medium, the code of Chinese characters, has played the role of an apparent, though imperfect, common medium of communicaton and a symbol of national unity. With greater mobility, central administration, broadcasting devices, and mass education, the need for a common spoken language and for an, at least partial, alphabetization has grown. The last need has become even stronger with the invention of computers and their use in communication. Considering Mandarin as the standard language and the other languages as its dialects evoked strong opposition, was problematic from linguistic points of view, and was also a great burden for non-Mandarin speakers. Therefore people who favoured a federal form of the Chinese nation sought a compromise, cf de Francis (1972:232): Mandarin should not be considered the Chinese standard language (which would make all other Chinese languages dialects), but it should be the 'common language' (p'u-t'ung hua). 'Thus a kind of "national common language" based on Northern Mandarin has been advanced along with the "regional common languages" of Canton and other areas' (de Francis 1972:234). This carefully balanced position has increased acceptability of Mandarin as the common national language, while next to it regional languages are accepted as languages and not just as dialects. As this compromise has supported the spread of Mandarin in China, the Indian compromise of the 'three-language formula' has enhanced the acceptance of Hindi. It says that Hindi–English–a regional language, often with an additional minority language, is a normal pattern of linguistic usage in India and has to be officially supported. This compromise has been more favourable for the spread of Hindi than a strong enforcement of Hindi would have been since that would have provoked strong opposition (cf Das Gupta 1976a; Apte 1976).

6.1.2 The choice and development of standard languages
This section addresses the question of what happens to the norms of a language in standardization. (It is a somewhat elaborated and improved version of Bartsch 1985b.) Language standardiz- ation involves a shift or change in the populational domains of existence (practice), acceptance, adoption, validity, and justifi- cation of the variety of a language that is chosen, or constructed, or that evolves as the standard of that language. (The language as a whole is a cluster of related varieties.) The same is true of the non-standard varieties of that language, though with an opposite effect. The situational domains of the norms of the stan- dard variety and those of the norms of the non-standard varieties change likewise in an opposite direction. Both kinds of shift, the ones in the situational domains and the ones in the populational domains, reinforce each other. In the process of standardization the cluster of related varieties is restructured such that a differ- ence between language (as a standard language) and dialects is established as an opposition that is socially determined. This social opposition has linguistic consequences.

In the following subsections these aspects will be investigated, discussed, and occasionally also evaluated. In particular, the topics will be the conditions under which standardization comes about, the role it plays in a population, whether it is a normative point of orientation or rather a range of certain kinds of language usage, what happens to the norms of the varieties involved in standardization, and whether a classical language, *ie* an earlier stage of the language for which literature of high value and prestige is the model, can be the basis of a standard language.

6.1.2.(1) Standardization and the role of the standard

Standardization can be developed in different areas of language. It comes about when language diversity is felt to be troublesome (Rubin 1976). Diversity is adverse when centralization and mobility are aimed at. This is the case when national states are formed of formerly independent tribes or states, and when mass media and mass communication, in particular printing, and recently the use of computers, require some uniformity in order to be effective and cheap. The choice of a common official language and its standardization promote the formation of central political power because linguistic unity makes people more easily controllable and available for mobilization, be it industrial, political, or military. A standard language is in the interest of people to the extent that they prefer broader areas for cultural activities, arts, sports, travelling, and generally for employment.

Standardization is a selection of one form or variety out of a number of existing ones, or a construction out of different varieties with a fixed amount of variants included. It further implies accepting, applying, and proposing the norms of the selected or constructed variety for a certain domain of situations of language use and for a population which has used different forms and varieties before.

To prevent the standard from being inelastic, at least a second-order regulation of a procedure by which new forms can be included and old forms can be cancelled belongs to the institutionalization of a standard. For a language this second-order aspect of standardization is taken care of by national linguistic institutes and organizations that provide the codifications of the standard, for example, a lexicon which is renewed regularly.

Rubin (1976:158) mentions the following aspects of the standardization process:

1. A reference point or system is set up or comes into being, *ie* a norm is isolated.
2. Value is assigned to the reference point or system, *ie* a judgement is passed by some significant group of people that it is 'good' or 'correct' or 'preferred' or 'appropriate'.

3. Specification is made or comes into being regarding when and for what purpose the norm is to be used.

Furthermore, agreement has to occur with regard to these points that they should serve as a basis for comparison in judging language behaviour, and this process has to be in effect for some time.

Standardization can be developed in the following areas of language:

1. A variety of a language can be selected or constructed as the standard language.
2. Pronunciation can be normalized, usually in connection with (1).
3. Spelling can be normalized for a written language.
4. A dictionary can be set up in which semantic norms are explicated and fixed to some degree.
5. Technical and scientific vocabulary can be standardized.
6. Registers, ie language use for certain situations and purposes can be standardized, for example the format, beginning, closure, and, generally, the style of certain types of texts, eg letters.

There is quite an amount of literature on the topic of standardization; cf the bibliography of Subbayya (1980), and for technical language use, Beier (1960).

Usually, standardization takes place together with literalization, ie with developing a written language, or after different written varieties of a language have been developed, and printing techniques have been invented in order to achieve a broad distribution of the literary works. This makes unification desirable against the high costs of diversity. However, a connection with literacy is not necessary for standardization to occur. Subbayya (1980:14) mentions that 'Amharic and Somali, two African languages, show a great deal of standardization in spoken form but very little uniformity in orthography. This may be so because these languages are already standardized on the spoken level while they have been put to writing recently.' Also in India, 'in the case of the Sema language spoken in Nagaland, Zhunoboto is treated as standard among six varieties. The reasons for the choice are the central location and military leadership of that group' (Subbayya 1980:14).

According to Subbayya, standards can evolve naturally in the course of history or can be planned by language-planning agencies. Certain factors contribute to both, the emergence of a standard and the successful implementation of a proposed standard.

Favourable for a variety becoming standard are the following factors:

1. The variety is spoken by a prestigious group, whereby prestige is defined in terms of political or economic power and education.

2. The variety has a history of literacy, especially literature written by 'great authors'.

3. The variety is located in an area in which several varieties of the language come into contact and therefore borrow from each other and assimilate. This can be an area that is located centrally or that has been inhabited by immigrants from various regions with different varieties of the language or that is central from the economic and political point of view as a centre for trade and political power, which implies that people from all parts of the country come here, and civil servants and merchants move from here to other parts of the country to deal, administer, and control.

In standardization always at least one of these factors obtains, but often several contribute to the development of the standard. In cases where proposed standards were not successful, none of these conditions was really fulfilled, or competing standards existed which were equally strong by fulfilling one or more of the conditions. As an example, let us consider the Norwegian case (cf Haugen 1966a, 1968), which is in the meantime merely of historical interest.

Bokmål, the Norwegian standard based on Danish, the language that had been used under Danish rule and influence, and the language variety of the majority of the upper-middle class and of the literature of the educated class generally, had the advantage of fulfilling conditions (1) and (2). Nevertheless, it had the disadvantage of being closely related to the language of a former foreign ruler or oppressor, which is negative from a patriotic point of view. An additional disadvantage for Bokmål was that a situation obtained which caused a reversal of condition (1). This can happen under certain political constellations: if there is a strong socialist movement favouring equality and equal opportunity for all people, and solidarity develops among working, rural, and underprivileged classes with sufficient support by part of the educated class, then a variety spoken by the élite groups (which under other political conditions have prestige) will be opposed by the masses and even more by their leaders. The new measure of prestige is what is of the people; 'people' or 'folk' has become a term loaded with positive value.

The two drawbacks of Bokmål in this political situation were enough to call its justification, and hereby also its validity, into question. For many progressively minded people of the educated class the acceptance of Bokmål had diminished, although it existed for them as their linguistic practice. But it was a practice they did not really approve of for political reasons. Thus some linguists, teachers, and politicians began to devise a new standard, Nynorsk, which comprises features of several varieties spoken in East Norwegian rural areas. In principle it follows the folk language Landsmål that had been constructed from several West Norwegian dialects in the second half of the nineteenth century in reaction against the urban colloquial standard related to Danish and normalized for writing as the official state's language, Riksmål, the predecessor of Bokmål. Landsmål had been used as a written language with official support in rural primary schools. Landsmål and its follower Nynorsk fulfilled conditions under (3), namely that they had features which made them germane to a whole range of varieties, West Norwegian dialects for Landsmål and, in addition, East Norwegian dialects for Nynorsk. However, it was a constructed variety, and people who favoured it made great efforts in order to implement it by writing books, newspapers, and teaching materials in this language, and by spreading these products. Socialistically oriented parties and government, as well as teachers, tried to promote the use of Nynorsk, which could be considered to be the written pendant of a cluster of regional varieties spoken by the people. The prestige of Nynorsk was that it was considered to be the written language of the people. This of course was only theoretically so, since, in fact, only the spoken language in all its diversity was of the people and the written version was a construct of generations of well-intentioned linguists. Despite all these efforts and governmental support, implementation of Nynorsk was not successful outside rural areas because it lacked support from large parts of the educated group and it lacked the history of great literature.

After years of competition the two conflicting standards began to show some tendency to merge, with regard to written language more in favour of Bokmål, which in fact was enriched by a few variants and became more liberal in the use of some stylistic devices typical for Nynorsk, while the spoken standard language became more influenced by the different vernaculars and in this way acquired features of Nynorsk. This vernacularization became more acceptable than it had been before. But note that the same was true also of other Western European countries where, with the student movements in the late 1960s, features marked for lower social class and everyday language became acceptable in the spoken standard language used in university seminars, public discussions, and radio commentaries. These features were an indication of showing solidarity with the 'people'. As a whole, Bokmål has been the stronger norm, even in spoken language on the radio and in formal public speeches. According to Jernudd, the question has become largely an academic dispute. Those people who advocated Nynorsk also mastered Bokmål, and thus the reason for the controversy was something other than real communication problems: ideological differences and socio-political matters have partly been fought out on the battleground of language (Jernudd 1971). In the last decade, serious efforts have been made to decide about matters of standardization by seeking to neutralize the old controversy between the two standards. The situation basically is now as Haugen (1968:685) had predicted: the colloquial standard that has been the back-up of Bokmål has moved somewhat towards the 'people's language' and in this form supports the Bokmål of today that, hereby, shows some concessions towards Nynorsk. But note that a similar course of more tolerance with respect to vernacular forms has also been taken by other European nations, although they did not have two competing written standards.

We shall now consider a few examples that show how the three factors mentioned above contribute to the development or to the successful implementation of a standard.

Firstly, we shall look at the standardization of Marathi, as it has been described by Subbayya (1980). Marathi is a language of the Aryan group, spoken as the main language in the Indian state of Maharashtra, and has been the official regional language of that state since 1956. Conditions (1) and (3) contributed to the successful implementation of Standard Marathi in the nineteenth century. Although several varieties of the Marathi language had a long tradition of written literature and thus fulfilled condition (2), Poona as the centre of political power under British rule became the source of the Marathi standard, devised by the director of education, Major Candy, and his staff. The language of the educated people of Poona was chosen as the standard, which then was implemented by a whole new literature, consisting first of translations from English, textbooks for schools, newspapers, and, after a while, original literature. This language, devised for the whole state of Maharashtra, met opposition from scholars, linguists, and journalists from other parts of the state, who could point out that their varieties had a long literary tradition, which had not been taken into account by the British and those who propagated the new standard. An influential opponent was the linguist Dadoba, who wrote a grammar of Marathi, by which he managed to introduce variations into the standard, originating from non-Poona varieties. He and his group published a lot of texts, which were not subsidized by the government, but by which they nevertheless managed to introduce variations that were accepted by the educated population of Maharashtra, and partly ultimately even by the planners of the standard, including Major Candy. With the rise of Bombay as the economically strongest city in the late nineteenth century, many variants from the Bombay variety of educated Marathi were included in Standard Marathi. Thus it became the variety of Marathi spoken by the educated people of Poona–Bombay.

The origin of the German standard language is an illustration of the influence of factor (3) in its beginning. Later factors (2) and (1) were responsible for its change, as well as its further stabilization, up to its present shape. (For details of the history of German see von Polenz 1970.)

Although there was a literary tradition in several northern and southern varieties of German, the middle-eastern German region became the area of origin and further development of Standard German. In the area, Thuringia and Upper Saxony, Luther worked on his Bible translation around 1520. It was based on several linguistic sources: his ideolect formed in this area, the accepted *Kanzlei-Sprache* of the Wettin chancellery with its centre in Meißen and a literature of sermons, writings by the Mystics, and older translations of the Bible, and it was also based on what Luther called "*den Leuten aufs Maul schauen*" ('to listen to how the people talk').

The area of Thuringia and Upper Saxony was not only located centrally within Germany, it was also an area through which, for centuries, streams of migrants had passed on their way to the east, where they settled in Silesia, Pomerania, and West and East Prussia. Many of the migrants from southern and western German states stayed on their way, and many got stranded in the towns of middle-eastern Germany. This town-language was favourable for the spread of Luther's translation of the Bible because, in this way, Luther's language is not founded on a single local dialect, but on a lingua franca based on many dialects from several parts of Germany, due to the migration movements. As the written language of the educated group in the area of Thuringia and Upper Saxony, Luther's language was oriented towards the norm of the Meißen chancellery (*cf* von Polenz 1970: 87–93).

A translation of the Bible into any of the traditional German dialects would not have gathered such a widely spread success because the base would not have contained enough features to make it linguistically acceptable in a wider area. Newly developed printing techniques and the Protestant opinion that the individual should have personal access to *the book*, *ie* the Bible, supported the spread of the variety used by Luther throughout all of Protestant Germany. Similar varieties arose as lingua francas in the towns of East Germany, which were founded by the Hansa, a northern German trade organization, and the 'Deutsche Ritterorden'. These towns were settled by streams of immigrants from all German states, among them in the sixteenth and seventeenth century many Protestants who had to leave southern and western German states where Catholicism had won the battle about souls and political power. The Bible played a central role in Protestant education and literacy of the masses, being the only book they owned and read. It was the model for the common language that was developed in the immigration cities of the east: Königsberg (East Prussia), Danzig (West Prussia), and Stettin (Pomerania). Here, the northern dialects of the first immigration waves, the southern and western varieties of the later immigration waves, and the written standard provided by the Bible as the model shaped the varieties of the lingua francas of former East Germany. In rural areas, other than in urban ones, the Bible remained the only model of high-standard written language until about 1914. In the cities, in the meantime, the influence of high literature had shaped the written standard and the colloquial standard of the upper classes.

In the centuries after Luther's translation of the Bible the importance of factor (2) is shown by the fact that the German literary language, and with it the standard, was further shaped by literary activities, with its centre again in middle-eastern Germany, branching out to the eastern parts: first there was Silesia in the seventeenth century with its great baroque literature, and then Leipzig in Upper Saxony with Gottsched's *Deutsche Sprachkunst* (1748) as a major contribution to the stabilization of the German written language (Blackhall 1966:102*ff*), further East Prussia in the eighteenth century with its philosophy and literature of the Enlightenment, *eg* Kant and Herder in Königsberg, and then Berlin, Leipzig, Jena, Weimar with the great authors of the eighteenth and nineteenth centuries, like Lessing, Goethe, Schiller as the classic, and von Humboldt, Schlegel, Brentano, Novalis as the romantic authors. The literary language reshaped the German standard. Bible-German was left behind as old-fashioned, but still played the major role in rural and lower-class education and literacy. The educated and urban class used the great authors of the eighteenth and nineteenth centuries as models in secondary schools and university education. The fact that the language of the great authors has been the model for educated people in Germany has been the main factor in stabilizing the German standard language within the population who had accepted the language of the prestigious group as their model for 'correct' and 'good', *ie* Standard German ('*Hochdeutsch*'). Thus, in the long run all three factors that support the promotion of a standard have been effective in the history of Standard German.

In the literature about standardization a standard has been identified among other varieties by the following criteria (*cf* Subbayya 1980:31).

1. The attitude of people towards it; it consists in attributing to it the properties 'spoken by the educated', 'good', 'pure', 'soft', 'melodious', 'like in the city', and in the Indian case quoted 'like a Brahmin';
2. Functional factors, namely by its being used in education, administration, trade, and at home by the educated class;
3. Linguistic features, such as the occurrence of unassimilated loan words, which lead to a larger phonemic inventory.

Historically, there is a hierarchy among these criteria: (1) and (2) are a prerequisite for being able to abstract the linguistic features that define a given standard. After having been identified as the features of the standard, the linguistic features may then serve for identifying standard usage in all kinds of situations by all kinds of people. In Marathi such a feature is the passive construction, borrowed from English. Furthermore, Sanskrit loans and, generally, Sanskritization are the features of highly formal (written) standard Indian languages. They can be found, for example, in the Marathi of leading newspapers and in formal speeches. Also English loans, which carry the prestige of belonging to the educated class, are indicators of standard speech as it is used in less formal situations, often by the young educated generation. In German, we find words of Latin origin as an indicator for the use of Standard German in formal situations and also words of French and English origin, the latter mainly with the younger generation and, like in India, in less formal situations. In Dutch we find Latin, French, and English words, and unintended Germanisms in language use that is accepted as standard. It is precisely the unassimilated loans that are an indicator of educated speech.

Subbayya (1980) has shown that Standard Marathi permits quite a range of variation according to specific factors of the situation of language use. With respect to each functional domain, be it education, news media, trade, language use at home and among friends, there is always a range of variations accepted as standard speech, depending on differentiating factors. With respect to education these are: lecture style, seminar style, generally the style of university and good high-school education, the styles of good city education, of rural education, and of slum education in primary schools. With respect to mass media these are: the styles of great newspapers, minor newspapers, and local newspapers, radio programmes for educated people and state broadcasting, local radio, radio programmes for the youth, radio programmes for housewives in urban or in rural areas. And with respect to trade these are: styles of linguistic usage in highbrow shopping centres, in supermarkets, in local shops and bazaars. In all these areas, standard language will be used on all or some occasions. According to the special needs of the situation, varieties are used that clearly are accepted as standard, or as 'still standard', and some varieties are what Subbayya calls 'approximate standard', a compromise between standard and vernacular, according to the requirements of the situation. The relevant aspects of a situation in this regard are: the education of the hearer or the audience, the formality of the topic, and the distance or solidarity between the partners in communication. In this way, the standard language has a range of flexibility in it, by which it is adapted to various needs, even within the areas of major functions mentioned above.

I shall now discuss the main topics of this section, namely what standardization amounts to in terms of norms and their properties. In particular, I want to attend to what happens to the norms that are singled out as the norms of the standard variety. I shall investigate further what happens to the norms of the varieties that are not selected to become the standard, and what kind of interaction takes place in the range that can be determined empirically as the standard by enquiring about attitudes, functions, and linguistic features with respect to linguistic usage, as had been done for Marathi in Rajyashree's dissertation, *ie* in Subbayya (1980). The last point will be treated first.

6.1.2.(2) Standard as a 'range' or as a 'point'?

From an empirical point of view, the standard is a range, namely a set of linguistic means and situations of their use, including a lot of variation recognized and accepted as standard by the population and by language specialists. The criteria used by Subbayya (1980) for the identification of a standard language, namely attitudes (determined by evaluation tests), functions, and linguistic features, have identified such a range of Standard Marathi.

From a normative point of view, the standard has rather been considered as a point, *ie* a single variety with no variation between forms.

These two points of view can be reconciled by seeing the range as being structured from an imagined point of reference, or an ultimate model. Methodologically, I shall distinguish the prescriptive standard as a normative concept of language planners, from the empirical standard as a descriptive concept of socio-linguistics. The prescriptive standard has an empirical reality as far as it plays a role as the ultimate model towards which the submodels for the standard linguistic usage are oriented. It is identified by linguistic experts, but it is more a construct or something postulated than something real. However, there are people in the speech community who are considered to be pretty close to it and are therefore its models. When people were asked who, according to them, was a model of correct speech, a hierarchy became apparent: in their answer people referred to others whom they considered models and who were closer to the prescriptive standard than they themselves were. When these models were then asked the same question they pointed to somebody they thought to be even closer to the prescriptive standard than they themselves (Rajyashree, personal communication, on the basis of her research enquiries). The hierarchy has an empirical reality in the opinions of people as a hierarchy of normative strength. It became apparent because Rajyashree (= Subbayya 1980) distinguished in her attitude tests the evaluation of the norms by experts from the evaluation by the educated group and the evaluation by the masses.

With respect to German pronunciation we also find such a structure in the range of the standard. The received pronunciation of German has been codified in Siebs's *Deutsche Hochsprache. Bühnenaussprache* (1898/1961 and in Siebs 1969). This codification has been a guideline for speech on theatrical stages throughout Germany and has been used in speech education at theatre schools, where not only actors, but also television- and radio-speakers receive their training, as well as the actors who synchronize foreign movies. Further on, Siebs was used in teacher training. I remember that a practical course of German pronunciation and speech based on Siebs was part of the Curriculum of German language and literature, when I took that course in 1961 at the university of Marburg. A similar role is played by English 'received pronunciation'. Although this normative standard has hardly ever been met perfectly, it still serves as a guideline for all those people who function as public models of standard language pronunciation on stage and screen, in broadcasting, and in schools.

In fact, there is quite a latitude in what counts as standard pronunciation of German or English in the different regions and is also accepted as such in educated speech across the whole population for which the standard is valid. This range is, in the terminology used here, the empirical standard of pronunciation of the respective language. This fact does not affect the claim that those people speak the 'best' German, or whatever language, whose speech is a standard speech that carries hardly any regional features, *ie* features that are typical for some regions but not for others. These speakers come closest to the normative idea on which the whole concept of a 'standard' is based, namely that there is one single measure that provides unity against diversity.

Something similar is true of grammar and lexicon. As soon as a language becomes codified (and that means a guideline is set out for further usage, especially for language learners), a prescriptive standard is selected within the range of the empirical standard. Usually, certain alternatives are noted as 'regional' or as belonging to a special social group or to a certain register, as, for example, is done in the German Duden Grammar and Duden Dictionary. Often the question is not decided, or the answer remains vague as to which of the alternatives belong to the standard as accepted and unmarked for the whole linguistic area, which belong to regionally accepted standards and are felt to be marked relatively to the whole area, and which are clearly non-standard under any of these judgements about what the standard language is. If a form is not marked in a codification, it is supposed to be valid for the whole linguistic area and users of the codification, for example, the grammar or the lexicon, should be able to rely on this. A codification should contain the overall, *ie* regionally unmarked, features of the standard language and the regionally marked ones that are part of the standard spoken and written in fairly broad regions, and these forms should be marked for regionality. It should not contain non-standard forms.

Not only with respect to different regions, but also with

respect to different functions, the judgement of what counts as standard usage in these functions can vary. With regard to the main functions of a standard we can, according to Subbayya (1980), speak of a range of linguistic usage acceptable as standard to a higher or lower degree, depending on the extent of vernacularization due to the special situation of use. Vernacularization does not only apply to purely linguistic features, but also to standard text features of the register, for example, in the amount of repetition, the use of examples, the type of vocabulary. In this way, there is a difference between a juridical and administrative style when used among specialists in the field and when used in communication with non-specialists. A standardization can be efficient only if it is sufficiently flexible in linguistic forms and stylistic means with respect to different parameters in the situation of use.

An example to illustrate this point is given by Srivastava *et al.* (1978), cited in Subbayya (1980:16): 'a health-manual prepared in a highly standardized variety of Hindi, which is the most efficient code among the élite, with the precision of meaning. But when these manuals were used for the purpose for which they were prepared, they proved to be inefficient, as the language could not convey the message.' Thus a flexibility is necessary within the standard, which Srivastava calls 'vernacularization'. An equilibrium between stability and flexibility had also been proposed by the Prague School, *eg* by Havrànek (1958). This flexibility guarantees that the standard can fulfil all communicative needs, and therefore ultimately contributes to its stability in the way of securing its further (practical) existence.

In accordance with the empirical work on identifying the standard of Marathi, we can represent the situation in the following way: for every function of language there are higher and lower varieties of the standard language, which are still identified as belonging to the standard. Below these, there are non-standard varieties, and above the acceptable standard there are hypercorrect versions of the standard, mainly produced by people who acquire the standard in secondary socialization (*ie* in school) or later in life and who overestimate the requirement of the use of the high standard forms in situations where they are not really adequate. The civil servant in Srivastava's example used the standard hypercorrectly with respect to the requirements of the situation. This notion of hypercorrectness, used by Subbayya (1980), is an extension of the parallel notion we know from phonology, where it means that non-standard speakers who want to speak standard over-generalize the use of phonemes that have to replace, from their point of view, typical non-standard phonemes in order to make the corresponding words of the standard.

I shall now argue that a normative standard is necessary as a distinguished part of the empirical standard. All language usage within the range of the empirical standard can serve as a model. People who judge it to be standard mean that it can serve as a model of linguistic usage. But these models themselves must be oriented towards a higher model because otherwise the range of the acceptable standard would grow repeatedly broader and would ultimately become a full range of language varieties, a situation contrary to what the standard is designed for. It is essential for the standard that it just overcome such diversity for the purpose of large-scale communication. This argument will be worked out in the following paragraphs.

If there were merely a range of standard varieties that are close enough to each other in order to facilitate mutual understandability and to count as **the** standard varieties of the language (which implies that they could be model), no degree of normality would be defined: new varieties and new forms, developed by children and newcomers, that are pretty close to one of the standard forms would also count as standard, and others pretty close to those would also count as standard. In this way, varieties would be developed at the opposite outer ends of the spectrum of linguistic usage that would be mutually incomprehensible or at least difficult to understand, but would still be standard. Such a situation obtains with regard to the range of dialects of a language, where the dialects from the opposite outer ends are mutually incomprehensible, as, for example, Bavarian and Lower Saxonian. This now is just what is to be prevented by the standard. The standard should be understandable for the whole population and, in particular, for all standard speakers. The following schema represents this adverse development:

$$(. .(. .(. . .). .). .)$$
$$\longleftarrow \qquad\qquad\qquad \longrightarrow$$

However, if there is a central orientation for the whole standard range, then the linguistic usage at the outer ends would be less acceptable as a model than the usage closer to the centre, and what deviates from the outer ends by being even further peripheral will be far less acceptable as a standard or model of a norm. Thus, there must be a decreasing value of normality or standardness towards the periphery. This way, we have a hierarchy of strength of the models, being great in the centre and weak at the periphery. The strength or weakness implies that correction takes place in one direction: the strong models over-rule the weaker ones, except if the situation requires some degree of vernacularization in order to guarantee the efficiency of language use. Therefore we can assume the following centrally oriented structure of degrees of standardness: a normative centre, the normative standard, is assumed as a point of orien-tation of corrective behaviour:

$$(. \ .(. \ .(. \ . \ .). \ .). \ .)$$
⟶   ⟵

In cases of doubt, similarity to forms or styles in the middle decides about correctness, and less so similarity to forms and styles that are more peripheral within the standard range. Codification, especially in dictionaries, grammar books, and style manuals, serve as centre models, which are also available to people who have little occasion to deal with language users who can serve as centre models. As far as the attitude of speakers is concerned, the range fo what they find acceptable as standard, and what not, will depend much on where in the scale the speaker is located himself: people in the centre will very likely accept a smaller range, people from the periphery will accept a broader range, which is at least as broad as to include the centre (and preferably also themselves).

The methodological distinction between the descriptive or empirical standard that fills the whole range and the prescriptive or normative standard that fills the imaginary centre point has an empirical reality, namely the reference to higher models by speakers and, in many cases, a codification of the standard that is made to fill the centre of the scale. Even children who in their primary socialization (*ie* at home) have acquired the standard language from their parents and educators may be corrected later in life by teachers of secondary schools and in language training at universities and theatre schools.

I now want to discuss what happens to the norms of a variety in standardization; firstly, what happens to the norms of the variety that becomes the standard and, secondly, what happens to the norms of the other varieties.

6.1.2.(3) *The norms of the standard*
When a variety becomes a standard, its norms are not just norms of the population for which they have already existed, *ie* for the population that speaks the variety anyway. Its norms will now be

considered to be valid for a much broader population who has spoken, and still speaks, their own varieties of the language. These norms are thus contrasted as valid norms in a whole range of functions with those norms that exist for this broader population and are from then on no more valid in these functions.

Sometimes the standard is used for new functions which had not been developed for the other varieties. Then the situation is less problematic: with new functions comes a new language, for example, with the introduction of literacy and its use in administration comes a new language variety. There is then no conflict with competing norms within this register, although the population that did not carry the standard variety as their language has more difficulties in acquiring the new register than the people for whom the standard existed as their primarily acquired language. From this point of view, introducing a standard language together with literacy is likely to create fewer conflicts than introducing it when other norms had sufficed up to then for the very same functions.

Applying this consideration to language teaching one would expect that children speaking dialect will experience fewer conflicts when learning the standard language together with writing, rather than after first having learned how to write in their own dialect. When they have already used the written dialect for several purposes, they then have afterwards to acquire a competing system in the same domains of usage. This surely leads to norm conflicts. But there seem to be other points of view which rather imply letting children acquire literacy first in their own dialect. Arguments for this option have to do with accepting and promoting the value of a dialect, with the integration of writing into the emotional life of a child as a technique for the expression of feelings, and with using the partial correspondence between the script and the phonological properties of the dialect in the teaching and learning process. The last argument implies that the written code is seen as a means of representation of the spoken language and that therefore to start out from the spoken language would promote learning how to write. This is a widely held view, for example in Ibrahim (1983), who argues for creating a new Arabic written language based on spoken Arabic, because this would help to overcome the illiteracy of the masses. But it is only partly true that the written code is a representation of spoken language because, necessarily and not just by tradition, written language has other properties than spoken language, due to the different medium and different functions it performs.

In the process of standardization the domains of validity of the norms of the chosen variety are extended within the population, and norm conflicts arise between them and the norms of the other varieties that exist in that domain. Validity supersedes existence, at least for the typical functions of a standard language, *ie* in the situational validity domain of the standard. This power of overruling is constituted by the fact that correction directed towards those who do not comply with the standard in these situations is justified officially by the standard's validity. The normative force of the norms of the standard variety is strengthened by acts of correction and official criticism, as well as by negative sanctions on non-standard usage.

A second important point is that the norm contents of the standard variety usually become codified, *ie* formulated officially and explicitly in manuals, grammar books, etc., next to an extensive availability of models for these norms in the form of written literature, officially approved of, and by radio broadcasting and teaching. The explicit formulation of the norms and the explicit indication of approval of models, as, for example, by the ministries of education of the German states, are stabilizing factors. Therefore these norms are more resistant to change than the norms of other varieties. This is only partly true, though, because the standard variety, by its broader spread over different regions, is more susceptible to the influences from different regional varieties, and because of its use in many functions, it is more susceptible to the influence of different registers that develop with changing communicative needs. The local varieties, and also the functional varieties, are less influenced by other varieties as long as they are self-contained and secluded, *ie* have not much contact with other varieties.

The Mennonites in Canada and the United States, for example, show the effect of seclusion in special registers, namely in communication at home and in religious and ritual language usage. Enninger (1979a, b; 1984) reports how the three languages of the 'Pennsylvania Dutch', namely Amish High German (AHG), the religious language, American English (AE), and Pennsylvania German (PG) are used in different functions and form. Between them exists a hierarchy of prestige, in the above order. The norms of the religiously bound AHG, and the ones of AE, are stronger than those of the dialect PG and therefore influence it considerably. This is the case because for PG there is no strict notion of correctness, since, as a dialect, it has no fixed norms of correctness (Enninger 1984:236). The dialect PG has only an occasional influence on the AE of the Amish on the phonological level: the Amish transfer German final devoicing of stops on to the AE (Enninger 1984:45). On the other hand, English words are borrowed into the PG on a large scale, and there are also trends of structural adaptation of the PG to the AE, as far as word order in main clauses is concerned. The AHG is secluded on two accounts: the religious function is clearly separated from other functions, which implies that the situational domain of AHG shows no overlap with situational domains of other norms, and the population domain of AHG is clearly separated from others, *ie* the Amish avoid contact with other groups.

The standard variety becomes rigidly normalized by codification. Some alternatives may be accidentally excluded by being overlooked. But they also may not be codified due to being disapproved of by the codifiers. This can happen for different reasons, because of social stigmatization or because these forms seems typically local and would mess up the 'neutrality' of the standard, and thus hinder its general acceptance. These two points of view are justified: transregional and transsocial neutrality are in principle essential for a standard, as is its general acceptability. That there is one point of view from which the standard is not neutral in these two respects has repeatedly been discussed in this book: it is the language of an educational élite and with that usually also favours the region where major parts of this élite live. The neutrality is thus only achieved with regard to the various non-standard varieties, *ie* the varieties spoken by people that do not belong to the leading or educated classes and that do not live in the areas which are the centres of political, economic, and cultural power.

Since the norms of the standard variety are the norms of the educated group and prestigious authors are the well-known models, they have attached to them a value that goes beyond the value they have as an effective means of broad-scale communication. An aesthetic value is attributed to them: linguistic usage conforming to the standard variety is 'good', 'pure', 'melodious', 'sweet', although there might not be any objective base for the assignment of these attributes. Rather they are carried over from the prestige of the great authors as exponents of cultural identity of the educated class and from the so-called 'finer' manners of the prestige of the great authors as exponents of the cultural ident-ity of the educated class and from the so-called 'finer' manners of demonstratively under the observing eye of the outside world, and also as a means of identification and solidarity among them-selves, in distinction to other groups. Norms of demeanour (other than norms of deference) are a marker of a group or class in

opposition to others, which serves for the identification as a
member of the class that complies with these norms (cf Goffman
1967). Note that this class is not something naturally given or
something of purely economic kind, but, since norms can be
acquired, people have the freedom of defining themselves as
belonging to that class provided they are really able to adopt the
norms. There is to some extent freedom of choice in identifying
oneself as belonging to one group or the other. These values are
assigned conventionally, possibly without an objective base.
Therefore they are not really descriptive terms, but emotional
and evaluative ones with a persuasive function. They are propagated by the educated class as part of its image.

In addition to its aesthetic value the standard language
acquires the value of an identity symbol for the whole population, nation, or state. It is a symbol that some part of the population carries better than the other parts. In this way people come
to consider it a more true and pure representation of national or
state identity than their own regional or social varieties of the
language.

Language purists and entire puristic movements try to keep
this symbol of national- or group-identity free from outside influences. They try to open native sources for lexical elaboration
(preferably from earlier stages of the language and not from
'vulgar' regional or social varieties) instead of non-native
resources. Even a classic language, though it has some prestige,
can be banned as a source, if it is not an ancestor of one's own
language, but rather one of a competing group of languages; see,
for example, Annamalai (1979a) about the purists' movement
that wants to free Tamil from Sanskrit loans. Usually purists do
not succeed for two reasons: firstly, the educated class prefers to
borrow foreign words not only because they are useful in
communication but also because they serve as an indicator of
broadmindedness and acquaintance with other cultures and
modern civilization. In general the élite tends to be internationally oriented. Secondly, the educated class also has the
lead in scientific and technical modernization and adapts vocabulary from this area, which is often foreign. In this way, it
intrudes into the standard language or, more positively, enriches
it and is thus one way of elaborating the language.

Standardization goes along with modernization. This implies
that the standard variety becomes elaborated because its use is
extended to new fields of technical and administrative activity,
whereby new registers are created that may have special syntactic
and lexical properties which will be partly incorporated into the

common standard language: every speaker of the standard is competent to some degree in some of these registers. Hereby his overall language behaviour is influenced, and by a cumulative effect special registers shape the standard language to some extent and it acquires a broad usability with respect to different functions and fields of common interest.

Standardization of a language is accompanied by cultivation. This has been pointed out by Subbayya (1980) for Marathi. There has also been cultivation throughout the growth of the standard of German, for example in the time of the great baroque literature by different linguistic associations, like 'Die fruchtbringende Gesellschaft' in Weimar, founded in 1617 (*cf* von Polenz 1970:110). The grammar of German became a topic of discussion and normalization, and grammar books were written to codify the norms to which one could agree in these linguistic circles. These activities imply that a certain variety of the language becomes cultivated along with the development of a literature written in this form. Written literature requires some normalization of syntax, lexicon, and spelling. In this process, standardization is achieved over a time, even without providing legal means for the implementation on the state level as an official or national linguistic standard. The vocabulary, grammar, spelling, and pronunciation of the regionally spread cultural and political lead of the population becomes normalized, *ie* the use of variants becomes more restricted under the influence of the literary language that serves as the model in a transregionally oriented education, which has mainly been secondary education.

6.1.2.(4) The norms of the non-standard varieties

With the creation of a standard the other varieties become the negative part of a new opposition, namely the opposition 'standard versus non-standard'. The standard is dominant. The other varieties have to be recessive in a whole range of situations of use in which they have been used before and also may have received cultivation as, for example, different varieties of Marathi with a classical literary tradition before the standardization of Marathi as a state language. By being declared non-standard, these varieties are prevented from being put to use in their old functions or in new functions that arise with modernization and are, therefore, no longer cultivated or elaborated. They become impoverished with respect to the functions they have fulfilled or otherwise could be developed to fulfil. This means that the situational domain of application of their norms becomes restricted and shrinks. Simply put, they become less

useful. There is thus less justification for the existence of these
norms, especially with regard to the range of primary functions
of linguistic norms. Usually the secondary function as a symbol
of group identity remains, and the norms will survive as long as
the group feels the need to stress its own identity against others
for whom the same standard language is valid. But if the
educational élite of such a group is more oriented towards
mobility and integration into transregional cultural and political
affairs, then the loss of primary functions, which are usually
supported by normalization and cultivation, is irreversible and
the variety will be used only by groups who are secluded and do
not feel a need to integrate into activities beyond the local level.
The non-standard variety, hereby, acquires an additional negative value as the language of those that are backward and un-
developed: as much as its speakers are despised the non-standard
variety will be despised and, combined with a low level of self-
esteem, even its own speakers will attribute a negative value to
their language, although it still carries the positive value of
solidarity. Dressler (1982:324) describes the situation as follows:

> In my opinion the basic mechanism of language decay starts with
> social change subordinating the respective speech community to
> another speech community. Speakers reflect this unfavorable change
> sociopsychologically by a less favorable evaluation of their language.
> A consequence is a socio-linguistically restricted use of their language,
> which results in an impoverished linguistic structure for their language.
> This impoverishment has a feedback on the speaker's socio-psycho-
> logical evaluation, because the quality of guaranteeing the prestige
> function and self-identification function . . . of the language has
> diminished. Also the socio-linguistically restricted use has a parallel
> feedback effect.

Dressler defines language decay as a loss of functions and structures without compensation within the same language. This, of
course, holds for dialects as well. Dressler (1982:325) also notices
another important aspect that involves language learning:

> Linguistic decay, I hypothesize, occurs predominantly during language
> acquisition. If children acquire the decaying language simultaneously
> with, or even after the victorious language and learn to use it only with
> family members, and if – due to low socio-linguistical evaluation –
> adults exercise weak social control of their acquisition process, the
> necessary conditions are present for pidginization of the decaying
> language in its reduced, auxiliary use.

I think that Dressler's restriction of this process to secondary
acquisition of a decaying language is unnecessary. A non-
standard variety is also in a bad position when it is acquired first,

in particular if the variety has received a negative value.

Then correction by parents of children's speech so as to keep it within the range of the norms of their variety will be less, especially if the child uses forms that are more similar to the standard than to their own dialect or variety. Such correction, if it took place at all, would be less justified because the norms of these varieties have no general validity but at most a limited one in house and kitchen, so to speak. Thus the child will normally follow his parents' speech as a model, but acts of correction would be less frequent or less intensive. In this way the child loses, or even never develops, the idea that anything in his mother tongue could be correct or incorrect. The notion of correctness will be developed mainly in school education, and then with respect to the standard. The child therefore will easily agree with the judgement passed about his dialect in school, namely that his speech is incorrect and needs to be corrected in order to become better, *ie* standard. In this way, the value 'correct speech' is never attached to the non-standard varieties although, in the light of the theory of norms, dialects are correct in themselves. Like any other language they have their own norms which determine correctness. But hardly anybody will realize this, because the standard is used as an outside measure of correctness such that non-standard speech seems to be incorrect speech, although it is only incorrect with respect to the norms of the standard varieties, which are not its norms. This constellation is essential to what a standard is and how it works.

But note that this is different if one consciously speaks (and thinks) about a 'common language' instead of a standard language and draws the consequences from this: only a standard is a measure of correctness or incorrectness for that which is supposed to be like it. A common language is nothing more than a second language next to regional languages that serves for inter-regional and super-regional communication. The regional languages are not supposed to be like it and it is therefore not a measure of correctness for them. Officially assigned validity of the standard makes it justified to judge other language use as correct or incorrect with respect to the norms of the standard. But these judgements should be restrained to just those situations in which the standard is valid and the other varieties are not. 'Correctness' is not merely a descriptive concept like 'difference' would be, but it implies appraisal, and 'incorrectness' or 'deviance' from the standard, *ie* from what is expected, implies disapproval.

Standard speech and writing are required in school and in

public life. It is expected from others by those who have to decide about careers, and this expectation is not an arbitrary one. It is the usual expectation one has with regard to one's own social group where everyone complies with the same norms. This expectation is extended, without much consideration of the differences within a nation or state, with the idea that, despite all its differences, a nation is a single speech community.

Norm contents of non-standard varieties are not made explicit and not codified, prestigious models are missing, and the existing models are not reinforced as models of linguistic usage. Even those linguists that provide a codification by writing a grammar and a lexicon of a dialect work under the assumption of descriptive science, namely that they merely write down factual linguistic usage and that their formulations are not codifications in the sense that they should serve as a model for the speakers of the dialect. (Linguists, naive or concerned with their reputation in the world of academics, have even written such grammars in theoretical frameworks like, for example, the Standard Theory of Transformational Grammar, and in this way have made their work more or less useless for matters of codification and teaching of the 'exotic' languages or dialects.) Working with this attitude they do not provide a means for cultivation of the dialect or language they describe, but rather provide a record of a language in a specific form which is merely of theoretical or historical interest: before a language dies out, a description and a record should have been made in order to preserve its very interesting properties for generations of further linguistic research.

From the above considerations we see that the situation brought about by declaring one variety to be the standard creates a great pressure on the norms of the other varieties. They are no longer valid in many functions, lose their normative force because of this, and are doomed to be extinguished unless secondary factors, such as group identity and solidarity or certain political and social goals connected with these, prolong their life or serve to revive them when they have almost died out. These political factors can lead to some cultivation activity, which could otherwise not be applied to these varieties. The old norms are cultivated for certain in-group activities with some positive status, such as rituals and local politics. In this way, a dialect sometimes gains the status of a recognized language, even in competition with a developed standard in several regional official functions, as has happened to the Konkani dialect of Marathi, and also with the Frisian dialect (or language) in the Netherlands. Subbayya (1980:93) writes about Konkani:

The Konkani speaking population started an anti-standard-Marathi movement which resulted in Konkani attaining the status of independent language in 1976. This shows that sometimes group identity may assert [itself] to such an extent that the speakers of a regional variety may claim separate language status.

This, of course, can only happen when the variety had an independent literary history and the educated élite of the minority and linguistic scholars work on codifying the dialect and produce modern literature and other texts of daily use in this variety, in order to preserve it. This has been the case with regard to Konkani: codification and cultivation were applied.

Such a support by the educated élite, however, was missing in other cases where language movements were unsuccessful and the varieties or minority languages were extinguished when the élite and the socially mobile group (*ie* economically upwardly and transregionally oriented) of a population accepted the standard or the majority language and thought of its own language variety as inferior. Compare, for example, Dua (1986), Pattanayak (1977), Misra (1979), Daswani (1979), and Ekka (1979), where the status of several Indian minority languages is described and analysed and the factors are investigated that are involved in success and failure of these languages with respect to being included in the eighth schedule of the Indian Constitution as recognized languages. In the case of the Kak-Borok language, a Tibeto-Burman language spoken by the Tripura tribes, its speakers, who have become a minority in their own state by massive Bengali immigration, want to change from the Bengali script to the Roman script because they associate the Bengali script with what they experience as Bengali suppression. In addition, Tripura nationalists want their language accepted as an official regional language in order to secure tribal identity against the Bengalis (Bhattacharya 1980). Besides these politically motivated movements for the preservation of minority languages or dialects, which under favourable circumstances with enough support from the educated élite can be successful, there is preservation without any language movement in those cases where speakers of minority languages or dialects are excluded from the social and economic development of a nation, like the isolated groups in slums, *cf* Rajyashree (1986), or in secluded villages with hardly any outside contact, or in those situations where religious sects isolate themselves from the influences of the outside world, as the Amish and other Mennonites have done, where old German dialects and the Bible-German of Luther's times have survived for centuries, *vis-à-vis* the majority language,

English. In all these constellations, conflicts between linguistic norms are prevented by denying contact with speakers outside the group.

6.1.2(5) Classical language as the norm of standard language?

A recurrent problem in standardization has been the overstated value attributed to classical languages as models of modern written and formal oral usage. We shall consider the cases of Telugu, Sinhala, and Arabic. The outcome with regard to Telugu and Sinhala is opposite to that with regard to Arabic.

Krishnamurti (1979) describes and discusses the controversy between the classical school, which devised classical Telugu as a modern standard language, and the modern school, which proposed a standard based on the polite speech of the educated Telugu speakers. Classical Telugu has as its model 'the language of the Kavitraya', which is the language of the three major poets from the eleventh, thirteenth, and fourteenth centuries. Any non-Kavitraya usage was considered as ungrammatical, and any mixture of colloquial language, called *gramya* (with a negative connotation) was prohibited. Teachers taught a language they themselves could not speak. Not until 1897 did a movement for the use of modern Telugu in writing gain ground.

The classical school argued that the Kavitraya has had a fixed standard for nine centuries with definite rules of grammar, which say what is correct or incorrect, while modern language varies from place to place, age to age, person to person, *ie* has no uniformity, and has no tradition of literary usage, and no grammar. If one could not stick with a fixed form, literature would become unintelligible for future generations and would be lost. It is therefore better to adjust modern language to classical language than to water down classical language. Besides, they pointed out, colloquial speech had been banned from written usage as vulgar ('gramya') by traditional grammarians (Krishnamurti 1979:11).

Against this position, the modernists argued that the archaic classical language might be suited for traditional poetry but not for textbooks and mass education. 'No scholar, however great, can write prose in classical language without committing blunders' (Krishnamurti 1979:12). The colloquial form of the language has a tradition in translations, epics, records, and commentaries. Furthermore, there is surely a distinction between polite colloquial speech and vulgar speech, and only the former is intended as a model of written language.

Although in 1913 a committee appointed by Madras University had ruled that modern Telugu was to be standard, school and college textbooks continued to be written in the classical or neo-classical style. Modern Telugu is based on the educated colloquial style of the central coastal regions of Godavari and Krishna, which were leading economically and intellectually. Since the mass media have been influenced by these speakers during the last forty years, the coastal educated speech spread over further areas. Standard Telugu is now the language of modern education and urbanization, and has become a prestigious model for all Telugu speakers.

According to Krishnamurti, the problem for the modernist movement at the beginning of the century had been the lack of models: 'there really was not any standard creative or scientific work which reflected current educated usage and could serve as a model for the style they were advocating' (1979:18). Only after around 1930 did models also emerge in creative literary writing.

The failure of the classicists was that they wanted to establish poetic language for uses and roles for which there was an established tradition of other styles. They did not see that the role of written language and literature had changed, and that it was no longer 'simply the preserve and privilege of a few, educated in Sanskrit and Telugu classics' (1979:17).

Krishnamurti reports that schools in the twentieth century had a choice of whether they wanted examinations written in classical or in modern Telugu. 'Teachers mostly preferred classical, because they did not know how to teach modern Telugu, without "high literature"' (1979:7). Teachers did not consider other texts. Only when, with modernization, classical educators and teachers lost their influence against people dominating modern science, theatre, and specially the mass media did modern Telugu become the standard language in writing as well.

The problems with Arabic are in fact very similar, but much more severe, and a solution is not in sight due to the religious fixation. Classical Arabic, the language of the Koran and other religious writings, is still the only model for teaching written Arabic (Ibrahim 1983). Classical Arabic differs from colloquial varieties in syntax, morphology, word order and lexicon. The distance between classical and colloquial Arabic seriously hinders the masses learning how to write and use written language as a medium of expression.

> The position accorded to Arabic by Islam is probably unique among the languages of the world. Not only is it the language of Islam's holy book, the Qu'ran, and of all religious rites and services among all Muslims, but it is probably the only language which provided its

speakers with a verbal miracle, the Qu'ran, which is miraculous by virtue of its having been revealed by God to the Prophet Muhammad in a form of language never to be surpassed or even equalled by any human being. This is the secret behind the position still enjoyed by standard Arabic. Muslims are spurred by their religion to use standard Arabic when they speak. (Ibrahim 1983:513)

Therefore it becomes very unrewarding to prepare books on colloquial Arabic for foreigners who come to Arabic countries to work there.

Anyone who deals with spoken Arabic, including Arab linguists who have studied certain aspects of their dialects, is looked upon with suspicion. Spoken Arabic, the native language of every Arab, is simply not worthy of any attention according to the overwhelming majority of Arabs who are willing to venture an opinion on this matter. (Ibrahim 1983:514)

Such a classical standard, by being too far away from colloquial educated speech, finally might lose its function as a standard altogether. Awareness of not complying with the norm may be lacking if the colloquial standard emerging from the variety of the educated speakers competes with the old classical standard in everyday life. People who fill important positions in state and society will neither be able nor willing to conform to the classical standard, but nevertheless, their speech (in a non-classical dialect) will be a model for many other speakers who recognize them as important people in official positions. These people, by way of their prestige, become models and that implies that their speech receives the certificate 'standard' or 'good speech' by the masses, though not by the religious and classical experts. This way, a competing colloquial standard arises that might have a chance as a basis for writing in the Arab countries if some secularization were to take place, without being repeatedly suppressed by fundamentalists. Another point is, of course, whether the varieties of colloquial Arabic in the various Arab countries are close enough to provide a common basis of one standard written language; or, if they are fairly different, whether one of these varieties is considerably stronger than the others because of literary activities and the political and economic power of its speakers, and thereby would be acceptable for the speakers of the other varieties. Furthermore, the Arabic influence on non-Arab Islamic nations plays a role because there classical Arabic is used merely for religious purposes without a parallel use of colloquial Arabic.

The problem of Sinhala is related, though again somewhat

different. It has an ethnic background, namely that the classical language and literature, which were close to being forgotten, should be revived to strengthen the solidarity and the self-respect of the Sinhalese majority against former English rule and Tamil supremacy connected with it. Musa (1981) reports that after Dutch and English colonialism the Sri Lankans decided to replace English by Sinhalese (also: Sinhala) as the official national language. Its standard was based on Sinhalese literature from the twelfth century: an archaic standard was selected and defended by language purists, who 'looked down upon the language of their own times' (Musa 1981:65). This group, the Hela Havula of Cumaratunga, and its followers, 'who were mostly school teachers, constantly endeavoured to popularize the idea that only by adopting the "hela" language could the Sinhalese race be civilized and dignified' (1981:65).

The major problem with the classical standard was that it was so distant from colloquial Sinhala, that even educated people could not use it properly. From 1955 to 1961 about 80 per cent of the civil servants who had to pass proficiency examinations in the Sinhalese language failed the test at the advanced level, and around 74 per cent failed at the ordinary level. During these years the failure rate did not drop, although repeatedly failing the exam could result in losing one's job. 'The first interim report of the language commission argued that as the language had been almost dead for centuries, "many government clerks and staff officers, though they possess a fairly good knowledge of Sinhalese, would never venture to write even a simple minute in Sinhalese, for fear of making some mistake or other" ' (Musa 1981:106).

The purists of the Hela Havula group succeeded in banning books whose language they did not consider to be pure or correct, and they also had great influence in the committee that was preparing school-books. Up to 1969, 'the committee specified a linguistic norm which could not conform to the speech habits of the people, but rather made the linguistic situation more difficult and confusing for the public' (Musa 1981:109). The dissatisfaction of the public resulted in the language departments of the four universities of Sri Lanka condemning the extreme position of the purists, and the textbooks proposed by the committee were withdrawn. Instead, efforts were made to provide texts written in modern colloquial Sinhala, for which standardization proceeds by providing such texts.

The problem created by the use of the classical standard of Sinhalese also aggravated the opposition of the Tamils. 'The Tamil community had started to learn Sinhalese in schools after the introduction of "Sinhalese only". But when the community lost confidence in Sinhalese "sincerity" they refused to learn Sinhala in school' (Musa 1981:112).

Now Sinhala and Tamil are accepted as two official languages of Sri Lanka, and since the colonial issue is no longer urgent, English is considered for reinstatement as a third official language, while in any case, it is used as an unofficial 'official language'.

If a language or variety is promoted for situations of use in which it is not really needed because another language or variety functions there, its acceptability is low. Its use is much better promoted if it is restricted to areas in which it is needed. So, according to Musa, it was counter-effective to enforce classical Sinhalese in administrative and governmental use. Also Dua (1980) stresses the point that acceptability depends on sentimental and on functional reasons.

The transition to the modern Bengali standard language proceeded more smoothly. The older Shadhu Bengali, with the great novelist Bankim Chandra as a nineteenth-century model, was replaced by Calit Bengali ('common Bengali') after 1913. It was promoted by Tagore and Chowdhury as the main literary models, and by Calcutta radio as the major mass medium (Musa 1984a). The establishment of the new standard was accompanied by efforts of language modernization and elaboration in the area of terminology, directed by the Bengali Academy of Language and Literature, and after 1934 aided by the Bengali Scientific Terminology Society. Next to the common Bengali style the old Shadhu style has been used in traditionally oriented literature, old-fashioned textbooks, and formal correspondence.

In all the cases considered here, the recruitment of civil servants with some, but not an effective, classical education has led to establishing a new standard: the civil servants, people of some standing, were supposed to speak standard, and they thought they did, as long as they were not confronted with language exams. In fact, many civil servants, schoolteachers, newspaper writers, and other text-writers did not comply with the classical norm. But because of their position they served as models of 'good' usage for other speakers who were eager to acquire the standard together with élite skills, power, status and economic advantages, and new beliefs (cf Dua 1980:33). In this way the standard changed by including colloquial forms from different vernaculars. The result was that there were two competing standards, and it depended on the classicists' strength for how long this situation would pertain. Writers about Arabic think that this situation will hold for a long time because of the force of Islamic influence. In the cases of Telugu, Bengali, and Sinhala the conflict has been decided in favour of the modern standard.

Also the struggles of 'classicists' or 'purists' for preventing non-native loans from English into Hebrew, or for eliminating Sanskrit loans from Tamil (cf Annamalai 1979a for Tamil), etc., have been decided in favour of functionally effective linguistic resources instead of native ones. Sometimes, such an opening of non-native resources in adjusting a language to modern needs has to be comouflaged ideologically in order to overcome sentimental objections. (These can only be overcome by even stronger sentimental arguments.) Thus, Heydt (1954) reports how the Turkish language was enriched by collecting words used in dialects and literature. But purists wanted only native sources to be used, and no loan words from Arabic, Persian, etc. Against this position the 'Sun-Language-Theory' (Günes-Dil teorisi) was invented and proposed, which claims that 'just as Central Asia, the ancient homeland of the Turks, was the cradle of human civilization, so Turkish was "the mother of all languages"' (Heydt 1954:34). In the vein of this 'theory' a lot of articles were published after 1935 which 'showed' that a great many Arabic, Persian, and European loan words in the Ottoman language were in fact of Turkish origin. Therefore, borrowing was no longer a problem. Purification became unnecessary.

6.1.2(6) Conclusion

It has been argued that standardization of language involves shifts or changes in the populational and situational domains of the linguistic norms involved. The lack of validity of the non-standard varieties for several types of linguistic use or function leads to non-acceptance, then to non-adoption and, in the end, to non-existence of the norms of these varieties. On the other hand, non-justification of a devised standard leads to conflicts with its official validity, and these conflicts lead to less acceptance and adoption of the valid standard, as the discussion of the implementation of classical languages as standard shows.

As a whole, the domains of existence, validity, acceptance, adoption, and justification grow for standard varieties and shrink for non-standard varieties. Likewise there is a shift in the situational domains that is also directed in an opposite direction for standard and non-standard varieties. Along with this change, language elaboration and cultivation take place with regard to the standard, but not with regard to other varieties, except in marginal situations of use. These different changes reinforce each other with an overall positive result for the standard and a negative one for the non-standard varieties. This development amounts to strengthening the linguistic norms of the standard and to weakening those of the non-standard varieties. This implies spread for the standard variety, and decay for the other varieties.

Besides this opposition there is a certain compromise between the standard variety and the others by vernacularization, resulting in borrowing from other varieties into the standard. This implies that the standard is itself a range of varieties. This range is centred and structured from an imaginary point of reference, which is carried out to a high degree by official models provided by lexica, grammar books, and school readers. These models, together with schoolteachers and speakers and writers of transregional mass media, perform an essential role in supporting the existence of a standard: only by being structured from a central point, can a standard be upheld as a range of varieties for which a transregional use and understandability are guaranteed. A common, though graded, notion of correctness of usage makes a standard different from just a set of varieties.

6.2 Linguistic norms in corpus planning

Corpus planning comprises language elaboration and cultivation. Firstly, it consists of developing grammar and lexicon as well as different registers and styles such that a language can meet old functions in a new way or new demands by fulfilling new functions. This is the aspect of elaboration. Secondly, it is language cultivation which consists in stabilizing the standard to the necessary degree by codification of its norms and by providing more and modern models for the different types of linguistic usage. This aspect also comprises criticism of 'bad' usage. In German these activities are called *Sprachkritik* and *Sprachpflege*; they are performed publicly by teachers, literary critics, and journalists in newspapers, magazines, educational journals, and on the radio.

I shall now deal with some aspects of linguistic elaboration and codification. Language cultivation will be the topic of the next section.

6.2.1 Linguistic norms in language elaboration
In the history of languages, elaboration has always occurred together with the development of literature, philosophy, and new

fields of science. In developing the disciplines, languages were elaborated in the area of vocabulary, stylistics, and even syntax. Complicated ideas and arguments gave rise to complicated syntactic constructions: nominalizations, complex attributes, subordinated clauses. Depending on the kind of activities, different styles were developed and, on the other hand, the availability of certain linguistic patterns promoted certain ways of thinking and arguing. This is, for example, evident for German philosophy, where a certain style, developed in the high days of Kantian philosophy, is still dominant in the writings of modern philosophers who have their roots in that tradition, such as Apel or Habermas, to mention just two. Likewise, literature and poetry were the origin of great elaborations in vocabularies and stylistic devices. Also other registers, being elaborations of the language in special fields, have partly been carried beyond the boundaries of their respective fields into other areas of linguistic usage and have even become part of everyday language. An example already mentioned is the passive construction in Marathi, which was introduced into the language by translations of administrative, juridical, technical, and educational English texts. Before the English influence the written varieties of Marathi were elaborated by Persian or Arabic loans in the area of law and administration (cf Subbayya 1980).

Generally, in the histories of languages, the areas of administration and law show extensive elaborations not only of the vocabulary by loan words, composita, and nominalizations, but also by new styles typical of the administrative and juridical registers, which are characterized by the regular use of agentless passives and impersonal constructions, and by nominalizations and subordinate clause constructions of great complexity. All this is aided by a partly new, or newly defined, vocabulary.

During colonialism Third World countries experienced how their traditional systems with councils for negotiating and straightening out conflicts were judged by Europeans from the point of view of efficiency in time saving, readiness for action, and centralization. 'Modern' law and administration were introduced parallel with the traditional councils and traditional law and partly replaced it (cf O'Barr and O'Barr 1976, especially with respect to Tanzania). According to different aims and conditions of interaction in councils, different styles in argumentation, turn-taking, and status orientation are typical of traditional institutional usage on the one hand, and modern institutional usage on the other. Modernization in this area implies either adopting the new institutional system with its linguistic registers, or finding a compromise between old and new by using, for example, the traditional system on the local and the modern system on the state level, with its special needs due to centralization.

Another field of language modernization that leads to elaboration is modern science and technology. Not only have new parts of the vocabulary been introduced, but linguistic usage in these areas has been very much rationalized with respect to the goal of representing states of affairs unambiguously. If the only aims of texts in a field are explanation and description, a restricted and rigid register is developed, which just fits these goals and no others. The extreme of this development is the construction of formalized and formal languages that serve one single goal, or a set of closely related goals that are pursued in one single type of situation that is completely controlled by very few defining factors.

Furthermore, English as an international language, a new variety, or more precisely a set of varieties, is in principle like this. It is the language of international science, trade, traffic, and politics, and it shows properties that are due to the restrictions with regard to the respective goals. Extreme varieties of this variety are the international language of air control, or the language of maritime control 'Seaspeak' (cf Strevens and Weeks 1985). International English is cut off from the cultural and literary development of English in the countries of native use and thus lacks a great deal of expressive power by syntactic as well as by lexical devices. On the other hand it is necessary that many of these culturally bound devices are excluded from the international language because they would create a lot of difficulties in understanding, and in particular they would create misunderstanding because the special cultural background (that determines the meaning of many words and stylistic devices for different groups of native speakers) is not available for a worldwide population that needs to use this language in different areas of international activities. An additional point is that the international language should not be overburdened with culture-specific vocabulary and stylistic patterns, because this would hinder its acquisition as a second language and would cause it to compete with other native languages in cultural and domestic affairs and thus would, because of patriotic reasons, diminish its acceptability as a common international means of communication.

There has been a rapid development of formal languages, formalized languages, and non-formalized but syntactically and semantically strictly delimited sub-languages of several natural languages. Examples are logic languages, computer languages, the language of mathematics with several sub-languages, and the languages of modern science generally. These languages are characterized by their strict limitations in function and expressive power. They are tailored for only one function, or very few functions of a technical and administrative kind. Being so much restricted, they are less ambiguous than natural languages and at the same time lack expressive power in all areas for which they are not constructed.

What do the different kinds of elaborations of natural languages imply with respect to the linguistic norms involved? Each elaboration is a restriction of the style of expression with regard to the amount of vocabulary, the use of the words in the field in question, and the use of syntactic forms. This has the effect that the pragmatic range of the sub-language is restricted. This aspect of elaboration can be seen as a selection out of the set of lexical items, meanings, syntactic devices, and, including all this, stylistic patterns. As far as the selection is one out of several variants, elaboration also includes normalization or standardization under the respective aim, as, for example, the normalization of technical vocabulary or registers. Restriction and normalization with regard to special fields of language use are a kind of elaboration, because lexical items and stylistic patterns are made explicit, as well as the functions to which the linguistic means will be put; the linguistic means and their ways of use are thus easily controllable and adjustable to the purpose they are designed for. Since the linguistic means are tailored to fit one purpose only they can do that well because they need not satisfy other purposes at the same time. The more purposes a formal language is going to serve the worse it will do for each of these, except if the purposes are very similar to each other. This is the Scylla and Charybdis for the construction of programming languages and also of computers. A machine, and likewise a language, that is excellent for one specific technical purpose is usually very weak on other counts. And what does reasonably well from several points of view is usually not excellent from any particular one. If, for example, a logical language is set up, the explicit rules of syntax and interpretation for this language make it usable for the formal calculations of logical truths and, in particular, implications that have been taken into account in its construction, and others that follow from these. The rules have been made such that at least certain implications are taken care of, and it is a nice outcome if this construction also automatically delivers further desirable implications. The concept of consequence is worked out in a restricted but precise way, in order to make logical calculations possible and their validity provable. The same happens in mathematical languages with respect to their specific vocabulary, defined in suitable terms, such that interesting theorems can be deduced. All these languages are completely fixed by codification. It is evident for these cases that normalization is accompanied by elaboration in the sense that limitation of use and, by this, precision, make it possible to define a concept of validity of formal operations.

'Validity' is not a fixed concept. Validity of operations can be defined with respect to different goals, for example, with respect to preserving truth. As it is possible to prove for a logical language validity of certain procedures (*eg* derivations) in the sense that they preserve truth, we can define certain operations and procedures in manipulating expressions while keeping intact other desirable properties they have, as, for example, meaning or information. This is a desirable property to be preserved in a whole set of manipulations, namely in 'translation'. Validity of certain operations in this field implies that meaning, or information, is preserved. Another notion of validity is the validity of computer programs, which have to be kept intact under certain operations. If certain changes have been performed on a computer program it should be provable that the program still is valid. This, of course, is true for the whole process of building a program: to prove its validity not only means to prove its consistency, but also that it will terminate, and that it will accomplish its task under all circumstances in which it should be appropriate.

That expressions of languages can be manipulated in certain ways which keep intact certain desirable properties is an elaboration of the possibilities of language use by restricting and normalizing, and by elaborating on this basis with respect to certain goals. Besides redefining and making old vocabulary precise, a range of definitions of new concepts can be provided if necessary, together with the device of new procedures for manipulating expressions while preserving certain desirable properties. What happens to linguistic norms in these processes?

By redefining the meaning of words already used in a language and by restricting their range of meanings to a single one and by making this meaning explicit, the content of semantic norms is narrowed down in the sense that the range of proper application of the word is reduced as far as the respective register is concerned. The word can be used correctly only in a smaller number of cases within the field of study. The restriction can be made by explicit definitions, by implicit definitions, or by 'definitions in use'.

Explicit definitions replace an expression by another expression that is supposed to have the same meaning as the replaced one in all contexts under consideration. *Implicit definitions* present a set of sentences (axioms) in which the word is used. Every further use is correctly possible only in sentences derived from these initial sentences via valid derivational processes. *Definitions in use* are such that a certain fixed sentence containing the word in question is, *per definitionem*, supposed to be equivalent to another sentence not containing this word. This way, the word can be eliminated by replacing the whole sentence by its equivalent. Operational definitions are definitions in use: a property 'A' of an object x can be defined operationally just by saying in what kind of operations x behaves in what way. These latter sentences, describing this behaviour, define the use of the symbol expressing 'A' with respect to x.

All definitions of symbols or words are restrictions on their use and thus are limitations or specifications of the notion of semantic correctness for these words or symbols. By such a procedure the norm content is specified and the normative force is strengthened because one is not allowed to treat the conditions of application of the word, *ie* the norm content, loosely.

If we investigate the use of a single word in different fields or, more generally, in different types of situations of use, we make explicit the whole polysemic structure of the meaning of this word. By thus clarifying its meanings in various types of use, an elaboration of the meaning structure of the word takes place to the effect that the procedures for creative use of the word in new types of situations are also made explicit. Thus the procedure of constructing new meanings belonging to a single polysemic complex becomes explicit, and with this, rules of semantic elaboration are established. These are the strategies of creative linguistic usage, which are second-order strategies that are inherent as a means of elaboration in the use of natural language.

Restricting or making the meaning of a word precise in one type of context or usage does not preclude elaboration of uses of the word in other contexts or fields. It does not imply restricting its use to precisely one meaning, but rather to one meaning in one type of context of use. One can do this for all types of usage of this word and in this way reconstruct its polysemic complex. To do this is not part of the different fields or registers where the word has just one single defined use, but it is part of the elaboration of a natural language as a whole, including the modes of application of its vocabulary in different fields or contexts of use.

From the point of view of a single field, or a single type of context, the procedure is a desired restriction, and from the point of view of language as a whole, comprising all the registers for different functions, the procedure is one of discrimination between different types of situations of use. In terms of the theory of norms this means that the domain of application of a norm becomes explicitly structured such that the different types of situations of use are incorporated as conditions of application, with the respective descriptions of the use of the expression in these types. An alternative view is that a norm content is split into several norm contents. This implies that a norm with a vague or complex content is replaced by several more specific norms that hold in the respective fields.

In extending linguistic usage and in creating new expressions in new fields it is important to notice that the correctness conditions for the use of words can only be developed as part of the content of the respective scientific or technical field. Elaboration is done by the scientists or technicians. If there appears a terminological diversity which is due to different structurings of the field, it is not the task of any linguist or term planner to do something about this. It is the task of the people in the field themselves to solve these differences or to proceed along different lines. Only if exactly one phenomenon is called by different names in the same context of use should normalization then take place. In such an act of standardization linguists could have a place in considering word formation in accordance with morphological principles of the respective language and bringing this aspect to bear in the process of decision.

Since scientists like to stick to vocabulary developed by themselves and their school, it is a question of social ties and power in the field which terminology will dominate. To push through one's own terminology is an act of power. A ruling by a linguistic agency will not be accepted by a disagreeing party if this party is strong enough. The problems reported about the Hebrew Academy's attempt to standardize and suggest vocabulary in technical and scientific fields have to do with this attitude about power in the respective fields, besides the uselessness of Hebrew scientific vocabulary in scientific communications outside the country. Scientists are not so much nationalists as rather internationalists since nowadays science is an international occupation. Jernudd (1977:221) comments:

The heritage of the Hebrew Academy with regard to the rebirth of Hebrew may now become a burden unless it adapts itself to new circumstances. As a matter of fact, the Hebrew Academy itself has moved to solve the conflict between the 'linguistically liberal' proposals that come from committees preparing terminologies (where technical people are in the majority) and the 'linguistically conservative' (ie Hebraizing) screening of proposals by members of the Academy in the Academy plenum. Instead of the plenum passing and rejecting the technical terminologies, a standing committee on terminology makes the decision. Members of the committee are selected for their understanding of professional needs, rather than ideology.

The Swedish Centre of Technical Nomenclature (TNC) works closely with people from various fields, and it is also open to international cooperation in devising terminology. The terminology has to be such that it can be used for communicating methods and results of technology and science to broader ranges of populations in schools and general education. The demands which the Swedish Centre formulates for adequate terminology are (Jernudd 1977:222):
1. Technical language shall be clear, unambiguous, effective, ie efficient within each speciality;
2. Technical language shall form a part of the national language;
3. Technical language shall be as internationally coordinated as possible with regard to definitions, terms, signs, and symbols.
It is evident that these requirements are in conflict with each other. A solution can be to devise two varieties, one that clearly fulfils conditions (1) and (3), and another that is stronger under condition (2) and is oriented more towards a broader group of people who have to learn and use the vocabulary. It is now an accepted point that planners for a certain field should not merely think of creating a compromise within one single register; two related registers might do better.

The whole terminological scene, which for the technical area is fairly clear, becomes somewhat unclear for science in progress because of rival schools in the respective fields, and it looks even somewhat chaotic with regard to the social sciences and humanities: the theory-ladenness of theoretical terms generally, together with the existence of competing theories and different schools supporting them, leads to the situation that a single term is used in competing theories meaning something different, or different terms are used for the same thing making theories look more different than they in fact are, or quite different sets of terms are used. The diversity is due to different perspectives, such as goals and interests, that determine the content and terminology of social theories.

Diversity in terminology becomes a battlefield of politics about power within a field. Neither an outsider, for example a linguist, nor an insider will be able to make a decision that will be generally approved of by at least the leading figures in the field. Therefore, the authority of terminological dictionaries or data banks will be questioned over and over again. This implies that in these cases the normative force of the proposed semantic correctness notions is low, and they will only be norms for those that agree with the direction or school that provided these terms with the definitions given in the dictionary. Decisions will be made by strength of the direction or school, which is only partly due to its scientific results or their truth. Terminological questions are political questions within a field of science, where the competing parties are motivated by the goal of attracting funds and satisfying the urge of being famous and influential. These struggles about the standardization of terminology are of the same kind as those that go along with standardizing natural languages. There are always 'strong men' who do not bother with the standard and claim 'correct or valid is what is according to my norm'. As long as these are just individuals it does not matter much, but if they are influential and can gather a group around them, or can speak for a group to begin with, they might succeed in making a standard ineffective by establishing a competing standard, at least in the areas over which their power extends. This area can be a population in a territory, a political party, or a school in one of the sciences.

Of course, instead of standardizing and codifying the devised standard one could, purely descriptively, register who uses which term in which way. But the result would not be a non-normative dictionary, as naive descriptivists might think. The result rather would force everybody to settle with one or the other of the people or groups whose terminological usage is registered. Thus, for the sake of being able to communicate at all, everyone would be forced to make himself a member of a party. The possibility of choice in such a situation does not take away the normative force of the dictionary or of the groups and persons that stand behind it as the ones whose terminological usage is recorded. We would have to settle with one of them. This implies that we would always be in a marked situation, so to speak, and this can be much worse than being in agreement with a 'neutral' norm. The trouble with such a situation of choice is that one would never have the choice of neutrality. On the other hand, if there is only the standard, we never have the choice of a party. This constellation makes it desirable that there be a standard, something that has the official status of a standard, a variety for which one does not have to fight permanently because it has official status and support. However, it is also desirable that there be some diversity, *ie* varieties from which one can choose, or can choose to fight for, even with the goal for a variety to become a new standard. A standard next to competing varieties provides an advantage as a relatively safe position to take, for example in university exams, or on cross-school conferences in scientific fields. Such a combined constellation is a situation of rest and unrest, stability and change. People have the right to both, and are in need of the one or the other, depending on the kind of situation they are in. These considerations have to do with aspects that touch on the manner in which human beings can exist. They are quite different from considerations of costs and benefits of having a standard in opposition to diversity. Although such economic considerations are certainly important, they are only of secondary importance compared to the points discussed in the preceding paragraphs.

6.2.2 Linguistic norms in language cultivation

Language cultivation is based on, and is a continuation of, the usual activity of correction and criticism of linguistic behaviour that people in a speech community direct towards each other, especially elders towards the young, and native speakers towards newcomers. In this way, language cultivation is primarily done with respect to spoken language. This activity is continued in speech education in schools, theatre schools, and speech classes at universities and teacher training colleges. Thus, Siebs's (1969) handbook of German pronunciation and other guides to pronunciation have not only contributed to the normalization of pronunciation, but also to cultivation in the sense that they have stabilized pronunciation of the respective standard language.

Another aspect of cultivation of spoken language is criticism of so-called 'bad words' which parents and guardians direct towards children. Hereby, certain words are kept within the taboo-sphere, which makes them useful linguistic means in situations of swearing and strong expression of emotion. Actually, this kind of language cultivation just contributes to the existence of this special register, which exists only by its opposition to cultivated speech, created by criticism. Forbidding the use of 'bad words' is, in fact, cultivation of the style which it supposedly bans. In this case, cultivation constitutes an opposition in style which is a useful linguistic means of expression. Looked at this way, cultivation implies a certain kind of elaboration of linguistic usage.

However, cultivation is mainly directed towards written language, and from there it is often enough transferred on to spoken language, which, at least in school situations and formal situations generally, is judged on the basis of written language, a practice that does not take into account the differences between spoken and written code and the conditions of appropriateness of these two codes that refer to situational and contextual factors (*cf* also Sandig 1976).

In particular, cultivation takes place in the wake of standardization and literalization. When standard forms are selected from alternatives and are codified in writing, their use will be enforced for broader domains of people and for broader domains of use. This is done by promoting models, such as literature by great authors, school-books screened from the point of view of normalization, and by recognizing civil servants and teachers as models. Since models are themselves creative language users, great authors genuinely and others also because of their heterogeneous backgrounds of different varieties and registers, language cultivation need not lead to a perfect fixation of the standard, but rather will provide a flexible stability, that permits slow change.

Cultivation of the standard variety takes place on a broad scale and in an official manner by theatres, schools, broadcasting, and newspapers. Only sometimes is it directed towards dialects or minority languages in order to promote their use at least in certain types of situations. Besides societies and institutions devoted to cultivating the standard or special registers of it, as, for example, high literature, there are also societies encouraging the production of literature and newspapers in certain dialects or minority languages. Without these activities, these languages would vanish much faster. Language cultivation and maintenance are the main means of keeping intact a language by promoting and sometimes even enforcing its use in a normalized form in certain types of situations.

It is the normalized form that has evoked opposition and ridicule against the activities of language cultivators and language critics, including teachers who try to enforce the accepted variety. The German linguists who oppose these activities handle a notion of 'norm' that applies merely to unsystematic features of language held alive by tradition against the linguistic regularity of which they are an exception. For example, von Polenz (1982) counts everything that is regular and functional in language as a part of the system of language ('Sprachsystem') which is, according to him, a social phenomenon, in distinction to the competence in a language ('Sprachkompetenz') which is a psychical entity. The norms of language are, according to von Polenz, merely the idiosyncratic peculiarities and deliberate fixations in the range of variants, *ie* in the range of linguistic expressions with the same meaning. He refers to acceptance and reinforcement of linguistic norms by the pejorative term *Sprachnormenfrömmigkeit* (von Polenz 1982:85), which implies a schoolmasterly clinging to linguistic peculiarities. Similarly, Heringer (1982a) calls regularities in language 'rules', and irregularities and deliberate prescriptions 'norms'. In his terminology, 'norms' are prescribed by those who select a variant as the standard one, and forbid others. He assumes that the rules are what everybody handles in any case and which thus do not need to be enforced. Obviously, he adheres to the myth of the homogeneous speech community where everyone, let us say every German, by some miracle uses the same rules of language. He writes: 'Understanding is secured by the commonality of the rules and not by conforming to norms' (1982a:99, my translation). Firstly, I want to argue that learning whatever linguistic rule is only possible via conforming to norms and, secondly, Heringer deliberately narrows down the notion of 'norm': he calls all norms that can be described by rules stating a systematic regularity of language 'rule', and calls 'norm' only those regularities of usage that are irregular from a systematic point of view, or are choices that have been made in the process of normalization and codification. Apparently, Heringer does not discriminate between the notions 'codification' and 'norm'. He calls 'norm' what in the theory of norms is called 'codification of a norm', and he does not distinguish norms from prescriptions.

Against the position of these two linguists, which to me seems typical for descriptively oriented broader linguistic circles, I want to restate and argue that the whole set of linguistic means can only function if it is regulated by norms that tell what the forms of the means are, *ie* delimit their appearance (and thus guarantee their recognizability and acceptability), and by norms that regulate how these means can be used semantically and pragmatically. These two kinds of regulations are the linguistic norms, no matter how regular or irregular their products might appear from points of view of linguistic systematization. That their systematic aspects can be formalized by means of those theoretical entities called 'linguistic rules', which depend very much on the theory advocated by the linguist who formulates them, is quite a different,

though important matter, and it has no bearing on the notion of
'norm' (cf 4.4).

The linguist Heringer (1982a) uses the provocative claim
'*Normen? Ja – aber meine!*' ('Norms? Yes, but mine!') as a title
for his attack against language cultivation and maintenance (in
German: *Sprachpflege*). His intention seems to be that everyone
may make this claim. But as a matter of fact and of principle,
I am afraid to say, this can only be claimed by someone who
accidentally belongs to the educational élite which determines,
whether he likes it or not, what the standard language is. His
claim is very true and, at the same time, very arrogant because
its truth is merely an accidental one: a member of other social
classes, like a worker or a peasant, or a pupil who is not a child
of the educational élite, will certainly get into trouble in public
life when saying 'Norms? Yes, but mine!' and living up to it. It
is typically an exclamation to which the saying pertains 'Quod
licet Jovi, non licet bovi'. If we were to take Heringer's claim
seriously as something everyone could claim, then there would
be no standard language, but only many small-scale dialects and
sociolects, the anarchist's paradise, so to speak, no market of
literary products (because this would be economically impossible
for small linguistic communities), and no transregional broadcasting. It is evident that people have to give up some of their
locally acquired linguistic norms if they want to take part in more
than strictly local affairs. Only those need not give up anything
and learn strange norms who are born into the educational élite,
which defines the standard: *ie* those fortunate ones who can play
the strong man by claiming 'Norms? Yes, but mine!', without
creating any trouble for themselves though possibly for others,
since norms are never a private matter. Imitation of Heringer's
suggestive claim by others than members of the higher social
classes is not advisable and should not be encouraged, not even
with the best intentions.

Creation and cultivation of a standard language are not only
a burden to many who have not acquired it in primary socialization and have to acquire it in school and later in life, but it also
adds to human freedom because it reduces the burden a lifelong
social identification with a group can be: if a person always and
everywhere, whenever he opens his mouth to speak, has to carry
the very distinct label of belonging to this or that region or social
group, he will be identified, whether he wants it or not, as a
member of this group and will be expected to act like someone
from this group, and he will be treated accordingly. Then it is
a blessing for many people in many situations that they cannot

be identified unambiguously because they speak standard. And even if an accent shows where they originally come from, they will be treated by what they are and want to be as a person in that situation if their language is roughly identified as standard, even though it shows an accent. The reason for this is that the standard counts as a neutral language, and use of it expresses some distance from the original background if that has been a non-standard speaking group. In addition to the possibility of transregional communication with sufficient ease in understanding, this freedom from overwhelming and very distinct markers is an achievement of normalization.

Cultivation, furthermore, provides a flexible stability for normal linguistic usage in different registers. It thus facilitates acceptance and adoption of the standard language, and it also promotes acceptability of the dialects and minority languages to which it is applied.

Language cultivation and maintenance create tension with respect to linguistic change if they are carried out solely with a backwards orientation. But this need not be so; cultivation activity rather can be a guide and control of change without trying to hold it back. Its function is one of holding back and giving way. By promoting the elaboration of styles, no matter whether literary or technical ones, cultivation leads to changes in any case because individual language users who acquire competence in different registers organize and reorganize their set of linguistic systematizations in such a way that features of one acquired register or style influence linguistic expression in others and are thus spreading to some extent into larger parts of the standard language. Recognizing these processes, considering their justification and acceptance, and possibly promoting them, is a task of language cultivation in schools and other institutions. At the same time conservatism in the cultivation of the linguistic standard is justified to the extent that changes should not affect understandability between at least living generations and parts of the population in a serious way. Cultural products in written form are worth handing down to new generations; and communication between different groups of the population should not be made too difficult by public everyday usage being overinfluenced by special registers, which happens when great amounts of vocabulary and stylistic devices are incorporated from special fields. The problem of cultural inheritance and understanding between generations lies in time: How far back should intelligibility reach? There will always be small changes adding up to a big change, finally requiring translation. Incorporating too many archaic forms leads to overburdening. Incorporating too many special register forms into everyday public language leads to the same result. Therefore a division of linguistic labour and translation is inevitable even in one single language.

The answer to the question what language cultivation does to linguistic norms is that it strengthens the normative force of norms by strengthening models and providing more models, and by codification, which formulates the results of normalization in a way that the norms can easily be referred to in situations of language teaching, or in case of doubt. The availability of more models extends the domain of acceptance and adoption of the normalized forms within a population. Thus cultivation helps to extend the domains of the norms of the standard language. It further helps to create new styles and strengthens the oppositions between them and, hereby, raises the expressive power of a language.

It is unwise to make fun of people who have doubts about what is correct or incorrect in language, *ie* who have doubts about what is accepted and what is not accepted as standard or normal form. I think that von Polenz's (1982) ironical label *Normenfrömmigkeit* is out of place. It expresses typically an attitude of someone who need not worry about his linguistic competence and usage. Caring about what is right or wrong, correct or incorrect, accepted or not accepted, is the necessary basis for all behaviour of humans for which they wish to take responsibility and of which they want to be in control, and it is a precondition for understanding: in interpreting (linguistic) behaviour we always presuppose that the (linguistic) means are used correctly, as long as evidence does not point to the contrary. To recognize a linguistic means by its form and to interpret it, is precisely to apply the conditions of correctness of appearance and use of this means to the situation of utterance. Understanding is only possible as far as common norms can be applied. Thus cultivation of linguistic norms is the labour that language users and people specifically appointed to this task do in order to **make** a language community and to keep it that way. A community, in whatever kind of norms, be it linguistic, ethical, religious, or juridical ones, does not fall from heaven as such, nor is it founded on a prestabilized harmony implanted in all its heads: rather it is an unstable product and result of permanent labour or coordination with regard to creating and preserving the norms that define it as a community, be it linguistic or of another kind. Language cultivation is this necessary work to create and keep intact a linguistic community, and people who care about correct or incorrect are taking part in this work by worrying about complying with the common norms which define the community as a set of people who understand each other to the extent that they are able to interpret (linguistic) behaviour as (linguistic) action by means of these common norms, *ie* by common expectations and expectations of expectations that should not be disappointed. That sometimes minor norms are the object of undue attention should not be used to discredit the basic attitude and the whole endeavour of language cultivation, at which a linguistic community as a whole works and for which some people feel more responsible than others, and for which even a great number of people are appointed and paid by the community.

Chapter 7

Kinds of norm conflict

7.1 A classification of norm conflicts in multicultural and multilingual societies

Norm conflicts can arise in different ways and they are of different kinds. Here I shall only treat those that are typical in multicultural and multilingual settings.

If two distant cultures are incompatible with respect to the norms holding in each and if they are not in contact with each other, there is not yet a conflict between norms, but merely an incompatibility of norm concepts. Two norm concepts are *incompatible* if there is no situation thinkable in which a person can realize both norm concepts at the same time or shortly after each other. The incompatibility can arise because two actions exclude each other physically, or the analysis and interpretation of behaviour according to one norm are distorted by realization of the other norm, or complying with one norm cannot be approved of as long as the other 'strange' norm is also complied with, especially if the latter is disapproved of in a society. Of course, there is no norm conflict as long as no one is required to realize both of the incompatible norm concepts.

A norm is a norm concept with some kind of existence in a population such that there are norm authorities, norm promulgators, norm enforcers and, generally, norm supporters or carriers. The existence of the norm concept as a norm is established by certain activities and interactions of these agents with respect to the norm concept.

A *culture* is the sum of repetitive, relevant, and deliberate actions, activities, and products produced by a population. This sum is reproduced and preserved by systems of norms practised in the population. A *culture shock* is the momentary loss of orientation due to a conflict between one's own norms and strange norms which results in the loss of functioning norms. A person experiences a loss of norms when others do not adhere to the norm, especially if the others are people of whom one expects that they would comply with the norm and expects that they expect the same of oneself.

Norm conflicts are problematic situations in which one or more persons and one or more norms are involved. For a norm conflict to arise it is not necessary that there are at least two incompatible norm concepts involved; a norm conflict can also arise with respect to a single norm, although often incompatible norm concepts are part of a norm conflict.

In what follows I shall distinguish cases where two different norms are involved from those in which the conflict arises with respect to a single norm or norm system, but where a competing norm system can be a cause of the problems that arise.

Before I start doing that a few remarks about the difference between norm conflicts and other conflicts, especially conflicts of interest, are in order.

Like norm conflicts, conflicts of interest can also arise between two or more individuals, and between groups; or they can arise between interests of a single individual or group. In the last case, an individual or group experiences a conflict between preferences it has.

An interest is constituted by a preference, its chance of realization and its cost. The higher the preference is compared with alternatively realizable preferences of the individual, the stronger is the interest; and the lower the chance of realization of the preference is compared to alternative preferences the weaker is the interest; the higher the costs are for the individual or the group the weaker is the interest. Thus, the strength of an interest is directly proportional to the relative strength of the preference and its chance of realization, and it is indirectly proportional to the costs of realizing the preference involved. Constituted like this, interests are clearly different from norms, and so are interest conflicts from norm conflicts. It is, of course, in the interest of people to realize one norm or the other. People are interested in coordination, and norms achieve coordination. But the interest in achieving coordination can be identical, though the ways to reach coordination differ according to different norms of different people. Thus, also with a single interest involved, norm conflicts can come up. And since norms of partiality (see Ullmann-Margalit 1977) are more to the advantage of one group than they are to the advantage of the other, norm conflicts that involve these kinds of norms, also involve conflicts of interest. There are many cases in which norms and interests are intimately connected. Thus, a certain interest can lead to conduct according to certain norms which define certain actions that are favourable to this interest. And somebody with opposite interests in the same situation will choose to behave according to other norms that define another action. In this case, we have a conflict between interests and not a norm conflict, because the reason for the conflict are different interests. If different interests lead to the realization of different norms or norm systems, the conflict is basically one of interests and not of norms.

7.1.1 Conflicts between two different norms or norm systems that are carried by two disjunct populations

For such norm conflicts to arise, two populations have to come into contact. But contact is not yet sufficient for norm conflicts to arise. Those populations, A and B, can come into contact and take notice of each others' norms. As long as A and B can just go on following their respective norms, no conflict arises. A contact that secures this peaceful coexistence would not amount to more than mutual observation, without interaction. As soon as the contact involves interaction, norm conflicts are likely to arise because interaction, as action where one partner takes into account goals, expectations, and image of the other, requires that the A-person or population takes into account the analysis of the situation of interaction, as supplied by the B-norms, and the B-person takes into account the analysis of the situation according to A-norms. A- and B-norms might give rise to different interpretations of the same situation, that means give rise to a different analysis of the situation from points of view that are relevant to actions to be performed under A- and B-norms respectively.

The following things can happen in such situations.

Situation 1

The A-person is not able to calculate the B-interpretation, and/or the B-person is not able to calculate the A-interpretation. Then the A- and B-persons do not understand each other and cannot interpret each others' behaviour as actions (according to the norms that guide the behaviour as action). If both partners realize this, they will terminate their attempt to interact and separate, with the knowledge that they do not understand each other, that means do not understand what the other is doing and will be doing.

The other possibility is that one of the partners, let us say the *A*-person, tries to interpret the behaviour of the other, the *B*-person, in terms of *A*-norms. This then amounts to situation (2).

Situation 2

The *A*-person interprets the behaviour of the *B*-person in terms of *A*-norms, and possibly vice versa. Then the *A*-person probably misunderstands what the *B*-person is doing and what his or her intentions are. If the interpretation is unfavourable to the *A*-person, conflict arises because the *A*-person feels attacked or finds his interests disregarded. If the misunderstood action of the *B*-person is favourable or neutral with respect to *A*'s interests, *A* will develop expectations with respect to *B*'s further conduct that very likely will be disappointed later, not because of ill will of the *B*-person, but because the *B*-person intended quite a different course of actions to begin with and even expressed this according to *B*-norms in the first situation, but was not understood properly, because his behaviour in that situation was already, wrongly, interpreted under *A*-assumptions and, especially, *A*-norms.

An example reported in the Dutch newspaper *NRC* of 15 January 1983: a North African worker goes to a Dutch post office to send home a parcel. He does not quite know how that has to be done, but at the counter he finds a helpful clerk who makes the parcel ready for dispatch. The Moroccan is impressed by what the clerk does for him (although it is normal efficient service under Dutch standards), and, on his next free day, he goes with a present to the post office to strengthen his newly won friendship with an official. The clerk does not even remember the Moroccan and pushes aside his present, saying that he is not allowed to accept presents, and turns to the next customer. The Moroccan feels insulted and deceived: first someone indicates that he wants to be his friend and then, some days later, he denies this.

Here we have a situation of misunderstanding due to handling different norm concepts in interpreting a situation and the behaviour of the other as a kind of action it was not meant to be. This misunderstanding can give rise to a conflict between interests, or to a conflict between the interests of one partner with the conception he, wrongly, holds about the interests of the other, that is, a conflict between his own interests with interests he, wrongly, attributes to the other.

Situation 3

In this third situation the *A*-person is willing and able to interpret the situation and the behaviour of the B-person in terms of B-norms, and the B-person is willing and able to interpret the situation and the behaviour of the A-person in terms of A-norms. At first sight, this situation seems ideal. It looks as if both partners understand each other. But precisely this understanding can make interaction impossible: the A-person sees that the B-person, according to his norms, is up to the course of actions f, and the A-person, on the basis of his norm, is up to the course of actions g. But interaction would require that they agree on which course of actions be taken, and f and g are incompatible in the sense that they cannot be followed up with respect to the same original situation at the same time, or after each other.

Here we have a true norm conflict between two partners that is understood by them and requires a solution.

If a solution is to be reached by negotiations, the partners need to have a common set of norms that constitute the institution of negotiation, and furthermore constitute it for both in the same way. But for different people, negotiation might be something different, and for some it might not exist at all, or not exist with respect to certain problems.

Two institutions of negotiation may differ in some of the rules of negotiation itself, for example in the role authority plays, or the role facts play, or the role norms play, or they may differ in the rules of turn-taking between the negotiating partners, in the way and degree self-image and partner-image is taken into account, and in the degree partner's interests have to be taken into account, in the rules determining the result, or in the rules about how to handle the results.

It may even be that some people do not know the institution of negotiation, but determine everything by some kind of authority, or they might have the institution of negotiation applying to certain kinds of differences, but not to others. Thus it might be possible that certain kinds of norms, and the actions required by them, are forbidden to be objects of negotiation; ie actions required by certain norms are not negotiable. In these cases a solution by negotiation is not possible. This leads us to situation (4), in which one partner or population extends the domain of validity of his own norms beyond the borders of his own population on to the culturally strange population he is in contact with. This is the situation of dominance as a solution to norm conflicts.

Situation 4
In the above situations, namely the one in which both partners

realize that they don't understand each other (1), or misunderstand each other (2), or understand each other and understand the conflict arising if interaction is insisted upon or is required (3), there are only two ways out: terminating interaction, at least in the areas that give rise to conflict, and trying to live in distant coexistence, or dominance by one of the two over the other, at least in the areas that give rise to conflict. The option of dominance is inevitable as long as negotiation is not possible according to the norms of the two involved persons or populations, and interaction is still required.

In opposition to Habermas (1974 and at other places) I do not see any *a priori* reason why negotiation about everything should always be possible, especially since I do not see that there is a universal institution called 'negotiation'. It is another thing, that just the problematic situation sketched here, that leads to dominance as the only alternative in interaction, will, hopefully, stimulate all people to strive towards establishing a general institution of negotiation, which, though incomplete, already exists between states. The argument that to establish such an institution already presupposes the universal existence of this very institution does not seem sound; instead of negotiating about what 'negotiation' should amount to and thus presupposing this very institution, people can slowly adjust to ways of negotiating behaviour by drawing conclusions from bad experiences with the alternative I called 'dominance'. I would think that all cultures have in some area of public or personal affairs, at least between persons that are considered equal in esteem or function, some form of negotiation. Especially, since social equality under certain respects can just be understood as having the right to negotiate about certain issues with those that belong to the same class. This class then is a class defined by equivalence from this point of view of having the right to negotiate among members of this class about certain issues. Generalizing these basic concepts of negotiation means to broaden the area of issues that are the object of negotiation and the domain of people that have the right to negotiate about these issues, and are equal from these points of view.

Dominance is the solution to norm conflicts in case negotiation is not possible or not wanted by one of the partners in interaction, and interaction is, nevertheless, wanted by at least one of them. The last condition excludes the solution provided by distant coexistence.

What does dominance mean as a solution to norm conflicts

that involve two different populations as norm carriers? 'Dominance' is a three-place notion:

A is *dominant* over B with respect to the norm or system of norms N if and only if A proposes and enforces validity of N for B.

A special case of dominance is that A devises validity of his own norms for B, *ie* claims and enforces that A-norms are valid for the B-population. Next to claiming validity of A-norms for B, there are also other ways in which B can adapt to A-norms. B can accept A-norms because they are prestigious or to B's advantage, or B can assimilate to A-norms, without even being aware, or even consciously resisting this assimilation. The latter are situations of weak dominance.

Dominance is not *per se* something bad or ethically wrong; it is often necessary as a solution of norm conflicts. But there are a whole range of norm conflicts that arise just in a situation of dominance. These I will treat in the next section. Further, dominance is temporally limited mainly to the first generation of the population B on which A-norms are imposed; the second generation finds itself with special problems because conflicts arise between B-norms still advocated by their parents, and public A-norms. This leads to a break with parental authority. In the third generation, normally, adaptation is completed, and there is no dominance relationship with respect to N, that were originally A-norms, but are now also the new B-norms, while the old B-norms become extinguished. B is now assimilated to A. But it is not quite that simple. As has been pointed out, for example by Fishman (1985) and by Jernudd and Thuan (1983), expressions from the old language, which generally is replaced by the new dominant language, will be used further on for expressing group identity. This way, relicts of the old language will still function with a symbolic value only: these expressions are no longer used because of their semantic value, but only because of their 'social connotation'. Merely symbolic gestures of adherence are a general means to express acceptance of norms that, in certain situations or even generally, one cannot practise.

The three-place notion of dominance includes the possibilities that A dominates B with respect to norms N_1, and that B dominates A with respect to norms N_2. Examples of this situation can be found in history: Greek slaves in the old Rome were subjected under Roman legal norms, but they dominated in cultural affairs, which gave rise to many Greek loan words in Latin (*cf* Bartsch and Vennemann 1982:162). Further, according to Hertzler (1965), French-speaking Normans established legal norms over the Anglo-Saxon population in England, *ie* dominated in legal and economic respects, but on the other hand adapted to kitchen English as their new language: the Anglo-Saxon kitchen maids, nannies, and servants raised the children of the upper, ruling class and imposed their linguistic norms (Anglo-Saxon language with some French vocabulary in the area of cooking and service) on the new generation of rulers. This language, together with a French-based vocabulary in the area of legal and military affairs, is the basis of the English language.

7.1.2 Norm conflicts which arise with respect to one norm (system) where this norm (system) exists heterogeneously in a population

In this section I want to define and illustrate a whole set of norm conflicts in which individuals and whole groups find themselves in situations of intercultural contact and subsequent dominance situations. To do this, I shall first repeat the concepts needed in the classification and description of these kinds of conflicts:

A norm N **exists** for a population P if and only if the norm concept N regulates behaviour (practice) of the population.

If a population has an external attitude towards the norm concept, *ie* follows it only under pressure, it exists for them only as a *prescription*. If the population has internalized the norm concept, *ie* uses it, without external pressure, as a guide for behaviour and correction, it exists for them as real norm.

A norm N is **accepted** by a population P, if and only if it is accepted as a guide for behaviour and correction.

A norm N is **adopted** by a population P, if and only if it has come to exist for the population.

Thus existence can be divided into 'natural' existence, *ie* where norms have been acquired in primary socialization of the child, and 'adoption', where the norms have been acquired later in life, in intercultural adaptation.

A norm N is **valid** for a population P, if and only if the members of P are justified in referring to N as the reason for certain behaviour, and as the reason for criticizing behaviour. That is, validity of a norm justifies certain conduct. Validity is backed up by norm authorities and norm enforcers.

A norm N is **justified** in a population with respect to a higher norm or value V adhered to by the population P, if and only if N is rational (*ie* goal directed and goal adequate) with respect to V. If N is rational with respect to V of P, and does not conflict with another norm or value of P, then N is justified for P. In the case of conflict, between favouring one higher value or norm and hindering another value or norm, there can only be justification to some degree, but not absolutely.

The group of people for which a norm N exists (as a practice) I call the **existence domain**, **E**, of N; the group of people by which a norm N is accepted I call the **acceptance domain**, **A**, of N; the group of people which has adopted norm N is the **adoption domain**, **O**, of N; the group of people for which N is valid I call the **validity domain**, **G**, of N; and the group of people for which N is justified I call the **justification domain**, **R**, of N.

Norm conflicts with respect to norm N arise if existence, acceptance, adoption, validity, and justification do not coincide in their domains within a population. These kinds of conflicts I shall illustrate mainly by examples from the areas of language contact, multilingualism, and language planning. In such cases we have to deal with populations that have a problematic status as a speech community.

Discrepancies between these different domains that are defined with respect to a norm or norm system N define different kinds of norm conflicts. There are the following possible discrepancies:

1. Existence domain $\neq$ adoption domain $E \neq O$
2. Existence domain $\neq$ acceptance domain $E \neq A$
3. Existence domain $\neq$ validity domain $E \neq G$
4. Existence domain $\neq$ justification domain $E \neq R$
5. Validity domain $\neq$ acceptance domain $G \neq A$
6. Validity domain $\neq$ justification domain $G \neq R$
7. Validity domain $\neq$ adoption domain $G \neq O$
8. Acceptance domain $\neq$ justification domain $A \neq R$
9. Acceptance domain $\neq$ adoption domain $A \neq O$
10. Adoption domain $\neq$ justification domain $O \neq R$

In case there is a dominant norm N_1 and a recessive norm N_2, conflicts of these kinds arise with respect to N_1 and also with respect to N_2.

For X and Y being E, A, G, O, R, the following four situations can arise: (1) X and Y are disjunct; (2) X and Y partly overlap; (3) X is included in Y; and (4) Y is included in X.

As long as there is no discrepancy between X and Y, *ie* $X = Y$, the differences $X - (X \cap Y)$ and $Y - (X \cap Y)$ are zero and there is homogeneity within the population with respect to existence, acceptance, validity and justification of the norm or norm system.

For $X \neq Y$ we have the problematic cases $X - (X \cap Y)$ and $Y - (X \cap Y)$; these are those people that belong to X but not

(1) $X \cap Y = \phi$

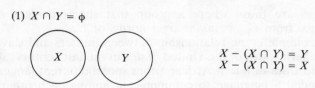

$$X - (X \cap Y) = Y$$
$$X - (X \cap Y) = X$$

(2) $X \cap Y \neq \phi$

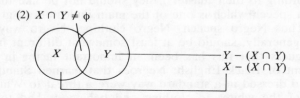

$$Y - (X \cap Y)$$
$$X - (X \cap Y)$$

(3) $X \subset Y$

$$Y - (Y \cap X) = Y - X$$

(4) $Y \subset Y$

$$X - (Y \cap X) = X - Y$$

to Y, and those people that belong to Y but not to X. We can distinguish nineteen cases.

(1a) $E \supset O$

There is no other case possible for $E \neq O$, and thus no case (1b). The difference $E - O$ is the domain where the norm N exists in a natural manner, E_{nat}. $E = E_{nat} \cup O$. This situation, generally, is unproblematic, except if the population E_{nat} does not approve of the population O adopting their norms. This, for example, can be the case if there is a strong feeling of group identity among members of E_{nat} such that E_{nat} feels threatened by seeing O adopting their norms that play an essential role in defining group identity. Examples that also involve group identity and group privileges are those where a group that shows evident racial difference from E_{nat} is taking over norms of E_{nat}.

An example is the relationship between masters and slaves in the southern states of the United States in the last century: slaves imported from different African tribes spoke different languages, and needed a language to communicate among each other and with their masters. They had to learn English. On the other hand, according to their masters, they should not be like them, also not in speech which is one of the main indicators of group identity. Thus Negro speech, Negro clothing, Negro way of behaving, generally, should be at least somewhat different from White. I guess that this has been an important factor in the development of Black English: Negroes that learned Standard English and dressed in a standard way were a threat to Whites. Imitation of the whites in clothing and behaviour had to be overstated such that it was funny, could not be taken seriously, and thus could not count as an entrance ticket into the privileged class. Therefore population E_{nat} hindered population O being fully adjusted to their norms.

$(2a)$ $(A \cap E) \subset A$

In this situation, problems arise for the group $A - (A \cap E)$, namely those people who have accepted norm N but cannot bring this norm into existence in the sense that their behaviour is regulated by N.

Examples are speakers of dialects who have accepted the norm of standard language, but cannot really speak according to this norm, or immigrants with respect to the language of the immigration country.

$(2b)$ $(A \cap E) \subset E$

The problematic group are people from $E - (A \cap E)$; they act according to certain norms, but do not really accept these norms. They would accept correction with the purpose of eliminating these norms and behaviour.

Examples are speakers of a dialect or a minority language, or a sociolect, who have a negative attitude towards their own language. Situations like this we find, for example, in India. Élites of minority languages value the culture and language of other economically successful minorities or majorities more positively than their own culture and language. They are eager to adopt these other standards and work towards loss of their old cultural and linguistic norms, especially if their language is not codified for, and used in, written communication (*cf* Dua 1986; Pattanayak 1977).

(3a) $(E \cap G) \subset G$
This situation is problematic for people from group $G - (E \cap G)$. For them there are certain valid norms although they do not exist for them as a practice. This means their behaviour or conduct is not in accordance with the norms that are valid for them.

Example 1: Dialect speakers and children of dialect speakers in situations in which speaking standard language is required, for example in school.

Example 2: Creole speakers on Mauritius for whom the norms of French are valid (*cf* Hookoomsing 1986).

Example 3: Children of foreign workers in the schools of Western Europe where the linguistic norms of the host country are valid, but do not yet exist for them.

(3b) $(E \cap G) \subset E$
The problematic group consists of people, $E - (E \cap G)$, who behave according to norms that are not valid for them.

Examples are speakers of a minority language within the area of another regional language which is valid for them. The minority language is not valid as a means of communication in many areas of daily life within the state. Nevertheless people use the minority language, and are punished or neglected because of that. We find examples in India, where a minority language may be a regional (majority) language in a state and thus is valid there, but is not valid in the states where it is a minority language.

(4a) $(E \cap R) \subset R$
For people of domain $R - (E \cap R)$ norms are justified that do not exist for them as a practice.

Examples are people for whom linguistic norms are proposed by language planners in the process of modernization. These norms are justified because they serve the needs for new lexical, grammatical, and stylistic means that develop with increasing technology and bureaucratization.

(4b) $(E \cap R) \subset E$
For people from $E - (R \cap E)$, there exist norms that they follow but that are not justified for them.

Example 1: People who follow ritual norms for preparation and consumption of food, and for clothing. In former times these norms might have been functional, but are no longer, except in a secondary function as markers of group identity or ethnicity.

Example 2: People who practise racist laws. They are not justified, but had been followed up, for example, in Germany under Hitler. To overcome the conflicts for people who practised these norms and realized that they were unjustified and even contradictory to accepted values, new values were proposed, such as racial superiority and purity, which helped to create a justification for the practices of these people.

$(5a)$ $(A \cap G) \subset A$

In this case people from $A - (A \cap G)$ have accepted norms that are not valid for them.

Example 1: People who accept norms of a prestige group they want to identify with, although these norms are not valid for them and can even lead to ridiculousness when realized in inappropriate situations outside the group and contexts they were originally designed for. Examples are lower-class speakers who imitate a sociolect of a higher class, or men who imitate behaviour of women, etc.

Example 2: Children of foreign workers who accept norms from their peer groups and from school and also try to practise them at home, although their fathers rule that these norms are not valid for them. The same problem arises for wives of Turkish and Moroccan workers in West Germany and the Netherlands (*cf* Nabantoglu 1981). Many of them are not allowed to go outside the house alone because they might learn and accept norms from the autochthons that are not valid for them, according to the man of the family, who rules which norms are valid for members of his family, and enforces the norms that are valid in his culture. The conflict is aggravated by the fact that these men base their self-image on this function within their family, often because they live in economically deprived situations that do not give them any other basis on which their self-esteem can be founded. And the problem is aggravated even more because their status as guest-workers justifies adherence to their traditional norms.

$(5b)$ $(G \cap A) \subset G$

For people of the problematic group $G - (G \cap A)$, norms are valid that are not, or not yet, accepted by them.

Example 1: People speaking creole on Mauritius, for whom

French is valid; but they do not accept French because it is, according to them, the language of the oppressor, the Franco-Mauritians. This way they are deprived of chances for economic betterment and remain underprivileged (cf Hookoomsing 1986).

Example 2: Negro youths in the ghettos of, for example, New York City who do not accept norms of the Whites that are valid for them in all areas of public life, especially in school. They also remain without chances, although they might preserve their pride and esteem within their peer groups.

Example 3: People from south India, especially Tamil speakers who do not accept Hindi as the official language. They rather stick to English as the second official language, and have always fought for preserving English as an official language of India (cf Annamalai 1979b; Srivastava 1979).

(6a) $(O \cap G) \subset O$
The problematic group are people, $O - (O \cap G)$, who have adopted norms that are not valid for them.

Example 1: Children and wives of Turkish and Moroccan workers in Western Europe who have adopted norms from their host country, although according to the authority in their families these norms are not valid for them. Results are conflicts within these families, illness of the threatened authority, and break-up of families.

Example 2: Slaves that had accepted norms from their masters, although, according to their masters, these norms were not valid for them. The masters, especially the Ku-Klux-Klan, did not approve of Blacks successfully imitating Whites.

(6b) $(O \cap G) \subset G$
The problematic group $G - (O \cap G)$ has certain norms that are valid for them, not, or not yet, adopted.

Example 1: Creole speakers from Mauritius for whom French is valid, but is not adopted by them.

Example 2: Dialect speakers for whom the standard language is valid but who, although they accept the standard norm, have not been able to adopt it.

Example 3: Immigrants in the United States of the first generation for whom English is válid, but who have not yet adopted English. For decriptions of these situations see Haugen (1972).

Example 4: Foreign workers and their children for whom in public life the language of the host country is valid, but who have not yet adopted this language.

(7a) $(R \cap G) \subset R$

For the problematic population $R - (R \cap G)$ there are norms justified that are not valid for them.

Example 1: People who are confronted with the beginning of language planning in the context of modernization. Then, norm concepts are justified and advocated by language-planning agencies. These norms are not yet valid for the population, but justified for them. People are in need of the new norms they do not yet have. Only after legislation and resolutions by the ministries of education and public affairs can these norm concepts be valid norms and be implemented.

Example 2: People for whom the norm concept that there should not be private property in land is justified, though it is not declared valid by the legislature.

(7b) $(G \cap R) \subset G$

For the problematic population $G - (R \cap G)$, norms are valid that are not justified.

Example: Germans in the Germany under Hitler, for whom the *Rassengesetze* were valid, although they were not justified for them. There were attempts made to justify these laws by claiming that they were justified on the basis of racial values, like superiority and purity of the so-called Aryan race. Many of those people who found themselves in these conflicts got into trouble because of resistance: they rated justification higher than validity.

(8a) $(R \cap A) \subset R$

People from the problematic group $R - (R \cap A)$ have found certain norms to be justified for themselves. But they have not accepted these norms. This often happens if the norms are not valid for them. They are then in the position to try to have them made valid by the legislature. If justified norms are also valid, acceptance normally follows.

Example: Again those people who think the norm concept 'No private property of land' justified, but do not accept it, because it is not valid.

(8b) $(A \cap R) \subset A$

Here, people from $A - (R \cap A)$ have accepted norms that are not justified for them.

Example 1: Those people who accepted racial laws, although they were not justified.

Example 2: People who accept for themselves norms of

another group because they want to identify with the group, even though it is not useful for them to do so.

(9a) $(O \cap A) \subset O$

Here, people from the problematic group $O - (O \cap A)$ have adopted norms that they have not accepted. This happens in automatic assimilation. Something similar also happens with respect to prescriptions which are forced upon people, and people adopt them, but have never accepted them in the sense that they would want correction in case they do not comply. In this case people have not adopted norms but comply, under pressure, to unaccepted prescriptions.

Example 1: Language purists who fight against all foreign borrowings in their own language but nevertheless find themselves using foreign borrowings in their speech.

Example 2: People who use slang expressions without accepting these kinds of expressions as part of their language. They find themselves behaving in accordance with language norms of others they do not accept.

(9b) $(A \cap O) \subset A$

Here, people of group $A - (O \cap A)$ have accepted norms that they have not yet adopted.

Example 1: People in India who have accepted Hindi as their language but are not able to speak it (properly or at all). In a census they honestly claim to speak Hindi or that Hindi is their language. This way they identify with prestige groups who speak Hindi (*cf* Khubchandani 1976).

Example 2: Speakers of a dialect that have accepted the standard language, but are not able to speak it (properly). Acceptance is proven by wanting and accepting corrections in favour of the standard, and in wanting their children to learn standard.

Example 3: Immigrants who accept the autochthons' language, but cannot speak it yet.

(10a) $(R \cap O) \subset R$

Here, people from the problematic group $R - (O \cap R)$ find that certain norms are justified for them, but have not adopted these norms yet.

Example 1: People who adhere to the norm concept 'No private property in land', but have not adopted this norm as a guide for their own conduct, maybe because it is not a valid norm.

Example 2: People who understand that modernization of their language is necessary, but are not able to adopt modernization readily.

Example 3: The majority in India think Hindi justified as their national language by Indian tradition. But many have not adopted Hindi themselves, especially since they can get along well enough with English as the second official language next to their regional state language.

$(10b)$ $(R \cap O) \subset O$

The problematic group $O - (R \cap O)$ has adopted norms that are not justified for them.

Example 1: Stylistic, phonetic, and behavioural imitation of a prestige group by people from another group. This leads to especially bad results if the one who has adopted the strange norms actualizes them within his own social group instead of complying to the norms that hold there. Also, the imitated group does not appreciate this kind of adherence. If these imitations happen on a large scale the imitated group sees its identity threatened and develops new norms of behaviour and style to create new distinctions.

Example 2: People who adopted the racial laws in the Germany under Hitler, but still felt that they were not justified. They tried, in many cases, to cover the conflict by rationalization of these laws on the basis of dubious values.

Existence of conflicts of the types discussed here means that a population is heterogeneous with respect to norms. A homogeneous population with respect to a norm or norm system N would be one in which the domains of existence, validity, adoption, and justification of N coincide. An example of a homogeneous population would be a village with hardly any contacts with the outside. Questions about validity, acceptance and justification do not arise here; these questions only become the focus of attention if there is some heterogeneity within the domains defined above.

7.1.3 Conflicts between different norms within one population

The kinds of conflicts described above become aggravated if, for example, the validity domains of two incompatible norms or norm systems, N^2 and N^3, overlap. Then, there are people, $G_{N^2} \cap G_{N^3}$, who have to obey both sets of norms. Often two different norm authorities and norm enforcers, who define and enforce validity, correspond with the two incompatible norms.

This is the case in the examples of wives and children of Turkish and Moroccan labourers in Western Europe.

A possible solution in these kinds of conflict is to restrict N^2 to certain kinds of situations, and N^3 to other kinds of situations. Often the two different situational domains of norm application are the domains of private life and of public life; or situations of interaction with members of group A, to which one restricts norms N^2, are distinguished from situations of interaction with members of group B, where norms N^3 are applied.

Examples of these kinds of conflicts in validity between two norms or norm systems are not only current in the lives of foreign workers and their families, but are also current in the life of women, who behave at home in their families very often according to those norms people think women should follow (for example, be especially protective with respect to the image of the partner), and in public, as business women or women in research and teaching, they have to behave according to norms that are functional there and traditionally are considered to be norms of conduct for men. Often such a clear discrimination between kinds of situations is not possible, and often one and the same situation exhibits features of both of the distinguished situational types.

For example, a secretary in business life has to be efficient and to the point in situations of information exchange, 'like a man', and at the same time she has to pay tribute to those norms that people think a real woman should comply with, that is, cleaning the ashtray, putting flowers on the boss's desk, preparing coffee, being tolerant towards all kinds of nonsense produced by the boss and – keep smiling. Such a woman, especially if intelligent, often finds herself in norm conflicts, for example between telling the truth and, by this, serving efficient handling of the business ('man's norms'), or protecting the image of her boss and keeping silent, although she knows better ('woman's norms').

Another strategy of solving conflicts between valid norms is, next to discriminating situations of application, to act according to N^2, and at the same time pay tribute to N^3 in a symbolic way. This, especially, is the only solution if a situation is at the same time both an N^2-type situation and an N^3-type situation, like that of the secretary, the businesswoman, and the career woman generally. Her make-up and dress, properly restrained, of course, are the symbolic tributes to the woman's norms in a business (man's) world. That women carry these social markers of group identity is approved of by men as well as by women.

Many examples of norm conflicts between two incompatible norm concepts in case of overlap in their respective domains of

existence, validity, acceptance, adoption, and justification can be
found in the area of multicultural settings, multilingual settings,
all kinds of immigrant situations and problems between cultures
and subcultures, and standard languages and dialects or sociolects. These types of norm conflicts can be represented by non-
empty $X_{N^2} \cap Y_{N^3}$, for $X = E, G, A, O, R$ and $Y = E, G, A, O,$
R. The cases $X_{N^2} \cap Y_{N^3}$ are identical in type with the cases
$Y_{N^2} \cap X_{N^3}$. This reduces the twenty-five combinations to fifteen
types:

$E_{N^2} \cap E_{N^3}$, $E_{N^2} \cap G_{N^3}$, $E_{N^2} \cap A_{N^3}$, $E_{N^2} \cap O_{N^3}$, $E_{N^2} \cap R_{N^3}$, $G_{N^2} \cap$
G_{N^3}, $G_{N^2} \cap A_{N^3}$, $G_{N^2} \cap O_{N^3}$, $G_{N^2} \cap R_{N^3}$, $A_{N^2} \cap A_{N^3}$, $A_{N^2} \cap O_{N^3}$,
$A_{N^2} \cap R_{N^3}$, $O_{N^2} \cap O_{N^3}$, $O_{N^2} \cap R_{N^3}$, and $R_{N^2} \cap R_{N^3}$.

In the discussion of some examples of these kinds of norm
conflicts, I shall point out the difference between the situation
of immigrants and the situation of foreign guest-workers with respect to norm conflicts.

In the immigrant situation, conflicts arise because the immigrants, from the beginning, have to be considered and have to
function as part of the society they immigrated into. The culture
and the legal system, as well as the linguistic norms of the autochthons are dominant, especially since the immigrants came
permanently to accept a function within the order and economic
system of the immigration country. This means that they come
there to be integrated, and thus dominance of culture and law
of the immigration country is presupposed. They did not come
as conquerors. In the United States, integration is normally
completed with the third generation, if not already with the
second. Descendants of immigrants who are economically
suppressed, often because they did not develop skills necessary
for progress in a modern society, stick with some, mostly ritual,
norms that still make their ethnical background apparent. Ethnical revival is, according to Fishman (1985), typically arising
within groups at the boundary of American society, who see
not much of a chance for economic betterment and esteem
provided by economic success. The function of ethnical revival
is to provide some symbol of an identity from which people can
derive some kind of self-esteem that, in deficiency of any other
background, is ethnical. It is noticeable that the ritual norms of
ethnicity do not really conflict with the norms of modern American society, although those people understand themselves as
adhering to both norm systems. Conflicts are prevented precisely
by the strategy indicated above, namely by making a clear
distinction between situations of life where the one, and situations where the other, norm applies. This has become possible

by restricting the ethnical norms to ritual forms of life that take place on Sundays or sabbatical days generally, in gatherings of ethnical and religious communities. Even use of languages other than English is restricted to ritual use. People who, in the course of ethnical revival, started to learn the languages of their fore-fathers, use these languages only in ritual settings and are not able to speak them in normal conversation. They pay a symbolic tribute to a set of norms that define, vaguely, their ethnicity. Often, clothing, hair-style, and the use of some ethnic vocabulary serve as markers of ethnic identity also outside ritual situations, in normal public life.

In a real immigrant situation dominance of the autochthons' law and culture is implied by this situation. This is different in cases where minorities conquer a country. There, dominance is reversed, although does not apply to all areas of life of the autochthons. Examples for this we find in colonialization. There, autochthonous populations, together with imported and immi-grating workers who did not belong to the conquerors, developed pidgin languages and creole languages that are oriented towards the language of the conquerors, in the scale of the so-called creole continuum, the development of a series of languages with an increasing similarity to the matrix language, which is the conqueror's language.

Still different from immigration on the one hand and conquest on the other, is the situation of the labourers who come from underdeveloped areas in Muslim countries to modern Western European countries. They came not as immigrants and not as conquerors. How is their status defined and what does that mean for the existing norm conflicts?

First, some remarks about the kind of norm conflicts those people are involved in: if one hears the stories and sees the sketches children of foreign workers tell and draw at school, it is very evident that many of the norms enforced on them at home are the same or very similar to those we had in our Western societies up to fifty years ago. The role of the patriarch in a family of a Muslim worker is the same as it was in our society not too long ago, and the kinds of norms he enforces are very similar to ours from not too long ago. They are not primarily religious; religion only supports these norms and backs up the norm enforcers. Further, it is noticeable that upper- and middle-class people from Muslim countries do not follow the traditional norms at home, for example in the larger Turkish cities; they are very European in behaviour and with regard to education and opportunities of their women. When these people come to work

and to live in Western Europe, they have hardly any problems
in the way of norm conflicts, except the linguistic ones. And
because of their intellectual training they are able to see differences and possible norm conflicts more easily, before they can
get into trouble. Taking this into account, we may conclude that
the problem of arising norm conflicts in the case of guest-workers
is very much related to lower social class, poor economic status,
and often even illiteracy. It is mainly a problem of modernization
and not so much of religion, which we in Europe took about
ninety years to solve, beginning with the first women who were
admitted to professional studies at universities.

The uniqueness of the situation of the guest-worker lies in the
fact that here no gradual change of norms towards modernization
is required, but people are required to conform at the same time
to different sets of norms, which means to be traditional and
modern at the same time, with both sets of norms still enforced
upon them by two different sets of norm authorities and norm
enforcers.

How does the status of these foreign workers differ from the
status of proper immigrants?

1. In principle, they themselves expect and they are expected to
   go home after having earned enough to build a house and
   found a small business in their home country.
2. They, in most cases, do not receive nationality (citizenship)
   of their host country.

These facts are of the utmost importance and put them in quite
a different position from immigrants, both with respect to their
own attitudes towards people and culture of the host country,
and with respect to the attitude of the autochthons, which is
described adequately by their use of the term 'guest'-worker.
Guest-workers are not expected to become citizens, and as
guests, they are expected to go home after having stayed a while.

On the other hand the development is such that most of the
foreign workers, especially their children, in fact will not go
home. They hope to go home some time, and at the same time
hope to stay for an indefinite time.

They are in an unclear position. If they were immigrants, also
legally, their position would be clarified, and all the norm
conflicts would finally be solved by dominance of the norms of
the host or immigration country, and rightly so. But as long as
these foreigners are expected to go back home, there is no
justification for dominance, because the perspective of going
home requires that the norms of their home communities are
enforced. Otherwise, reintegration in the home communities

would be impossible. Thus the position of the norm authority in the family, the father, cannot be weakened in order to relieve the norm conflicts in favour of the norms of the host country. For foreigners who have become immigrants it is justified to weaken the norm authority in the family, and that will automatically happen because family members are now in the position to exert pressure on the head of the family, because they have a stronger legal status; and enforcing the traditional norms is no longer justified for an immigrant. Weakening the authority in the family will lead to problems for the man in saving his self-image, but the safe legal status will make it easier for him to adjust to the dominating culture and norms, and still feel some security. Such an immigrant can, with some pain, adjust to modern society, and will, rightly, be required to do so.

A guest-worker, who is a non-immigrant, has to expect to go back and has to remain prepared for that. To internalize norms of modern society would make this impossible. He and his family could not reintegrate into the larger family in his village in, let us say, Anatolia, but would rather have to go to one of the major cities, where he would live in anonymity, and probably without adequate supplies and support. This makes it rational to stick to the traditional norms, and it is a justification for keeping intact the role of the patriarch in families of Muslim workers.

At the same time, he and his family are required to conform to modern society because they want to earn money and want to have a position as workers in this society. This gives some justification to accept and comply with the autochthons' norms that are functional in this kind of society.

We can conclude that the unclear chameleon situation of the guest-worker is such that it justifies and requires both sticking to the traditional norms and accepting the traditional norm enforcers and authorities, and learning to conform to the norms of the modern host society, and accepting their norm enforcers and authorities. This situation is one of a genuine conflict with two equally strong back-ups for validity of two conflicting sets of norms. The seriousness of the problem, that makes it worse in comparison with the kind of conflicts the immigrant finds himself in, lies in the fact that both sets of norms are valid in a justified manner, and both sets of norm authorities and norm enforcers are justified in their function.

This is a strong argument for offering the status of immigrant to guest-workers, although even this status would still involve problems in the area of norm conflicts. But these people would then at least not be in the most problematic categories

$G_{N^2} \cap G_{N^3}$, and $R_{N^2} \cap R_{N^3}$, $G_{N^2} \cap R_{N^3}$, $R_{N^2} \cap G_{N^3}$
but in
$E_{N^2} \cap G_{N^3}$, $E_{N^2} \cap A_{N^3}$, $A_{N^2} \cap A_{N^3}$, $A_{N^2} \cap G_{N^3}$, and others.

These latter categories are less problematic because in these categories norm conflicts can be solved clearly according to the principle of dominance, because those people no longer belong to G_{N^2} and R_{N^2}. This means that their traditional norms are no longer valid or justified for them, although they still, at least for some time, exist for them. Conflicts will have to be solved in favour of the valid N_3 norms of the host country that is now the immigration country.

7.1.4 Conclusion
In this section thirty-four types of norm conflicts have been defined, and many of them have been illustrated.

The definitions of norm conflicts given in this chapter can serve as an analytic tool for detecting certain kinds of norm conflicts and constellations of several norm conflicts taking place in one single situation. The next step in this area of research would then be to investigate what the kinds and strategies of solution are in certain constellations of norm conflicts.

7.2 Norm conflicts in situations of communication

The norm conflicts treated in this chapter concern the use of communicational means, also called 'communication forms' if they are complexes of communicational means which are of certain text-linguistic form, as, for example, different sorts of text. I shall distinguish five types of norm conflict.

Situations have properties which satisfy the conditions for the application of certain norms; this means that in situations of, let us say, type c, behaviour according to norm N is suitable or even required. The sets of situations which permit or require the realization of a certain norm content I call the *situative validity domain*; or shorter 'the situative domain' $S(N)$ of the optional or obligatory norm N.

It is possible that the situative domains of two norms overlap without it being possible that both norms can be fulfilled at the same time, or after each other. In such a case the two norms are incompatible. There are overlaps between the situational domains of one or more norms or even whole norm systems or groups of norms. These can be unproblematic, but there can also be problematic situations. The latter are of interest here.

Two norms or norm systems A and B are *incompatible* with each other if there are situations in which people are permitted to or ought to act according to A and to B but the one excludes the other.

Examples for these kinds of incompatible groups of norms we find in situations in which women with a career often find themselves, who, in their work, have to fulfil norms of efficiency and competence (A-norms) and at the same time have to fulfil norms that fit to the image of a woman in our society (B-norms). Conflicts of this kind can be avoided by distinguishing the situational domains of A- and B-norms clearly, for example by restricting the application of A-norms to public life and the application of B-norms to the private sphere. But this is not generallly possible, because the A- and B-norms serve certain functions which cannot be distinguished as belonging to the area of public or of private life exclusively. Likewise it is not generally possible to restrict the situational domain of A-norms to dealings with certain people and the domain of B-norms to dealings with others.

Nevertheless, both points of view provide in many cases a rough delineation between behaviour according to A-norms and according to B-norms, and there are possibilities to satisfy the A-norms or the B-norms in certain situations to a higher or lower degree, depending on which side of the delineations the situation of norm application lies. Thus, we read in newspapers – no matter whether is true or not – that such an able and efficient politician (A-norms) as Margaret Thatcher is a good wife for Denis since she cooks him bacon and eggs for breakfast (B-norms). Also, by her way of dressing, bending down to little children and talking with common women as 'woman to woman', etc., she fulfils in a symbolic manner the norms that are held to be valid for women. By symbolic acts like these, people express that they accept the group of norms that are valid for them, although the circumstances require satisfying another group of norms that make it impossible really to fulfil the norms of the first group satisfactorily.

Not only female but also male politicians commit in public symbolic acts in favour of B-norms to prove that they, in principle, accept these norms of behaviour that exist for people 'with a heart', although their office requires them to deal with all kinds of matters according to A-norms. Lifting up little children or kissing them in public is a symbolic act often carried out to this effect.

Sometimes a situation admits two interpretations, namely as a situation from $S(A)$ and as a situation from $S(B)$, without giving any clues as to whether the situation is more an A-situation or more a B-situation. This can be the case in interaction between men and women in business life. Interaction with a man makes it proper for a woman to behave according to B-norms, while the business situation and the goal of efficiency require behaviour according to A-norms. This conflict is reflected in the partly contradicting advice given in handbooks for secretaries.

In situations in which pertinent information exchange is aimed at, we generally find a source of norm conflicts in the fact that here on the one hand A-norms are valid, which are oriented towards Grice's principle of cooperation in efficient information exchange, and on the other, B-norms are valid, which are founded on Goffman's principle of cooperation in image support and politeness. The kinds of expectations and conflicts resulting from this constellation between A- and B-norms have been investigated by Boeren (1982), as far as they especially pertain to women. It is evident that men also experience norm conflicts in this area; but in our society men are expected to have a clear preference for the principle of effective information exchange, while women are expected to prefer the principle of image support which guarantees smooth interaction and helps to avoid conflicts between people. Boeren points out that for men and women in our society there are different directions in strategies for solving conflicts between A- and B-norms by giving preference to the one or the other cooperation principle, respectively. This seems to be a culture-dependent phenomenon, since, for example, Malagasy men and women are expected to have just the opposite preferences and thus to follow the opposite strategies (cf Keenan 1974). It is going too far to work out the consequences of this constellation in our society. As far as the careers of women are concerned, these opposite expectations of preference are disadvantages.

There can even arise conflicts with regard to the Gricean principle alone because the different maxims that explicate it from the points of view of quality, quantity, relation, and manner can come into conflict with each other. These conflicts are exploited in the procedures of conversational implicatures (cf 1.2.6).

Also under Goffman's principle of image support alone, conflicts can arise. The strategies and rules for support and strengthening of one's own image can come into conflict with those for support of the image of the interaction partner. Often, one can only be achieved against costs for the other. In these cases the strategies for solving these conflicts are of second order; and also here something different is expected from men than from women, namely that women have to prefer norms of behaviour that support the partner image, especially the 'male' image, while men may very well support their own image. And so both do. A good example are the long and overly elaborate speeches that some men deliver in gatherings and seminars, and especially as members of Ph.D. committees in public examinations, without considering that time is scarce, that every member of the committee should have a chance to pose a question, and that the defendant should have time enough to answer. This is cocky behaviuor and largely an unconsciously used means to strengthen one's own image. In this there is no difference from the Malagasy community described by Keenan (1974), where men have the privilege of producing very elaborate, though polite, speeches in a high ceremonial style called *kabary*. For women only the simple style, *resaka*, is appropriate. This is also the style of conducting real business, fighting out conflicts, shouting, gossiping, etc., and women are usually expected to be involved in these dealings. They are sent out by their men to perform these acts, that they themselves can devote their time to higher values and activities, performed in *kabary*.

People in our society have generally to keep a certain balance between supporting their own image and supporting the partner's image. Certainly in the northern and middle European countries one is expected to work carefully on both and not to overdo one or the other. In other cultures the conflict between both is solved differently: we can observe that in the United States people are allowed to praise their own achievements. Counterbalancing this boasting behaviour, however, they may be attacked severely by critics, who again show off by this kind of criticism. In Japan, on the other hand, people are not allowed to strengthen their own image explicitly by showing off and praising themselves. They have to humiliate themselves and give a very modest appearance, while the partner in communication is obliged to compensate this by praising the other and performing all kinds of acts of honour and respect. Women, above this, use even more polite forms than Japanese men in comparable situations; their speech generally expresses more distance and carefulness (Ide *et al.* 1986).

What is common in these different cultures is that generally the plus and minus of own-image-support and other-image-support have to be in balance such that the result is, in principle, an equality of the interaction partners. In our culture this second-order principle is evident when we have to praise somebody who presents himself with uttermost modesty. For some people, being modest has become a strategy to receive praise: 'fishing for compliments'. People who present themselves as very modest, shy, somewhat embarrassed, and vulnerable ask much of other people, because these then have to work on strengthening the image of the first if they want to be able to interact and negotiate with them on the basis of equality.

In the examples given above a strategy for solving norm conflicts has been illustrated. This strategy consists of fulfilling in a situation of conflict one of the conflicting norms and paying tribute to the other in a symbolic way. In this way, frozen patterns of politeness have a symbolic function: in behaving according to these patterns we express respect towards others without really doing anything to strengthen their image or doing something to their advantage. Traditional politeness towards women rests on this function: the more this ritual form of politeness had been complied with, the less it was necessary to do some real actions to support their image and to prove acceptance of women as equal partners. Ritual politeness was offered as a compensation for equal rights and had been accepted by the majority of women. (It is not easy to judge to what extent this is still so.)

The following strategy is based on the same principle: the exaggerated use of forms and rituals of politeness serves as a symbolic counterpoise or compensation for an especially severe attack on the other. His or her image is damaged by the attack, and at the same time the appearance or fiction of respect is preserved, necessary to maintain at least in principle the equality that is a precondition for further interaction. Often it is unavoidable to oppose explicitly the opinions and actions of others. Such an opposition is understood as an offence. It is 'face-threatening'. By supporting and strengthening the image of the other in at least a symbolic manner the attack can be performed in a 'decent' way and thus be bearable. (Expressing opinions indirectly and softening strong statements is another method to give a less threatening appearance.) Hereby the possibility, and the necessity, for an aggressive counter-action is taken away from the other, and he has the chance to react to the criticism in a reasonable way. Rituals of politeness and the ritual of assuring the other that one, in no way, wants to attack him personally serve to smooth a conflict between persons. Since the image of people largely consists of the opinions and attitudes assigned to them it is unavoidable that a conflict around opinions and actions is always also an attack on the image of the other.

Generally speaking, norms need not and cannot be complied with in all situations in which they are valid, but they have, at least, to be strengthened by showing acceptance and paying tribute to them. This can be done by apologizing for not following them, by correcting oneself if that is possible, or by expressing acceptance of them symbolically. These proofs of reference to a community's norms are a method to reinforce one's membership.

As has been pointed out, certain situations of interaction require certain forms of behaviour, *ie* the application of norms is dependent on the type of the situation. This relationship between situational type and norm or group of norms can also be made use of in the reverse way by language users: by applying a certain norm A in a situation s which does not belong to the situational validity domain of A, the actor tries to define or to reconstruct s as a situation belonging to $S(A)$, the situational domain of A. Thus, one interaction partner – or even both if the second cooperates – can try to redefine a situation of a type belonging to $S(B)$ as a situation of a type belonging to $S(A)$. This is known in Goffman's (1974) terminology as a 'frame'-shift.

Examples of conflicts between definitions of situations and frames we find in Quasthoff (1980), where in an institutionally defined situation, namely in office conversations between clients and social workers, one interaction partner, the social worker, communicates according to the norms of the institutional frame and the other partner, the client, tries to redefine the institutional situation as a personal conversation between friends by applying norms of behaviour that are valid for such private situations.

The official uses the forms of communication that are suited for the goal of obtaining information necessary for deciding on the kind and amount of aid for the client. These means of communication are questions directed to this goal, which require as an answer a short report by the clients about their household tasks, the performance of these tasks, and their bodily or mental disabilities.

The clients, on the other hand, do not accept these forms of communication: they do not provide the required information, or treat it as merely an accessory matter. Instead they tell about a stay in a hospital, about the old times, about adventures when going shopping, etc.

Some of these stories function as illustrations of a point relevant for the official, or function as explanations in an argumentation about a certain claim for official support. The officials usually accept these stories, at least as far as they are able to recognize the illustrative and argumentative functions of the stories. Often, these functions are not recognized at the beginning of a story, or they are difficult to extrapolate from the story. Then the officials try to stop the course of story-telling by pointing out what the real topic of conversation is and requiring the client to return to it. Such admonitions do not need to disturb the clients if they do speak to the point. But instead of getting confused because their argumentational strategy is not accepted, or instead of merely continuing with the story, the clients should point out to the official in a meta-communicative way what the function of their story is with respect to the theme of the conversation. But this does not happen. Apparently, most clients, often being of lower class, are not at all trained in meta-communicative talk about conversational strategies. But there are' also cases where the story is not to the official point, and the client knows this and uses story-telling as a means of changing the situation into a more private one.

According to Quasthoff, many of these stories have the function of psychic relief, or serve for strengthening the self-image of the client, or serve the client's intention to entertain the hearer by fantastic and amusing stories.

The clients often take great pains to break the institutional frame and to deliver their story even if the official does not cooperate. They then try to raise the curiosity of the interaction partners such that they are willing to grant some opening for the story within the conversation.

Quasthoff (1980:177, 186) mentions three possible analyses of these situations of conflict between actualized communicational norms and communicational norms required by the kind of situation:

1. One of the partners misconceives the situation type or frame; he has misunderstood the situation, ie he finds himself in a 'frame confusion'.

Quasthoff supposes that it is the client who must have misunderstood the situation. This is so because the more powerful, that is the institution or its representative, defines the frame of interaction. The official is present in his function, the client approaches him and therefore does not have the right to define the situation or to negotiate about redefining it. As a result, the client can be mistaken about the analysis of the situation, but the official cannot, since the situation is defined by himself in his function.

2. Both interaction partners have the correct notion of the situation. The client knows that his form of communication does not fit a situation of this type, but he or she feels the need to

prolong communication to achieve some psychic relief, for example.

This need, then, is in conflict with the realization of the communicational norms of the institutional frame. The client and, in the most fortunate case, also the social worker defer the institutional frame for the moment to find some opening for fulfilling the communicational need of the client. This is a compromise between two aims in which both, the norms bound to the institutional frame and the norms bound to private conversation, are realized to some extent. The whole situation remains institutionally defined by reserving only a limited space for the story within the institutionally defined discourse.

3. Both interaction partners perceive the situation correctly, *ie* understand the frame, but one of them does not accept it.

The client wants to change the frame: he wants to rid the conversation of its matter-of-fact character, directed towards obtaining information and giving advice. He wants to engage the other into a private conversation with the aim of winning a friend. In these cases, the stories have, according to Quasthoff (1980:177), a 'frame-defining' function.

If the official were to cooperate with the client without reserve, this would count as accepting the new situation which the client tries to create by his manner of communicating. From this, obligations would arise which the official could not comply with later on. To avoid disappointing the client, the official has to resist the redefinition of the situation by the client and therefore cannot accept his stories, except with obvious signs of disapproval. The behaviour of the client has to be marked as inappropriate by the official; accepting it as appropriate would mean that the situation would be fitted to the behaviour and thus would be redefined. The official will usually refuse to listen to the story given in this way, will indicate that it is irrelevant, will endeavour to persuade the client to return to the point.

The frame-defining role of story-telling sometimes makes it difficult to accept stories where they have an argumentative function to the point. By blocking these stories, too, officials deprive clients of all their argumentational means in a conversation. Particularly clients of lower class are trained in arguing by means of illustrative and explanatory stories, more than by means of arguments that consist of propositionally formulated premises and conclusions. These people, hindered in using their group-specific means of communication, then come to stand literally speechless, *ie* 'without language', before the official.

Especially in situations in which argumentation is required, hearers of higher social strata perceive stories told by socially deprived speakers as deviating from the topic, being fussy, concerned with secondary matters, not to the point, and avoiding the issue. The behaviour of the speaker is experienced as irrational, because it does not appear goal directed and goal adequate. It is not realized that stories also serve for argumentation and illustration of central points in the discussion. The lack of knowledge about the social determinateness of speech strategies leads to disqualification of interaction partners. They are not taken seriously, one does not listen to them, except to catch some funny remarks the relevance of which is not noticed.

An illustration of this is a discussion that took place in the talk show *Sonja* by the Dutch television producer VARA, from 4 March 1983; this talk show has been analysed in a working group directed by Dorothea Franck at the University of Amsterdam:

Sonja talks with an inhabitant of a mobile-home camp at the outskirts of Amstelveen, a houseowner, and a local politician of that community about the question whether the camp should be allowed to remain in that place, despite the protest of the houseowners in the area.

After having listened to the tape for the first time, the members of the working group had negative reactions towards the inhabitant of the mobile-home camp (let us call him 'John'): John deviates from the theme, he does not speak to the point, he speaks in unconnected sentences, he uses an unintelligible pictorial style, he prevents others from having their turn, he only wants to be funny, make a show, make the others laugh, play the clown.

Only after hearing the tape in parts, and for a second time after analysing the transcript carefully, could the working group recognize the argumentative value of John's stories and apreciate his talk as a contribution to the discussion. But, other than this group, John's listeners were not in the position to make such an analysis and therefore his contribution did not have the intended effect in the discussion and was not understood, except, of course, by his own people who watched this show on television in their caravans. Among middle-class speakers, this man made a somewhat irrational appearance as a mentally less developed, funny, and rude fellow, who has missed the point of the discussion.

Only after recognizing the argumentative role of the stories, did the working group judge the repeated blockades and interruptions of this man by the show hostess Sonja to be inappropriate; Sonja called John to order and tried to make him speak to the point. And this was wrong because she did not realize that he was speaking to the point in his way, namely according to the speech norms and argumentational strategies of his social group.

Both speakers understood the kind of situation they were in, and what the goals were, namely argumentation *pro* and *contra* with regard to the question of where the camp should be placed. Furthermore, some show effect and entertainment of the public were certainly intended. Even then a conflict arose between the norms of communication that were applicable in a situation of this kind, because these norms were different according to the different social background of the communication partners.

The camp inhabitant would have improved his chance of being understood if he had used some meta-communicational means to mark his stories as contributions to one or the other point in the discussion. But it also belongs to the style of this social group that these means are not used, or at least are not used sufficiently often, probably since in such closed communities people understand each other very well anyway because of their background of common knowledge which makes such means of steering conversation superfluous.

A further complicating factor that might have contributed to the norm conflict in this discussion was the fact that John had to discuss, on the one hand, with his (middle-class) opponents in the show, had to take into account the audience in the hall, and also his people at home, who certainly were watching the live show. Thus, his contributions had to be triple-addressed. And above all he had to make an appearance that could be valued positively according to the norms of his own group: for them he speaks, and they will judge his performance. In a similar manner Sonja pays attention to her public, mainly middle class like herself, although the VARA is the workers' broadcasting organization. She is bound to the norms of argumentation of the educated class. In addition to these complicating factors, Sonja is not only a partner in the discussion but, at the same time, chairperson and show hostess. In this way she is a partner in the discussion with a clearly dominating role: she defines the situation and her (middle-class) norms are the norms that determine the course of the conversation. As far as she is concerned there is no conflict; but for the camp inhabitant there is a conflict, namely between the communicational norms of Sonja (and her social background), which dominate in this situation, and the communicational norms of his social group.

Controlling this norm conflict would have required that the

chairperson of this discussion had some knowledge or at least some feeling of the social differences in communicational norms between herself and her partner in discussion.

7.3 Conclusion

In this chapter five different kinds of norm conflict were analysed or at least mentioned.

1. Norm conflicts arise when a situation admits different interpretations and thus at the same time shows features requiring the application of A-norms and features requiring the application of B-norms, where A- and B-norms cannot be realized together. Then the acceptance of the more recessive norms is merely indicated symbolically.

2. Norm conflicts arise in situations that have a unique interpretation, or admit only one interpretation due to clear institutional frames and power relationships. Here a conflict can arise between, on the one hand, communicational norms bound to an institutional frame in a situation defined by this frame, and on the other, communicational norms which serve to fulfil needs and interests outside this frame and which require other communicational forms than the ones required by the institutional frame. Within the institutional frame some space will be reserved for the weaker part in those cases in which some readiness for cooperation exists with regard to the interests and goals that are strange compared with the institutional ones.

3. Norm conflicts arise even when the situation is uniquely defined if one of the partners does not accept the definition of the situation provided by the other, or given independently. The one who does not accept the situational frame will break this frame and create a newly defined situation. Conflicts of this kind can only be solved if one of the partners gives way and makes concessions. In most cases the more powerful will carry through the frame which he thinks is provided by the situation, or which fits his purposes. Defining situational frames is part of having power.

4. Norm conflicts arise in cases of unique interpretation of a situation if interaction- and communication-strategies are not recognized or even misunderstood because of group differences or differences in social strata.

5. Norm conflicts arise if speech is multiply addressed and the addressees differ in communicational norms such that different styles are appropriate for them.

References

AL, B. P. F. (1977) *Normatieve Taalkunde*. Muiderberg: Coutinho.

ALISJAHBANA, S. T. (1974) 'Language policy, language engineering, and literacy in Indonesia and Malaysia', in Fishman (1974c) *pp* 391–416.

ALLWOOD, J. (1976) *Linguistic Communication as Action and Cooperation: A Study in Pragmatics*. Gothenburg Monographs in Linguistics 2. Dept of Linguistics: University of Göteborg.

ALLWOOD. J. (1977) 'Negation and the strength of presuppositions', in Dahl, Ö (ed.), *Logic, Pragmatics, and Grammar*. Dept of Linguistics: University of Göteborg, *pp* 11–52.

ANNAMALAI, E. (1979a) 'Movement for linguistic purism: the case of Tamil', in Annamalai (1979b) *pp* 35–59.

ANNAMALAI, E. (ed.) (1979b) *Language Movements in India*. Central Institute of Indian Languages: Mansagangotri, Mysore-570006.

ANNAMALAI, E., B. JERNUDD, and J.RUBIN (eds) (1986) Language Planning. Proceedings of an Institute. Central Institute of Indian Languages. Mysore, India, and Institute of Culture and Communication. East-West-Center. Honolulu, Hawaii, USA.

APEL, K.-O. (ed.) (1976) *Sprachpragmatik und Philosophie*. Frankfurt: Suhrkamp Verlag.

APTE, M. L. (1976a) 'Language controversies in the Indian Parliament 1952–1960', in O'Barr and O'Barr (1976) *pp* 213–34.

APTE, M. L. (1976b) 'Multilingualism in India and its socio-political implications: an overview', in O'Barr and O'Barr (1976) *pp* 141–64.

BAHRDT, H. P. (1973) 'Der Deutschunterricht aus der Sicht eines Soziologen', in Gidion, J, and Bahrdt, H. P., *Praxis des Deutschunterrichts. Überlegungen und Materialien*. Göttingen: Vandenhoek und Ruprecht, *pp* 75–104.

BAILEY, CH.-J. (1973) *Variation and Linguistic Theory*. Arlington: Center for Applied Linguistics.

BAILEY, CH.-J. (1974) 'Some suggestions for greater consensus in creole terminology', in DeCamp and Hancock (1974) *pp* 88–91.

BARON, D. (1982) *Grammar and Good Taste. Reforming the American*

Language. New Haven: Yale University Press.

BARTSCH, R. (1969) 'Grundzüge einer empiristischen Bedeutungstheorie'. Dissertation, University of Heidelberg.

BARTSCH, R. (1973) 'Gibt es einen sinnvollen Begriff von linguistischer Komplexität?', *Zeitschrift für Germanistische Linguistik*, **1**(1), 6–31.

BARTSCH, R. (1975) 'Topik–Fokus Struktur und kategoriale Syntax', in Ehrich and Finke (1975) *pp* 85–100.

BARTSCH, R. (1976) 'The role of categorial syntax in grammatical theory', in Kasher (1976b) *pp* 503–39.

BARTSCH, R. (1978) 'Satzreihung, Satzgefüge, oder Adverbialkonstruktion? Über pragmatische und kontextuelle Unterschiede zwischen semantisch gleichwertigen Aussagen', in Hartmann, D., Linke, H., and Ludwig, O. (eds), *Sprache in Gegenwart und Geschichte. Festschrift für Heinrich Matthias Heinrichs*. Cologne: Böhlau Verlag, *pp* 1–18.

BARTSCH, R. (1979a) 'Semantical and pragmatical correctness as basic notions in the theory of meaning', *Journal of Pragmatics*, **3**, 1–43.

BARTSCH, R. (1979b) 'Die Rolle von pragmatischen Korrektheitsbedingungen bei der Interpretation von Äußerungen', in Grewendorf, G. (ed.), *Semantik und Sprechakttheorie*. Frankfurt: Suhrkamp, *pp* 217–46.

BARTSCH, R. (1979c) 'Die Unterscheidung zwischen Wahrheitsbedingungen und anderen Gebrauchsbedingungen in einer Bedeutungstheorie für Partikeln', in Weydt (1979) *pp* 365–77.

BARTSCH, R. (1981) 'Kommunikatienormen en lexicale verandering', *Tijdschrift voor Taal- en Textwetenschap* (*TTT*), **2**, 83–101.

BARTSCH, R. (1982a) 'The concepts "rule" and "norm" in linguistics', *Lingua*, **58**, 51–81.

BARTSCH, R. (1984a) 'The structure of word meaning', in Landman F., and Veltman, F. (eds), *Varieties of Formal Semantics*. Dordrecht: Foris Publications, *pp* 25–54.

BARTSCH, R. (1984b) 'Norms, tolerance, lexical change, and context-dependence of meaning', *Journal of Pragmatics*, **8**, 367–93.

BARTSCH, R. (1984c) 'Context-dependent interpretation of lexical items'. Paper given at the 5th Amsterdam Colloquium, Aug. 1984. In: Groenendijk, J., de Jongh, D., and Stokhof, M. (eds), *Foundations of Pragmatics and Lexical Semantics*. GRASS 7, Dordrecht: Foris Publications, 1986, *pp* 1–28.

BARTSCH, R. (1985a) 'Concept formation, truth, and norm', in Seuren, P. (ed.), *Meaning and the Lexicon*. Dordrecht: Foris Publications.

BARTSCH, R. (1985b) 'The influence of language standardization on linguistic norms', *Studia Linguistica*, **39**(1), 23–50.

BARTSCH, R., and VENNEMANN, TH. (1982) *Grundzüge der Sprachtheorie*. Tübingen: Niemeyer Verlag.

BEIER, E. (1960) 'Wege und Grenzen der Sprachnormung in der Technik. Beobachtungen aus dem Bereich der deutschen technischen Sprachnormung'. Dissertation, Rheinische Friedrich-Wilhelms University, Bonn.

BENEŠ, E., and VACHEK, J. (eds) (1971) *Stilistik und Soziolinguistik*

Beiträge der Prager Schule zur strukturellen Sprachbetrachtung und Spracherziehung. Munich: List Verlag.

BERITS, J. (1983) 'Proposed spelling reform for Dutch', *Language Planning News Letter.* July 1983. East-West Center, Honolulu.

BHATTACHARYA, S. S. (1980) 'Socio-economic movement, language identity, and emergence of standard language – a case study of Tripura'. Paper given at the 1980 conference at the Central Institute of Indian Languages, Mysore-6.

BICKERTON, D. (1975) *Dynamics of a Creole System.* New York: Cambridge University Press.

BICKERTON, D. (1977) 'Some problems of acceptability and grammaticality in pidgins and creoles', in Greenbaum, S. (ed.), *Acceptability in Language.* The Hague: Mouton, *pp* 27–37.

BIERWISCH, M. (1970) 'Fehlerlinguistik', *Linguistic Inquiry*, 1, 397–414.

BLACKALL, E. A. (1966) *Die Entwicklung des Deutschen zur Literatursprache 1700–1775.* Translated by H. G. Schürmann, Stuttgart, 1966. English version: *The Emergence of German as a Literary Language 1700–1775.* Cambridge, 1959.

BLOM, J. P. and GUMPERZ, J. J. (1972) 'Social meaning in linguistic structure: code-switching in Norway', in Gumperz, J. J., and Hymes, D. (eds), *The Ethnography of Communication.* New York: Holt, Rinehart, and Winston, *pp* 407–34.

BLOOMFIELD, L. (1933) *Language.* New York and Chicago: Holt, Rinehart, and Winston.

BODINE, A. (1975) 'Sex differentiation in language', in Thorne, B., and Henley, N. (eds), *Language and Sex. Difference and Dominance.* Rowley, Mass.: Newbury House Publishers, *pp* 130–51.

BOEREN, A. (1982) 'Vrouwentaal en Vooronderstellingen', *Tijdschrift voor Taalbeheersing*, 3(3), 210–19.

BOOIJ, G. E. *et al.* (1979) *Spelling.* Spektator Cahiers 2. Groningen: Wolters-Noordhoff.

BRESNAN, J. (1978) 'A realistic transformational grammar', in Halle, M., Bresnan, J., and Miller, G. A. (eds), *Linguistic Theory and Psychological Reality.* Cambridge, Mass.: MIT Press, *pp* 1–59.

BYNON, TH. (1977) *Historical Linguistics.* Cambridge–London: Cambridge University Press.

CARE, N. S., and LANDESMAN, CH. (eds) (1968) *Readings in the Theory of Action.* Bloomington: Indiana University Press.

CARNAP, R. (1928) *Der Logische Aufbau der Welt.* 2nd edn. Hamburg 1961.

CARNAP, R. (1956) 'Meaning and synonymy in natural languages', in *Meaning and Necessity.* University of Chicago Press, 2nd enlarged edn, *pp* 233–47.

CHOMSKY, N. (1957) *Syntactic Structures.* The Hague: Mouton.

CHOMSKY, N. (1965) *Aspects of the Theory of Syntax.* Cambridge, Mass.: MIT Press.

CHOMSKY, N. (1966) *Topics in the Theory of Generative Grammar.* The Hague: Mouton.

CHOMSKY, N. (1977) *Essays on Form and Interpretation*. Amsterdam: Elsevier–North Holland Publishing Company.

CHOMSKY, N. (1980) *Rules and Representations*. New York: Columbia University Press.

CHOMSKY, N. (1981) *Lectures on Government and Binding*. Dordrecht: Foris Publications.

CLARK, E., and CLARK, H. (1979) 'When nouns surface as verbs', *Language*, **55**, 767–811.

COBARRUBIAS, J. (1983) 'Ethical issues in status planning', in Cobarrubias, J., and Fishman, J. A. (eds), *Progress in Language Planning*. Berlin: Mouton, *pp* 41–85.

COLE, P., and MORGAN, J. L. (eds) (1975) *Syntax and Semantics*. Vol. 3: *Speech Acts*. New York: Academic Press.

COOPER, R. L. (1982a) 'A framework for the study of language spread', in Cooper (1982b) *pp* 5–36.

COOPER, R. L. (ed.) (1982b) *Language Spread. Studies in Diffusion and Social Change*. Bloomington: Indiana University Press.

COSERIU, E. (1970) 'Sprache, Strukturen, Funktionen. Darin: "System, Norm und Rede" und "Synchronie, Diachronie, Typologie"', *Tübinger Beiträge zur Linguistik*. Tübinger: G. Narr Verlag.

COSERIU, E. (1974) *Synchronie, Diachronie und Geschichte*. Munich: Fink Verlag.

DANES, F. (1968) 'Einige soziolinguistische Aspekte der Schriftsprachen', *Die Welt der Slaven*, **13**.

DASCAL, M., and MARGALIT. A. (1974) 'A new revolution in linguistics? – "Text grammars" versus "sentence grammars"', *Theoretical Linguistics*, **1**, 195–213.

DAS GUPTA, J. (1976) 'Practice and theory of language planning: the Indian policy process', in O'Barr and O'Barr (1976) *pp* 195–212.

DASWANI, C. J. (1979) 'Movement for the recognition of Sindhi, and for the choice of a script for Sindhi', in Annamalai (1979b) *pp* 60–70.

DAVIDSON, D. (1969) 'Truth and meaning', in Davis, J., Hockney, D., and Wilson, W. (eds), *Philosophical Logic*. Dordrecht: De Reidel, *pp* 1–20.

DAY, R. R. (1974) 'Decreolization: co-existent systems and the post-creole continuum', in De Camp and Hancock (1974) *pp* 38–45.

DECAMP, D. (1971) 'Towards a generative analysis of a post-creole speech continuum', in Hymes (1971) *pp* 349–70.

DECAMP, D., and HANCOCK, I. F. (eds) (1974) *Pidgins and Creoles: Current Trends and Prospects*. Washington: Georgetown University Press.

DEUTSCHE AKADEMIE FUR SPRACHE UND DICHTUNG (eds) (1980) *Der öffentliche Sprachgebrauch*. Vol. 1: *Die Sprachnorm-Diskussion in Presse, Hörfunk und Fernsehen*. Stuttgart: Klett-Cotta Verlag.

DIGGS, B. J. (1968) 'Rules and utilitarianism', in Care and Landesman (1968) *pp* 341–72.

DIJK, T. A. VAN (1972) *Some Aspects of Text Grammars*. The Hague: Mouton.

DIJK, T. A. VAN (1977) *Text and Context. Explorations in the Semantics and Pragmatics of Discourse*. London: Longman.

DIJK, T. A. VAN (1980) *Textwissenschaft. Eine interdisziplinäre Einführung.* Munich: Deutscher Taschenbuc Verlag.

DIK, S. (1978) *Functional Grammar*. Dordrecht: Foris Publications.

DIK, S. (1980) *Studies in Functional Grammar*. London and New York: Academic Press.

DOKULIL, M. (1971), 'Zur Frage der Norm der Schriftsprache und ihrer Kodifizierung', in Benes and Vachek (1971). 94–101.

DONNELLAN, K. (1962) 'Necessity and criteria', *Journal of Philosophy*, **59**, 647–58.

DRESSLER, W. U. (1982) 'Acceleration, retardation, and reversal of language decay?', in Cooper (1982b) *pp* 321–36.

DROP, W., and DE VRIES, J. H. L. (1980) *Taalbeheersing. Handboek voor Taalhantering*. Groningen: Wolters-Noordhoff.

DUA, H. R. (1980) *Language Planning. An Overview*. Mysore: Central Institute of Indian Languages.

DUA, H. R. (1986) 'Language planning and linguistic minorities'. Paper presented at the 1980 conference at the Central Institute of Indian languages, Mansagangotri, Mysore-570006, *pp* 133–73.

EHRICH, V., and FINKE, P. (eds) (1975) *Beiträge zur Grammatik und Pragmatik*. Kronberg, Ts.: Scriptor Verlag.

EHRICH, V. and SAILE, G. (1972) 'Über nicht-direkte Sprechakte', in Wunderlich, D. (ed.), *Linguistische Pragmatik*. Frankfurt: Athenäum, *pp* 255–84.

EKKA, F. (1979) 'Language loyalty and maintenance among the Kuruxs', in Annamalai (1979b) *pp* 99–106.

ENNINGER, W. (1979a) 'Language convergence in a stable triglossia plus trilingualism situation', in Freese, P. *et al.* (eds), *Anglistik. Beiträge zur Fachwissenschaft und Fachdidaktik, Festschrift für Eleonore Cladder*. Münster, *pp* 43–65.

ENNINGER, W. (1979b) 'Social roles and language choice in an old order Amish community', *Sociologica Internationalis*, **17**, 47–70.

ENNINGER, W. (1984) 'Funktion, Struktur und Erwerb der Varietäten Pennsylvaniadeutsch, Amish Hochdeutsch und Amerikanisches Englisch bei den Altamischen', in Oksaar, E. (ed.), *Spracherwerb – Sprachkontakt – Sprachkonflikt*. Berlin–New York: de Gruyter, *pp* 220–41.

ERVIN-TRIPP, S. M. (1972) 'Sociolinguistic rules of address', in Pride, J. B., and Holmes, J. (eds), *Sociolinguistics*. Penguin Modern Linguistic Readings, *pp* 225–40.

FELLMAN, J. (1977) 'The Hebrew Academy: orientation and operation', in Rubin *et al.* (1977) *pp* 97–110.

FELLMAN, J., and FISHMAN, J. A. (1977) 'Language planning in Israel: solving terminological problems', in Rubin *et al.* (1977) *pp* 79–96.

FERGUSON, CH. A. (1977) 'Sociolinguistic settings of language planning', in Rubin *et al.* (1977) *pp* 9–30.

FISHMAN, J. A. (ed.) (1968) *Readings in the Sociology of Language*. The

Hague: Mouton.

FISHMAN, J. A. (1974a) 'Language planning and language planning research: the state of the art', in Fishman (1974c) *pp* 15–36.

FISHMAN, J. A. (1974b) 'Language modernization and planning in comparison with other types of modernization and planning', in Fishman (1974c) *pp* 79–102.

FISHMAN, J. A. (ed.) (1974c) *Advances in Language Planning*. The Hague: Mouton.

FISHMAN, J. A. (ed.) (1978) *Advances in the Study of Societal Multilingualism*. The Hague: Mouton.

FISHMAN, J. A. (ed.) (1985) *The Rise and Fall of Ethnic Revival*. Berlin – New York–Amsterdam: Mouton.

FRANCIS, J. DE (1972) *Nationalism and Language Reform in China*. New York: Octagon Books.

FRANCK, D. (1975) 'Zur Analyse indirekter Sprechakte', in Ehrich and Finke (1975) *pp* 219–32.

FRANCK, D. (1980) *Grammatik und Konversation*. Königstein Ts.: Scriptor Verlag.

FROMKIN, V. A. (ed.) (1973) *Speech Errors as Linguistic Evidence*. The Hague: Mouton.

FROMKIN, V. A. (ed.) (1980) *Errors in Linguistic Performance: Slip of the Tongue, Ear, Pen, and Hand*. New York: Academic Press.

GAZDAR, G. (1979) *Pragmatics*. New York: Academic Press.

GAZDAR, G. *et al.* (1985) *Generalized Phrase Structure Grammar*. Oxford: Basil Blackwell.

GLOY, K. (1975) *Sprachnormen 1. Linguistische und soziologische Analysen. Reihe: Problemata 46*. Stuttgart–Bad Cannstadt: Frommann-Holzboog.

GLOY, K., and PRESCH, G. (eds) (1976) *Sprachnormen 3. Kommunikationsorientierte Linguistik – Sprachdidaktik. Reihe: Problemata 48*. Stuttgart–Bad Cannstadt: Frommann-Holzboog.

GOFFMAN, E. (1967) 'The nature of deference and demeanor' in *Interaction Ritual*. New York: Pantheon Books, *pp* 47–96.

GOFFMAN, E. (1974) *Frame Analysis*. New York: Harper and Row.

GOODY, E. N. (1978) 'Towards a theory of questions', in Goody, E. N. (ed.), *Questions and Politeness*. Cambridge: Cambridge University Press.

GREBE, P. (1968) 'Sprachnorm und Sprachwirklichkeit', in Institut für deutsche Sprache (1968) *pp* 28–44.

GRICE, P. (1975) 'Logic and conversation', in Cole and Morgan (1975) *pp* 41–58.

GROENENDIJK, J., and STOKHOF, M. (1975) 'Modality and conversational information', *Theoretical Linguistics*, 2, 61–112.

GROENENDIJK, J., and STOKHOF, M. (1978) 'Semantics, pragmatics, and the theory of meaning', *Journal of Pragmatics*, 2, 49–70.

GROENENDIJK, J., and STOKHOF, M. (1984) 'Studies in the semantics of questions and the pragmatics of answers'. Dissertation, University of Amsterdam. (To be published by Oxford University Press in 1988.)

GUMPERZ, J. J. (1971) *Language in Social Groups* (ed. by A. S. Dil). Stanford: University Press.

HABERMAS, J. (1974) 'Vorbemerkungen zu einer Theorie der kommunikativen Kompetenz, in Habermas, J., and Luhmann, N., *Theorie der Gesellschaft oder Sozialtechnologie – Was leistet die Systemforschung?* Frankfurt: Suhrkamp Verlag, *pp* 101–41.

HABERMAS, J. (1976) 'Was heißt Universalpragmatik?', in Apel (1976b) *pp* 174–272.

HALL, R. A. JR (1950) *Leave Your Language Alone!* Ithaca, New York; and (1960) *Linguistics and Your Language*. Second revised edition of 'Leave Your Language Alone'. A Doubleday Anchor Book. New York: Anchor Books.

HARRIS, Z. (1970) *Papers in Structural and Transformational Linguistics*. Formal Linguistic Series 1. Dordrecht: Reidel.

HART, H. (1961) *The Concept of Norm*. Oxford: University Press.

HARTMANN, D. (1973) 'Thesen zum Gebrauch von Anredeformen und Bezeichnungen dritter Personen in der direkten Kommunikation', *Zeitschrift für Literaturwissenschaft und Linguistik*. Beiheft: *Soziolinguistik*.

HARTMANN, D. (1977) 'Aussagesätze, Behauptungshandlungen und die kommunikative Funktion der Satzpartikel *ja, nämlich*, und *einfach*', in Weydt (1977) *pp* 101–14.

HARTUNG, W. (1977) 'Zum Inhalt des Normbegriffs in der Linguistik', in Hartung, W. (ed.), *Normen der sprachlichen Kommunikation. Reihe Sprache und Gesellschaft*. Vol. 11. Berlin (DDR): Akademie Verlag, *pp* 9–69.

HARTVELDT, D. (1978) *Taal en samenleving*. Baarn: Basis Boeken, Ambo.

HAUGEN, E. (1966a) *Language Conflict and Language Planning. The Case of Modern Norweigan*. Cambridge, Mass.: Harvard University Press.

HAUGEN, E. (1966b) 'Linguistics and language planning', in *Ecology of Language* (ed. by A. S. Dil). Stanford: University Press, *pp* 159–79.

HAUGEN, E. (1968) 'Language planning in modern Norway', in Fishman (1968) *pp* 673–87.

HAUGEN, E. (1971) 'Instrumentalism in language planning', in Rubin and Jernudd (eds) *pp* 281–292.

HAUGEN, E. (1972) *The Ecology of Language* (ed. by A. S. Dil). Stanford: University Press.

HAVRÀNEK, B. (1958) 'The functional differentiation of the standard language', in Garvin, P. L. (ed.), *A Prague School Reader on Esthetics, Literary Structure, and Style*, 2nd edn. Washington: *pp* 1–18.

HAVRÀNEK, B. (1964) 'Zum Problem der Norm in der heutigen Sprachwissenschaft und Sprachkultur', in Vachek (1964b) *pp* 413–20.

HAVRÀNEK, B. (1971) 'Die Theorie der Schriftsprache', in Beneš and Vachek (1971) *pp* 19–37.

HELLWIG, P. (1982) 'Grundzüge einer Theorie des Textzusammenhanges', in Rotkegel, A., Sandig, B., and Weissgerber, M. (eds), *Text – Textsorten – Semantik. Linguistische Modelle und maschinelle*

Anwendung. Proceedings of the International Colloquium, Saarbrücken, 18–20 November 1982.

HERINGER, H. J (1982a) 'Normen? Ja – aber meinel', in Heringer (1982b) *pp* 94–105. Also in: Deutsche Akademie für Sprache und Dichtung (1980) *pp* 58–72.

HERINGER, H. J. (ed.) (1982b) *Holzfeuer im hölzernen Often. Aufsätze zur politischen Sprachkritik,* Tübingen: G. Narr Verlag.

HERTZLER, J. O. (1965) *A Sociology of Language.* New York: Random House.

HEYDT, U. (1954) *Language Reform in Modern Turkey.* Jerusalem: Oriental Notes and Studies, publ. by the Israeli Oriental Society, no. 5.

HJELMSLEV, L. (1942) *Langue et Parole. Cahiers Ferdinand de Saussure, 3.* German translation: Langue und Parole. In: L. Hjelmslev (1974) Aufsätze zur Sprache-Wissenschaft. Stuttgarf: Klett Verlag. *pp* 44–55.

HJELMSLEV, L. (1943/1969) *Prolegomena to a Theory of Language.* Madison, Milwaukee, and London: The University of Wisconsin Press.

HOCKETT, C. (1948) 'A note on "structure"', *IJAL*, **14**, 269–71. Reprinted in Joos (1957) *pp* 279–81.

HOCKETT, C. (1954) 'Two models of grammatical description', *World*, **10**, 210–31. Reprinted in Joos (1957) *pp* 386–400.

HOOKOOMSING, V. Y. (1986) 'Creole and the language situation in Mauritius'. Paper given at the 1980 conference at the Institute of Indian Languages. In: Annamalai, Jernudd and Rubin (1986) *pp* 309–37.

HYMES, D. (ed.) (1971) *Pidginization and Creolization of Languages.* Cambridge: University Press.

IBRAHIM, M. H. (1983) 'Linguistic distance and literacy in Arabic', *Journal of Pragmmatics,* **7**, 507–16.

IDE, S. (1986) 'Sex difference and politeness in Japanese'. *Int'l. J. Soc. Lang.* 58: 25–36.

INSTITUT FUR DEUTSCHE SPRACHE (eds) (1968) *Sprachnorm, Sprachpflege, Sprachkritik. Jahrbuch des Instituts für deutsche Sprache 1966/67* (= Moser 1968).

ITKONEN, E. (1974) *Linguistics and Metascience.* Studia Philosophica Turkuensia, Fasc. II. Kokemäki: Societas Philosophica et Phaenomenologica Finlandiae.

ITKONEN, E. (1976) 'Was für eine Wissenschaft ist die Linguistik eigentlich?', in Wunderlich, D. (ed.), *Wissenschaftstheorie der Linguistik.* Fischer-Athenäum Taschenbuch, *pp* 56–76.

JÄGER, S. (1971) 'Zum Problem der sprachlichen Norm und seiner Relevanz für die Schule' *Muttersprache,* **81**, 162–75.

JAKOBSON, R. (1960/1971) 'Der Doppelcharakter der Sprache. Die Polarität zwischen Metaphorik und Metonymik', in Ihwe, J. (ed.), *Literaturwissenschaft und Linguistik.* Vol. 1: *Grundlagen und Voraussetzungen.* Frankfurt: Athenäum Verlag, *pp* 323–33.

JERNUDD, B. (1971) 'Review of "Language conflict and language planning: the case of modern Norwegian. By Einar Haugen"', *Language*, 47, 490–3.

JERNUDD, B. (1977) 'Linguistic sources for terminological innovation: policy and opinion', in Rubin *et al.* (1977) *pp* 215–36.

JERNUDD, B., and THUAN, E. (1980) *Naming Fish.* Report, Institute of Culture and Communication, East-West Center, Honolulu.

JERNUDD, B., and THUAN, E. (1983) 'Control of language through correction in speaking', *The International Journal in the Sociology of Language*, 44, 71–97.

JESPERSEN, O. (1922) *Language. Its Nature, Development, and Origin.* London: Allen & Unwin (paperback edn 1969).

JOOS, M. (ed.) (1957) *Readings in Linguistics I. The Development of Descriptive Linguistics in America 1925–56.* Chicago: The University of Chicago Press.

KAPLAN, D. (1979) 'The logic of demonstratives', *Journal of Philosophical Logic*, 8, 81–98.

KASHER, A. (1976a) 'Conversational maxims and rationality', in Kasher (1976b) *pp* 197–216.

KASHER, A. (ed.) (1976b) *Language in Focus: Foundations, Methods, and Systems. Essays in Memory of Y. Bar-Hillel.* Dordrecht: De Reidel.

KEENAN, E. (1974) 'Norm-makers, norm-breakers: uses of speech by men and women in a Malagasy community', in Bauman, R. and Sherzer, J. (eds), *Explorations in the Ethnography of Speaking.* London: Cambridge University Press.

KHUBCHANDANI, L. M. (1976) 'Language factor in census: a sociolinguistic perspective', in A. Verdoodt and R. Kjolseth (eds) *Language in Sociology.* Louvain: E. Peters, *pp* 93–123.

KHUBCHANDANI, L. M. (1978) 'Distribution of contact languages in India. A study of the 1961 bilingualism returns', in Fishman (1978) *pp* 553–86.

KLOSS, H. (1967) '"Abstand" languages and "Ausbau" languages', *Anthropological Linguistics* 9(7), 29–41.

KLOSS, M. (1971) 'Language rights of immigrant groups', *International Migration Review*, 5(2), 250–68.

KLOSS, H. (1977) *The American Bilingual Tradition.* Rowley, Mass.: Newbury House.

KRISHNAMURTI, BH. (1979) 'Classical or modern – a controversy of styles in education in Telugu', in Annamalai (1979b) *pp* 1–25.

KUCHLER, R., and JÄGER, S. (1976) 'Zur Sanktionierung von Sprachnormverstößen, in Presch and Gloy (1976) *pp* 125–39.

KUTSCHERA, F. (1973) *Einführung in die Logik der Normen, Werte und Entscheidungen.* Freiburg–Munich: Alber Verlag.

LABOV, W. (1972a) 'The study of language in its social context', in *Sociolinguistic Patterns.* Philadelphia: University of Pennsylvania Press, *pp* 183–259.

LABOV, W. (1972b) *Language in the Inner City: Studies in the Black*

English Vernacular. Philadelphia: University of Pennsylvania Press.

LANDMAN, F., and MOERDIJK, I. (1983) 'Compositionality and the analysis of anaphora', *Linguistics and Philosophy*, 6, 89–114.

LEECH, G. (1983) *Principles of Pragmatics*. London: Longman.

LEWIS, D. (1969) *Convention: A Philosophical Study*. Harvard: University Press.

LO CASCIO, V. (1978) *De ideale spreker. De relatie tussen kompetentie en ideologie*. Lisse: The Peter de Ridder Press.

LORWIN, V. R. (1972) 'Linguistic pluralism and political tension in modern Belgium', in Fishman, J. (ed.), *Advances in the Sociology of Language*. Vol. II. The Hague: Mouton. *pp* 386–412.

LUHMANN, N. (1972) *Rechtssoziologie*. Vol. 1. Reinbek: Rowohlt Verlag.

LUTZEIER, P. (1981) *Wort und Feld*. Tübingen: Niemeyer Verlag.

MACNAMARA, J. (1971) 'Successes and failures in the movement for the restoration of Irish', in Rubin and Jernudd (1971/1975) *pp* 65–94.

MAHMUD, U. A. (1979) 'Processes of language change in the southern Sudan'. Dissertation, Institute of African and Asian Studies, University of Khartoum.

MAHMUD, U. A. (1982) 'Language spread in a wavelike diffusion process: Arabic in the southern Sudan', in Cooper (1982b) *pp* 158–83.

MAZRUI, A. (1971) 'Islam and the English language in East- and West-Africa', in Whiteley (1971) *pp* 179–97.

MEY, J. (1985) *Whose Language? A Study in Linguistic Pragmatics*. Amsterdam and Philadelphia: John Benjamins Publishing Company.

MISRA, B. J. (1979) 'Language movements in the Hindi region', in Annamalai (1979b) *pp* 70–9.

MISRA, B. G. (1982) 'Language spread in a multilingual setting: the spread of Hindi as a case study', in Cooper (1982b) *pp* 148–57.

MONTAGUE, R. (1974) *Formal Philosophy. Selected Papers of Richard Montague* (ed. by R. H. Thomason). New Haven: Yale University Press.

MOSER, H. (1967) *Sprache – Freiheit order Lenkung? Zum Verhältnis von Sprachnorm, Sprachwandel, Sprachpflege*. Mannheim: Bibliographisches Institut: Duden Beiträge No. 25.

MOSER, H. (ed.) (1968) *Sprache der Gegenwart II. Schriften des Instituts für deutsche Sprache*. Düsseldorf: Schwann Verlag.

MUSA, M. (1981) *Language Planning in Sri Lanka*. Dacca: Bhuiyan Muhammed Imram P.W.D. Bungalow No. 3. Fuller Road, Dacca 2. Bangladesh.

MUSA, M. (1984a) Language Planning for Language Development: The Modernization of Bengali. MS, Institute of Culture and Communication. East-West Center. Honolulu.

MUSA, M. (1984b) The Ekushe: A Ritual of Language and Liberty. MS, Institute of Culture and Communication. East-West Center, Honolulu.

MYERS SCOTTON, C. (1982) 'Learning lingua francas and socioeconomic integration: evidence from Africa', in Cooper (1982b) *pp* 63–94.

NABANTOGLU, P. (1981) *Aysel en anderen. Turkse Vrouwen in Nederland*.

Amsterdam: Feministische Uitgeverij Sara.

NEUSTUPNÝ, J. V. (1974a) 'Basic types of treatment of language problems', in Fishman (1974c) *pp* 37–48.

NEUSTUPNÝ, J. V. (1974b) 'The modernization of the Japanese system of communication', *Language in Society*, **3**, 33–50.

NEUSTUPNÝ, J. V. (1978) *Post-Structural Approaches to Language. Language Theory in a Japanese Context*. Tokyo: University of Tokyo Press.

NEUSTUPNÝ, J. V. (n.d.) Language Planning and Human Rights. Dept of Japanese, Monash University, Clayton, Vic. 3168. Australia.

O'BARR, W. M., and O'BARR, J. F. (eds) (1976) *Language and Politics*. The Hague: Mouton.

OMAR, H. A. (1982) 'Language spread and recession in Malaysia and the Malay archipelago', in Cooper (1982b) *pp* 198–213.

PATTANAYAK, D. P. (1977) 'Language planning and language development', in P. G. Sharma and L. S. Kumar (eds), *Indian Bilingualism*. Agra: Kendriya Hindi Sansthan.

PAUL, H. (1880/1970) *Prinzipien der Sprachgeschichte*. 8th edn. Tübingen: Niemeyer Verlag.

POLENZ, P. VON (1969) 'Sprachkritik und sprachwissenschaftliche Methodik', in Moser (1968) *pp* 159–84.

POLENZ, P. VON (1970) *Geschichte der deutschen Sprache*. Sammlung Göschen, Vol. 915/915a. Berlin: De Gruyter.

POLENZ, P. VON (1982) 'Sprachkritik und Sprachnormenkritik', in Heringer (1982b) *pp* 70–93.

PRESCH, G., and GLOY, K. (eds) (1976) *Sprachnormen II. Theoretische Begründungen – außerschulische Sprachnormenpraxis. Reihe: Problemata 47*. Stuttgart–Bad Cannstadt: Frommann-Holzboog.

PUTNAM, H. (1975) 'The meaning of "Meaning"', in *Mind, Language, Reality*. Philosophical papers. Vol. 2. Cambridge: University Press, *pp* 215–71.

QUASTHOFF, U. (1980) *Erzählen in Gesprächen*. Tübingen: Gunter Narr Verlag.

QUINE, W. V. O. (1963) 'Two dogmas of Empiricism', in *From a Logical Point of View*. Harper Torchbooks, *pp* 20–46.

QUINE, W. V. O. (1964) *Word and Object*. Cambridge, Mass.: The MIT Press.

QUINE, W. V. O. (1973) *Roots of Reference*. La Salle, Ill.: Open Court.

RAJYASHREE, K. S. (1986) *An Ethnolinguistic Survey of Dharavi. A Slum in Bombay*. Central Institute of Indian Languages. Mysore 570006.

RAWLS, J. (1968) 'Two concepts of rules', in Care and Landesman (1968) *pp* 306–40.

RAY, P. S. (1963) *Language Standardization: Studies in Prescriptive Linguistics*. Janua Linguarum. Series minor, No. 29. The Hague: Mouton.

RAZ, J. (1975) *Practical Reason and Norms*. London: Hutchinson University Library.

REINERS, L. (1963/1969) *Stilfibel*. Munich: DTV, No. 154.

338   REFERENCES

RIESEL, E. 1959. *Stilistk der deutschen Sprache*. Moscow: Verlag für fremdsprachliche Literatur.

RIESEL, E. (1970) *Der Stil der deutschen Alltagssprache*. Leipzig: Reclam.

RUBIN, J. (1977a) 'Attitudes towards language planning', in Elert, C.-Ch. *et al.* (eds), *Dialectology and Sociolinguistics. Essays in Honour of Karl-Hampus Dahlstedt*. Umeå: Centraltryckeriet, *pp* 166–74.

RUBIN. J. (1977b) 'Language stadardization in Indonesia', in Rubin *et al.* (1977) *pp* 157–80.

RUBIN, J., and JERNUDD, B. (eds) (1971/1975) *Can Language be Planned?* An East-West Center Book. Honolulu: The University of Hawaii Press.

RUBIN, J. *et al.* (eds) (1977) *Language Planning Processes*. The Hague: Mouton.

SAG, I. (1981) 'Formal semantics and extra-linguistic context', in Cole, P. (ed.), *Radical Pragmatics*. New York: Academic Press, *pp* 295–318.

SANDIG, B. (1976) 'Schriftsprachliche Norm und die Beschreibung und Beurteilung spontan gesprochener Sprache', in Presch and Gloy (1976) *pp* 93–105.

SAUSSURE, F. DE (1916/1967) *Grundfragen der Allgemeinen Sprachwissenschaft*. (Translation from the French *Cours de linguistique générale*). Berlin: De Gruyter.

SCHAAP, G. C. (ed.) (1980) *De Spelling van de Nederlandse Taal. Derde bijgewerkte druk*. Publikatie van de Centrale Directie Voorlichting van het Ministerie van Onderwijs en Wetenschappen. The Hague: Staatsuitgeverij.

SCHAFF, A. (1968) 'Unscharfe Ausdrücke und die Grenzen ihrer Präzisierungen', in *Essays über die Philosophie der Sprache*. Frankfurt: Europäische Verlagsanstalt, *pp* 65–94.

SCHIPPAN, TH. (1975) *Einführung in die Semasiologie*. 2nd rev. edn. Leipzig: VEB Bibliographisches Institut.

SCHNELLE, H. (1976) 'Empirische und transzendentale Sprachgemeinschaften', in Apel (1976b) *pp* 394–440.

SCHWARZE, CHR. (1980) 'Sprachpflege – Sprachkritik – Spracherziehung. Thesen und Empfehlungen zum Sprachgebrauch in den Medien', in Deutsche Akademie für Sprache und Dichtung (1980) *pp* 25–37.

SEARLE, J. (1969) *Speech Acts*. Cambridge: University Press.

SEARLE, J. (1975) 'Indirect speech acts', in Cole and Morgan (1975) *pp* 59–82.

SIBAYAN, B. P. (1974) 'Language policy, language engineering, and literacy in the Philippines', in Fishman (1974c) *pp* 221–54.

SIEBS, TH. (1898/1961) *Deutsche Hochsprache. Bühnenaussprache*. 18th rev. edn (ed. by H. de Boor and P. Diels). Berlin 1961.

SIEBS, TH. (1969) *Deutsche Aussprache. Reine und gemäßigte Hochlautung mit Aussprachewörterbuch*. 19th rev. edn (ed. by H. de Boor, H. Moser and Chr. Wrinkler). Berlin: De Gruyter.

SKUTNABB-KANGAS, T. and R. PHILLIPSON (1968). 1. English: the Language of Widest Colonisation 2. The Legitimacy of the Arguments for the

Spread of English 3. Denial of Linguistic Rights: the New Mental Slavery. Papers presented at the 11th World Congress of Sociology, New Delhi, India, 18–24 August 1986, and at the Post-Congress on Ethnocentrism in Sociolinguistics, Central Institute of Indian Languages, Mysore, India. 26–28 August 1986.

SLAUGHTER, M. M. (1982) *Universal Languages and Scientific Taxonomy in the 17th Century*. Cambridge: Cambridge University Press.

SLAUGHTER, M. M. (1985) 'Literacy and Society', in *The International Journal of the Sociology of Language*, **56**: 113–39.

SRIVASTAVA, R. N. *et al.* (1978) *Evaluation Report: Communicability and Comprehensibility of the Manual for Community Health Workers*. Parts 1 and 2. Delhi: UNICEF.

SRIVASTAVA, R. N. (1979) 'Language movements against Hindi as an official language', in Annamalai (1979b) *pp* 80–90.

STEGER, H. (1980) 'Normprobleme', in Deutsche Akademie für Sprache und Dichtung (1980) *pp* 210–19.

STERN, G. (1931/1974) 'Allgemeine Theorie des Bedeutungswandels', in Dinser, G. (ed.) (1974), *Zur Theorie der Sprachveränderung*. Kronberg Ts.: Scriptor Verlag, *pp* 67–112.

STREVENS, P., and WEEKS, F. (1985) 'The creation of a regularized subset of English for mandatory use in maritime communications: SEASPEAK', *Language Planning Newsletter*, **11**, 2 May, 1–6.

SUBBAYYA R. (= K. S. RAJYASHREE) (1980) 'The Standardization of language. A case study of Marathi'. Dissertation, University of Mysore. MS, Central Institute of Indian Languages. Manasagangotri, Mysore 570006. To appear as a book under the name K. S. Rajyashree, published by the same Institute in 1986.

TAULI, V. (1974) 'The theory of language planning', in Fishman (1974c) *pp* 49–67.

THOMASON, R. (ed.) (1974) *Formal Philosophy. Selected Papers of Richard Montague* (Introduction by R. Thomason). New Haven and London: Yale University Press.

ULLMANN, ST. (1964) *Semantics. An Introduction into the Science of Meaning*. Oxford: Basil Blackwell.

ULLMANN-MARGALIT, E. (1977) *The Emergence of Norms*. Oxford: Oxford University Press.

VACHEK, J. (1964a) 'Zum Problem der geschriebenen Sprache', in Vachek (1964b) *pp* 441–52.

VACHEK, J. (ed.) (1964b) *A Prague School Reader in Linguistics*. Bloomington: Indiana University Press.

VALDMAN, A. (ed.) (1977) *Pidgin and Creole Linguistics*. Bloomington and London: Indiana University Press.

VENNEMANN, TH. (1972) 'Phonetic analogy and conceptual analogy', in Vennemann, Th., and Wilbur, T. H. (eds) *Schuchardt, the Neogrammarians, and the Transformational Theory of Phonological Change*. Frankfurt: Athenäum Verlag, *pp* 180–204.

VISSER, F. TH. (1973) *A Historical Syntax of the English Language*. Part III, 2. Leiden: E. J. Brill.

WASHABOUGH, W. (1977) 'Constraining variation in decreolization', *Language*, **53**, 329–52.

WEYDT, H. (ed.) (1977) *Aspekte der Modalpartikeln*. Tübingen: Niemeyer.

WEYDT, H. (ed.) (1979) *Die Partikeln der deutschen Sprache*. Berlin: De Gruyter.

WHITELEY, W. H. (1969) *Swahili. The Rise of a National Language*. London: Methuen & Co. Ltd.

WHITELEY, W. H. (ed.) (1971) *Language Use and Social Change. Problems of Multilingualism with Special Reference to Eastern Africa*. London: Oxford University Press.

WITTGENSTEIN, L. (1960) *Philosophische Untersuchungen*. Frankfurt: Suhrkamp.

WRIGHT, G. H. VON (1963) *Norm and Action*. London: Routledge & Kegan Paul.

ZIFF, P. (1960) *Semantic Analysis*. Ithaca, New York: Cornell University Press.

Index of Normtheoretic and Linguistic Terms